European and American

MUSICAL
INSTRUMENTS

Anthony Baines

A Studio Book · THE VIKING PRESS · New York

PUBLISHED IN 1966 BY THE VIKING PRESS, INC.,
625 MADISON AVENUE, NEW YORK, N.Y. 10022

LIBRARY OF CONGRESS CATALOG CARD NUMBER 66–25611
REPRODUCED AND PRINTED IN GREAT BRITAIN BY
REDWOOD PRESS LIMITED, TROWBRIDGE & LONDON

PREFACE

This pictorial museum is intended primarily for collectors and curators who are not already specialists in musical instruments, as a help to identification of types and varieties of the non-keyboard instruments of Western Society from the Renaissance onwards. A general acknowledgment must at once be paid to those in past and present who have built up the private and public collections which make a book of this kind possible.

In order to provide a typological survey of this wide subject, the ruling procedure in the illustrations is to show many specimens in single view, in preference to detailed illustration of fewer. Even so, limitations of space have forced the omission of certain classes in addition to keyboard instruments, like the free-reed class (accordions, etc., though in fact many of this class are with keyboard), bells and many other percussion instruments, also mechanical musical instruments. With more regret, regional folk instruments have had to be treated very sparsely; some of the most distinctive species are shown and some others for comparative reasons. But the book is principally concerned with products of professional town workshops, even if a fair number of these are of the smallest interest to music history, though yet good and appreciated musical instruments in their day and usually designed and constructed with expert thought and care.

As to the selection of examples for inclusion, emphasis is naturally placed upon the classic models of successive periods, but at the same time unusual, even apparently unique specimens are not totally excluded: our historical knowledge is not so complete that what may now appear a freak can be assumed in every case to have been equally freakish at the date of its construction. Secondly, as to state of preservation, a perfect original state throughout is an ideal probably unattainable with musical instruments. Among stringed instruments especially, the choice often lies between specimens partially depleted of fittings or altered at a subsequent date, or else restored in modern times to what the restorer believes to be original condition; I personally feel that all these imperfect states of preservation can be equally informative, each after its own fashion.

The specimens are numbered in one continuous series, and brief individual particulars are supplied at relevant points in the text, thus saving space in the captions without, I hope, causing inconvenience to the reader. An effort has been made to show all instruments in a given Plate on approximately the same scale. The text is no more than a compressed companion to the illustrations, and therefore references are in the main confined to acknowledgments of recent research (a good proportion of which, on this subject of musical instruments, has appeared in the *Galpin Society Journal*, London, from 1948, cited as *GSJ*). I should like to add that this book, from fiddles to drums, enters many very different fields, each of them highly specialized, and to apologize now for any statement of fact or opinion which an expert in one of these fields may consider unsound.

For help and suggestions I am especially indebted to Philip Bate, Dr Alfred Berner, Otto Bess, William A. Cocks, Reuben Greene, W. E. Hill & Sons, Mrs Roland A. Hoover, Mrs Jean Jenkins, R. Morley-Pegge, Marco Pallis, Michael W. Prynne, José Ricart Matas, Miss Joan Rimmer, Mme Thibault Comtesse de Chambure, and Dr J. H. van der Meer; also to Miss Mary Scriven of B. T. Batsford Ltd who has borne the brunt of the secretarial work involved in the preparation of the book and to my wife for her encouragement and patience through a long requisitioning of my 'spare time'.

London, 1966   Anthony Baines

v

CONTENTS

Contents

ACKNOWLEDGMENT

The Author and Publishers wish to thank the following for permission to reproduce the illustrations which appear in this book:

The Curator of the Sammlung alter Musikinstrumente, Kunsthistorisches Museum, Vienna, for Figs 1, 7, 8, 13, 14, 64, 65, 83, 87, 159, 168–70, 174, 179–81, 197, 198, 228, 231, 241, 281, 282, 458, 514–16, 585, 590, 663, 667, 736, 750 (property of the Gesellschaft der Musikfreunde in Vienna), 788, 810 and 824.

The Keeper of the Ashmolean Museum, Oxford, for Figs 2–4, 15–21, 25–8, 76–9, 88–97, 229, 230, 249, 290 and 738.

The Director of the Royal College of Music, London, for Figs 5, 6, 44, 49, 72, 130, 145, 146, 151, 153, 157, 192, 193, 195, 196, 207–12, 214, 255, 275, 283, 284, 390, 391, 401, 413, 497, 500, 562, 578, 580, 617, 681, 697, 702 and 731.

The Director of the Conservatório Nacional, Lisbon, for Figs 9, 38, 39, 59, 110, 149, 203, 204 and 673.

The Director of the Musée instrumentale, Conservatoire royal de Musique, Brussels, and A.C.L., Brussels, for Figs 10, 12, 37, 45–7, 50, 51, 54, 58, 69, 86, 116–18, 121, 122, 133, 171, 184, 186, 219, 220, 259, 261, 264, 269, 270, 274, 285–9, 296, 317–19, 326, 327, 340, 354, 371, 382, 388, 389, 405, 409, 414, 420, 454–7, 474, 509, 513, 519, 520, 525, 529, 539, 550, 555, 586, 593, 614, 674, 708, 805 and 806.

Musikinstrumenten-Museum der Karl-Marx-Universität, Leipzig, for Figs 11, 57, 101, 102, 106, 109, 141, 260, 304, 329, 421, 517, 536, 561, 579, 588, 604, 628, 631, 646, 660, 683, 687 and 690.

Vestlandske Kunstindustri Museum, Bergen, for Fig 22.

William E. Hill & Sons, London, for Figs 23, 24, 29–31, 36, 43, 98, 99, 218, 246, 291, 294, and 295.

The Director of Haags Gemeentemuseum, The Hague, for Figs 32, 33, 84, 85, 140, 172, 236, 238, 360, 535, 540, 600, 643, 650 and 722.

Istituto Luigi Cherubini (Museo), Florence, for Figs 34, 35, 55 and 56.

The Curator of the Horniman Museum, London, for Figs 40, 73, 191, 276, 277, 359, 376, 406, 435, 444, 460, 472, 475, 486, 499, 551, 552, 581, 601, 602, 606, 658, 684, 707, 755, 771, 772, 784, 790, 795 and 807.

The Stearns Collection of Musical Instruments, The University of Michigan, Ann Arbor, for Figs 41, 311, 330, 348, 351, 373, 374, 395, 607, 652, 671, 694, 757 and 820.

The Trustees of the Victoria and Albert Museum, London, for the frontispiece and for Figs 42, 74, 100, 132, 134, 136–9, 147, 148, 183, 187, 201, 202, 205, 206, 213, 215–17, 245, 250, 253, 254, 256, 257, 268, 292, 293, 300, 310, 316, 325, 328, 335–7, 339, 341, 364, 394, 398, 400, 403, 404, 468, 548, 654, 726 and 727 (Crown Copyright).

Staatliches Institut für Musikforschung, Sammlung alter Musikinstrumente, Berlin, for Figs 48, 101, 102, 107, 119, 120, 128, 144, 185, 237, 247, 297, 312, 350, 352, 353, 355, 370, 387, 424, 466, 512, 518, 521, 522, 524, 527, 528, 530–4, 559, 587, 591, 598, 630, 651, 699, 700, 709, 718, 735, 754, 785, 786, 796, 798 and 812.

The Dolmetsch Collection, Haslemere, for Figs 52, 53, 62, 63, 80–2, 103–5 and 108.

Raymond Elgar Esq, for Figs 60 and 61.

Musikhistorisk Museum, Copenhagen, for Figs 66, 165, 194, 199, 200, 221, 223, 242–4, 248, 331, 358, 378, 715, 733 and 756.

Pitt Rivers Museum, University of Oxford, for Figs 67, 68, 332, 372, 377, 506–8, 546, 680 and 823.

Musée Instrumental du Conservatoire National de Musique, Paris, for Figs 70, 113, 114, 150, 173, 175–8, 224–7, 232–4, 262, 263, 265–7, 271–3, 298, 299, 320, 321, 367, 381, 399, 423, 425–30, 433, 439, 452, 453, 467, 469, 470, 543, 584, 657, 665, 666, 676–8, 695, 696, 703, 710, 717, 747 and 753.

The Commandant of the Royal Military School of Music, Kneller Hall, for Figs 71, 375, 440, 553, 567, 655, 661, 681, 704, 743, 745, 765, 775, 778, 801, 811 and 819.

The Municipal Museum and Art Gallery, Warrington, for Fig 75.

The General Director of the Bayerisches Nationalmuseum, Munich, for Figs 111, 112, 618, 620, 645 and 693.

The Director of the Museo Municipál de Música de Barcelona, for Figs 115, 182, 305–7, 411, 526, 542, 545, 547, 675, 759 and 789.

The Museum of Fine Arts, Boston, Mass. (Leslie Lindsey Mason Collection), for Figs 123, 124, 365, 556, 649, 723, 729, 764 and 779.

The Chief Director of the Germanisches Nationalmuseum, Nuremberg, for Figs 125, 126, 129, 379, 380, 386, 564, 621, 701, 739, 742, 748, 763, 809 and 822; and for Figs 397, 644, 669, 679, 716, 728, 758, 768, 769, 804 and 816 (from the Rück Collection in the Germanisches Nationalmuseum).

The Historisches Museum, Basel, for Figs 127, 142, 143, 303, 369, 592, 711, 719, 734 and 813–15.

The Director of the Royal Pavilion, Art Gallery and Museums, Brighton, for Figs 131, 334, 338, 345, 446, 627, 705, 762 and 792.

Reuben Greene Esq, London, for Figs 135, 301, 302, 342, 346, 347, 357, 366, 402 and 443.

The Director of the Museum für Hamburgische Geschichte, for Figs 152, 154, 511, 589, 599, 605, 641 and 688.

The Director of the National Museum of Ireland, for Figs 155, 384, 385, 504 and 610.

The Director of the Salzburger Museum, Carolino Augusteum, Salzburg, for Figs 156, 349, 356, 537, 544, 622, 713 and 799.

The Musikhistoriska Museet, Stockholm, for Figs 158, 258, 309, 361, 618, 619, 642, 647, 664, 752, 783 and 803.

Acknowledgment

The Folger Shakespeare Library, Washington, for Figs 160 and 161.

The Warwick Museum, for Figs 162–4.

The Director of the Museo Civico, Bologna, for Figs 166, 167, 392, 393 and 558.

Mecklenburgische Landesbibliothek, Schwerin, for Figs 188–90.

The Metropolitan Museum of Art, New York (The Crosby Brown Collection of Musical Instruments, 1889), for Figs 222, 315, 324, 333, 362, 396, 407, 498, 557, 639 and 767.

The Director of the Historisches Museum, Frankfurt-am-Main, for Figs 235, 251, 252, 415–18, 422, 538 and 730.

Lord Tollemache, for Figs 239 and 240.

Musée Jacquemart-André, Paris, for Figs 278–80.

The Smithsonian Institution, Washington, for Figs 308, 343, 344, 363, 629 and 802.

Yale University (Belle Skinner Collection), for Figs 313, 314, 322, 323, 760 and 782.

The Curator of the Städtisches Museum, Brunswick, for Figs 368, 624 and 672.

The Keeper of the National Museum of Antiquities of Scotland, for Fig 383.

Arthur Guinness & Co (Dublin) Ltd, for Fig 384.

The Director of the Galleria Estense, Modena, for Fig 408 (photograph by Fratelli Alinari, Florence, and The Mansell Collection, London).

The Music Division, The Library of Congress, Washington (The Dayton Miller Flute Collection), for Figs 410, 412, 431, 432, 434, 436–8, 442, 445, 447–50, 459, 461, 462, 464, 465, 471, 473, 476, 480–3, 485, 487–93, 495, 496, 549 and 554.

Musée Vleeshuis, Antwerp, for Fig 414.

The Bach Museum, Eisenach, for Figs 419 and 776.

The Principal of Birmingham School of Music, for Fig 441.

The Director of the Bankfield Museum, Halifax, for Figs 451 and 766.

The Chief Curator of the Musée d'Art et d'Histoire, Geneva, for Figs 463, 568, 569 and 668.

Eric Halfpenny Esq, Ilford, for Figs 468 and 623.

Luton Museum and Art Gallery (The Ridley Collection of Musical Wind Instruments), for Figs 477, 572 and 640.

R. Morley Pegge Esq, Stoke d'Abernon, Cobham, Surrey, for Figs 478, 479, 571, 582, 626, 685, 686, 721, 773, 787 and 794.

Philip Bate Esq, London, for Figs 484, 565, 566, 570, 573–6, 583, 594–7, 603, 609, 615, 616, 625, 632–8, 648 and 653.

The Collection of the late Rev Charles Overy, for Figs 494, 774, 780, 781, 797 and 808. (*Collection now dispersed*)

William A. Cocks Esq, F.S.A. Scot., Ryton-on-Tyne, for Figs 501–3, 505 and 510.

The Director of the Narodni Museum, Prague, for Fig 523.

The Historical Museum, Bern, for Fig 541.

The Director of Glasgow Art Galleries and Museum, for Fig 563.

Rushworth & Dreaper Ltd, Liverpool, for Fig 577.

Kunst und Historisches Museum, Neuchâtel, for Fig 608.

Mr Philip Young, Yale, for Figs 611 and 612.

F. Rendell Esq, for Fig. 613.

James A. MacGillivray Esq, for Fig 656.

Miss W. N. Bartlett, Dartington Hall, for Fig 670.

The Curator of the National Museum of Wales, Welsh Folk Museum, for Fig 682.

The Director of the Schweizerisches Landesmuseum, Zürich, for Figs 689, 698 and 741.

Dienst voor 's Rijks Verspreide Kunstvoorwerpen (loan Haags Gemeentemuseum, The Hague), for Figs 691, 749 and 751.

The Trustees of the Wallace Collection, London, for Figs 692, 714 and 740.

Bradford Corporation Libraries, Art Gallery and Museums Committee, for Fig 706.

Staatliche Historisches Museum, Dresden, for Fig 712.

City of Norwich Museums, Strangers Hall, for Figs 720 and 821.

City of Gloucester Museum, for Figs 724 and 725.

The Trustees of the London Museum, for Figs 737 and 744.

Joseph Wheeler Esq, London, for Fig 746.

The Director of Keighley Art Gallery and Museum, for Fig 761.

The Commanding Officer, U.S.S. Constitution, Boston, Mass., for Fig 770.

Professor C. G. Widstrand, Uppsala, for Fig 791.

Christopher Baines Esq, London, for Fig 793.

Hornboskapen, Södermanlands-Nerikes Nation, Uppsala, for Fig 800.

The Curator of the Dorset Military Museum, Dorchester, for Fig 817 (on loan from Dorset County Museum).

George Potter & Co, Aldershot, for Fig 818.

I Stringed Instruments

I Stringed Instruments

Non-keyboard stringed instruments can be placed for descriptive purposes in three principal groups: (1) Those like violins and lutes, in which the soundbox is attached to a projecting neck along which the strings are stopped by the player's left hand. (2) Those like zithers and dulcimers, in which the soundbox requires no projecting neck. (3) Harps, in which the soundbox forms one side of an open triangular structure traversed by the strings.

Of these groups the first, by far the most numerous and complex, requires some preliminary generalized description. The soundbox is bipartite in the sense that one component, the soundboard or 'belly', is normally of pine while the rest is of harder wood, to which the belly is usually attached with glue of a relatively weak strength in order to facilitate its removal for repair or other work on the interior. The classic material for this rest of the body, traditional counterpart to the pine of the belly, is sycamore (often simply called maple), though other materials may be employed alternatively or for decorative effects. To make a round body, as for a lute, strips of the material (ribs[1]) are laid against each other over a humped wooden mould, the construction being strengthened internally with paper or cloth. For a body with separate back and sides, as a guitar, the pieces for the sides are bent to their required curvatures over a heated bar or pipe; the back, of one or more pieces with the grain normally running towards the sides, may be flat or bent to a slight curve, or, as with violins, carved from thicker wood to a vaulted shape. Another possible construction, alike for round bodies and those with perpendicular sides, is to carve the whole from a single piece of wood, though this is rare in professional European work later than the sixteenth century. Flat backs are normally strengthened internally by transverse bars, one of which also serves to bear the pressure of the soundpost in flat-backed bowed instruments like viols and double basses. With both these last, the back is usually bent in near the top ('half cut'), the bend being made along a transverse saw-cut which is afterwards glued and papered over. This saves weight in the neck block and neck root, besides in some cases adding to the comfort of the player.

The neck block is a substantial piece of pine around which the back and sides (or the ribs of a lute) are gathered at their upper ends during assembly of the body. It forms a structural focus for the completed instrument, the neck being joined to the body by means of it. In early work, up to the end of the eighteenth century, the root of the neck abuts the block, the glued junction being reinforced by one or more iron nails driven in from the inner face of the block. Later practice is to mortise the neck into the neck block. At the bottom end of the body there is a corresponding bottom block, often of slighter dimensions than the neck block. It has an added use in serving to hold exterior fittings like tailpins or hitchpins for the strings, slinging button, etc. Other interior reinforcements include side linings and corner blocks. In much early work there are no linings of the junction of back and sides other than perhaps paper or canvas strips. Pinewood linings came in early on violins, but on other kinds of instruments are infrequent before the eighteenth century.

[1] The term 'ribs' is also commonly used for the sides of the violin, etc, though not in the present work.

3

The three primary materials for the strings before the nylon age are mentioned in a source of the thirteenth century: 'Chordalia sunt ea, quae per chordas metallines, intestinales vel sericines exerceri videntur' (anon, *Summa Musicae*; Gerbert, *Scriptores*, III). Metal strings are usually steel or brass, and where both materials are used on the same instrument, steel is for the higher-tuned strings and brass for the lower. Gut strings are spun from sheep's gut, an industry formerly associated particularly with Naples and Rome. Silk, occasionally used for strings of the finest gauge, is better known as a core for overspun strings. In these the unit weight of the string is increased by a winding of metal wire in order to give satisfactory tonal results in deep tunings without excessive thickness, stiffness or slackness of tension. Overspun silk is often thus employed alternatively to overspun gut for the lower strings of gut-strung instruments, and overspun brass with metal-strung instruments. Early reports of them are believed to be mid-seventeenth-century references to 'twisted strings' (Trichet, c. 1640; Playford, *Booke of New Lessons for the Cithren and Gittern* [cittern and guitar], 1652).

The strings are almost invariably arranged with the highest-tuned or 'first' string running down the left side of the neck—'left' and 'right' being understood in terms of the instrument as a standing figure

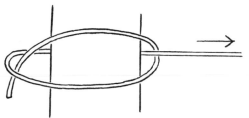

Fig 1 String hitch for tied bridge

with belly and strings to the front. The left side is therefore often described as the 'treble side', the 'bass side' being the other. Further lateral distinctions may follow from this, for instance the belly wood is in many cases left a little thicker on the bass side. Transference of string-vibration to the belly is through a bridge, which in some instruments, as lute and guitar, is a shaped bar of ebony or other hard material glued to the belly, the strings being directly tied or otherwise fastened to it. In the older bridge, still commonly employed on the Spanish guitar, the strings are passed through holes running parallel with the belly and tied with a simple hitch of the kind shown in Fig 1. The later 'pin bridge' has wider holes, drilled perpendicularly to the surface of the belly to penetrate both bridge and belly; the strings are gripped in these holes by ebony pins (e.g. **298**).

Differing from this 'tension' bridge is the 'pressure' bridge, over which the strings pass to their attachment further down, either to a floating tailpiece as on most bowed instruments, or to hitch pins or studs at the bottom. When such a bridge is a low one, as on the mandolin, it is usually glued in its correct position. The expression 'string length' signifies the full vibrating length of a string from the bridge up to the nut, this last being a small transverse bar upon which the strings bear immediately below the tuning pins.

Tuning is either by pegs (Fig 2), by square-topped metal wrest pins turned with a separate key (as in a pianoforte), by screw devices or by worm gears ('machines'). Some specimen tunings are given on p. 70. More important here is the question of arrangement of strings in 'courses'. Many types of instrument include paired strings, i.e. two adjacent strings tuned to the same note (or, in an 'octave course', to a note and its octave) and struck by the player as one string, as on the mandolin today (**215**). Especially common among the plucked types of instrument up to the end of the eighteenth century, such pairings of strings add to the vibrance of the sound as well as allowing the player to continue should one string break (though old sources do not allude to this second point). Moreover, it has been the practice on many instruments to have some strings paired and others single, or some paired, others tripled. Hence, when discussing such instruments, it is customary to speak not so much of the number of actual strings but of the number of 'courses'. An 11-course lute may have one single course and ten

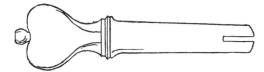

Fig 2 A typical form of peg, pre-nineteenth-century

double courses, making 21 strings, though the musician regards himself as playing on 11. In the absence of strings the pegs or peg holes may indicate their total number, but in order to identify the nature, period, or individual history of an instrument it will probably be necessary to examine the spacing of the grooves in the nut or holes in the bridge for evidence of multiple courses, whether original or as the specimen may have been altered at some time.

The neck of the instrument carries a fingerboard of ebony or other hard material, in many cases a veneer, and in many types of instrument this is fretted at semitone intervals. With viols, lutes and early guitars the frets are of gut, tied round the neck with a knot of the kind shown in Fig. 3. Such frets can be adjusted or replaced by the player, but since their number is restricted by the length of the neck, technical considerations may have required their con-tinuation by a few fixed frets glued to the belly. Other fretted instruments, like citterns and the later guitars, have fixed frets throughout, generally of brass or silver and let into the fingerboard. In their older forms they are of flat wire set on edge. Special fret-wire of a T or mushroom section was introduced about the middle of the nineteenth century, though flat frets may be found even today in the products of small workshops. As to the position of frets, the twelfth (the nut not being counted) divides the string length into two equal parts

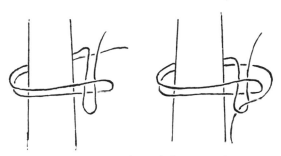

Fig 3 A Fret knot (after Hayes)

and gives the octave of the open string. The seventh fret gives the musical fifth above the open string, and so on. One old rule for placing gut frets is to tie the second fret at one ninth of the open string length from nut to bridge; the fourth at one ninth of the distance from the second fret to the bridge; the fifth at one quarter of the open string length and the seventh at one third. The intervening frets are then placed by eye. Position dots of ivory, etc, marking principal frets like the fifth, seventh and twelfth, are rare before the nineteenth century and not common until after *c.* 1840.

A tricky matter with stringed instruments is that of signatures. Branded, stamped or painted signatures being exceptions rather than the rule, one is confronted in most cases with the printed or manuscript label pasted inside the back of the body, and the fact is well known that labels are not always trust-worthy. An authentic label may have been transplanted to another instrument; a label may be a forgery; or it may be a fictitious label giving the name of a maker who never existed. The great works of von Lütgendorff and of Vannes (see Bibliography) afford assistance here with their reproductions of genuine labels and are anyhow indispensable reference books in matters concerning stringed-instrument makers. But, especially in the case of an instrument like the violin, forgeries can often be detected only by experts, and needless to say there is no short cut to acquisition of the experienced eye of such an expert: no one can learn from a book—least of all this one—how to tell a genuine Stradivarius from a good copy, or a genuine Tieffenbrucker lute from a good forgery. With instruments of other kinds, among which choice old examples have not on the whole found such high market prices either in the past or in the present, one can, preferably with the help of Vannes or von Lütgendorff, treat labels more optimistically if technical features and decoration are of a likely character—bearing in mind that decorative styles and motifs can be very conservative in stringed instruments as compared with other woodwork like furni-ture. Well into the eighteenth century motifs recur of those oriental types introduced long previously by the Venetians, just as harp makers still preserve much of the neo-classical and neo-Gothic ornament of some 150 years ago.

1 Liras and Early Violas

Fiddles had been leading instruments of Western music for five centuries before the period of the violin (which began in the mid sixteenth century) but no fiddle exists that can be dated with certainty before 1500. In pictures from the late thirteenth century to the late fifteenth, the viola[1] with an elliptical body outline predominates, tending to the shape of a rounded rectangle (similar to guitar **277**) often with the sides slightly incurved. Pine bellies are mentioned in the fourteenth century (Bachmann, 87) but it is impossible to state whether these were carved to a vaulted form before the second half of the fifteenth century, when there is clear evidence of this in Italian paintings. Some indirect light on the question may be thrown by 'folk' fiddles made up to recently in Wendish areas of Germany and in Bohemia and Moravia still, apparently uninfluenced by the violin in design and construction. An example shown (**66**) has an elementary barrel-arched belly evidently achieved simply by bending, flat back, also the flat head with upright pegs characteristic of all violas before the sixteenth century. Inside the body a soundpost is present in the normal position under the left foot of the bridge, but the bass bar, which in violins is glued longitudinally underneath the bass side of the belly, is absent. The number of strings, three, was typical up to the fifteenth century, though two of these might be double courses (e.g. a unison first or principal melody course, and an octave second course, as described by Jerome of Moravia, early fourteenth century) making five strings in all and presumably a rich sonorous effect when the instrument was played alone, or alone with the voice, as it had been regularly during the *trouvère* period. The fifth of the strings (third course) was mainly a *bourdon*, i.e. a bass or drone, always sounded open and sometimes arranged to pass clear of the neck to the bass side, struck either by the bow or by the left thumb, as on the Welsh crwth (**74**). The bow was haired with horse-hair rubbed with pitch, later with resin; Praetorius (*Syntagma*, 1619) mentions both.

A culminating form of the medieval viola is an Italian instrument introduced in the last quarter of the fifteenth century, known in that time as *viola*, though now referred to by the later sixteenth-century name *lira*, or as amplified in some sources *lira da braccio*. Of this, four complete specimens are known, plus one or two others which are thought to be liras converted at later dates for use as modern violas. The strings run in five courses of which the lower two are octave courses, making in all seven strings, the legendary number of the lyre of Orpheus. The second of these octave courses is the bourdon, lying off the fingerboard. The lira retains the medieval flat head, improved in an elegant leaf outline with the pegs inserted from the front and the strings led to them through small holes above the nut and, for the bourdon, in the side (**2, 3**).

Illustrations: Liras and Early Violas

1 Lira da braccio. Giovanni d'Andrea, Verona, 1511. *Vienna, Kunsthist. Mus., C.94.* MS label *Joannes Andree. Veronen . . . 1511.* Scrolled shoulders. Concave sides. No linings or bass bar. Carved head with detachable back plate. Original fittings including bridge. *Length* 80·5 cm, body 51·5 cm. *Depth* 4·5 cm.

[1] The word *viola* already described the instrument in the troubadour language, also in Latin texts of the early fourteenth century, while neighbouring Romance languages employed other forms of the word, as Old French *vièle*. 'Fiddle' names (*Vidill*, etc) were used in Germanic languages and the term used now in Germany for a medieval or early Renaissance viola is *Fiedel*.

2–4 Lira da braccio. Giovanni Maria (dalla Corna) of Brescia, Venice, *c.* 1540 or earlier. *Oxford, Ashmol. Mus.* Label *Gioan maria bresiano in Venetia.* Belly and back each in one piece. No linings or bass bar. Flat fingerboard. Head decorated with gilt arabesques. *Length* 65 cm, body 39 cm. *Depth* 3·3 cm.

5, 6 Lira da braccio. *London, R. Coll. of Music, 52.* Presumed false inscription on back inside in ink *Joan Karlino Brescia 1452.* Back in one piece. Neck at some time restored, and later fingerboard. *Length* 72·5 cm, body 46 cm. *Depth* 3·8 cm. (Shown on reduced scale.)

7 Lira da gamba. Wendelin Tieffenbrucker, Padua, *c.* 1590. *Vienna, Kunsthist. Mus., C.95.* MS label *in Padua Vendelinus Tieffenbrucker. Length* 112·5 cm, body 68 cm. *Depth* 7 cm.

8 Viola da braccio. Italian, *c.* 1500. *Vienna, Kunsthist. Mus., C.70.* Early build with concave sides. Present four-stringed condition not necessarily original. *Length* 66 cm, body 40 cm. *Depth* 4·5 cm.

9 Viola da braccio. Label printed in capitals, though in type seemingly of a later character than the date given, *Nicolaus Franciscus Constantini. 1508. Lisbon, Conserv. nacional, 58.* Vaulted back in one piece. Edges of back and belly flush with the sides. Bass bar but no linings. Thick neck with old fingerboard and head carved in the form of a faun's head. *Length* 73 cm, body 39 cm. *Depth* 6 cm. (See p. 8.)

10 Lira da gamba ('*lirone perfetto*'). Unsigned. *Brussels, Conserv. royal, 1444.* Flat back. Small rose in belly. *Length* 106 cm, body 72 cm. *Depth* 6·4–6 cm.

11 Lira da gamba. Unsigned. Italian, ? 1659. *Leipzig, former Heyer Collection* **784.** Destroyed in the last war. Back and sides of walnut. 'Dolphin'-shaped soundholes and parchment rose. *Length* 107 cm, body 66 cm. *Depth* 7·5 cm above, 11 cm below. (Shown on reduced scale.)

In some pictures of around 1500 the lira da braccio still has a guitar-shaped body without corners at the waist; or the body possesses a lower pair of corners only, as in Fig 4, sketched from Carpaccio's 'Christ at the Temple' of 1510. Or again, as painted by Bellini in 1505, there are both pairs of corners at the waist, making the classic three bouts of the violin group, though the corners are still but tentatively pointed. Among the known specimens, the earliest, dating from the same years as these pictures, is the splendid Veronese instrument in the Vienna Collection (**1**). The back and belly are shaped to a gentle arch. The two-lobed bottom outline is typical of liras, though also seen occasionally among violins and viols (**15**). The scrolled shoulders are matched in some contemporary illustrations and the exuberant soundholes retain the basic form of the inwards-facing C-holes of earlier fiddles. A remarkable feature is the carved concavity of the sides, also matched in contemporary pictures.

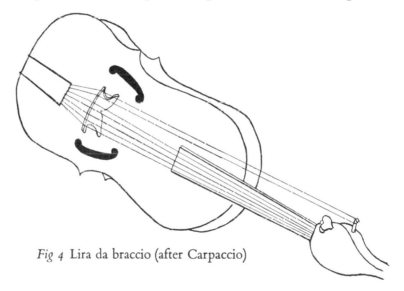

Fig 4 Lira da braccio (after Carpaccio)

The lira da braccio varies in size though not with any known differentiation of musical purpose. The Andrea lira is one of the largest, exceeded in body length only by an example by Ventura Linarol, Venice, 1577 (Leipzig, 780), restored as a lira from a later four-stringed condition, with a body length of 59 cm. The Maria[1] lira (**2**), the smallest of those known, has the size of a smallish modern viola; suggested

[1] David Boyden, *The History of Violin Playing*, p. 17, identifies this maker as Giovanni Maria dalla Corna, and suggests *c.* 1525 as a likely date for this lira.

dates for it put it from 20 to 45 years before the earliest known violins, yet its form is fairly well advanced with a high-arched belly and neat though plain *f*-holes. A third example (**5**) is of a medium-sized lira, with soundholes as seen in the work of Linarol; the unsigned lira at Brussels (1443) is rather like it and has body length of 43·2 cm, and depth of 3·6 cm. It is unlikely that many lire da braccio were built after the turn of the sixteenth century.

Lira da gamba. Also known as *lirone*, this is a larger instrument played downwards like a cello. Also it has a greater number of strings, some of which are bourdons, though not invariably. Like the preceding liras, these larger instruments were intended to be played much in chords (in both solo work and accompaniment), with curious tunings evidently calculated to assist this. Their period is rather later than that of the lira da braccio, namely *c.* 1550–*c.* 1660. The example by the Paduan Tieffenbrucker (**7**) is a rare instance of a bowed instrument by this celebrated lute maker. The anonymous Leipzig example, now destroyed (**11**), was also in original state; its curious blunt-cornered model, with the corners 3 cm wide, is matched in a mid-seventeenth-century painting by Le Valentin. A specimen at Brussels (**10**) may also be an original lira da gamba, of a variety without bourdons named in one source *lirone perfetto*. There are further specimens resembling it in body form but with necks and heads which are the work of modern restorers.

Early violas. Coexistent with the Renaissance lira were violas of more straightforward types without offset bourdons, in this respect closer in a direct line to the violin. One specimen (**8**) is without doubt a genuine example of *c.* 1500 or very early in the sixteenth century. The body is of an average modern viola length and depth. The middle bouts have an early short character, with mildly pointed corners like those of the Andrea lira (**1**) and the sides are carved in a similar concave way. Likewise linings and bass bar are absent, but the *C*-holes are back to back as often with early viols. Though re-necked at some later date the feature of a scroll pegbox, giving a strong two-point bearing for the pegs, had long previously been known in Asia, and in Europe on the rebec and the mandore; also from the late fifteenth century on the viol, and of course later with the violins. Other examples of seemingly early viola exist, over the authenticity of which one must feel less certain. One of these (**9**) has a body without linings, and the neck, though perhaps not original, is yet of an early thick kind, carrying a head for six strings. The small distance between the soundholes diminishes the likelihood of this instrument having been built as a viol however. The inwards-facing *C*-holes with central points are an early type frequently imitated later, e.g. in kits and hurdy-gurdies. Lütgendorff reasonably suggested 1608 as the more likely date for this specimen.

2 The Violin Group

Illustrations

42   Kit. Dimanche Drouyn, Paris, seventeenth century. *London, Victoria and Albert Mus., 519–1872.* Narrow shape, of ivory. Purfling simulated with twisted silver wire. Ivory fittings. *Length* 37 cm, belly 23 cm. With ivory bow, *length* 38 cm.

43   Kit. Joachim Tielke, Hamburg, 1675. *London, W. E. Hill & Sons.* Narrow shape. *Length* 40 cm. With tubular case of cardboard covered with cloth.

44   Pochette d'amour. Battista, Genoa, eighteenth century. *London, R. Coll. Music, 38.* Rounded back hollowed in one piece; no separate sides. *Length* 53 cm, body 21 cm.

45   Kit. Gaspar Borbon, Brussels, 1686. *Brussels, Conserv. royal, 2764.* Festooned body. *Length* 48·5 cm.

46   Kit. Unsigned. *Brussels, Conserv. royal, 493.* Violin form, in one piece. *Length* 39 cm.

47   Miniature violin. Unsigned. *Brussels, Conserv. royal, 2766.* Short, waisted shape. *Length* 30·5 cm.

48   Practice violin (*Brettgeige*). Johann Schorn, Salzburg, 1695. *Berlin, Inst. f. Musikforschung, 282.* Supposed to have belonged to Mozart when a boy. Carved lion head. *Length* 57·5 cm.

49   Mute violin. English, nineteenth century. *London, R. Coll. of Music. 43.* Small body with rounded back in one piece. Belly with open soundhole encircled by purfled rings. *Length* 60 cm.

50   Violino-harpa. Th. Zach, Vienna, 1873. *Brussels, Conserv. royal, 1359. Width* 36 cm.

51   Contra-alto. J. B. Vuillaume, Paris, 1851. *Brussels, Conserv. royal, 235. Length* 68 cm. *Width* 36·5 cm.

52, 53 Violoncello piccolo. Jakob Stainer, Absom, seventeenth century. *Haslemere, Dolmetsch Coll.* Rose carved in belly. Five strings. *Length* 95 cm.

54   Violoncello. Martin Kaiser, Venice, 1679. *Brussels, Conserv. royal, 1441.* Heart-shaped rose. Original neck with marks of gut frets. Slinging holes in back. *Length* 120 cm, body 71·5 cm, fingerboard 40·5 cm. *Depth* 13 cm.

55, 56 Violoncello. Antonio Stradivari, 1690. *Florence, Istituto Cherubini, 6.* 'The Medici.' New neck. *Length* body 79·7 cm.

Double Bass, Violone

57   Double bass. Gottfried Tielke, (Königsberg), 1662. *Leipzig, K.-M. Univers., 940.* Label reads, *Santo Maggini Brescia: Gottfried Thielke: me fecit. Anno 1662.* (Instrument possibly made by G.T. while on visit to Brescia.) Violin form. Double purfling. Belly inscribed with the signatures of players. Lion's head. Five strings. *Length* 202 cm, body 115·5 cm. *Depth* 22 cm.

58   Double bass. Pietro Zenatto, Treviso, 1683. *Brussels, Conserv. royal, 1437.* Normal form with flat back. Belly with double purfling. Entirely in original condition, with the remains of five gut frets. *Length* 199 cm, body 120 cm. *Depth* 24 cm.

59   Double bass. Barbieri Francesco, Verona, 1697. *Lisbon, Conserv. nacional, 90.* Viol form. Original neck and fittings. Five strings. *Length* 172 cm, body 104 cm.

60   Double bass. Carlo Giuseppe Testore, Milan, 1694. *London, in private ownership (photo lent by Raymond Elgar Esq).* The solo instrument of Giovanni Bottesini (b. 1821), since converted from three strings to four. The shoulders have been a little shortened. *Length* body 110·3 cm.

61   Double bass. John Frederick Lott, London, first half of nineteenth century. *In private ownership (photo lent by Raymond Elgar Esq).* In original three-stringed condition. *Length* body 113 cm.

62, 63 Violone. Gio: Paolo Maggini, Brescia, early seventeenth century. *Haslemere, Dolmetsch Coll.* Overhanging edges, double purfling. *Length* 170 cm, body 98 cm.

64, 65 Violone. Ventura Linarol, Padua, 1585. *Vienna, Kunsthist. Mus., C.78.* Nearly original condition. Inlaid fingerboard and tailpiece. *Length* 173 cm, body 100 cm. *Depth* 20 cm.

Other Fiddles

66   Husla. Nineteenth century. *Copenhagen, Muskhist. Mus., D.56.* Three strings. *Length* 61 cm. (See p. 6)

67, 68 Harding fiddle. Norwegian, 1841. *Oxford, Pitt Rivers Mus., 131.H.12.* With 'crémaillère' bow (notch tensioning).

69 Violin. François Chanot, Paris, 1818. *Brussels, Conserv. royal, 1332.* Chanot model with tailpiece.

70 Violin. Félix Savart, Paris, *c.* 1819. *Paris, Conserv., C.19.* Trapezoid model of 1819.

71 Violin. Rigart Rubus, St Petersburg, 1850. *London, Kneller Hall, 195.* 'Russian' model with flush edges.

72 Violin. Thomas Howell, Bristol, *c.* 1835. *London, R. Coll. of Music, 54.* Howell's patent, model with fixed tailpiece.

73 Philomele. German, second half of nineteenth century. *London, Horniman Mus., 15.10.48/30. Length* 60 cm. *String length* 31·7 cm.

74 Crwth (Welsh fiddle). *London, Victoria and Albert Mus., 175-1882.* Copy of 1742 crwth in Welsh Folk Museum, St Fagans. Belly without bass bar. *Length* 56 cm, belly 32 cm. *Depth* (mean) 4·5 cm.

75 Crwth. Welsh, eighteenth century. *Warrington, Museum.* Fingerboard and fittings missing. (Back.)

Historians have cited a fresco of *c.* 1535 in Saronna Cathedral, Lombardy, by Gaudenzio Ferrari, as the earliest depiction of a violin, shown beside two larger instruments which might be a tenor and a bass corresponding to the present viola and violoncello. Thus by the 1530s the violin, then only three-stringed, was already in existence in Italy and was already played in consort with its deeper-pitched congeners. No specimens earlier than of the 1560s are now known to exist.[1] These of the 1560s are by Andrea Amati of Cremona, the earliest of the violin makers whose work has survived, and by Gapsaro da Salò, whom it will here be convenient to notice first. Gasparo (1540–1609) was apprenticed to his father, F. Bertolotti, at Salò, near Brescia, whither he went in about 1562 to work under the luthier Girolamo Virchi, making viols, violins and citterns and becoming a master luthier in 1580 (Vannes). Gasparo's instruments are seldom dated. One violin dates from 1562, when the maker would have been some 22 years old. Less than ten of the numerous violins ascribed to him are now considered genuine, and of violas five, cellos possibly four, and double basses five (Henley). The 'Ole Bull' violin, named after the Norwegian virtuoso of the last century, is doubtful, though a fine example of a decorated violin of the early period (**22**). Two of Gasparo's violas are shown ('viola' here and henceforth having its modern connotation as the middle member of the violin group). The viola in normal format (**16**) shows early characteristics: long, wide and upright *f*-holes; a relative simplicity of the middle bouts, their curve descending at once from the upper corners; and plain scroll. The other viola (**15**), dated 1561, is modelled with no upper pair of corners, in this respect, also in the two-lobed bottom, recalling Carpaccio's liras of 50 years earlier. Otherwise this early Gasparo instrument is decisive and forward-looking. An instrument of similar model (**12**), though possibly not a genuine Gasparo, is considerably larger, with ornamental inwards-facing *C*-holes and a later neck with four-stringed pegbox. It is interesting for its size. Contemporary Italian and German sources now and then mention a member of the *viole da braccio* (the violin group) tuned a fourth or fifth below the viola and presumably between viola and cello in size. No doubt it had uses as a small bass, perhaps by those who preferred a g–c–G(F) consort like the viols to the g–c–C of the normal violins. This unique specimen with body length of 53 cm and 5·5 cm sides may be an example of such an instrument (rather than a converted large lira; and compare a modern attempt at the same pitch and size by Zorzi, p. 14).

A surviving violin by the younger Linarol (**13, 14**) points to a Venetian thrust of independence during this still early time in the instrument's history. The soundholes are most individual, while the curve of the middle bouts at the upper corners points well to the future and the upper bouts are proportionately quite wide. This violin is one which has the additional interest of remaining in its original condition, in this case even to the bridge. Most old violins have undergone, from about 1800 onwards, certain pro-

[1] See Boyden, *op. cit.*, Chap. 1, who cites works by Ferrari depicting the violin as early as 1529–30, and also mentions two violins by Andrea Amati dated 1542 and 1546 said to have been formerly in existence, both originally three-stringed and neither traceable today.

cesses of modernization through the demands of higher playing pitch, larger concert rooms and developments in players' technique. Alterations concern the bass bar, bridge and the neck and fingerboard. The old neck seen in profile (**14, 31, 33**) is set straight in line with the edges of the belly, and often begins to deepen long before the root is reached. The fingerboard is canted up by a wedge. A characteristic notch is usually cut in the underside of the fingerboard at the point where it flies over the rim of the belly.

The record of the great Cremona school begins with Andrea Amati, the grandfather of Nicolò Amati, who was in turn followed by Antonio Stradivari in whom the craft is recognized to have reached its summit. Examples of their work illustrate something of the evolution of body proportions, shoulder lines, curve of the middle bouts, modelling of the corners; also the degree of arching of the belly and the shape of the soundholes. Andrea Amati (b. before 1511, d. *c.* 1580) was already a master luthier in 1526 (Vannes) and may be presumed at that time to have been making precursive forms of the violin, possibly three-stringed as described by Lanfranco (*Scintille*, 1533) and shown in the Saronna fresco. Amati must have played a considerable part in the creation of the violin (**17–19**), though other luthiers, possibly in France too, no doubt contributed. Certainly the *violon* was being sold in Paris in 1551 (Lesure, *GSJ*, VII, 22), probably made there, and also in Lyons, as well as imported from Italy, though no such early French violins are known.

Among the violins of Nicolò Amati (1596–1684) the later examples have been regarded as marking a great step forward (**23, 24**). At the time, the rise of the great Italian school of virtuoso violinists like Corelli must have powerfully stimulated the luthiers' efforts to increase the instrument's tonal resources and brilliance of response to the soloist's bow (of which a dated example of the period is shown, **29**). Stradivari (*c.* 1642–1737) may not have been a regular pupil of Amati as was once thought, but an apprentice wood-carver who veered into violin making through acquaintanceship with the Amati household (A. Baruzzi, *La Casa Nuziale*, transl. Desmond Hill, London, 1962). This would well account for the expert inlay of a number of his earlier violins. Generally, violin inlay rarely exceeds designs in purfling, on the whole a commoner feature among viols (**94**, etc). In the inlaid example shown (**25, 26**) the maker has already begun to lower the vaulting of the belly as well as to strengthen the appearance of the instrument, his perfected form of which is shown in the celebrated 'Messiah' violin (**27, 28**), so-called after the romantic story of its discovery in mint condition by Vuillaume in the last century. The upper and lower bouts are wide and bold, and the *f*-holes are more slanted. In all, more than 600 violins are known to exist from the hand of this master craftsman, of whom the authoritative account is by the brothers Hill (see Bibliography).

By the first half of the eighteenth century, when pupils and successors of Amati were perfecting the craft throughout Italy, the northern countries were in the main dominated by the prototypes of Jakob Stainer (1621–83) of the Tyrol, the only maker outside Italy to become counted among the greatest (**30, 31**). His influence extended to England, though as the eighteenth century progressed English makers, led by Banks of Salisbury and Parker in London, turned to Amati models. The climax of violin design having by then been reached, the era mainly devoted to copying, which has continued up to the present, had commenced. Stradivari's models took some time to dominate this field. Credit for the international recognition of Stradivari goes to French luthiers of the second half of the eighteenth century and after, notably N. Lupot and J. B. Vuillaume. A recent analysis of the situation by Skeaping (*GSJ*, VIII, 1955) has shown that the successes of Stradivari models thenceforth were partly due to the favourable response of these low-arched violins to the processes of modernization already mentioned. Stradivari, along with his most distinguished contemporaries like Joseph Guarnerius, have since provided prototypes not only for high-class work but also for mass-production in centres like Mirecourt, Mittenwald and Markneukirchen, each an old centre of fine violin making and the home of many excellent makers both before and after the rise of the 'factory fiddle' in the nineteenth century.

Miniature violins, down to the total size of a hand's length, sometimes in fancy shapes (**47**), have been made as souvenirs or gifts—though there are violinists who can perform electrifyingly upon them. *Small-sized violins* for children reached some degree of standardization of sizes with the production methods of the nineteenth century: quarter size, with body length approx. 28–30 cm; half size, approx. 31–32 cm; three-quarter size, 33–33·5 cm. In earlier times, however, small violins were also made for professional use, as by Andrea Amati (**17**), while the *violino piccolo* named in some works, of which the best known is Bach's First Brandenburg Concerto, though no contemporary specification of its size exists, may have approximated to 'three-quarter' dimensions, to judge by what has been found suitable in modern performances of this work.

Rebec. Second in importance among fifteenth-century fiddles after the viola, the rebec retained the general form of a medieval species of perhaps Byzantine origin. It had an elongated pear shape with round back and flat belly, and three strings with about the string length of a violin. An odd feature is the flat fingerboard which spans out over the upper part of the belly. The body was either carved from a single piece integral with neck and pegbox, or moulded from ribs. Tinctoris (Naples, *c.* 1487) thought highly of the rebec as a musical instrument, and it may have been one of the first bowed instruments to have been built in various sizes for playing in consort, there being an indication of this in some Italian sonnets of *c.* 1420 by Prudenzani. In the course of the sixteenth century it became supplanted by the violin (itself frequently referred to as *ribecchino* in Italy up to *c.* 1600). Nevertheless rebecs continued to be made in Italy and France up to the eighteenth century and some of these later instruments survive (**38, 39**). Their average total length is from 50 to 56 cm.

In Eastern Europe several species of rebec-like instrument exist in folk music, some, like the Bulgarian *gadulka* and Greek *lyra*, probably stemming directly from the Byzantine prototype, while others like the Dalmatian *liritsa* (**40**) show some influence of the Italian rebec and have sometimes been mistaken for it by collectors.

Kit. This pocket violin (Fr. *poche*, *pochette*) is the dancing master's violin, made from the mid sixteenth century to the end of the eighteenth. Most specimens are seventeenth or early eighteenth century. The sound of the kit is adequate for private dancing lessons without disturbing adjacent apartments. The characteristic form is narrow and truncheon-like (**42, 43**), hollowed from one piece to present five longitudinal rear facets, or built from separate ribs or even from a stick of cane. The narrow belly is highly arched and often has soundholes of an antique *C*-form with notches, also a small heart-shaped hole higher up. A slender soundpost is employed but there is no need for a bass bar. The string length is around 21–24 cm, and the player no doubt tuned to a suitably high pitch (Mersenne gives a tone higher than the violin). Many specimens are so beautifully made that they must have been aristocratic possessions. The instrument was carried with its bow (about 38–45 cm long) in a tubular case (**43**). Kits were also made with a small violin-like body—distinguishable from miniature violins by the proportionately longer neck (**46**)—and in oblong shapes, festooned shapes (**45**), or any that took the maker's fancy. A few carry four wire sympathetic strings in addition to the four playing strings (**44**) and have been described as *pochette d'amour* on the analogy of the viola d'amore. *Walking-stick violins* (**41**), mainly of the nineteenth century, bear some resemblance to the kit in construction and musical effect. *Practice or mute violins*, intended for violin practice without disturbance to neighbours, have taken various forms, of which two common ones are illustrated: the *Brettgeige* (**48**), with no back and virtually no sides; and a later kind with very small soundbox and a solid T-piece to rest against the shoulder (**49**).

Some variant forms of violin are noticed later (**67–72**, also **50**).

The Viola, of which some early specimens have already been noticed, was built by most makers up to the beginning of the eighteenth century in two sizes following the common lay-out of violin-orchestra music up to that time with two middle parts below the second violin. Stradivari termed his smaller viola *contralto viola* and the larger *tenore viola*, the 'Medici' viola (**34, 35**) being a fine example of the latter. During the eighteenth century, as the musical distinction grew obsolete, players generally preferred the smaller instrument (37·5–41 cm body) and large numbers of the old 'tenors' (43–48 cm) were cut down in size, the body being shortened at top and bottom and possibly a slice removed down the centre. An impossible cut being straight across the middle, a cut-down instrument may look disproportionately long in the centre bouts. A traditional and pretty feature of violas, though sometimes omitted, is the semicircular continuation of the back of the pegbox by the neck, as on cellos. The *viola pomposa* is a large five-stringed German species of the first half of the eighteenth century, with J. C. Hoffmann of Leipzig (37) its best-known maker (examples dated 1720, 1732), and Telemann, the best-known of its few composers; body length 46–50 cm. A large-bodied viola by Vuillaume, Paris, 1855 (51) illustrates one of many attempts that have been made to assuage a lurking feeling, formerly expressed on the whole more by theorists than by musicians, that the customary violas are not as big as an instrument tuned a fifth below the violin should be. Vuillaume's design is calculated, according to Heron Allen, to contain an air mass sufficient to resonate to a note pitched a fifth below that of the violin; the resulting tone was said to be powerful but too much like that of a violin. Attempts were also made during the nineteenth century to introduce instruments midway in pitch between the viola and the cello, corresponding to the rather obscure sixteenth-century size mentioned earlier (p. 11), e.g. Stelzner's *violotta* (Wiesbaden, 1891), and Zorzi's *controviolino* (Florence, 1902) with 54 cm body and 5·8 cm sides, played in cello position.

Small violoncellos, down to as little as 46 cm in body length, though distinguishable always from violas by their deep sides, have been built for children at all times. The rare *violoncello piccolo*, however, is an instrument in its own right. Like the viola pomposa it emanates from Germany and from Leipzig in particular, one of the makers again being J. C. Hoffmann (examples between 1731 and 1741). It is five-stringed, the extra string being above the normal A string, and most examples have a rose carved in the belly, as in the Stainer instrument shown (52, 53); body lengths, *c.* 58–60 cm. The violoncello piccolo *may* be the cello *à cinq acordes* for which Bach wrote the Sixth Suite for unaccompanied cello, but authorities are not agreed on this. Certainly there were plenty of ordinary-sized five-stringed cellos still about in Bach's time.

The Violoncello itself for the first 150 years of its existence was usually a slightly larger instrument than played today and intended solely for the bass part of the violin orchestra. Its name up to *c.* 1700 was in fact simply 'bass violin' (*basse de violon*, etc, 54). It had either four or five strings, several examples being preserved in collections with five, e.g. by Willems, Ghent, 1717 (Brussels, 2876). The original straight-set neck may deepen almost evenly throughout the length and give a very massive appearance from the side. Traces of gut frets are sometimes visible, and in the back of the body there may be two holes by which the instrument could be suspended with its head against the player's shoulder for playing while standing, whence an eighteenth-century name for the instrument in Germany, *viola da spalla*. The change to a rather smaller, more elegant model was hastened towards the end of the seventeenth century by musical development of the bass violin as a solo instrument, under the name *violoncino*, later *violoncello*. Stradivari's earlier cellos are of the older large dimensions with 79–80 cm bodies (55, 56). After about 1701 they get smaller, down to 75 cm or less and narrower in proportion. The brothers Hill (*Antonio Stradivari*) suggest that Stradivari's work on the cello might be counted as of even greater revolutionary importance than his work on the violin. As with violas, many of the old large cellos have since been cut down, including many by Italian makers particularly celebrated for their cellos, as Francesco Rugeri, Cremona.

Double basses. Dating from the second half of the sixteenth century, the double bass, familiar and precious instrument in so much of our music, is even now the least standardized member of the violin group. Its variations, leaving out of consideration those of the bow, may be summarized under three headings: stringing, dimensions and model. The number of strings on a double bass has varied from three to six. In basses preserved intact from the seventeenth and early eighteenth centuries, five is the commonest number. These five-stringers are mostly German (57), but there are Italian examples too

(59). They were usually fitted with gut frets (58), claimed to give a clearer tone on the stopped notes (Quantz). Many have been converted to three or four strings in accordance with later practice.

In size, double basses range from exceptional giant basses down to portable and chamber basses sometimes little larger than cellos. Numbers of small basses with body length from *c.* 84 cm upwards were made in Italy and Germany in the seventeenth and eighteenth centuries (*bassetto, Bassl*) for use on serenades, in country bands, etc, and many exist in collections, some with only three strings. A little above this, with bodies from *c.* 90 to 105 cm, are the best 'chamber basses', with examples by leading Italian violin makers, like a fine Andrea Guarneri of 1650 in a sturdy cello format, body 90 cm, from Queen Victoria's private band (Kneller Hall Coll.). The normal double bass with a body length of 112–117 cm and average height six feet used to be termed in the trade a 'three-quarter' bass, in distinction from the now little used 'full' bass with body length of *c.* 122 cm. At the top of the scale is the seventeenth-century Italian giant bass from Dragonetti's collection (Victoria and Albert Museum, 487–1872) with body length 200 cm, depth of sides 30·5 cm, and total height 288 cm. In some respects more interesting since it comes just within practical size, is a large bass from the Correr Collection (Brussels, 1438) with body length 142 cm, mean depth of sides 27 cm and total height 228 cm. This remains in its original five-string condition.

Both these extra-large examples have the classic model of the double bass. This is basically that of the violin and cello save that for various reasons, among them economy in wood and weight, and considerations of player's comfort, the back is flat, half cut towards the top, and the shoulders are sloped to the neck. The edges are often strengthened by beading applied along the sides, and from early in the last century the old tuning pegs (sometimes with ratchet) were replaced by a machine head. The model has been executed with much individual variation, as may be seen by comparing the Testore bass of the celebrated soloist Bottesini (60) with a bass by Lott, an original three-stringer by the best remembered of English double bass makers (61). The squaring of the shoulders of the Lott bass close by the neck is intended to make a strong, imposing appearance despite the narrow three-string neck. One alternative to the classic model is the complete 'violin form', with vaulted back and square shoulders, making a splendid-looking instrument, but rather bulky to manage (57). On the other extreme is a sloping 'viol form' with flush edges and unpointed corners (59), not rare, though in the last century associated mainly with the cheaper German instruments.

Violone. Though up to the eighteenth century this term could include the double bass, in modern usage it is reserved for the double bass viol, a rare instrument made from the second half of the sixteenth century to the third quarter of the seventeenth for use with other viols when desired, and with mixed ensembles. The body size ranges from *c.* 94–110 cm. The build should be lighter than that of a double bass and six strings are normal. In model, the violone may take any of the forms mentioned above for the double bass. In theory, a way of distinguishing the two instruments is by the proportions of body length to string length. With a viol the former is about equal to or a little less than the latter; with a double bass, as with other instruments of the violin group, the body length is the greater. Viol proportions are seen in two violoni illustrated (62–5), that by Gasparo da Salò's celebrated pupil Maggini being built with overhanging edges and other violin-like features.

Other Fiddles and Violin Variants

The primitive *husla* (66) has been mentioned earlier (p. 6); further primitive fiddles have been made as folk instruments in the remoter districts from Portugal to Russia, many of them simple versions of the violin. A sophisticated species is the *Harding fiddle* (67, 68), named from the Hardanger district in West

Norway, where it goes back to the mid seventeenth century. It has a very highly arched belly and four metal sympathetic strings which pass below the playing strings. The Harding fiddle is interesting not only for the individual character of its music but also for the traditional Norwegian motifs with which it is liberally decorated. The Swedish keyed fiddle, *nyckelharpa*, is described later (**158**, p. 27).

Violins built by recognized luthiers and others in different shapes from the classic form have appeared at all periods: festooned, oblong, figure-of-eight, etc. While many are fanciful, the nineteenth century brought endeavours to rationalize the form of the instrument, also of the cello, on scientific precepts, as in the designs of Chanot and of Savart in Paris from 1817. Chanot made the body in 'guitar' shape with flush edges (**69**). In a later model he fitted a short tailpiece attached directly to the belly and reversed the scroll to curl backwards. He made cellos of similar pattern. Staufer's violin, Vienna, 1828, was much the same. Savart adopted a trapezoidal shape (**70**). Both designs were reported to have come well through behind-the-screen tests against the conventional model; nevertheless neither could successfully contest the maxim that to the musician an instrument which looks wrong sounds wrong. In England, Howell (**72**) sought among other things to facilitate playing in the higher positions of the hand (patent of 1835). A Russian model of the mid-century, with chamfered edges flush with the sides, enjoyed some local success (**71**). Finally among the oddities which are shown here, since specimens still turn up, Zach's *violino-harpa*, Vienna, 1873, a hideous attempt to increase tone through soundbox enlargement (**50**).

Philomele. This differs in being a wire-strung fiddle evolved by the Munich zither makers about the middle of the last century (**73**). In early models the body has flat plates, the edges flush with the sides, and no tailpiece: the bridge is joined to the end of the metal-fretted fingerboard and the strings are hitched directly to it. In later models, as illustrated, the strings run to a tailpiece and the body may be more violin-like, with vaulted plates and with a violin soundpost instead of the block of pine glued inside centrally under the bridge as found in the earlier type. Tuning is by machines.

Crwth. The post-classical lyre or 'rote' lingered into medieval Europe and during the eleventh century people began to play it with the then recently imported fiddle bow. For this the strings were reduced in number, though at first remaining spread out fanwise in the lyre fashion. The melody would have been mainly stopped on one string, by the ancient manner of using simple pressure (with no fingerboard), and other strings would have been sounded as bourdons. An active survival of this stage is the Finno-Estonian bowed lyre described by Otto Andersson, whose work (*The Bowed Harp*) also contains the fullest modern account of the Welsh *crwth*. In Britain by the beginning of the fourteenth century the instrument was being modernized, with the strings brought together over a central fingerboard for playing with the more advanced fiddle techniques that had then come into use. This was the 'crowd' which survived up to the end of the eighteenth century in Wales as *crwth* (**74, 75**). No more than four authentic specimens appear to be known. They are carved from one piece of wood which provides flat-backed body, sides, arms, cross-bar and central neck. Added components are the flat pine belly, the fingerboard, tailpiece and bridge. One foot of the bridge passes through one of the soundholes to rest against the back like a soundpost. Details in some cases (**74**) indicate the hand of one who made or played the violin, and the string length is about that of the violin. The six strings form three octave courses, one of which is a bourdon course lying off the fingerboard and struck with bow or thumb. At the cross-bar the strings pass through holes to wrest pins in the rear.

3 Viols

Some twelfth-century pictures show fiddles with figure-of-eight-shaped bodies rested on the lap or slung body-downwards from a cord, but no specific technical particulars are known about them. The history of the viol as a species is best begun in the second half of the fifteenth century, when a demand seems to have arisen for a bowed instrument corresponding in compass, tuning and string length to fingered instruments like the lute and the Spanish large guitar *vihuela*. A few late fifteenth-century paintings show an instrument of this description, and foreshadowing viol models of the next century, by the beginning of which viols were being developed as a consort for the performance of music in parts on viols of appropriate different sizes. Thenceforth the interest of viols from the musical point of view is shared between the music of the consort and that of bass viols employed in solo capacities. The instruments are in general lightly built, resembling other fiddles in overall structure but provided with six strings of finer gut, tuned in the manner of the Renaissance lute. As with the lute, the fingerboard is tied with gut frets. The viols are played with the body downwards, resting on the lap or between the knees according to the size—whence the Italian term for a viol, *viola da gamba*.[1] For each nominal size there exists some dimensional latitude. Some seventeenth-century English treble viols are a good deal larger than the average and are now often termed alto viols. There are also small tenors. Players could choose sizes which suited their consort ideas best. Smaller than the full-sized consort bass are two sizes intended for solo playing: the division viol, and the rarer and smaller lyra-viol. Approximate size-ranges are (body length): treble, 35–39 cm ('alto', up to 41 cm); small tenor, 42–46 cm; tenor, 47·5–53 cm; lyra-viol, 54–60 cm; division viol, 62–67 cm; consort bass, 68–71 cm. (Among sixteenth- and seventeenth-century Italian viols there are instruments which do not correspond to the above scheme of sizes and over which there has been some discussion.) A full set of viols during the greatest days of the consort—from the end of the sixteenth century to the latter part of the next—might comprise two trebles, two tenors and one or two basses. For the double-bass viol or violone, see p. 15.

It should be added here that though the typical number of strings on a viol is six, five is not rare and occurs at every period, while bass viols may have five, six or seven. Numerous viols have come down to us in four-stringed condition, having been altered during the eighteenth century or after for use as violas or cellos.

Illustrations: Viols

76–9   Treble viol. Giovanni Maria (dalla Corna) of Brescia, Venice, c. 1540 or earlier (cf note, p. 7). *Oxford, Ashmol. Mus.* Label, *Juan Maria da Bressa fece in Venecia*. Model without corners. Back in one piece. Original neck, head and fittings, including end-pin. *Length* 61 cm, body 35·7 cm. *Depth* 7 cm.

80–2   Bass viol. Hans Vohar (? Vienna, late fifteenth century or perhaps later). *Haslemere, Dolmetsch Coll.* Cornerless model with shaped back. Open scroll decorated with a single-headed eagle. *Length* 112 cm, body 66 cm. *Depth* 11·8 cm.

83   Tenor viol. Gasparo da Salò, Brescia, second half of sixteenth century. *Vienna, Kunsthist. Mus., C.72.* Label, *Gaspar da Salo in Brescia*. *Length* 86 cm, body 48 cm. *Depth* 8·5 cm.

1 Whence in turn the now prevalent German expression *Gamba*. Early sixteenth-century names for viols are different, including *viole da tasti* ('fretted violas'). The English word is presumably from the French *viole;* old spellings like 'vyalle' indicate the pronunciation.

84, 85 Bass viol. Gaspard Duiffoprugcar, Lyons, *c.* 1560. *The Hague, Gemeentemus.* Model without lower corners. Beaded edges. Divided soundholes. Inlaid back, fingerboard and tailpiece. Finial in form of a horse's head. *Length* 116 cm, body 64 cm. *Depth* 12 cm.

86 Bass viol. Battista Ciciliano, Venice, ? sixteenth century. *Brussels, Conserv. royal, 1426.* Label, *Batista fiel d'Ant° Cicilian in V*ª. Shaped end of fingerboard. *Length* 106·5 cm, body (back) 61 cm, (belly) 59·7 cm. *Depth* 11·4 cm.

87 Tenor viol. Francesco Linarol, Venice, *c.* 1540. *Vienna, Kunsthist. Mus. C.71.* Label, *Franciscus Linarolus Bergomensis Venetiis faciebat. Length* 81 cm, body 51 cm. *Depth* 6 cm.

88–90 Bass viol. Gasparo da Salò, Brescia. *Oxford, Ashmol. Mus.* Wide model. Flat two-piece back, half-cut close to upper end. Beaded sides. Double purfled. Inset carved rose. Original neck and fingerboard. *Length* 114 cm, body 64·5 cm. *Depth* at upper end 12 cm, at bottom 14 cm.

91, 92 Bass viol. Antonio and Geronimo Amati, Cremona, 1611. *Oxford, Ashmol. Mus.* Medici 'M' device branded on the back. Overhanging edges. Shaped back, half-cut. Scroll. Neck, fingerboard, etc not original. *Length* 110 cm, body 62 cm. *Depth* 10 cm.

93 Bass viol. Venetian, sixteenth century. *Oxford, Ashmol. Mus.* Similar to **88** but with inlaid plaques set in belly. *Length* 108 cm, body 59 cm.

94–6 Lyra viol. John Rose, London, 1598. *Oxford, Ashmol. Mus.* Back and sides purfled with trellis patterns. Belly, neck and fittings are replacements by Messrs Hill, *c.* 1900. Original head. *Length* 104 cm, body 54 cm. *Depth* 11·5 cm.

97 Bass viol. Ascribed to John Rose, London, late sixteenth century. *Oxford, Ashmol. Mus.* Festooned model. Flat back and sides decorated with purfled trellis patterns. Belly painted with the arms of Somerset, and with floral designs by hot needle. Original neck and fittings (though not the pegs). *Length* 130 cm, body 70·5 cm. *Depth* 12 cm.

98, 99 Bass viol. Henry Jaye, Southwark (London), 1619. *London, W. E. Hill & Sons.* Decorated back and belly. Renewed tailpiece. *Length* 130 cm.

100 Bass viol. Richard Meares, London, 1677. *London, Victoria and Albert Mus., 170–1882.* Decorated belly. Back and sides renewed. *Length* 121 cm, body 67 cm. *Depth* 11·6 cm.

101, 102 Bass viol. Barak Norman, London, 1697. *Berlin, Instit. f. Musikforschung, 168.* Decorated belly, etc. Inlaid fittings. Open scroll.

103, 104 Division viol. Barak Norman, London, 1712. *Haslemere, Dolmetsch Coll.* Decorated belly, double purfled. Open scroll. *Length* body 68 cm.

105 Tenor viol. John Baker, 'Exon' (on label, but ? Oxford), 1660. *Haslemere, Dolmetsch Coll.* Decorated belly. Scroll. *Length* body 41 cm.

106 Division viol. Ernst Busch, Nuremberg, 1644. *Leipzig, K.-M.-Univ., 808.* Festooned form. Bird's-eye maple. Flame holes, and parchment rose. Carved scroll. *Length* 112·5 cm, body 62 cm. *Depth* 13 cm.

107 Bass viol. Vincenzo Rugeri, Cremona, 1702. *Berlin, Instit. f. Musikforschung, 164.* 'Cello' format. Inset rose. Flame holes. Neck and head renewed in 1884. *Length* 136·5 cm, body 75·5 cm.

108 Bass viol. Jakob Stainer, Absom, 1655. *Haslemere, Dolmetsch Coll.* Square shoulders. Seven strings. *Length* 124 cm, body 68 cm.

109 Tenor viol. Johann Ulrich Eberle, Prague, 1749. *Leipzig, K.-M.-Univ., 796.* Festooned model. Back and sides of figured sycamore. Flame holes. Five strings. *Length* 79·5 cm, body 46 cm. *Depth* 7 cm.

110 Bass viol. Zenatto, Treviso, 1643. *Lisbon, Conserv. nacional, 65.* Narrow form, with bevelled flush edges. Flat back. *Length* 117 cm, body 66 cm. *Depth* 9·5 cm. *Max. width* 37 cm.

111, 112 Bass viol. Joachim Tielke, Hamburg, 1691. *Munich, Bayer. Nationalmus., 39.* Made for the Elector Johann Wilhelm of Pfalz. Inlaid back, sides and fittings. Rose. Ivory head.

113, 114 Bass viol. Claude Pierray, Paris, 1713. *Paris, Conserv., E.1006, C.173.* Inlaid fleurs-de-lys at corners. *Length* 120 cm.

115 Head of bass viol. Joachim Tielke, Hamburg, 1694. *Barcelona, Mus. de musica, 693.* Five strings.

116, 117 Bass viol. Joachim Tielke, Hamburg, 1701. *Brussels, Conserv. royal, 229.* Back of rosewood with ivory fillets. Ivory neck, head and fittings including tailpiece in the form of a cornucopia.

118 Quinton. Nicolas Louis Gilbert, Metz, 1701. *Brussels, Conserv. royal, 1396.*

119, 120 Pardessus de viole. Paul François Grosset, Paris, 1742. *Berlin, Instit. f. Musikforschung, 4220. Length* 59·7 cm, body 33 cm. *Depth* 4·7–5·5 *cm.*

121, 122 Pardessus de viole. Louis Guersan, Paris, 1754, *Brussels, Conserv. royal, 480.* Striped back. *Length* 62 cm, body 33 cm. *Depth* 6 *cm.*

123, 124 Alto viol. Richard Duke, London, 1786. *Boston, Mus. of Fine Arts, 277.* Five strings. Inset rose. Flame holes and square finial. *Length* 69·5 cm, body 41·5 cm. *Depth* 3·5 *cm.*

Early viols. The model of the viol varied much in the early part of its 300 years of use, and the present illustrations are selected partly with a view to demonstrating this aspect of what the late Gerald Hayes called 'a very Proteus among instruments'. Before the end of the sixteenth century Italian specimens predominate. Models without corners, with either sloping or squared shoulders (**76–83**), were built in Italy until possibly quite late: a remarkable set of some 14 cornerless viols at Brussels, from the Correr collection, bear among them labels of Pietro Zenatto (not Zanetto, a better-known name in lutherie), Treviso, some with the date 1683, though it is conceivable that this little-known maker did not construct, but salvaged and restored this stock of instruments of which the belly lengths are 39, 51, 60–62 (the majority) and 71 cm. The fine cornerless viol (**80**) with shaped back and a signature *Hanss Vohar* which is not recorded elsewhere, shows the open scroll (a scroll pierced right through) much used by seventeenth-century viol makers alternatively to a finial in the form of a carved figure.

A rarer model of the sixteenth century (**84, 85**) is that in which the waist has an upper pair of corners but not a lower (the opposite of the arrangement seen in early pictures of the lira da braccio and in the early Gasparo viola, **15**). This model has the importance of being associated with one of the celebrated early luthiers outside Italy, Gaspard Duiffoprugcar of Lyons (1514 71), possibly related to the Tieffen-bruckers of Venice and Padua. The body is without linings and the tailpiece is attached to a wooden hook-bar fixed to the base of the body, as in most later viols. In the early Italian viols the tailpiece is usually attached to an end-pin or simply to a metal staple driven into the base of the belly.

The two principal early treatises on viol playing, by Hans Gerle, Nuremberg, 1532, and by Sylvestro Ganassi, Venice, 1543, both illustrate a viol with the complete four corners to the waist of the body, anticipating the classic form of the seventeenth century. Its model is approached among the early specimens by certain Venetian instruments (**86, 87**). As with some of the cornerless viols, the back is for some unexplained reason (perhaps to do with comfort) longer than the belly, so that the sides of the shoulders take an upwards inclination towards the back. The upper corners are distinctly pointed but the lower scarcely so, also recalling the woodcuts in Gerle and Ganassi. Ganassi actually mentions a Gioanbattista Ciciliano (*cf.* **86**), though other evidence has suggested that this Venetian family were making similar viols in the second half of the seventeenth century.

Another early Italian model with completed corners differs in being wide and square-built, with short upper bouts and very deeply-cut centre bouts. The belly is peculiarly carved to form very distinct ridges running towards each of the four strongly pointed corners (**88, 93**). A small rose is carved in the belly (as quite often in viols) and the soundholes are of an antique *E* pattern. Three are ascribed to Gasparo da Salò and a dated example is by Antonio Brensio, Bologna, 1592 (Leipzig, 782). Most are six-stringed, but some show signs of having been altered and the question has been asked whether any of them were built as *lire da gamba* (p. 8). The Brensio instrument at Leipzig has been restored as such from the four-stringed state in which it was obtained. On the other hand, a fine viol by the brothers Amati (**92**) has a similar overall model, though the belly is not carved with the ridges and the back is arched. The reason behind these different early viol models is unknown. There is no apparent evidence of differentiated musical function. Yet their existence seems strange since most other leading types of instrument soon in their history take on a classic form. Yet another curious model is known by at least two examples, one by Zenatto (**110**): the form is very thin with elongated centre bouts and the belly edges are carved all the way round to a wide bevel. In an unsigned example (Brussels, 1429) the waist is no more than 14 cm; in this the back is arched.

Classic forms. The classic viol, which has the most interest alike for players and connoisseurs today, is known by examples dating from the end of the sixteenth century. The graceful economy of its form is beautifully illustrated by a lyra viol by John Rose (**94, 95**), the earliest of the English makers whose work has survived. The English were at this time on the way to leading Europe in every aspect of the viol and its music, though how much the classic viol in England may owe to the Italian musicians who thronged the Court in the sixteenth century is as yet hard to say. The purfled or incised geometrical ornament which is so frequent on the seventeenth-century English viols is seen on a viol in a picture by Tintoretto, *c.* 1550, while striped backs and sides of woods of contrasting hues are also inherited from Italian Renaissance lutherie. The shallow, lute-like neck may be a new feature (and one with which some ancient viols have been re-fitted). Refinements of musical technique no doubt demanded it. Its root is usually shaped to a ridge. The backs and bellies are sometimes made from as many as five pieces of wood. Their edges are flush with the sides and the interior of the body is without wooden linings, though these may appear in viols made late in the seventeenth century. The tailpiece is carried on a hook-bar, and the C-holes in the belly face outwards and tend to become narrower with the makers who followed Rose, as Henry Jaye (**98**), Richard Meares (**100**), John Baker (**105**) and lastly Barak Norman (d. 1746) (**102, 103**).

Concurrently, festooned models occur. These, which would appear to be derived from the older viol model without lower corners like the Duiffoprugcar (**84**), are seen in Venetian mid-sixteenth-century paintings and in an extant large bass viol, 77 cm in body length, with a label bearing the name of Pellegrino Zanetto, Brescia, 1547 (Paris, E.504). Later examples are by Rose (**97**) and especially by the Nuremberg makers Paul Hiltz and Ernest Busch (**106**), both working through most of the earlier part of the seventeenth century. In all these festooned viols 'flame' soundholes are characteristic.

Towards the end of the century there appears much fine viol making after the classic form in France, the Netherlands and Germany. Among leading names are Peter Rombouts, Amsterdam (especially seven-stringed bass viols); J. C. Hoffmann; Joachim Tielke of Hamburg (**111, 112, 115-17**), noted for the elaborate decoration found on his instruments of all kinds; and in Paris, Claude Pierray (**113, 114**). Others include makers better known for their work on the violin group, the influence of which may show in their viols, as Stainer and V. Rugeri (**108, 107**). From the time of Pierray until past the middle of the eighteenth century, viol playing was revived in France with combinations like harpsichord and bass viol accompanying one or more small viols of fresh types; the *pardessus de viole* (**119-22**), which is a small treble viol (body *c.* 32 cm) with the sixth string usually omitted; and shallow-sided five-stringed instruments known as *quintons*, with body *c.* 32-35 cm, often a shaped back, and intended for playing at the shoulder (**118**). Guersan, pupil of Pierray, and Grosset are among the best-known makers of the pardessus. Instruments similar to the quinton were made outside France by Tielke and others, and in England by violin makers like Wamsley and Duke (**123, 124**), this last example showing decorative traits of the latter part of the eighteenth century.

4 Viola D'Amore, Cither Viol, Baryton

Illustrations

125, 126 Viola d'amore. Caspar Stadler, Trabant (Munich), 1714. *Nuremberg, German. Nationalmus., MI.208.* Back inlaid with floral scrolls and musical scenes. Six strings and six sympathetic.

127 Viola d'amore. J. B. Wassner, Passau, 1707. *Basel, Hist. Mus., 1956–431.* Open pegbox. Six plus six strings.

128 Viola d'amore. Max Zacher, Breslau, 1733. *Berlin, Instit. f. Musikforschung, 4526.* Festooned model. Rose. Seven plus seven strings. *Length* 86 cm, body 43·5 cm. *Depth* 4·5–5·2 cm.

129 Viola d'amore (*Englisches Violett*). Johann Paul Schorn, Salzburg, 1712. *Nuremberg, German. Nationalmus., Rück Collection.* Festooned model. Rose. Seven playing strings and 14 sympathetic. *Length* 90·5 cm, body 45·5 cm.

130 Viola d'amore (*Englisches Violett*). J. U. Eberle, Prague, 1737. *London, R. Coll. Music, 33.* Eight playing strings and 24 sympathetic, the latter tuned at traps in the base of the body. *Length* 78 cm, body 43 cm. *Depth* 6·4 cm.

131 Bow of viola d'amore. Italian. *Brighton, Museum.* Accompanying a viola d'amore by V. Rugeri, 1701.

132 Viola d'amore. Probably French. *London, Victoria and Albert Mus., 157–1882.* Seven playing strings, seven sympathetic. (Back of pegbox.)

133 Violon d'amour. Salomon, Paris, 174–. *Brussels, Conserv. royal, 481.* Label, *Salomon, Lutier . . . a Paris 174.* Five playing strings and six sympathetic. *Length* 66 cm.

134 Cither viol. John Perry, Dublin, 1767. *London, Victoria and Albert Mus., 156–1882.* Shaped back and high-arched belly each in one piece. Flush edges. Pearl inlay round edges. Ivory fittings. Machine head with attached brass ring-buttons, possibly replacing an earlier peg head. Square finial. Six metal strings. *Length* 76 cm, body 36 cm. *Depth* 4·3 cm. *String length c.* 34 cm.

135 Cither viol. Stewart & Son (? London), 1828. *London, Reuben Greene Collection.* Shaped back. Five double courses of metal strings, with screw tuning by separate watchkey.

136–8 Baryton. Jacques Sainprae, Berlin, first half of eighteenth century. *London, Victoria and Albert Mus., 1444–1870.* Originally six playing strings and 25 sympathetic, the latter attached to fixed rail below a fixed and oblique bridge. Marquetry tailpiece and fingerboard. Carved neck plate, the face veneered with engraved ivory pierced with a scroll pattern. Partitioned pegbox surmounted by a figure of Orpheus. *Length* 133 cm, body 70 cm. *Depth* 14 cm.

139 Baryton. Joachim Tielke, Hamburg, 1686. *London, Victoria and Albert Mus., 115–1865.* Belly has 'flame' holes. Six playing strings. Twenty-five sympathetic strings, attached to oblique fixed bridge and tuned at the head by wrest pins. *Length* 135 cm, body 69 cm. *Depth* 13 cm. *String length c.* 67 cm.

140 Bass viol (*viola bastarda*). Unsigned, German, second half of seventeenth century. *The Hague, Gemeentemus.* Festooned model. Rose. Open pegbox. Seven strings and seven wire sympathetic strings attached to hitch pins at base of body. Neck renewed. *Length* 127 cm, body 70 cm.

141 Arpeggione. J. Georg Staufer, Vienna, 1824. *Leipzig, K.-M.-Univ., 609.* Arched belly. Brass frets. Six strings. *Length* 115 cm, body 64 cm.

Viola d'amore. This was built in most countries from the late seventeenth century to the third quarter of the eighteenth, English examples being the fewest. There are, however, earlier and later dates in extant specimens, e.g. 1660 (Tielke, Boston, 281) and 1828 (A. Gagliano, Brighton Museum). The six or seven playing strings are usually stated to have been of gut, but Majer (1741) mentions second, third and fourth strings of steel and brass, and the lower of gut overspun with silver. Six or seven sympathetic wires pass down the neck concealed in a hollow under the fingerboard. The early Tielke instrument just referred to has, however, five playing strings with seven wires. The body outline is generally somewhat viol-like, with flush edges (**127**), though there exist a number of German and Italian festooned instruments (**128**) and many with shaped backs. The depth of the sides averages 4 cm in the ordinary models with body 35–41 cm, and 6·5 cm in those which are rather larger, with 42·5–44·5 cm body. Flame ('flaming sword') soundholes are typical and so is a carved blindfold cupid or cherub surmounting the head. The instrument is played at the shoulder and without frets. The normal pegbox is long and graceful, and is open for at least half of its back. The pegs for the wires are placed higher up than those for the playing strings (**132**). In a rarer arrangement the wires are hitched at the head and tuned by wrest pins concealed in traps cut in the bottom block of the body. Many viole d'amore were later converted for use as violas, some still so in use among amateur players of the older generation.

Englisches Violett. Leopold Mozart gives this name for a type of viola d'amore with additional sympathetic strings, and the name has stuck, though most examples are Austrian. That by Schorn (**129**) has 14 wires. Eberle made almost identical instruments and also a version with 24 wires tuned in traps at the base of the body (**130**).

Violon d'amour. A rare French species of the mid eighteenth century, smaller than the viola d'amore and with a varying number of strings (**133**).

Cither viol. Also named *sultana*, this was introduced by Thomas Perry, Dublin, in the 1760s (**134**). Though in some respects it brings to mind early descriptions of the viola d'amore as a species with wire playing strings and without mention of sympathetics, Perry, a fine violin maker trained in London under Duke, seems to have intended a bowed companion to the popular 'English Guitar' of the period, which is a kind of cittern or 'cither' (p. 42). From this instrument the cither viol took its tunings and the materials of the strings (three steel, one brass, two overspun brass), though the string length is approximately that of the violin. The body has a shaped back and a free-lance outline somewhat recalling that of the viola d'amore, while the style of ornamentation is mostly derived from the English Guitar. Later specimens, by Perry & Wilkinson, are strung in various ways, sometimes with five double courses (1794, etc), while a late example by Stewart (**135**) indicates that the cither viol had more than a few years of dilettante success.

Baryton. A very distinctive variant of bass viol, played from the mid seventeenth century to the end of the eighteenth, mainly in Germany and Austria (**136**). It is the first European instrument known to have regularly carried additional strings of metal, running underneath the playing strings. Such strings, already noticed on the viola d'amore and other instruments, were earlier in use on Asiatic instruments like the Indian *sitar*, vibrating in sympathy with the playing strings and adding very considerably to the effect of the instrument in performance. But on the baryton the wires are arranged so that they can also be struck by the left thumb in accompaniment to the gut bowed strings. This is made possible by constructing the neck in the form of a frame, with two pieces placed parallel at some distance from each other and together supporting the pegbox. Bridging the intervening space down one side is the fingerboard, with, on its right, a wide board or grill behind which the wires pass exposed to the rear (**137, 138**). The characteristic body form is of the upper-corners-only viol type, quietly festooned in the lower part and two-lobed along the bottom so that the instrument will stand without support. The soundholes are often of a 'double comma' form (**136**), and the body length is from 62–70 cm.

A reference by Mersenne in 1644 (*Cogitata Physico-Mathematica*, quoted by Fruchtman, 1962) is to an English viol which appears to have been a true form of baryton, with auxiliary metal strings which were plucked. In a baryton by Magnus Feldlen, Vienna, with a date 1647 which may be presumed genuine (London, R. College of Music, 204) the fingerboard is raised sufficiently clear of the neck member beneath it to allow tying of gut frets, of which the example has seven. Otherwise the baryton was played without frets. In this same example the wires, numbering 13, are hitched at the base of the pegbox and tuned by wrest pins set in a diagonal fixed bridge. Usually the wires are hitched to the fixed bridge or to hitch pins at the bottom, and tuned by pegs or wrest pins in the pegbox. They number up to 40, tuned chromatically. The baryton is best remembered in music history for the numerous Divertimenti written by Joseph Haydn for his patron Prince Nicolas Esterhazy.

An earlier use of wire sympathetic strings had apparently been made in England, on the lyra viol. Praetorius, describing the lyra viol under the name *viola bastarda*, mentions an English form with eight wires. Playford (*Musick's Recreation on the Viol, Lyra-way*, 1661) ascribes the idea to the violist and composer Daniel Farrant, earlier in the century; Playford says that the wires ran through a hollow passage in the neck (cf the viola d'amore), over a bridge about half an inch high, to the tail of the viol. Playford adds that he had seen many such viols, though they had passed out of use. Among surviving viols, a small number of bass viols, one English (Brussels, 487, by Francis Baker, 1696, with 12 wires), the other Continental (**140**), have wire sympathetic strings arranged much in the way Playford describes, though in some cases (as with the Baker) possibly representing a later alteration. Boivin's big festooned bass viols with shaped backs made in Paris in 1734, etc, were, however, built originally with sympathetic strings.

Arpeggione. A short-lived recurrence of the Renaissance idea of a bowed guitar. Its inventor, J. G. Staufer, Vienna, 1823, also named it *guitare d'amour* (**141**). The body has something of the appearance of Staufer's cornerless cellos but the neck has metal frets. Schubert wrote a pleasant Sonata for the arpeggione, now often played on other instruments.

5 Trumpet Marine

This (Italian *tromba marina*, German *Trumscheit*) stands on the average some 200 cm high from the open bottom of the soundbox to the top of the tuning head, which is normally for one long gut string. Mersenne recommends a stout racquet string. The player bows the string with a short box close to its upper end, meanwhile touching it with the thumb at points below the bow where it will vibrate in harmonics of the note it is tuned to. By this means simple diatonic melodies are played in the register of the treble voice, and since the notes are restricted to those of one harmonic series the music, in scope as in intonation, bears a resemblance to that of the old natural trumpet—whence no doubt 'trumpet', though why 'marine' is not adequately explained. The instrument was played from the sixteenth century, before which there were smaller-sized precursive forms not known by extant specimens, to the nineteenth, largely during the later centuries in religious houses to accompany chant, and in folk music.

Illustrations: Trumpet Marine

142, 143   Trumpet marine. German, seventeenth century. *Basel, Hist. Mus., 1876.21; Nef 151.* From Kloster Wittichen, Bädischen Schwarzwald. Seven staves of lime. Vertical tuning screw. *Height* 200 cm.

144   Trumpet marine. Hornsteiner, Mittenwald, 1790. *Berlin, Instit. f. Musikforschung, 158.* MS label *Mathias Hornsteiner in midten waldt an der isser grätz geigen macher 1790.* Six staves of pine. Vertical tuning screw. *Height* 195 cm.

145   Trumpet marine. German, eighteenth century. *London, R. Coll. of Music, 244.* Body of seven staves. Neck attached by an iron plate. Finial in form of human head. *Height* 194 cm, body 117 cm. *String length* 140 cm.

146   Trumpet marine. Renault, Paris, second half of eighteenth century. *London, R. Coll. of Music, 289.* Normal form. Body of seven staves, forming two longitudinal parts bolted together on the inside. Belly with two roses and inlaid surrounds. Neck marked with bone strips. The notes are marked by harmonic numbers, 3, 4, 5, 6, 8, and so on up to 13 (9, 11 and 13 in smaller figures). Body stamped *RENAULT*. Tuning peg with ratchet. *Height* 198 cm, body 120 cm. *String length* 155 cm.

147, 148   Trumpet marine. ? German, c. 1700. *London, Victoria and Albert Mus., 174–1882.* With sympathetic strings. Body of five staves of pine. Belly with oval soundhole with ebony moulding surround. The 41 wire sympathetic strings run inside, close to the belly, from wrest pins at the top of the body, accessible through a sliding trap, to hitch pins at the base. Ratchet tuning by separate key. *Height* 191 cm. *String length c.* 144 cm.

149   Trumpet marine. Italian, eighteenth century. *Lisbon, Conserv. nacional, 100.* Two-stringed. Belly with rose and 'flame' soundholes. Two gut strings pass over an ordinary symmetrical bridge and are attached below to the belly. Pegbox with two pegs. *String length c.* 128 cm.

Praetorius and Mersenne both show a pyramidal body which, including soundboard, reaches to the head. The known examples, however, have a separate neck, the body thus being shorter. Evidently this represents a mid or late seventeenth-century modification. The body is usually of seven or five tapered staves over which is placed a flat belly. The neck is often inscribed with letters to show where the string is to be touched for the different notes. Tuning is either by a vertical screw turned by a round knob like a door-handle placed at the extreme top (**142**), or by an ordinary peg, often furnished with pawl and ratchet. The vertical screw is the rarer, and is generally accompanied by a bell-bottomed shape of body, though the reason for the coincidence of these features remains to be explained.

The lower end of the string passes over a bridge which is normally asymmetric, having a lengthened left leg which is intended to jar against the belly like a primitive amplifier. Below the bridge the string is held in the belly by a toggle or similar device. Most specimens of trumpet marine are work-a-day instruments with no decoration whatever (**145**). Two of those shown (**146, 148**) belong, however, to a period when the instrument took some part in public and private concerts, chiefly in France and England, and these examples are modestly decorated.

Internal sympathetic strings are found in several examples (**147**). Praetorius describes three sympathetics, but mounted on the belly. The internal arrangement dates from the second half of the seventeenth century. Examples with an additional playing string are more scarce. In an Italian eighteenth-century specimen (Leipzig, 704) the second string is shorter than the main string, as shown by Mersenne. The instrument illustrated (**149**) has two strings of the same length, no doubt to be tuned to two different notes and so add to the musical resources.

6 Hurdy-Gurdy

Wheel fiddles, in which gut strings are sounded by turning a resined boxwood wheel mounted on an axle placed inside the body of the instrument, are first shown in manuscripts of the twelfth century (see Bachmann, 122). Wooden keys, by which the strings are stopped, were arranged in various manners in medieval church and secular forms of the instrument, none of which has survived. In later instruments, from the fifteenth century up to the present, the keys are mounted in a keybox fixed on top of the body and there is virtually no neck (**150–6**). Throughout this period the hurdy-gurdy (formerly in England *cymbal*; Fr. *vielle*, Ger. *Leier*) has been chiefly a folk instrument, known in many parts of Europe, often in the hands of street musicians. In France, however, it was reintroduced to higher society along with other peasant instruments during the reign of Louis XIV. It was then developed by the Paris makers in 'lute' (**153**) and 'guitar' (**151**) forms and though the fashion expired during the eighteenth century, the hurdy-gurdy has since retained a certain air of respectability in French provinces like Berry and Auvergne, handsomely made by local craftsmen for folk music.

Illustrations: Hurdy-Gurdy

150 Hurdy-gurdy. French, sixteenth century. *Paris, Conserv., E.2057.* Tapered body. Two roses. Heart-shaped head with side struts. Six strings. Two rows of keys. *Length* 60 cm.

151 Hurdy-gurdy (*vielle en guitare*). French, eighteenth century. *London, R. Coll. of Music, 120.* Guitar-shaped body with C-holes. Sides of dark wood with ivory fillets. Wheel guard removed. Two rows of keys and six strings (two melody, four drones). *Length* 58 cm.

152 Hurdy-gurdy. German, 1787. *Hamburg, Mus. f. Hamburg. Geschichte, 1924, 223.* Body with sharp waist. Square head. Peasant-style decoration and notch carving. Three strings and one row of diatonic keys. *Length* 70 cm.

153 Hurdy-gurdy (*vielle en luth*). Varquain, Paris, 1742. *London, R. Coll. of Music. 123.* Lute-shaped body, two C-holes. Six strings.

154 Hurdy-gurdy. German, 1714. *Hamburg, Mus. f. Hamburg. Geschichte, 1924, 222.* Body with sharp waist. Two roses, and a C-hole on the right side. Belly overlaps sides. Square head. Four strings of which two (melody and drone) pass through keybox and two pass outside, one on each side. One row of 11 keys. Date inlaid with brass wire on keybox lid. *Length* 70 cm.

155 Hurdy-gurdy. Quig, Ireland, late eighteenth or early nineteenth century. *Dublin, Nat. Mus. of Ireland.* Long 'guitar' shape. Soundholes in quatrefoil pattern. Scroll head. Two rows of keys and four strings. Shown with keybox opened. Wheel guard missing.

156 Hurdy-gurdy. Austrian, seventeenth or eighteenth century. *Salzburg, Mus. Carolino Augusteum, 162, Geir. 106.* Violin form, the sides nailed. C-hole on right side of belly, and decorative date 1528. Single diatonic row of 12 keys. Five pegs (three new) but four strings (two melody, two drones outside keybox). *Length* 64 cm. *Depth* 10·5 cm.

157 Organ hurdy-gurdy (*vielle organisée*). *London, R. Coll. of Music, 122.* Six strings and 23 organ pipes. *Length* without handle 74 cm.

158 Keyed fiddle (*nyckelharpa*). Swedish, nineteenth century. *Stockholm, Musikhist. Mus., 2344.* Waisted body of pine. Flat head with rear pegs. Seven strings and bow. *Length c.* 87 cm.

The hurdy-gurdy is carried on a sling with the keys sloping a little downwards and pushed inwards by the fingers of the left hand. The right hand turns the handle. The body shape and the 'chair-leg' struts of an early French specimen (**150**) recall a painting by Bosch, though the six strings and double row of keys indicate a later date. Three or four strings are usual among the peasant instruments of Germany and countries to the east, two or three of the strings being drones, not touched by the blades of the keys. In France the head imitates that of a viol and is carved with a figure or scroll, though it keeps to the old fiddle arrangement of upright pegs inserted from the front (**151**). Also in France, two unison melody strings pass through the keybox and two drones pass on each side. Of the drones to the left side (key side) one, the *trompette*, is arranged to give a rasping sound by means of a loose, juddering bridge, the string being adjusted by a loop of gut.

Organ hurdy-gurdies, incorporating one or two ranks of stopped organ pipes in addition to the strings, belong to late eighteenth-century France (**157**). The keys act as organ keys as well as stopping the strings and the handle works the bellows as well as turning the wheel. Many different patterns were made.

There have also been, from the later Middle Ages onwards, fiddles which fall half-way between ordinary fiddles and the hurdy-gurdy, possessing the wheel action or the key action but not both. Wheel action alone is illustrated by Praetorius in a type of peasant hurdy-gurdy, no example of which appears to have survived. Key action without wheel is a feature of the Swedish *nyckelharpa* (**158**), known from the sixteenth century, perhaps earlier. This is played with a short bow. An old form had three strings (one melody, two drone) and also wire sympathetic strings. About the beginning of the nineteenth century another string was added (Panum, 314), placed next to the old melody string and provided with about five keys of its own, making it possible to play in harmony, e.g. in thirds and sixths. To make way for this string's key action which is placed lowermost, some of the primary set of keys have their rods in the shape of an open circle. The blade of the lower key comes up through this opening from below. Like the hurdy-gurdy, the nyckelharpa is slung on a strap, leaving both hands wholly free for manipulation of the instrument.

7 Lutes

This classic musical instrument of Arab culture, introduced into European music in the thirteenth century, rose during the fifteenth to a position of unique importance which it held until a decline set in towards the end of the seventeenth century, though lutes were still built in the mid eighteenth century. By the end of the fifteenth century the lute was properly Europeanized, the Arab plectrum styles having given place to polyphonic performance with the fingers, the tuning altered to suit. At that time the chief centre of lute making was Bologna, where worked Laux (Luke) Maler (d. 1552), whose lutes remained in highest demand for over two centuries. Hans Frei ran Maler, possibly his instructor in the craft, a close second in this respect. By the mid sixteenth century Venice had risen as a lute-making centre, followed by Padua and Rome, nearly all the great makers in these cities having also been of German extraction. In Lyons, too, there were German makers, led by Gaspard Duiffoprugcar (p. 19), while important centres in Germany itself included Nuremberg and Augsburg. There were makers in England but none of their lutes have survived.

Under the general heading 'lute' may be included various forms known by different names, as theorbo and chitarrone, both two-headed lutes or 'archlutes' with one pegbox surmounting the other. They will be noticed separately later, but they have constantly to be borne in mind when considering old lutes. All employ the same kind of body construction, moulded from ribs numbering from nine to over 50, and events have shown that in the past bodies became regarded as interchangeable from one kind of lute to another. From the second half of the seventeenth century onwards old lute bodies were frequently commandeered for rebuilding as archlutes. This, coupled with alterations to lute stringing and neck-width as a result of changes in playing practice—in some cases going back to the mid sixteenth century—drastically diminishes the chances of finding an old lute still in the condition in which it left its maker's workshop. Collections abound with archlutes embodying the remains of a genuine old lute, not to mention lutes converted into guitars or large mandolins during the latter part of the eighteenth century and after, as well as collectors' pieces fabricated in the last century from old parts and crude accretions. But at least it can be said that through these things a large number of fine lute bodies are preserved which would otherwise have passed into limbo. The majority of the earlier examples illustrated here have, or may be suspected of having undergone some alteration, though of honest kinds associated with playing requirements during the active era of the lute.

Illustrations: Lutes

159   Lute. Laux Maler, Bologna, c. 1520. *Vienna, Kunsthist. Mus., C.32.* Label in ink, *Laux Maller.* Eleven ribs. Plait-work Renaissance rose. Eleven-course (two single, nine double) and raised treble peg. *Length* 81 cm, body 51 cm.

160, 161   Lute. Michielle Harton, Padua, 1598. *Washington, Folger Shakespeare Library.* Thirty-five ribs. Two frets on the belly. Ivory stringing on fingerboard. Nine-course (raised treble peg added by modern restorer). *Length* 74·3 cm, body 52 cm. *String length* 65 cm.

162–4   Lute. Hans Frei, Bologna, c. 1550. *Warwick, Museum. Ex-Halfpenny Coll.* Eleven ribs of figured sycamore. Fingerboard inlaid with floral pattern with contrepartie on back of neck, this neck probably a replacement of c. 1600. Eleven-course (two single, the rest double, the first now absent). *Length* 78 cm, body 50 cm.

165 Lute. Gaspar Duiffoprugcar, Lyons, *c. 1550. Copenhagen, Claudius Coll., 91A.* Nine sycamore ribs. Later head with bracket for four bass strings in addition to the ten main courses. *Length* 103 cm, body 50 cm. *String length* 68 cm.

166, 167 Bass lute. Magnus Stegher, Venice, second half of sixteenth century. *Bologna, Mus. civico, 12.* Forty-three ribs. Triple rose. Neck with ivory stringing. Twenty pegs (probably for 11 courses). *Length* 102 cm, body 69 cm. *String length* 89·8 cm.

168 Lute. Wendelin Tieffenbrucker, Padua, 1582. *Vienna, Kunsthist. Mus., C.36.* Label, *Padova Vvendelino Venere de Leonardo Tiefenbrucker 1582.* Thirteen ribs. Plait-work rose. Five double courses. *Length* 76 cm, body 51 cm.

169, 170 Descant lute. Wendelin Tieffenbrucker, Padua. *Vienna, Kunsthist. Mus., C.39.* Nineteen ribs. Brand mark *W.E.* with anchor. Seven-course (single treble course). *Length* 50 cm, body 32·5 cm.

171 Treble lute. Giovanni Hieber, Venice, late sixteenth century. *Brussels, Conserv. royal, 1561.* Seven-course. *Length* 67·5 cm, body 43 cm. *String length* 60 cm.

172 Theorbo-lute. P. Massaini, Rome, 1570. *The Hague, Gemeentemus.* Fifteen ribs with ivory fillets. Altered in seventeenth century with two heads, one reflexed, one upright. Six double courses from the main head, eight single from the upper. *Length* 102 cm, body 50 cm. *String lengths* 63, 70 cm.

173, 175 Theorbo-lute. Sebastian Schelle, Nuremberg, 1727. *Paris, Conserv., E.233.* Striped body of nine ribs. Raised treble peg and bracket for the bass courses.

174 Lute. Hans Burkholtzer, Füssen, 1596. *Vienna, Kunsthist. Mus., N.E.48.* Twenty-one ivory ribs. Rebuilt by Thos. Edlinger in 1705 as theorbo-lute with ten courses and three doubled bass courses. *Length* 80 cm, body 50 cm.

176–8 Small theorbo. Matteo Sellas, Venice, 1638. *Paris, Conserv., E.1028, C.1052.* Back of ebony and ivory ribs. Engraved panels on fingerboard and arabesques. 'Swan-head' upper pegbox. Seven double courses and seven doubled bass courses. *Length* 108 cm, body 38 cm. *String lengths* 61, 85 cm.

179 Theorbo. Wendelin Tieffenbrucker, Padua, 1611. *Vienna, Kunsthist. Mus., C.47.* Label *Padova Vvendelio Venere 1611.* Brand mark *W.E.* and anchor. Twenty-seven ribs with dark intervening fillets. Plait-work rose. *Length* 146 cm, body 56·5 cm.

180, 181 Chitarrone. Magno Tieffenbrucker, Venice, second half of sixteenth century. *Vienna, Kunsthist. Mus., C.45.* Label, *Magno Diefopruchar a Venetia.* Twenty-one shaded ribs with dark intervening fillets. Triple rose. Inlaid neck and fingerboard. Six double courses and eight single basses. *Length* 163·5 cm, body 46·5 cm.

182 Theorbo. Magno Tieffenbrucker, Venice. *Barcelona, Mus. de musica, 404.* Back with ivory fillets. Neck inlaid with ivory in floral and scroll patterns. (Detail of neck.)

183 Rose of chitarrone. Matteo Buechenberg, Rome, 1614. *London, Victoria and Albert Mus., 190–1882.*

184 Chitarrone. Matteo Buechenberg, Rome, 1608. *Brussels, Conserv. royal, 1570.* Triple rose. Repair to neck. Six and eight courses, all single. *Length* 192 cm, body 70 cm. *String lengths* 99, 170 cm.

185 Theorbo. Johann Christian Hoffmann, Leipzig, 1717. *Berlin, Instit. f. Musikforschung, 129.* Hoffmann label, and also repair label of Seb. Schelle, Nuremberg, 1738. Nine sycamore ribs. Eight main courses (the first two single) and five doubled basses. *Length* 121 cm, body 51 cm.

186 Theorbo. Matteo Sellas, Venice, first half of seventeenth century. *Brussels, Conserv. royal, 1565.* Triple-headed. Twenty-one ribs. Seven courses (single treble) from main head, four double from the second, and three double from the highest. *Length* 123 cm, body 41 cm. *String lengths* 59·2, 82, 100·8 cm.

187 Theorbo. Jacob Heinrich Goldt, Hamburg, 1734. *London, Victoria and Albert Mus., 4274–1856.* Eleven rosewood ribs with ivory fillets. Marquetry neck and fingerboard. Eight main courses (the first two single) and five doubled basses. Thumb-lever sprung device for changing pitch of basses added later. *Length* 133 cm, body 54 cm. *String lengths* 76, 105 cm.

188 Angel lute. J. Chr. Fleischer. *Schwerin, Mecklenburg. Landesbibliothek.* Back of neck and head.

189, 190 Angel lute. Joachim Tielke, Hamburg, 1704. *Schwerin, Mecklenburg. Landesbibliothek.* Eleven ribs. Ten courses from main head, six from upper, all single. *Length* 127 cm, body 53 cm.

191 Cobsa. Moldavian, nineteenth century. *London, Horniman Mus., 28.4.56/238.* Deep body of five ribs of pine. Crude rose carved in belly. Tied bridge. Gut and overspun strings, the first and third courses triple, the second and fourth double. **Frets missing.** *Length* from base to the angle of the head 52 cm. *Depth* 20 cm.

192, 193 Swedish lute. Lorents Mollenberg, Stockholm, *1817*. *London, R. Coll. of Music, 135.* Back of seven ribs with separate forwards-sloping sides. Maker's MS. number, *82*. Eight strings from main head and seven (overspun) from upper, attached to a pin bridge. Brass thumb-lever attachment for changing the pitch of the bass strings. *Length* 104 cm, body 50 cm. *Depth of sides* 9·7 cm.

194 Lute. Mattias Griesser, Innsbruck, *1756*. *Copenhagen, Claudius Coll., 99A.* Nine sycamore ribs. Six courses. *Length* 98 cm, body 46 cm. *String length* 69·5 cm.

195 Russian theorbo. First half of nineteenth century. *London, R. Coll. of Music, 151.* Label illegible. Body of 11 ribs with a longitudinal strut inside. Purfled belly. Four single and four double courses from the main head. Four single basses from the upper head. Twelve single trebles across the left side of the body, with rear pegs. All strings gut, attached to one long bridge. *Length* 120 cm.

196 Russian bandura. *London, R. Coll. of Music, 286.* Body, flat-backed with rounded sides, carved from two pieces of wood, the right hand of which continues upward to form the neck and scroll head. The neck is hollow under the fingerboard. Inside the body is a longitudinal wooden strut. Inset rose with moulding surround. Eight strings over fingerboard and 36 across the left-hand part of the belly, all strings being tuned by wrest pins. *Length* 99 cm.

The classic form of the lute body, described in old sources as the 'pearl mould', was credited by later generations to Laux Maler (**159**). The greatest width and depth come low down, at around 70 per cent of the belly length from top to bottom. This mould, of which makers executed their individual varia-

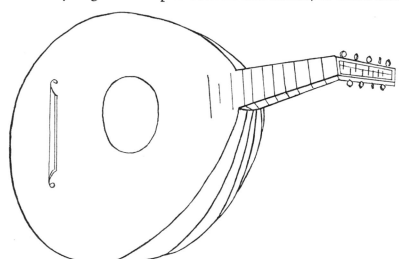

tions, supplanted an older form commonly seen in Renaissance paintings and a common one among Arab lutes still. The widest point here comes higher up, giving a plump appearance further emphasized by the narrow neck and the absence of those pointed ebony 'beards' which continue the fingerboard of the classic models. Fig 5, sketched from Ercole dei Roberti's 'The Consort' (late fifteenth century) gives an idea of this shape, which is also re-called in some lutes by later makers, as Sellas, a versatile artist

Fig 5 Lute, late fifteenth century (after Ercole dei Roberti)

who also made lutes of a model in which the widest point comes extremely low down, giving a kind of triangular appearance. Woods employed in the sixteenth century besides sycamore include cypress, 'Brazil wood', sandal wood, etc. (An interesting seventeenth-century account of early makers, lute shapes and materials, is in the Mary Burwell Instruction Book, *GSJ*, XI, 10–11.)

The pine belly is carved with a rose (**160**)—often in the case of large bellies a 'triple rose' of three joined circles (**183**)—and is lightly reinforced on the underside with barring. Even so a tendency for the belly to collapse under the pull of the numerous strings made necessary its periodic removal for ironing flat, an operation fully described by Thomas Mace (1676). A shaped strip of wood, the 'lace' is applied round the edge of the body, protecting the lower edges of the belly (visible in **167, 177** among the instruments in the illustrations). Extra frets were sometimes glued to the belly (**161, 175**) in order to supplement the gut frets (numbering from seven to ten) with which the neck was tied. Decoration was on the whole sparsely applied save in lutes made for presentation purposes; regular lavish ornamentation was a feature rather of amateur instruments like the guitar. The ribs of Italian lutes are often 'shaded', i.e. darkened along half the width, emphasizing the contours of the body, especially when the ribs are numerous and narrow (**181**). A fluted effect is said by lute makers to arise naturally, in most cases, as the ribs are laid over the mould. A musical result of the lute type of soundbox is a curiously 'black-and white' timbre by contrast with the colourful sound of a guitar.

The head of a lute—though not of an archlute—is reflexed, pointing backwards at an angle of 90 degrees more or less, and it is perfectly straight and plain-ended, all for lightness and balance. A gentle S-curve can usually be taken as a sign of an Arab, Persian or Turkish lute, many handsome examples of which masquerade in collections as European. (An exception to this is a form of theorbo-lute, **172**, see below). Other oriental features include an ogival plaque at the end of the fingerboard instead of the European 'beards', and a protector plate in the belly. A common addition to the head of a European lute is a 'raised treble peg' for the first string, held in a small raised mounting in order to ease the bend of this very fine gut string over the nut (**159**); it may occur as an original feature from *c.* 1600, though often it is a later addition. A raised bracket on the bass side of the head is a late device (p. 32), also often added to old lutes (**165**).

An ordinary or 'mean' lute has a belly length in the region of 48–51 cm. Smaller and larger sizes were built chiefly in the second half of the sixteenth century for use in consort with the mean lute. Descant lutes (**169**) have a belly of about 33 cm, and treble lutes are a little larger (**171**). Bass lutes, with dimensions in the ratio 4:3 to the mean lutes and body length *c.* 68·5 cm, are very rare (**166**), most of them probably having been converted into archlutes during the seventeenth century.

The interest of sixteenth-century musicians in employment of deep sounds is shown in deep-pitched bowed and wind instruments, in downwards extensions of keyboard compass, and again in 'bass' strings added to the bass side of the traditional six courses of the lute. Maler's lutes, and probably Frei's (**162**) would have been built for six courses (tuned very much as the present strings of the guitar) and with a correspondingly narrow neck akin to that of the Wendelin Tieffenbrucker instrument shown (**168**, though its present stringing is probably not original). It is not absolutely certain when the extra bass strings first came in on the lute, but it may have been around 1550, the neck being widened to accommodate them. A nicely plain Venetian lute by Hieber (**171**) has one extra course. An almost intact and perfect example of a nine-course lute of the end of the century is that by Harton (**161**); on such an instrument John Dowland might have performed his lute songs. After this, 11 courses became common, and since they mostly lay beyond practicable reach of the player's left-hand fingers the bass courses were tuned to follow a diatonic sequence like harp strings and were struck always 'open'. This led to theorbo-lutes.

Theorbo-lutes. Before the advent of overspun strings, the deeper bass courses, when sharing the string length of the primary courses, needed a thickness of gut disadvantageous to their sonorous effect. Soon after 1600, therefore, recourse was made to the structural principle of the already-invented theorbo, with a pegbox for the bass courses elevated above the main pegbox and allowing these courses extra length. A lute embodying this arrangement was a 'theorbo-lute', or, as the meaning of the term is more clearly expressed on the Continent, *luth théorbé, theorbierte Laute.* About the middle of the seventeenth century a modified design appeared in which the reflexed head is retained for the main courses, restoring something of the traditional balance in the hands, while an upright head is set beside it to give some 7 cm extra length to the basses; the two pegboxes are usually given matching curves (**172**). Though many pictures show this type of theorbo-lute, examples are curiously rare and even then are conversions of older lutes. Two of the famous names in the later seventeenth-century history of the lute, Gaultier the French soloist, and Mace the writer, are both associated with a variant of it (in Mace, 'French lute') in which the upright head is stepped, having four nuts, one for each of four bass courses, disposed in echelon one above the other. No good example seems to have survived, so a sketch from Gerard Terborch, 'Lute player', is given (Fig 6). A later equivalent, made possible by developments with overspun strings, is the raised ebony bracket for bass courses, fixed to the bass side of a reflexed head, with pegs for two or three double courses. This arrangement is associated particularly with the revival of lute playing in Germany in the first third of the eighteenth century, when excellent instruments were made by Schelle of Nuremberg (**173**), Hoffmann and others, who also fitted the bracket to earlier lutes, thus to keep them in commission.

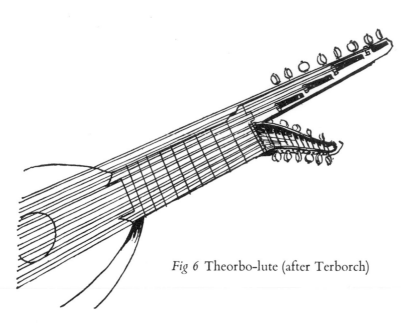

Fig 6 Theorbo-lute (after Terborch)

Theorbo. This is the first of the large two-headed lutes or archlutes (some sources give the name 'archlute' only for the chitarrone). An inventory of the Accademia Filarmonica, Verona, 1544, includes *una tiorba*—perhaps the earliest mention of the name (Turrini, 1941, 41). A normal theorbo is longer necked than a normal lute, so that the main courses are relatively long, while the upper pegbox provides for long basses. The theorbo (the name is unexplained) remained an important instrument of accompaniment up to the middle of the eighteenth century. At first it was strung with single courses but in the seventeenth century often in double or mixed single and double courses, typically numbering from seven to eight main and six to seven bass. The height of the true theorbo varies, 140 cm being a rough figure. There are two chief ways of building the two heads. First, with a straight head (**176–9**). Here the main pegbox is a slot cut near the base of a long straight-sided and slightly tapered member which rises from the back of the neck and carries the bass pegbox at its top. The bass pegbox typically has a 'swan-head' form (**177**) which economises total length. This is provided with a high square nut of ivory which in most instruments projects over to the bass side to lead the bass courses clear of the others; to assist this, the neck is often set slightly askew to the belly centre-line. This seems to be the older construction. Secondly, the jinked head. Here an upright main pegbox is surmounted by a crooked bracket upon which the bass head is aligned to the bass side of the centre-line (**185, 187**). This is the more usual construction from about 1630 onwards, and the fine theorbos of eighteenth-century Germany keep to it.

Besides full-sized theorbos, small instruments (*tiorbini*) were built, some pretty examples being by Sellas (**176**), by whom is also a not so pretty model with three heads (**186**). Their bodies are about 36–40 cm long and the string lengths correspondingly short as if they were intended for small hands. There are also numerous theorbos or theorbo-lutes of nondescript size, probably in many cases decorative rebuilds from old pieces.

Chitarrone. This taller version (**180, 184**) of the theorbo appeared shortly after the theorbo itself. Praetorius terms it 'Roman theorbo', and remains of examples by Buechenberg of Rome, with bodies up to 70 cm long, figure prominently among the earlier specimens. The height is from 175 up to 200 cm, though as with the theorbo some small-sized models were made, scaled-down chitarroni being about 140 cm tall. The chitarrone pegboxes are built according to the first of the two methods mentioned above for the theorbo. The usual stringing is six double courses plus eight single basses, the latter often of metal and giving an especially good effect in music. The chitarrone could also be strung entirely with metal. Most examples are Italian, but there are fine seventeenth-century Spanish specimens, with inlaid surround to the rose.

Angel lute (angélique). The idea of an archlute with the strings tuned diatonically throughout, harpwise in single courses, is mentioned by Praetorius as a minor novelty (Sciagr., XXXIV), and then again between 1660 and 1713 as 'angel lute'. One of the few known specimens, by Tielke (**189, 190**), provides another example of this maker's fine decorative work.

Late and Regional Lutes

The cobsa (191) is a Rumanian and Moldavian folk lute used chiefly to accompany the violin. The deep scoop-like body is of a few broad ribs, the centre rib maintaining its full width right to the point where it joins the base of the belly. The neck is extremely short, *c.* 7 cm, with room for only five frets. The strings run in double and triple courses from the reflexed head to the bridge.

Modern lute. After the decline of the lute in the eighteenth century a lingering affection for its pleasing contours led to the construction of simplified instruments more suited to the day, strung in the manner of the guitar, i.e. at first, up to *c.* 1790, with five or six double courses and thereafter with six single strings. To these the name 'modern lute' or 'German lute' has been given. There are early German examples (**194**) and French, and such instruments are still manufactured today.

The Russian theorbo (torban) or **Ukrainian lute** of the late eighteenth and early nineteenth centuries (**195**) has a round body strengthened by a wooden pole which traverses the interior space from neck block to bottom block. The gut strings run in single and double courses over the frets and there are three or four basses mounted in theorbo fashion. In addition, 12 gut strings are mounted across the treble side of the belly, their pegs held in a stout ledge fixed to the edge of the body. These strings (*pristrunki*) are tuned in diatonic sequence, and bring into use the player's right little finger, which in normal lute playing is generally rested on the belly. These extra treble strings were no doubt suggested, via the *bandura* (below), by the old Russian *gusli*, a form of psaltery (shown in the belly decoration of the balalaika **223**). A few instruments elsewhere also have them, however, since if one wishes to match the common provision of diatonic basses by corresponding trebles, the latter must not get in the way of the player's left hand on the fingerboard, i.e. they must be pegged low down, at or close to the edge of the belly.

In the Ukrainian *bandura* (**196**) there are up to 36 of these diatonic trebles arranged in a fan. The fingerboard strings are here termed basses. The body is hollowed out in the form of a shallow bowl. An early example is dated 1740 (Vertkov, *Atlas*, 126). This has five strings plus 18 trebles.

The Swedish lute or Swedish theorbo was made from *c.* 1780 onwards, even into the second half of the nineteenth century, by Stockholm luthiers led by Peter Kraft. Instruments by Kraft, Mollenberg, Jerner, etc are not uncommon in collections today (**192, 193**). The body form is asymmetric, the neck being placed over to the treble side. The back is either a shallow bowl made with ribs, or it is flat. In either case it is joined to separate sides. The strings are tuned largely diatonically and on the majority of examples a thumb mechanism is provided by which the basses can be raised a semitone or more in pitch whilst playing. For selection of the bass-raising interval, an adjustable plate with holes for a capotasto is mounted at the back of the head.

8 Mandores

Small, normally round-bodied instruments bearing a superficial resemblance to miniature lutes range from the Renaissance mandore to the mandolin of the modern era.[1] Their body lengths vary between about 21 and 28 cm. The earlier forms are strung primarily, like the modern mandolin, to serve as melodic instruments, with few courses of strings, most typically four, and an 'open' tuning in fourths or fifths as used on fiddles. Counterbalancing their negligible importance in the higher flights of musical art are the labours on the part of makers to make the instruments pleasing objects to possess; particularly in the later periods, from the mid seventeenth century, as much ornament is often crammed onto their small bodies as room can be found for. They are most simply considered in two groups; first, the older mandores, with gut strings tied to the bridge as on a lute; second, the mandolin, with strings at least partially of metal and attached to the bottom of the instrument.

Illustrations: Mandores and Mandolins

197, 198 Mandore. Italian, ? sixteenth century. *Vienna, Kunsthist. Mus., C.43.* Eleven ribs alternately of a dark wood and ivory, the neck being of the same materials with the colours reversed. Carved rose. Square finial. Four strings. *Length* 46 cm, body 26 cm.

199, 200 Mandore. Sixteenth or seventeenth century. *Copenhagen, Musikhist. Mus., 300.* Ivory body. Carved rose. Reflexed head. Four courses (three double). *Length* 41 cm.

201, 202 Mandore. French, seventeenth century. *London, Victoria and Albert Mus., 219–1866.* In ink on edge of body, *Boissart 1640.* Carved in one piece of pear, forming body, neck and head. The back carved in relief with strapwork and scrolls and a scene depicting the Judgement of Paris. On the back of the neck a Medusa's head. Rose carved in belly. Six pegs. Later bridge for five strings. *Length* 42 cm, belly 21 cm. *Depth of body* 3·5 cm. *String length* 28·3 cm.

203, 204 Mandore. Jacques Dumesnil, Paris, mid seventeenth century. *Lisbon, Conserv. nacional.* Flat back carved in relief recalling **202**. Five courses. Fingerboard probably and belly are later replacements.

205, 206 Mandore. Pietro Antonio Gavelli, Perugia, 1690. *London, Victoria and Albert Mus., 504–1868.* Nine ribs alternately of ivory with engraved scrollwork, and tortoiseshell on metal foil. Sunk triple rose of wood. Inlaid fingerboard and square finial. Four courses. *Length* 50 cm, body 24 cm. *String length* 33·5 cm.

207 Mandore. Francesco Presbler, Milan, 1733. *London, Royal Coll. of Music, 109.* Body of a gourd. Belly with carved rose with ebony and pearl surround, and ivory edging. Six double courses. *Length* 48 cm. *String length* 28·5 cm.

208, 209 Mandore. Giovanni Smorsone, Rome, 1714. *London, R. Coll. of Music, 201.* Body of 13 sycamore ribs with intervening ivory fillets matched by ivory stringing up the neck and head. Carved rose. Six double courses. *Length* 57·5 cm, belly 23·5 cm. *String length* 34 cm.

210 Mandore (Milanese mandolin). Giuseppe Presbler, Milan, 1775. *London, R. Coll. of Music, 202.* Label, *Francesco Presbler e Giuseppe figlio . . .* Body of 15 rosewood ribs with ivory fillets. Belly carved with a

---

[1] *Mandore* is the French name from the sixteenth century to the eighteenth, equivalent to the Italian *mandora* and customarily pronounced by English speakers as if it were also an Italian word. It is the most convenient generic term for the earlier species of these instruments, i.e. those before the Neapolitan mandolin. Use of the Italian (in some cases German–Italian) terms *mandora, pandurina, mandola* tends to lead to confusion, though the last of these, *mandola*, is useful in its modern professional sense of a large mandolin.

rose and edged with pearl and inlaid ornament. Fingerboard of pearl with stringing in light-coloured wood. Back of neck covered with tortoiseshell. Open-backed pegbox with pearl-faced finial. Now strung with six double courses of metal. *Length 54 cm. String length 30·5 cm.*

211, 212   Mandore. Joseph Gallina, Brescia, 17—. *London, R. Coll. of Music, 19.* Back of a diamond pattern of pearl and four different woods on canvas base. Pearl and ebony ornament on belly, etc. Rose is missing. Silver frets. Finial in the form of a winged bust of a woman with circlet of mother-of-pearl. Four single strings. *Length 49 cm. String length 33·7 cm.*

213   Mandore. J. N. Lambert, Paris, 1752 (last two figures unclear). *London, Victoria and Albert Mus., 503–1868.* Body of 13 ivory ribs with ebony fillets. Parchment rose surrounded by pearl and ebony chequers. Metal frets. Finial in form of a turbaned Moor's head. Originally five-course. *Length 56 cm, belly 22·5 cm. String length 31 cm.*

214   Mandore. David, Paris, 1786. *London, R. Coll. of Music, 165.* Label, *David faciebat Anno 1786 A Paris* (cf Vannes). Flat back of sycamore bent to slight curve. Belly painted with a badge of fleur-de-lys and a royal figure in red coat wearing Maltese cross. Open soundhole. Later fingerboard, reaching to the soundhole, with ivory frets. Later flat head with rear pegs for six strings. *Length 55 cm. String length 31 cm.*

215, 216   Mandolin. Antonio Vinaccia, Naples, 1772. *London, Victoria and Albert Mus., 10–1894.* Twenty-one sycamore ribs with ivory fillets. Round soundhole with marquetry surround. Tortoiseshell protector plate. Silver frets. *Length 57 cm, belly 28 cm. String length 32·5 cm.*

217   Mandolin. Petroni, Rome, 1865. *London, Victoria and Albert Mus., 924–1902.* Said to have been made for Queen Margherita of Italy. Deep body of six wide ribs dotted with pearl. Fingerboard with brass frets. Head with radial screw tuning. Four double courses of metal. *Length 51 cm, belly 28 cm. String length 33·2 cm.*

218   Mandola. Antonio Vinaccia, Naples, 1773. *London, W. E. Hill & Sons.* Twenty-five ribs, the outer with applied wooden strap-work. Belly with round soundhole and two fancy *f*-holes. Silver frets plus ebony frets on belly. *Length 76 cm, belly 40 cm.*

219   Mandola. Gaetano Vinaccia, Naples, 1744. *Brussels, Conserv. royal, 3182.* Body of 24 rosewood ribs. Tortoiseshell protector plate in belly. Four double courses of metal strings, the lower two overspun. *Length 108 cm, belly 53 cm. String length 77·5 cm.*

In the second half of the sixteenth century at least three body constructions of the mandore are mentioned in French records (Lesure, *GSJ*, VII), the instrument having then been especially popular in France. One method is by carving from one piece, integral with the neck. A beautiful example of this, though of the next century (**201, 202**) was probably built for four courses, including two double. As with other early specimens the carved rose and the beards of the fingerboard recall lute making. The second method is by moulding from ribs: a Paris inventory of 1587 mentions *mandores à costes* of ebony and ivory. Some fine examples here are Italian (**197** and probably **199**). The third construction is with flat back and separate sides (*mandore plat* in these inventories). Again a later French specimen is shown (**203, 204**). All these mandores have some kind of reclining pegbox and have the gut frets employed on nearly all fretted instruments of the period except citterns. The musical effect of the four-course mandore, including *tremolando* playing with a plectrum, is enthusiastically described by Mersenne.

During the second half of the seventeenth century a trend began for increasing the number of strings to five and in the eighteenth century to six double courses, the bodies becoming correspondingly wider, and sometimes also deeper through incorporation of an extra wide outer rib. The eighteenth-century result has become known as the *Milanese mandolin*, through the abundant and pretty examples by the Presbler family of Milan (**210**). Another expression, *mandore luthée*, which already appears in a 1639 Paris inventory (Lesure, *GSJ*, X, 88), is used again by Walther (*Lexicon*) who observes that with these added strings the mandore loses its nature to become a thing for imitating lute music on. Nevertheless the type was a popular amateur instrument for most of the eighteenth century, made not only by

Presbler (including examples made from a gourd, **207**) but by makers in other Italian cities, as Smorsone in Rome (**208**) and others (**206**). Makers allowed themselves great freedom in model and decoration, as instanced by an example from Brescia (**211, 212**), though scores of others could be chosen. A five-course mandore was now made in France (**213**), again sometimes flat-backed (**214**). Large Italian versions were made by Presbler and also by earlier makers, e.g. a five-course example by Stefano Franco, 1692 (Florence, Instit. Cherubini, 59), but many large specimens are simply conversions from lutes. Talbot mentions an *arch-mandore* with six main courses and seven single basses mounted in the theorbo manner, but whether an example survives is doubtful.

The **Neapolitan mandolin** has many distinctive features (**215, 216**). The body, with up to 35 narrow ribs, deepens very markedly in the lower part, largely through an outer rib of greatly exaggerated width (partly concealed by a broad lace). The belly is bent inwards at the level of the bridge. The soundhole is open, in earlier models round, later often oval. A tortoiseshell plate is inlaid in the belly just above the bridge to protect the wood from the plectrum or 'pick' with which the instrument is always played (with the earlier mandores a plectrum was optional). The head is flat, as on the guitar, with rear pegs until machines came in during the nineteenth century. The strings restore the early nature of the mandore by running in four courses, all double, and tuned like a violin. All-metal stringing was not invariably used; a favourite alternative in the past was a treble course of fine gut (said to have been spun from only three strips of the prepared sheep's intestine, as against five or six for a violin gut *E* string), steel second course, the third brass and the fourth of overspun silk. During the first half of the nineteenth century the old type of fingerboard flush with the belly was replaced by an extended fingerboard reaching onto the belly. From the beginning the Neapolitan mandolin was fretted with metal or ivory.

The Neapolitan mandolin would seem to be compounded from every kind of fretted instrument, oriental or Western, known in eighteenth-century Naples. As to the time of its appearance, Bonanni (*Gabinetto Armonico*, 1722) has an interesting passage in which he says that *pandura* was the Neapolitan name for an instrument 'in shape like a mandola but much bigger, and with eight metal strings struck with a plectrum'. This was evidently a fairly large instrument, and it is curious that among early specimens of the Neapolitan type those of large 'mandolas' appear to have the earliest dates, namely of the 1740s (**219**). Among these already appears the name of Vinaccia, the Neapolitan family with whom the early development of the mandolin is particularly associated. The early dates for the small mandolin seem to be some 20 years later. Antonio is regarded as the finest maker of the family (**215**). After him the work starts to grow more perfunctory, leading eventually to the popular models of the later nineteenth century with ornament mass-produced in Italian and German factories. Many local modifications appeared up and down Italy from the end of the eighteenth century and preliminary attempts to classify them regionally have been made by Sachs (*Reallexikon*) and others. Some types include triple courses and have been termed 'Sicilian' though they were also made in Naples. Others include hybrids with the 'Milanese mandolin', while many specimens of the latter were partially converted to 'Neapolitan'. A late Roman variant (**217**) uses the Portuguese type of radial screw-head. There are also flat-backed models, including French and fancy Neapolitan designs of the early nineteenth century with the shoulders raised in 'horns' no doubt inspired by the lyre-guitars of the period.

The ordinary Neapolitan *mandola* (**218**) has a body length of *c.* 50 cm, old lute bodies having been sometimes employed. Among local versions, a 'Roman lute' with two or more bass strings lying off the fingerboard, was made from the mid eighteenth century by Ferrari of Rome. A whole series of large mandolins was developed in the second half of the nineteenth century for use in mandolin orchestras: 'mandola' or 'tenor mandola' (corresponding in size to the mandola just mentioned); 'mandoloncello' (larger, body *c.* 65 cm, with cello tuning); and a three-stringed 'bass mandolin' with a spike for resting on the floor.

9 Long Lutes, Colascione

Among the plectrum instruments of the Near East, the type second in importance after the lute itself is a wire-strung instrument with relatively small round-backed body and long narrow neck (**221**). It is still played in many countries formerly under Ottoman rule, being known in Arab lands as *buzuk*, in Turkey as *saz*, in Greece *bouzouki* and in Yugoslavia *tamboritsa* (from the classical Arabic name *tanbur*). A Western version is the now-extinct *colascione*.

Illustrations

220   Colascione. Italian, seventeenth century. *Brussels, Conserv. royal, 1567.* Body of ebony and ivory ribs. Neck with ivory inlay. Ivory finial in the form of a dog's head. Three strings. *Length 94 cm.*

221   Bouzouki. Athens, nineteenth century. *Copenhagen, Musikhist. Mus., 317.* Belly of woods of two colours. Rosette of small soundholes. Gut frets. Two triple courses (or three double) of metal strings. *Length 80 cm, body 27 cm.*

222   Bouzouki (*cavonto*). Greek, late nineteenth century. *New York, Metropol. Mus., 1018.* Body with rose and protector plate. Gut frets. Unfretted extension of fingerboard. Three double courses of metal strings.

223   Balalaika. Russian, nineteenth century. *Copenhagen, Musikhist. Mus., 319.* Triangular belly painted with floral designs and inlaid with the figure of a man playing a *gusli* beside a log house. Rear pegs. Three strings. Position dots and five capotasto holes. *Length 67 cm.*

An old *bouzouki* (**221**) shows traditional oriental features: stump-ended neck with T-shaped pegs in two rows, one in front and one on the right side (handiest for the player); gut frets, but wire strings, usually in three double courses; belly bent to an arch, with a strip of darker wood like cedar joined to the pine on each flank, and with minimal soundhole (indeed the Turkish *saz* may have no soundhole whatever, yet radiate sound perfectly effectively). More recent bouzoukis are much influenced by the Italian mandolin, with flat belly, large soundhole or rose, extended fingerboard with inset brass frets, pearl borders, etc. An example (**222**) illustrates a stage in these developments.

Instruments of this type were introduced into Italy via Naples in the fifteenth century to become Westernized—taking on characteristics of Italian lute-construction—under the name *colascione* (from which the French phonetic equivalent *colachon*). In the seventeenth century the colascione (**220**) became quite well known in the northern countries and lasted therein as a bye-attraction for the dilettante into the eighteenth. The round body varies from 16 cm in length up to almost lute dimensions. One example has a tortoiseshell body. The belly, though normally of pine, could be, according to old writers, of vellum, or half wood and half vellum, as found in various Asiatic and other non-European instruments. The neck is tied with 16 or more gut frets and the strings run in two or three single or double courses, properly of metal though gut seems to have been much employed. The head is a small pegbox with a finial which takes, among other things, the form of a dog's head, presumably commemorating the Turk. A few sixteenth-century colascioni exist, including handsome specimens with ivory and ebony ribs. One of these has an early label: *Antonio Baraptutio, (Naples) 1535* (London, W. E. Hill & Sons), a name with a Turkish or pseudo-Turkish ring about it, as again in a large example (length 147 cm, body 44·8 cm) at Brussels (1566), labelled *Bárrata Eméntoti . . Padoúa . . 1564.*

The balalaika (**223**) is an eighteenth-century modification of the older, round-bodied Russian *domra* which has been regarded as another member of the long lute family. The triangular body is made from ribs. As with other popular stringed instruments it gained an extended fingerboard, machine head, etc, during the last century, and towards the end of which large sizes, up to contrabass, were built for balalaika orchestras.

10 Citterns

Citterns are characterized in the first place by metal stringing. This is also met, of course, among other kinds of fretted instrument as mandolins and guitars. But with citterns it is the rule, and has been a main contributor to the high popularity of these instruments at certain periods in the past when society has felt the desire for a cheerful strumming or accompanying instrument on which the strings seldom break and are able to keep their tuning pretty well when the instrument is idle. Generally, citterns have a flat back and separate sides, and a rounded outline often described as pear-shaped (apt enough inasmuch as every shape a pear can have can be matched among the shapes of citterns). The fingerboard is always extended onto the belly. It is usually fairly thick and is fretted with fixed frets, normally metal. The strings pass over a bridge, usually two-footed, to their attachment at the base of the body.

Nothing definite is known about a medieval instrument that went by the name *citole* and was possibly a cittern ancestor. The known types up to the eighteenth century fall into two distinct groups. First, those which may be termed 'old' citterns. In these, of which the first clear evidence is from the late fifteenth century, the sides of the body narrow from the neck towards the base. Second, 'late' citterns, appearing in the eighteenth century; here the body is on the whole deeper, with sides which are of constant width or else narrow slightly towards the neck, the build being more guitar-like. Among the old citterns it is convenient also to consider the orpharion and some other less common species.

Illustrations: Old Citterns

224–6 Cittern. Italian, *c.* 1600. *Paris, Conserv., E.543, C.250.* Label, *D.P. Jovanni Salvatori.* Ascribed to Maggini, Brescia. Purfled decoration. Solid head with finial in the form of a female head with ruff. Six double courses. *Length* 83 cm, belly 36 cm.

227 Cittern. Italian, 1536. *Paris, Conserv., E.1131, C.1054.* Label, *Franciscus Antonius Plebanus 1536.* On the back, *AF.P.* and decoration. Divided pegbox with carved figure. Ivory frets. Six double courses. *Length* 64 cm, belly 33 cm. *Depth* above 5 cm, below 3 cm. *String length* 54 cm.

228 Cittern. Girolamo de Virchis, Brescia, 1574. *Vienna, Kunsthist. Mus., A.61.* Made for the Archduke Ferdinand of the Tyrol. Branded on head *Hieronymus Brixiensis* and initials *I.V.* Date written on label. Body of palisander, superbly carved, including the arms of the Archduke. Carved rose in belly, painted and gilt and with the red eagle of the Tyrol. Solid head carved with figure of Lucretia Romana, her earrings of real pearls. Six double courses. *Length* 73·5 cm, body 35 cm. *Depth* above 4·5 cm, below 2 cm.

229, 230 Cittern. Italian, seventeenth century. *Oxford, Ashmolean Mus.* Purfling simulated in ink. Brass frets in scalloped fingerboard. Open-backed pegbox with nine pegs, originally probably for four courses including one triple. Sunk rose. Carved finial in form of a Moor's head. *Length* 76 cm, belly 33 cm. *Depth* above 5 cm, at base 2·7 cm. *String length* 46 cm.

231 Cittern. ? Paduan, sixteenth or seventeenth century. *Vienna, Kunsthist. Mus., C.64.* Back and sides carved in one piece. Brand mark, barely legible, *Padova* (?). Solid head with plain finial. Six double courses. *Length* 88 cm, body 35 cm. *Depth* above 8·5 cm, below 7 cm.

232–4 Cittern. Ascribed to Antonio Stradivari, Cremona, *c.* 1700. *Paris, Conserv., E.1271, C.1055.* Fan back. Solid carved head. Fingerboard flies over belly. Six double courses. *Length* 73 cm, body 33 cm. *Depth* above 4·8 cm, at base 1·6 cm. *String length* 54 cm.

235 Cittern. ? German, 1705. *Frankfurt, Hist. Mus., Epstein, 51.* Inscribed *A.I.* (coat of arms) *D.G.A.° 1705.*

Striped back. Belly partly renewed. Sunk paper rose. Five courses. *Length* 84 cm, body 37·5 cm. *Depth* at neck 4·5 cm, at base 2 cm.

236 Arch-cittern. Johann Gottfried Klemm, Radeberg, 1756. *The Hague, Gemeentemus.* Festooned body in a rather square format. Two roses. Sides narrow slightly towards base. Four double courses and eight single basses.

237 Arch-cittern. Andreas Ernst Kram, Nuremberg, 1768. *Berlin, Instit. f. Musikforschung, 4080.* Four double courses and nine single basses, attached to brass hooks at base of body. *Length* 97 cm, body 42 cm. *Depth* 6·8 to 3·4 cm at base. *String lengths* 46, 67 cm.

238 Cittern (*Waldzither*). Georg Nicol Köllmar, Krawinkel, 1816. *The Hague, Gemeentemus.* Even sides, and plates overlap sides. Belly with three roses. Neck cut away down bass side. Five course (four double, one single).

239, 240 Orpharion. John Rose, London, 1580. *Lord Tollemache, Helmingham Hall, Suffolk.* Label, *Johanne Rose Londini fecit In Bridewell, the 27th of July. 1580.* Carved shell back, inlaid belly with jewelled rose centre. Sides carved with the words *cymbalum decachordum* (from the Psalms). Shallow head, the pegs passing right though (pegs should be in front). Six double courses. *Length* 89 cm, body 40·5 cm. *Depth* above 6·7 cm, at base 4·2 cm. *String length* 59·8 cm.

241 'Harp-cittern.' Wendelin Tieffenbrucker, Padua, c. 1590. *Vienna, Kunsthist. Mus., C.67.* Label, *In Padova Vvendelio di Leonardo Tiefenbrucker.* Body with lute-like outline and three separate roses. Three bridges, the outer two set at an angle. Original gut frets. Main head is for nine courses (single, six double, and two single). Harp-like frame on right side for 20 single basses. Fifteen single treble strings across left side of belly. *Length* 118 cm, body 60 cm. *Depth* above 8·5 cm, at base 10·5 cm.

242-4 Orpharion. Francis Palmer, London, 1617. *Copenhagen, Claudius Coll., 139 (23).* Back of seven pieces alternately brown and red. Even sides. Neck cut away on bass side. Pegbox with carved figure. Oblique frets and bridge. Nine double courses. *Length* 100 cm, body 43 cm. *Depth* 7·5 cm. *String lengths* from 53·5–60·5 cm.

245 Bell cittern. Joachim Tielke, Hamburg, c. 1700. *London, Victoria and Albert Mus., 1122–1869.* Back slightly arched. Marquetry decoration with inset gems of coloured glass. Three deep roses. Neck cut away on bass side. Inscribed *cest trop tard. 1539.* Bridge and most pegs missing. *Length* 64 cm, body 28 cm. *String length* 36 cm.

246 Bell cittern. Joachim Tielke, Hamburg. *London, W. E. Hill & Sons.* Inlaid ivory back, neck and head.

247 Bell cittern. Heinrich Kopp, Hamburg, 1702. *Berlin, Instit. f. Musikforschung, 4798.* Five double courses. *Length* 67 cm, body 29 cm. *Depth* 3·9–3·3 cm.

248 Bell cittern. Michael Paiker, Copenhagen, 1739. *Copenhagen, Musikhist. Mus., 327.* Engraved brass tail-piece. Ivory pegs for six courses. *Length* 70 cm.

Tinctoris (*De usu, c.* 1487) claims the *cetula* as Italian, describing it as flat-bodied with four metal strings (possibly meaning four double courses) and wooden frets. Instruments which might fit this brief description are seen in the *intarsie* of decorated rooms as those from Gubbio (New York, Metropolitan Museum of Art). Fig 7 is sketched from one of these. The staircase-like frets are evidently diatonic, not, as with the brass frets of subsequent citterns, chromatic. Among extant early Italian citterns one bears the date 1536 (**227**). Its sides both taper downwards and slope inwards towards the back as in a frying pan. The shoulder lines are very straight. Among other examples with this form of body, at least one (**231**) has back and sides carved from a single piece. Otherwise the back is separate. The belly is sometimes slightly

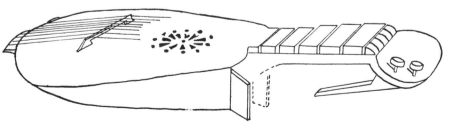

Fig 7 Cittern, late fifteenth century (after Gubbio *intarsie*)

raised, usually purfled round the edge and strengthened by light barring underneath. Such examples are from Padua, Urbino (a large instrument in the Victoria and Albert Museum, 392–1871, inscribed *Augustus Citaraedus 1582*, body 45 cm) and possibly Brescia (**224**). The classic Brescian model, however, has vertical sides, and shoulder lines which curve gracefully to the neck (**229**). A superb example is that which was made for the Archduke Ferdinand in 1574 by Virchi (**228**), the luthier noticed earlier as a teacher of Gasparo da Salò, who himself made citterns on the same model (Ashmolean Museum) as also did his pupil Maggini (Vienna Collection, C.32). There are many other instances of cittern and violin making in the same workshop, though doubt has been expressed over the attribution of two fine examples to Stradivari, one with a fan back (**232–4**).

Some further features of these early Italian citterns may be noticed. A split baluster or equivalent ornament is often applied at the junction of side and neck on each side. The neck is cut away down the bass side so that only the treble side of the fingerboard is in contact with it—probably to provide a strong depth of neck while yet making things comfortable for the player's thumb and preserving a good balance in the whole instrument. The head is either a normal pegbox (**227, 229**), or else a solid head in which the two rows of pegs (or the two outer rows of three) are inclined away from each other to facilitate manipulation (**224, 231**). The back of such a head is generally carved in a hook form for suspension of the instrument. The fingerboard, of walnut or similar wood rather than ebony, has an asymmetrically shaped end extending towards the rose furthest on the treble side, and it is sometimes scalloped between frets. Among the frets, the fourth is often omitted owing to a problem of intonation that arose when a favourite tuning (not unlike that of the modern ukulele) was used. For similar reasons some of the higher frets may be of fractional width (**227**). Though most of the extant specimens are six-course, a popular arrangement was four-course, especially in France and England, though no early specimens are known from these countries. With four courses, from one to three might be triple, so that the total number of pegs might be anything up to 11. With a spare peg hole added, the instrument could have been convertible to six double courses. Contemporary sources do not allude to this, but among the specimens one finds much evidence of alteration to the stringing, even on more than one successive occasion.

Orpharion and Bandora. Though not properly citterns these were similar in many ways and the bandora was often associated with the cittern in performance. The orpharion has from six to nine metal courses tuned like a lute and attached to hitch pins in the bridge. The bandora, similar but rather larger, was said to have been invented by John Rose in 1562, the orpharion following some years later. Both became known abroad, and the bandora, if not the orpharion, is still heard of around 1650. Only the orpharion is known by surviving specimens, these numbering two, both with festooned bodies. One, a beautiful instrument by Rose himself (**239**) shows decorative features in common with Rose's festooned viols (**97**). It has cittern-like tapered sides and a graceful solid head. The other, by Francis Palmer (**242**) has sides of even depth and a pegbox; its nut, frets and bridge are set obliquely, converging towards the treble side of the instrument, reducing the tension on the higher strings, the open-strung compass being wide and the mean string length some 10 cm greater than in the average cittern of the time. A number of replicas based on the Palmer instrument or on the illustration in Praetorius exist in collections. (For a fuller description of the orpharion and the bandora, see Gill, *GSJ*, XIII, 1960.)

A number of collections possess examples of a curious type of instrument, rather heavily built with a three-lobed body, with some ten courses of strings (generally gut) tied to a bridge in the lute manner (**270**). The name *bandora* has been commonly attached to it, though old sources indicate that the bandora was like the orpharion but about 12 cm longer in the body (Gill). The three-lobed instrument is, however, illustrated in the Lutherie section of the Diderot *Encyclopédie* above the name *pandore en luth*. The crude drawing there omits the rose (as also in the cittern on the same plate). The specimen at Brussels makes up for this by having a paper rose placed in the back. Against the conclusion that all these specimens may be of some eighteenth-century variety of instrument, it should in fairness be added that the example formerly in the Galpin Collection, now in the possession of Professor Thurston Dart, was found to contain sixteenth-century Italian printed paper in its linings.

A complex instrument sometimes mentioned along with the orpharion and bandora is the *polyphant* or *polyphone*. Playford (*Introduction to the Art of Descant*, 1683) writes that Queen Elizabeth 'did often recreate herself on an excellent instrument called polyphant, not much unlike a lute, but strung with wire'. No example is known, but a fairly good technical description is given by Talbot. Though space forbids quoting this here (see Gill, *GSJ*, XV, 1962), an illustration is included of a unique compound cittern in the Vienna Collection, by Wendelin Tieffenbrucker (**241**), which if not actually a polyphant seems to be something of a similar nature. It has three sets of strings. On the bass side, a curving harp-like frame supports 20 basses, while on the treble side, across the left side of the belly are 15 diatonic strings. (Talbot describes 16 bass strings arranged in two levels, and six diatonic trebles on the opposite side; another source, of 1655, quoted by M. Tilmouth, *GSJ*, X, 1957, gives for the 'polyphon' eight or ten short trebles and 40 basses.)

South German citterns. During the second half of the seventeenth century the cittern lost much of its former popularity save in Germany. Cittern making in the old style continued there without interruption through the eighteenth century (**235**), and indeed up to modern times as a folk instrument, Thuringian *Waldzither*, though in this old features become to some degree lost and one may find sides of even depth, overhanging plates, etc (**238**). The South German eighteenth-century cittern makers, headed by Kram of Nuremberg, are especially noted for their arch-citterns, those of Kram dating from the 1760s to the 1780s (**237**). They have four double courses for the fingerboard and up to nine single basses, sometimes attached to long brass hooks below the bridge. For changing the pitch of the basses there may be a wooden cylinder with small projecting nuts, attached below the bass head in such a manner that it can be rotated to raise the pitch of selected combinations of the basses to suit different keys. In outline, a rather square festooned shape is among the typical ones (**236**).

Bell cittern. This is a small cittern with the body outline of a swinging bell (**245**), introduced in the second half of the seventeenth century in North Germany, possibly by Joachim Tielke, one of whose labels has the date 1676 (London, R. College of Music, 27) and who seems not to have made citterns of normal type. In Germany the bell cittern was known best as *Hamburger Cithrinchen*, while Talbot in England calls it 'bell guittern'. The body, about 28 cm long, retains the old tapered sides, also the cutaway neck (**246**). Belly and back are slightly raised and the belly has three roses, two of them placed low, by the points of the body. The strings are in five courses. Various models appeared from other North German luthiers, also Danish (**247, 248**), mostly less ornate than Tielke's. Few seem to have been made after the mid-eighteenth century.

Late Citterns

The later kind of cittern is exemplified by the instrument well known to English collectors under the name *English guitar* (**249**, etc). Built from perhaps as early as 1740 (an example by Hintz bearing this date is listed in the catalogue of the Music Loan Exhibition, London, 1904) up to near the end of the century, it was intended chiefly for the feminine amateur and much enterprising invention and handsome workmanship was put into its construction, many of the makers having been violin makers of considerable repute. The source of the species is very uncertain. Bremner's *Instructions* of 1758 says that the instrument was 'but lately introduced' into Britain. There exist unsigned instruments in collections with rather similar types of body and with decorative features suggesting Italian or German work of earlier eighteenth century date, while the Italianate term 'cetra' instead of the old 'cittern' or 'cithren' in the title of

Hintz's *Psalms . . . for the Cetra or Guittar* (*c.* 1760) may also suggest recent foreign provenance. In France, instruments similar to the English, some among the early examples having identical rose and finial patterns, date from the 1760s, and Le Blond, one of the first French makers in the field, is said by Vannes to have had early business connections with London. However, Parisian trade cards of the 1770s advertise the *cistre ou guitare allemande*. However again, the attested German examples of the late cittern appear to be of the end of the century or even later. Another country that enters into the question is Portugal, where the *guitarra* has been played continuously from the eighteenth century up to today. Early Portuguese examples closely resemble the English, but are rarely dated. A credible conjecture would be that the whole genus was derived from or suggested by some obscure Portuguese instrument related to the bandurria.

Though these late citterns are normally flat-backed, there were also made round-backed models with bodies of nine or more ribs (**252**). The majority of these are French, apparently sold under the name *pandore*.

Illustrations: Late Citterns (English Guitar, etc)

249 English guitar. John Preston, London, *c.* 1770. *Oxford, Ashmol. Mus.* Plain shape. Star rose and finial ornament. Simple pegbox. Capotasto affixed. *Length* 73 cm, body 35 cm. *Sides* 5·3 cm above, 7 cm at base. *String length* 42 cm.

250 English guitar. Rudiman, Aberdeen, third quarter of eighteenth century. *London, Victoria and Albert Mus., 375–1882.* Plain shape. Sides with feather banding. Stamped gilt metal rose. Fingerboard of red tortoiseshell with silver frets and four capotasto holes. Simple pegbox. *Length* 73 cm, body 34 cm. *Sides* 6·5 cm above, 7·5 cm at base. *String length* 42·5 cm.

251, 252 English guitar. John Zumpe, London, 1762. *Frankfurt, Hist. Mus., Epstein 53.* Round back of 19 sycamore ribs with ebony fillets intervening. Ivory star rose and finial ornament. Brass frets and three capotasto holes. Simple pegbox. *Length* 74·5 cm, body 36 cm. *Depth* 12 cm. Leather case (not shown) has Zumpe's trade sign *At the Sign of the Golden Guittar.*

253 English guitar. Remerus Liessem, London, 1756. *London, Victoria and Albert Mus., 230–1882.* Festooned model with watchkey screw tuning. Purfling simulated in ink. Star rose of ebony and ivory. Long ebony fingerboard, perhaps a later replacement, with 19 brass frets and five capotasto holes. *Length* 70 cm, body 32 cm. *Depth* 6 cm. *String length* 44·4 cm.

254 English guitar. Frederick Hintz, London. *London, Victoria and Albert Mus., 37–1870.* Purfling simulated in ink. Stamped copper gilt rose. Ebony fingerboard. Renewed head with screw tuning by watchkey, stamped *Preston Inventor.* Also a detachable key mechanism stamped *Smith's Patent Box. Length* 69 cm, body 34 cm. *Depth* 7·5 cm. *String length* 41·5 cm.

255 English guitar. J. C. Elschleger, England, third quarter of eighteenth century. *London, R. Coll. of Music, 21.* The name is engraved on ivory panel in back of head. A pearl panel on back of body is engraved *M C. of GF.* Head with finial in form of carved head of a woman, and tuning by worm-and-pinion machines with ivory pins, turned by separate watchkey from the front. *Length* 82 cm, body 35 cm.

256 English guitar. Claus & Co., London. *London, Victoria and Albert Mus.* Interior key action with hammers. (View of belly, with strings and bridge removed.)

257 English guitar. William Gibson, Dublin, 1765. *London, Victoria and Albert Mus., W.17–1919.* Large size with pointed shoulders. Original worm-gear machines with ring touches. Bass side of neck slightly hollowed. Capotasto fitted. *Length* 90 cm, body 40·5 cm. *Depth* at centre 7·2 cm. *String length* 53 cm.

258 Norwegian cittern. Armund Hansen, Friederichshald, *c.* 1790. *Stockholm, Musikhist. Mus., 999.* Body with lower points. Rose and two crescent soundholes. Four double courses and two single.

259 Cittern. Gérard J. Deleplanque, Lille, 1764. *Brussels, Conserv. royal, 1525.* Round back. Ebony borders inlaid with ivory. Ebony and ivory star rose. Finial a carved woman's head. Three double courses and four single. *Length* 86 cm.

260   Cittern. G. le Blond, Dunkirk, 1773. *Leipzig, K.-M.-Univ., 618.* Barber's-pole borders of ebony and ivory. Sunk paper rose. Screw tuning and square finial. Four double courses and two single. *Length* 77 cm, body 35 cm. *Depth* 7·5 cm.

261   Arch-cittern. G. Deleplanque, Lille; keybox dated 1792. *Brussels, Conserv. royal, 2916.* Keybox added by Hoebrechts. Divided pegbox. Four double and three single courses, plus two single basses.

262, 265   Arch-cittern. Renault, Paris, late eighteenth century. *Paris, Conserv., C.260.* Asymmetrical body, reduced on treble side. Five basses.

263, 266, 267   Arch-cittern, Renault & Chatelain, Paris, 1787. *Paris, Conserv., E.1662.* Body extended as far as the nut on the bass side. Enclosed machines with ring touches. Eleven courses with five overspun basses. *Length* 108·5 cm, body 33 cm (67 cm on bass side). *Depth* 12 cm. *String lengths* 50, 77–79·5 cm.

264   Arch-cittern. Louis S. Laurent, Paris, 1775. *Brussels, Conserv. royal, 252.* Label, *Au cytre allemand, Laurent ... 1775.* Round-backed, with 11 ribs. Four double and three single courses, plus two bass strings. *Length* 99 cm, body 38 cm.

268   Portuguese guitar. Jaco Vieira da Silva, Lisbon, 17... *London, Victoria and Albert Mus., 208–1882.* Body with blunt points. Ivory and wood mosaic purfling. Brass openwork rose and small fancy *f*-holes. Twelve brass frets. Capotasto attached. Screw tuning by watchkey. Six double courses. *Length* 72 cm, body 34 cm. *Depth* 7·5 cm. *String length* 43·2 cm.

269   Portuguese guitar. Rosa & Caldeira, Lisbon, mid nineteenth century. *Brussels, Conserv. royal, 2494.* Radial screw tuning with attached buttons. Open soundhole. Six double courses (the lower three in octaves). *Length* 71·5 cm.

270   Pandore en luth. ? Eighteenth century. *Brussels, Conserv. royal, 1555.* Two-piece back with inset rose. Five-piece belly. Divided pegbox with carved figure and 18 pegs. *Length* 119 cm, body 61·5 cm. *Depth* above 9·5 cm, at base 8·1 cm. *String length* 75·5 cm.

The normal flat-backed instruments have internal side-linings in the manner of violin making and the backs are often pressed to curve inwards to the neck as seen from the side. Bellies vary in length between 33 and 42 cm, and the sides are between 6 and 7·5 cm deep. Typical forms of the inset rose include an inlaid star pattern in different colours, and a musical trophy or other design in stamped copper gilt. At the base of the body is a row of ivory studs for the lower ends of the strings. The neck is of full width throughout, though on large-sized instruments it may be hollowed a little down the bass side. The ebony or tortoiseshell fingerboard is curved and its lower end is shaped symmetrically. There are usually from 12 to 15 ivory or metal frets in English instruments but 17 in French. The English stringing is six-course (four doubles of steel and brass, with two overspun singles below them). This is found among the earlier of the French instruments but the typical French arrangement adds another single course, making seven in all. The tunings employed differ from those of the old citterns, being based on a common chord, as in some lute tunings, and suitable for the *arpeggiato* accompaniment that had grown fashionable during the period.

Fingerboard and neck are pierced with holes between certain of the frets for the attachment, by a wing nut, of a capotasto, seen in position in **249** and other examples illustrated. A capotasto is an ancient and still common device on fretted instruments, having the function of a movable nut, allowing the player to transpose into a higher key without different fingering. In other instruments, as the guitar, it is often secured by a gut loop, or by screw-clip encircling the neck.

The initial form of head is a pegbox (**249**), typically surmounted by a square finial as in the older mandores. Then tuning by enclosed screwed rods came in (screw tuning), an early instance being a guitar by Liessem, 1756 (**253**). Sometimes (**254**) this mechanism is engraved 'Preston, Inventor' (no patent recorded). The screws are turned by a separate watchkey, the head of the instrument being brought up in a wide curve in order to make room for the key. A third method of tuning is by worm gears, in modern parlance 'machines'. In some instances the machines are turned by separate watchkey, as in a curious undated English example (**255**). More commonly the ten machines are enclosed, each with its own attached key in the form of a ring touch (**257**).

In 1783 Claus of London patented a *Keyed guitar*, with an action for striking the strings mechanically, avoiding the chance of damage to the fingernails. Six small keys like pianoforte keys actuate six small felted hammers which emerge to strike the strings through holes in the rose or in the place where the rose should be (**256**). More commonly found, however, is an external keybox, detachable at will and in English examples often stamped 'Smith's Patent Box' (no patent recorded). It consists of an oval wooden box containing the keys and hammers, clamped to the body of the instrument by wooden arms (**254**).

Portuguese guitars (**268**) were strung with five or six double courses (today six). An individual later feature is the radially arranged screw tuning (**269**), which gives room for fixed buttons, replacing the old separate watchkey which was apt to wear out. During the nineteenth century the Portuguese guitar became influenced by the extravagances of mandolin decoration, though additional soundholes in *f* and 'tear-drop' forms appear to go back to the late eighteenth century (**268**). Other late citterns appeared in Scandinavia, e.g. the Norwegian cittern of Armund Hansen (**258**), slightly reminiscent in outline and soundholes of the bell citterns previously so popular in the north. In Stockholm, makers of the Swedish lute also made wire-strung versions of it, including an arch-cittern with screw tuning throughout.

A notable feature in France, perhaps reflecting the not too distant memory of the theorbo, is the number of arch-citterns (*arcicistre*) made especially by the Parisian luthiers from the 1770s until just after 1800. A name for them was in fact *théorbe*. Some are round-backed (**264**). The flat-backed instruments favour an elliptical outline, while in some models the body is asymmetrical, diminished on the treble side (**262, 265**) and sometimes, from the 1780s, extended along the full length of the neck, presumably to offer the bass courses extra soundbox volume (**266, 267**). The nut of the upper pegbox is usually set at a slant. Most instruments are tuned by pegs, but Renault also used small enclosed machines mounted individually in a head with a flat face, and tuned by side rings (**263**) or by separate watchkey. Some of these instruments have gut frets, as again on the 'double' model by Savains here placed with the guitars (**326**), though possibly meant originally for wire strings ('double arch-cittern').

11 Bandurria

Illustrations

271–3 Bandurria. Eighteenth century. *Paris, Conserv., E535, C.247.* Decorated with marquetry. Rose in belly. One fixed fret, the others gut. Six double courses of gut. *Length* 54 cm, body 22 cm. *Depth* 6 cm. *String length* 29·7 cm.

274 Bandurria. Late nineteenth century. *Brussels, Conserv. royal, 3185. Length* 55 cm. *Depth* 7·4 cm.

This little Spanish instrument, in appearance something like a squat English guitar, typologically falls between the citterns and guitars. It is flat-backed and strung sometimes with gut, sometimes with metal. The body length is from about 19 to 24 cm, though 6 to 8·5 cm deep, and the shoulders are typically squared off (**271**), though also rounded (**274**). The instrument is used chiefly for playing the melody over guitar accompaniment in popular ensemble and dance music, much as the mandolin in Italy. A bandurria is mentioned in early sources, as Bermudo (1555), though without divulging much about the size and shape. The present form is attested from the mid-eighteenth century (Minguet y Yrol, 1754). With wire strings, the attachment is to the tail end of the body; with gut, normally to the bridge, though both materials may be employed together. Five double courses were usual in the eighteenth century, subsequently six. One of two prettily decorated bandurrias in the Paris Collection (C.248) is strung with four triple courses of wire and has the obliquely placed nut, frets and bridge seen in the work of Minguet (one of the few Spanish instrument books of the eighteenth century). As with other instruments the fingerboard was extended onto the belly in the nineteenth century and the soundhole left open. The head is of guitar type, with rear pegs, though machine tuning may be found in late models, some of these made in France and Germany. There have also been 'lyre' models, copied from the lyre-guitar, and so on.

Further Spanish popular instruments include the larger *bandolon*, and the nineteenth-century *laúd*, which is not a lute but a long-necked cittern, sometimes built with scalloped outline rather like that of the old orpharion.

12 Guitars

Links between the guitar of the sixteenth century and earlier instruments in medieval pictures which look faintly like guitars, or are named by poets with guitar-like names such as 'gittern', remain imperfectly elucidated. By the middle of the sixteenth century, however, the *guiterne* or *guiterre* was well known in France and was a small guitar of probably Spanish evolution (see Heartz, *GSJ*, XVI, 1963). From this point the history of the guitar can be considered: firstly, up to the second half of the eighteenth century; secondly, the ensuing period, during which the modern six-stringed guitar was created.

Illustrations: Guitars

275 Treble guitar (*cavaquinho*). Portuguese, nineteenth century. *London, R. Coll. of Music, 130.* Pin bridge. Twelve brass frets. Five strings. *Length* 50 cm, body 22·5 cm. *Depth* 5 cm. *String length* 34 cm.

276 Rajão (guitar in form of a fish). Portuguese, nineteenth century. *London, Horniman Mus., 28.4.56/220.* Body carved from two pieces of pine, the upper including rounded belly and the neck. Incised scales. Mouth and eyes in red, black and white paint. Five strings. *Length* 65 cm. *String length* 39 cm.

277 Guitar. Joze F. Coelho, Lisbon, *c.* 1820. *London, Horniman Mus.* Straight-sided model, crudely made. Brass frets. Tied bridge. Six strings. *Length* 77 cm, body 42 cm. *Depth* 4·2 cm. *String length* 56 cm.

278-80 Vihuela. Spanish, sixteenth century. *Paris, Musée Jacquemart-André.* Engraved on side of head *GVADALVPE*. Flat back of alternate sectors of dark and light wood, and sides of interlacing pattern of similar woods. Five parchment roses. Narrow head originally for 12 rear pegs. *Length* 109 cm, body 58·4 cm. *Depth* 7·2 cm. *String length c.* 76 cm (with an earlier position of the bridge, *c.* 80 cm).

281 Guitar. Giovanni Smit, Milan, 1646. *Vienna, Kunsthist. Mus., C.53.* Small size, with vaulted back of black ribs and ivory fillets. Sunk rose. Fingerboard inlaid with *genre* figures. Four double courses of gut strings. *Length* 56·5 cm, body 26 cm. *Depth* 5·5 cm.

282 Guitar. Giovanni Smit, Milan, 1646. *Vienna, Kunsthist. Mus., C.52.* Similar to the preceding though strung with five courses as a *chitarra battente*.

283, 284 Guitar. Belchior Dias, 1581. *London, R. Coll. of Music, 171.* Label, *Belchior dias a fez . . . lx^a nomes de dez^ro 1581.* Carved on head, *BCHIOR DIAS LXA.* Small size. Vaulted back of seven deeply fluted ribs of chestnut (?) with ivory fillets. Sides of the same materials. Rose missing. Holes for ten pegs in flat head. *Length* 77 cm, body 36 cm. *Max. depth* 6·5 cm. *String length* 55 cm.

285-7 Guitar. Matteo Sellas, Venice, *c.* 1630. *Brussels, Conserv. royal, 550.* Vaulted back of rosewood ribs with ivory fillets. Sides of the same. Floral marquetry on the belly and a rose of lead, gilt, in wide marquetry surround. Engraved ivory panels on fingerboard represent scenes from Aesop's Fables. Five double courses. *Length* 87 cm.

288, 289 Guitar. Giorgio Jungmann, Genoa, 1633. *Brussels, Conserv. royal, 3183.* Flat back of dark wood with ivory fillets. Inlaid floral designs on belly and fingerboard. No rose. Fixed frets. Five double courses. *Length* 97·5 cm.

290 Guitar. René Voboam, Paris, 1641. *Oxford, Ashmol. Mus.* Flat back and sides of tortoiseshell strips with inlaid ivory zig-zag pattern. Ebony and ivory barber's-pole ornament along edges and bridge. Sunk rose. Five double courses. *Length* 92·5 cm, body 45·5 cm. *Depth* above 8 cm, below 9 cm. *Widths* 21·5, 18·2, 25 cm.

291 Chitarra battente. Jakob Stadler, Munich, 1624. *London, W. E. Hill & Sons.* Vaulted back of ebony and ivory ribs. Belly bent inwards at bridge level and decorated with hunting scenes. Sunk rose. Engraved ivory pegs for five double courses. *Length* 86 cm, body 44 cm. *Depth* of sides 11 cm.

292, 293 Guitar. Joachim Tielke, Hamburg, *c.* 1700. *London, Victoria and Albert Mus., 676–1872.* Vaulted back of five broad ribs of engraved marquetry of tortoiseshell, ivory and pewter, and sides similar. Sunk rose of paper, partly gilded. Neck with tortoiseshell and ivory marquetry. Ebony fingerboard. Openwork ivory head. Eleven pegs. Six-course (treble single, the others double). *Length* 101 cm, body 50 cm. *Depth* of sides 12 cm. *String length* 72 cm.

294, 295 Chitarra battente. Italian, seventeenth or eighteenth century. *London, W. E. Hill & Sons.* Vaulted back with flat ribs and sides also of ribs. Sunk rose with inlaid surround. Belly bent inwards at bridge level. Marquetry neck and fingerboard. Five triple courses of wire. *Length* 96 cm, body 46 cm. *Depth* of sides 14 cm.

Later Guitars

296 Guitar. Lamblain, Ghent, 1795. *Brussels, Conserv. royal, 2909.* Walnut body. Belly with pearl borders and open soundhole. Five double courses.

297 Guitar. Thielemann, Berlin, 1814. *Berlin, Instit. f. Musikforschung, 4676.* Six strings. Pin bridge. *Length* 93·4 cm, body 45 cm. *Depth* 7·7 cm above, 8·6 cm at base.

298, 299 Guitar. Grobert, Mirecourt, first half of nineteenth century. *Paris, Conserv., E.375, C.278.* Inscribed with the names of Berlioz and Paganini. Figure-of-eight head. Six strings. Pin bridge.

300 Guitar. José Pages, Cadiz, 1798. *London, Victoria and Albert Mus., 415–1905.* Four fan bars under lower part of belly. Open soundhole surrounded with chequers of mother-of-pearl and dark wood. Head and bridge for six double courses. Shallow extended fingerboard of rosewood with 18 brass frets, is apparently an early addition to the instrument. Six double courses. *Length* 98 cm, body 45 cm. *Depth* 9·4 cm. *String length* 64·5 cm.

301 Guitar. Gennaro Fabricatore, Naples, *c.* 1805. *London, Reuben Greene Coll.* Curved fingerboard with inlaid edges and silver frets. Tied bridge. Six strings.

302 Guitar. Louis Panormo, London, *c.* 1820. *London, Reuben Greene Coll.* Pin bridge, extended fingerboard. Machine head.

303 Guitar. Harlot, Mirecourt, early nineteenth century. *Basel, Hist. Mus., 1897:28.* 'Shield' model. Sycamore body, with pearl borders. Figure-of-eight head. Six strings. Pin bridge. *Length* 98 cm. *Depth* 8 cm.

304 Guitar. Louis Panormo, London, 1829. *Leipzig, K.-M.-Univ., 566.* Wide model, curved fingerboard with silver frets. Machine head. *Length* 98 cm, body 48 cm. *Depth* 8·5 cm.

305, 306 Guitar. Antonio Torres, Almeria, 1859. *Barcelona, Mus. de musica, 626.* Formerly the property of the soloist Miguel Lopez. Spanish bridge, flat fingerboard, heel at neck root, machine head.

307 Guitar. Porcel, Barcelona, 1867. *Barcelona, Mus. de musica, 445.* With 19 metal sympathetic strings which pass across the body from peg plate on right shoulder to a bridge on the left side. Figure-of-eight head.

308 Guitar. Martin & Coupa, New York City, *c.* 1835–50. *Washington, Smithsonian Instit., loaned by Walter Lipton.*

309 Guitar. O. F. Selling, Stockholm, *c.* 1835. *Stockholm, Musikhist. Mus., 1462.* Flat scroll head with the six pegs in line, of a guitar in 'shield' form.

310 Guitar. Altimira, Barcelona, 184–, *London, Victoria and Albert Mus., W.15–1915.* Belonged to the daughter of General de Rosas, Dictator of Argentina. Back and sides of amboyna wood. Belly decorated with mother-of-pearl painted with floral designs, and hunting scenes painted on the wood. Pin bridge. Seventeen frets separated by engraved and painted mother-of-pearl panels. *Length* 95 cm, body 45 cm. *Depth* 9·5 cm. *String length* 62·5 cm.

311 Guitar. G. Tiefenbrunner, Munich, mid nineteenth century. *Ann Arbor, Univ. of Michigan, 1117.* Cittern shape. Three soundholes with simple roses. Pin bridge. Figure-of-eight head. *Length* 94 cm. *Depth* 9 cm.

The first guitar to figure importantly in musical history is the Spanish *vihuela*, which held a place in courtly music during the later fifteenth century and the sixteenth roughly corresponding with that held by the lute in other countries. Only one specimen has been identified (**278–80**), a large, shallow-bodied guitar with a curious disposition of soundholes matched in contemporary illustration of the instrument. This unique relic has been fully described by M. W. Prynne, who first drew attention to it, in *GSJ*, XVI, 1963.[1]

The ordinary guitar of the same period (Spanish *guitarra*) differed in having a rather lower musical status and a smaller size with fewer courses. Descendants of it abound in the Peninsula as regional forms like the small *tiple* ('treble') guitar or (in Madeira) *machete* (275) with four or five strings (parent of the ukulele), and others built in shapes recalling medieval instruments (277) and in the form of a fish (276), most of them now with single courses. The small sixteenth-century instrument is shown in French illustrations from *c.* 1550 with four courses, of which the first is single, and with a body shape similar to that of subsequent guitars up to the eighteenth century, i.e. narrow-bodied with unobtrusive waist, rose in belly, and gut frets. The head is flat as later, or, outside Spain, it may have a mandore-like pegbox. Early Spanish specimens seem very scarce. A guitar with the date 1581 and label of an otherwise obscure Lisbon maker (283, 284) may be genuine, though somewhat altered through restoration. Two small seventeenth-century Italian guitars at Vienna (281, 282), one of them still in four-course condition, similarly have vaulted backs moulded from ribs with an appearance of deep fluting. This construction, which makers may have felt to be a particularly strong one, is common up to the beginning of the eighteenth century in Italy, France and Germany. The sides of such instruments are usually also made from ribs matching the colours and decoration of the back. Almost invariably the belly wood is continued a little way up the face of the neck before abutting the fingerboard proper, presumably as a strength member rather like the deck of a ship, for though the guitar is sonorously one of the most perfect of instruments it tends to be structurally not the most robust. The guitar through the seventeenth century in Italy and France seems to have been an instrument—by no means the last—which many sought to possess as a handsome object not necessarily to be learnt studiously. Ornate decorations include sunk roses intricately constructed from cylinders and tiered elements in ivory and parchment; extravagant twirled moustaches to the bridge; finely shaped heads surmounting richly inlaid neck and fingerboard (285–9). Five courses are usual, though sometimes in the eighteenth century there are six (292). Voboam was the leading maker in Paris around the middle of the seventeenth century (290). In Italy, after the generation of Sellas, some large guitars survive from the workshop of Stradivari (Ashmolean Museum and Paris Conservatoire). Many instruments were given fixed frets during the eighteenth century and in the nineteenth large numbers were converted into six-string guitars.

Wire-strung guitars. Metal strings have been used on the guitar in certain forms from the seventeenth century up to today, a traditional form still in use being the Portuguese 'Braga guitar' (*viola bragueza*), often still built with the old type of flush fingerboard. The wire strings are said to be advantageous when the instrument is used for accompaniment for long hours in hot sun. Best-known of earlier types is an Italian form of the seventeenth century onwards which historians term *chitarra battente* (signifying a guitar strummed with a plectrum)—a term which, according to the late Professor Kinsky, was gathered from Tuscan vernacular in the last century by the collector Paul de Wit. In this species, in which the body normally has the vaulted form of back, the belly is bent inwards at bridge level as in the Neapolitan mandolin and the wire strings are attached to hitch pins at the base (294, 295). A protector plate may be fixed to the belly. The neck has fixed frets and the head may contain as many as 15 pegs, since any number of the five courses may be triple courses. Italian specimens are rarely signed; signed examples are generally conversions from ordinary guitars, though not invariably (291).

Later Guitars. The middle of the eighteenth century was a quiet era in guitar design, even though

---

[1] The word *vihuela* is the Castilian form (mute h) of 'viola', this last being still the term by which the guitar is known in Portugal, pointing to a close connection felt between guitars and fiddles in the Peninsula in early times. The full name of this courtly guitar was *vihuela de mano*, distinguishing it from the *v. de arco* or viol. The inventories of Henry VIII include 'guitterons . . . also caulled Spanishe Vialles' (Galpin, 1910, p. 296).

'Spanish guitars' were sold in most capitals. Yet one can see in the proportions of some examples (e.g. by Deleplanque of Lille [Brussels, 2915], dated 1761) the beginnings of the changes which were accelerated in the last 20 years of the century. Average measurement across the body of a full-sized guitar of the old type are of the order of: upper part, 21 cm, waist 18 cm, lower part, 25 cm. By the end of the century the corresponding figures might be 23, 16 and 28, thus wider, though narrower in the waist. At this point the great creative period in the guitar's history may be said to have begun, bringing in a host of new features, some of which must now be noticed.

A typical early transitional guitar is by Lamblin (**296**). By this time, vaulted backs were no longer made, save sometimes in peasant instruments. The interior, previously lined only with paper, has wooden kerfing strips or rows of separated triangular blocks. Soundholes are usually left vacant. Pages of Cadiz had already introduced fan-barring of the lower part of the belly before 1800, for acoustical gain. The change from double courses to six single strings commenced also before 1800, first probably not in Spain but somewhere along a Paris–Naples axis passing through Marseilles. From Naples, a guitar in the Claudius Collection, Copenhagen (**172**), with the label of Antonio Vinaccia, 1785, appears to have been built with six strings. In the *arpi-guitare* by Pacquet of Marseilles, 1784 (**318**), the single courses are already attached to a pin bridge—a device taken from harp practice. The lyre-guitars also seem to have been single-strung from the first. (The six single strings of the guitar have been normally three of gut and three of overspun silk.)

Alternative shapes of the head enter after 1800, including a figure-of-eight form (**298**), also machine heads from *c.* 1802, though not common until later. The guitars played by celebrated musicians like Weber, Schubert, Paganini and Berlioz would have been of the later transitional types with pin bridge, etc, as illustrated by an example by Grobert (**298, 299**) signed with the names of the last two of these musicians. The fingerboards are still mostly of the old type, flush with the belly and occasionally still fretted with gut. The extended fingerboard came in gradually after 1800 and is uncommon before 1830 save in advanced models like those of Louis Panormo of London, who had been introduced by the soloist Fernando Sor, *c.* 1809, to the latest Spanish models of the time. Two Panormo examples (**302, 304**) show this maker's own development of the Spanish model and the enormous progress made in advanced guitar design by 1830. Further enlargements of the body, especially in the lower part, relocation of the bridge to the centre point of the lower bouts, and reduction of ornament, took place in the following 20 years, resulting in the mid-century models of Antonio Torres (**305, 306**), often cited as the creator of the modern Spanish guitar, and of other forward-looking luthiers like Martin of New York (**308**). Torres developed the Spanish tied bridge, rejecting the pin bridge which had made inroads into Spain as it had elsewhere. For a *flamenco* guitar the old peg head has been preferred to machines, for its relative lightness. (For fuller details of the early nineteenth-century development of the guitar and its fittings, see Usher, *GSJ*, IX, 1956.)

Besides these developments, guitars of less advanced models continued to be made up to the end of the century, particularly highly decorated 'ladies' models' (**310**). Also there have been innumerable variant forms, the most successful being that which is known in Germany as a *Wappengitarre*, 'shield guitar' (**303**), evolved in Vienna about 1810 on the premise that the upper swell of the body contributes little to the tone and might as well be omitted, or rather, for sake of appearance, be reduced to points. The model was copied to some extent in other countries and is in manufacture still. Other basically round outlines include cittern-like (**311**) and crescent forms (**319**) and many others. They are identified as guitars by their six strings (but in Russia often seven) and their guitar string length of around 64 cm. There are also early nineteenth-century lyre-guitars with the arms reduced to squared-off stumps. An American 'harp-guitar' dating from *c.* 1834 and still used recently by some soloists has an oval body with a long hollow prolongation which reaches to the floor (**324**). 'Bass guitars', with bass strings arranged theorbo-wise, are mentioned in the next section.

13 Lyre-Guitars, Bass and Compound Guitars, Harp-Lutes

These are here grouped together for convenience. Some are technically guitars, with or without extra strings, while others, including Light's harp-lutes, are hybrids or developments from hybrids, strictly speaking forming small categories of their own. They date mainly from the late eighteenth century onwards.

Illustrations: Lyres and Lyre-guitars

312 Lyre-guitar. J. G. Thielemann, Berlin, c. 1800. *Berlin, Instit. f. Musikforschung, 4677.* Flat base. Swell back. Two quatrefoil soundholes. Pin bridge. Flush fingerboard extending to edge of belly. Rear pegs. Six strings. *Length* 86 cm, body 38 cm. *Depth* at points 1·1 cm, at neck 8·4 cm.

313, 314 French lyre. Charles, Marseilles, 1785. *Yale, Univ. Coll.* Striped back. Rose on each side of bridge. Rounded fingerboard with shaped end. Triangular head with gilt dolphins and trophy. Ivory frets, capotasto holes and rear pegs. Nine strings.

315 Lyre-guitar. Lupot, Orleans, 1778. *New York, Metropol. Mus., 2590.* Flat base. Open soundhole and applied brass ornaments. Tied bridge. Flush fingerboard with ivory frets. Flat head with rear pegs. Six strings. *Length* 83 cm.

316 Apollo lyre. Robert Wornum, London, before 1815. *London, Victoria and Albert Mus., 891–1875.* Marked *R. Wornum, Inventor & Maker.* Body painted green. Attached gilt foot. Gilt crescent in soundhole held on interior bracket. Bridge of L-section with ivory-bushed holes in which the strings are hitched without pins. Flat ebony fingerboard with silver frets and four ivory position dots. Gesso head of Apollo carried on a hinge to give access to the wrest pins for the six strings. *Length* 85 cm, body 31 cm. *Depth* at neck 7 cm. *String length* 54 cm.

317 French lyre. Boulan, Arras, 17—. *Brussels, Conserv. royal, 3180.* Label, *Fait par Boulan luthier de Paris en 17*— (the last two figures barely legible); stamped on cross-bars, *Boulan à Arras.* Round soundhole and two antique C-holes. Curved fingerboard. Seven metal strings from rear pegs. *Length* 78 cm.

318 Arpi-guitare. Pacquet, Marseilles, 1784. *Brussels, Conserv. royal, 3177.* Seven-stave body with rose in belly. A curved neck carries a pegbox surmounted by a carved lion's head from which runs a fingerboard with 18 ivory frets and ten capotasto holes. Seven strings. Pin bridge. *Length* 94 cm, soundbox 70 cm.

319 Guitar. Gennaro Fabricatore, Naples, 1817. *Brussels, Conserv. royal, 1537.* Crescent model. Tied bridge. Six strings. *Length* 91 cm.

Bass and other Guitars

320, 321 Bissex. H. Naderman, Paris, 1773. *Paris, Conserv., E.2372.* Round-backed body with rose. Six gut strings and six basses, running from rear pegs in flat head to the bridge. *Crochet* action by thumb-lever for eight strings. *Length* 87 cm, body 46 cm. *String length* 60–65 cm.

322, 323 Guitare décacorde. Caron, Versailles, 1784. *Yale, Univ. Coll.* Oval-shaped round-backed body. Two open pegboxes. Six gut strings and four basses, all passing over the fingerboard. String attachment to base of body. Gut frets.

324 Guitar ('harp guitar'). Jos. Beckhaus, Philadelphia, late nineteenth century. *New York, Metrop. Mus., 1519.* Body extended far below the bridge. Two soundholes, the lower with a simple metal rose bearing the maker's name.

325 Guitar. Rafael Vallejo, Baza (Granada), 1789–92. *London, Victoria and Albert Museum, 389–1871.* Decorated with Royal Arms of Spain and Imperial Double Eagle, also inscription indicating the instrument as a possession of Charles IV. Large body with incised and inlaid decoration. Short neck with six double courses and five frets. Attached board on left shoulder of body has 20 rear pegs from which ten double courses of metal treble strings run over a wooden bar and under an iron wire at the belly edge, and so across the left side of the belly to a slanting extension of the bridge. *Length* 102 cm, body 50 cm. *Depth* above 10·5 cm, at base 12 cm. *String length* 67 cm; of the treble strings, 21·5–38 cm.

326 Double arch-guitar. Savains, Paris, *c.* 1783. *Brussels, Conserv. royal, 1534.* Two necks with fingerboards in length proportion 2:3. Five gut strings over each fingerboard. The upper pegboxes with oblique nuts carry five basses (longer neck) and three (shorter neck). Belly with paper rose and tied bridge. Gut frets. *Length,* max. 115 cm.

327 Harpolyre. J.-F. Salomon (Besançon; patent 1829). *Brussels, Conserv. royal, 3176.* Three necks and fingerboards, arranged in a fan. Guitar strings in the middle, eight gut trebles on the left and seven basses on the right fingerboard. Three soundholes.

328 Double harp-guitar. John Frederick Grosjean, London, *c.* 1840. *London, Victoria and Albert Mus., 201–1872.* Rosewood soundbox 79 cm long, 4 cm deep at top, 10 cm at base. Two flush fingerboards with nickel-silver frets and position dots (placed across the frets). Two elongated soundholes in the narrow side of the body, and slinging buttons. *Length* 96 cm. *Depth* at top 4 cm, at bottom 10 cm. *String lengths* 63, 31·5 cm.

329 Bass guitar. Vissenaire, Lyon, 1825. *Leipzig, K.-M.-Univ., 597.* Shield form. Bird's-eye maple. Brass frets. Six strings, three basses. *Length* 101 cm, body 43 cm. *Depth* 7 cm.

330 Bass guitar. Lacôte, Paris, 182–. *Ann Arbor, Univ. of Michigan, 1127.* Pin bridge. Flush fingerboard reaching edge of belly. Five basses of overspun silk. *Length* 91·5 cm.

331 Bass guitar. (?) J. G. Schirzer, Vienna, *c.* 1865. *Copenhagen, Musikhist. Mus., 351, C.34.* Inside the body a supplementary soundboard over which run wire sympathetic strings. Pin bridge, machine head. Six basses. *Length* 110 cm.

Harp-lutes, etc

332 Harp-lute-guitar (harp-theorbo). Harley, London, early nineteenth century. *Oxford, Pitt Rivers Mus., Balfour 1939, 609.* Black-painted body with flat back and sides. Crescent in soundhole. Pin bridge. Three basses.

333 Harp-guitar. Levien, Paris, early nineteenth century. *New York, Metropol. Mus. of Art, 1515.* Round back with soundhole in it. Pin bridge. Three semitone buttons on rear of neck. Seven strings of gut and overspun silk. *Length* 84 cm.

334 Harp-lute-guitar. Barry, London, *c.* 1800. *Brighton, Museum.* Body of three staves with oblong soundhole in back. Gilt rose. Tied bridge. Seven gut strings and four overspun basses. *Length* 91 cm. *String lengths* 44·5–62·5 cm.

335 Harp-lute. (Light), London, *c.* 1810. *London, Victoria and Albert Mus., 37–1873.* Inscribed *675. Light. Foley Place, London.* Seven-stave back. Belly painted blue with gilt decoration. Inserted rose. Ivory frets. Twelve gut and overspun silk strings tuned by wrest pins. Four of the long strings can be raised a semitone by brass ring stops, one of these being turned by left thumb knob and connecting levers. *Length* 82 cm. *String lengths* from 35 to 63 cm.

336 Harp-lute. London, *c.* 1815. *London, Victoria and Albert Mus., 252–1882.* Body similar to the preceding, painted green and with pin bridge. Stepped fingerboard. Fourteen strings, three of which have ring stops while two have movable nuts actuated by sprung levers. *Length* 83 cm. *String lengths* 26·5–66 cm.

337 British harp-lute. (Light), London, *c.* 1816. *London, Victoria and Albert Mus., W.33–1925.* Marked *Light. Foley Place. London. Patent No 58.* Varnished body with composition base. Pin bridge (not slanted). Two ring stops and ten ditals. *Length* 83 cm.

338 Dital harp. (Light), London, 1819. *Brighton, Museum.* Marked *Dital harp. 363.* Painted light blue. Slanting bridge. Nineteen strings of which the longer 13 have ditals. *Length* 89 cm.

339 Harp Ventura. A. G. Ventura, London, after 1828. *London, Victoria and Albert Mus., 248–1882.* Flat back with elevated central panel. Tortoiseshell sides. Belly painted cream colour, with cameo ornament in soundhole. Recess in top of body for tuning key. Nineteen strings. Ten *fourchette* mechanisms encased in brass plates and actuated by seven brass thumb levers each with locking device. *Length* 62 cm.

340 Harpe ditale. Pfeiffer, Paris, *c.* 1830. *Brussels, Conserv. royal, 248.* Seven levers actuating *fourchettes. Length* 89 cm. *Depth* of body 6·4 cm above, 9 cm below.

Certain types of instrument built between *c.* 1770 and *c.* 1840, often lumped together under the name *lyre-guitar* (**312–17**), reflect times when ladies' fashions extended to small musical instruments, in this case married to the neo–classical pose. The *French lyre* comes closest to the Grecian lyre in build, having a wide and deep body from the shoulders of which rise two solid curving arms, each fixed to its own 'neck block' in the body. These arms support a shaped and decorated flat head, to which is attached a broad fretted fingerboard that runs down towards the body without reaching it; there is no central neck. The strings, of gut or wire, the deeper overspun, number from six to nine single courses running to hitch pins at the base. Probably they were tuned in a similar way to the contemporary French cittern, the string length averaging some 51 cm, too short for a guitar. In a lyre by Charles, Marseilles, 1785 (**313–14**) the arms meet the head directly, but in a version by Boulan, Arras (**317**), a short cross-piece links them to the head; the unclear date on this last has been read as 1747 though this seems improbably early.

Examples of the ordinary *lyre-guitar* are much commoner, this instrument having been made in most countries. It is simply a six-stringed guitar with the body carried up in two hollow arms which continue the soundbox space, yet are really no more than decorative. The neck and fingerboard are as in a guitar and the gilt or painted wooden rods which join the head to the tips of the arms form no part of the essential structure (**312**). The base of the body is generally flat for standing the instrument upright on a table. A pair of quatrefoil soundholes is characteristic, or else a single soundhole often containing a gilt crescent supported by an internal bracket. An early example (**315**) with tied bridge and ivory frets is ascribed by its label (the authenticity of which has been questioned) to Lupot, Orleans, 1778. Most specimens are late eighteenth-century or of the first third of the nineteenth. A few include from two to five open bass strings. A London-made variant is the *Apollo lyre*, introduced *c.* 1810 either by Edward Light or Robert Wornum (**316**). Here, too, the fingerboard is carried by the neck which, however, is given a shorter string length than that of the lyre-guitar, being around 54 cm. The painted body rises in two short 'horns', each surmounted by a solid piece connected to the head by a sinuous gilt wooden rod, though this last is sometimes omitted. A gilt gesso head of Apollo is mounted at the top of the head on a hinge, so that it can be lifted to gain access to the wrest pins underneath. Again, some have bass strings.

The *arpi-guitare* of Pacquet d'Aix, Marseilles (**318**), is, despite the curious adjunction of a harp-like soundbox (70 cm long, built of seven ribs), a seven-stringed guitar, with a string length of 62·5 cm. The example shown, dated 1784 (or as Vannes reads it, 1774), must be one of the earliest examples of the use of the pin bridge in instruments other than harps. The body has a slinging button and ring for playing in guitar position.

The expression *bass guitar* has generally been taken to mean a guitar provided with open diatonic bass strings corresponding to those of a theorbo or arch-cittern. Two precursive forms are shown, each a Parisian free-lance design of the late eighteenth century. The *bissex* (**320, 321**) was first built by Naderman, the famous harp maker, from 1773, following an idea of one van Hecke. It amounts to an early instance of a six-stringed guitar or lute, with six basses added (thus in all 'bis sex'). Each bass is provided with a *crochet* mechanism derived from the Naderman harp (**400**) and actuated by a thumb lever at the back of the head to raise the pitch of the string by a semitone. The moulded back is of an original form with the centre rib wider than the others. The *guitare décacorde* by Caron (**322, 323**) dates from 1785, though Mahillon has suggested that it was not the first instrument to go by this name (nor the last, since Lacôte used it for one of his own bass guitars). The strings all run over a wide gut-fretted neck to the base of the body. There are six main courses and four basses which in an example at Paris can be raised a semitone by a lever which acts upon all four simultaneously. The body, moulded from ribs, has an unusual neo-classical oval form.

More conventional is a theorbo-style guitar by Villaume & Giron, Troyes, 1791 (Leipzig Collection, 596) with double courses and four basses. Later models include those by the noted Parisian guitar maker Lacôte, 1826, etc (**330**). One of these has 'ditals' (p. 55) for raising the pitch of the basses. A bass guitar in 'shield' form (**329**) is by Vissenaire, Lyons, 1825. Provincial France figures prominently beside Paris throughout this era of experimentation from the lyre-guitars onwards, most of the makers having been in the first place violin makers, some of them quite well known in violin lore. A later bass guitar (**331**) illustrates a design due to J. G. Schirzer, Vienna, *c.* 1865. Another Schirzer model, *Gitarre-harfe*, 1862, has the body extended upwards on the bass side alongside the neck under three basses. Instruments of these last types became widely used in Russia.

Among guitars in which a diatonic set of treble strings is added on the left side of the body (cf Russian theorbo, **195**) an early example is Andalusian (**325**), with ten double courses of metal trebles. The short neck with five frets suffices for simple chords in accompaniment to melodies played on the trebles. Another is the *guitare multicorde* of Charpentier and Munch, Paris, *c.* 1832 (Brussels, 2490, etc). Here 11 single gut trebles ('jeu de harpe') are tuned at a cross bar which reaches from low on the neck across to a raised arm in the left side of the body. The neck carries the normal six strings ('jeu de guitare') and an extension of the head carries eight basses. The inventors claimed that the diatonic trebles circumvented difficulties of playing on the higher frets of the guitar fingerboard. A *harpo-lyre* patented in 1829 by Salomon, a guitar professor in Besançon, adopts a similar principle (**327**), though using three necks, the outer two of which are equally provided with fretted fingerboards, for affixing capotastos, etc.

Guitars with two fingerboards strung in a normal way go back to 'twin' guitars of the seventeenth century, in which a small guitar is joined to a full-sized one in Siamese twin fashion; a fine example by Voboam is in the Vienna Collection (C.57). From the late eighteenth century an undated two-necked instrument by Savains (**326**) has the appearance of a two-necked arch-cittern (cf. p. 45) but has gut strings. It is almost identical with another specimen which is unsigned but bears the date 1783 with the arms of the House of Orleans (Brussels, 547). The fingerboards have a length ratio of 2:3. A later design is a *double harp-guitar* by the London harp maker J. F. Grosjean, *c.* 1840 (**328**). The long wedge-shaped sound-box is combined with a curved solid upper arm and a guitar neck with a fingerboard of normal proportions to form an open triangle. Across this is fixed a shorter fingerboard, half the length of the first and presumably with its strings tuned an octave higher, allowing the performer an easy change of register.

Harp-lutes, etc

A series of amateur stringed instruments invented by the London organist Edward Light (*b.* 1747) includes, in order of appearance, *harp-guitar*, *harp-lute* and *dital harp*, the first being a kind of gut-strung English guitar and the last almost a lyre (**333–8**). All are distinguished by a body construction borrowed from harps, with back and sides of seven flat staves (**337**) or of a single piece bent round. The bottom is closed by a curved plate of wood and there are one or more slot-shaped soundholes in the centre stave. The consequent resonance is full, as Light intended, but of a rather neutral character. The instruments, though marked with Light's name in most cases, were mostly if not all built by professional London craftsmen including Barry and Harley, and over their period, *c.* 1798–1820, were sold in fair quantities and are now common objects in collections. Their bodies are generally lacquered black or brightly painted, with gilt borders in contemporary decorative styles.

The *harp-guitar* (1798) has seven or eight gut strings of English guitar string length, attached to the bridge. The *harp-lute-guitar* (**334**) has the addition of a 'theorbo' head for three or four basses. It was also made by Harley with a more conventional type of soundbox (**332**). An improved harp-guitar (**333**) was brought out in Paris, by Levein, an ex-associate of Light, with the strings tuned by separate key and three of them with 'ditals' (below).

The *harp-lute*, advertised in 1815, introduces Light's thenceforth standard arrangement of a pillar on the bass side and a neck on the other which is extended in a curve to join the top of the pillar (**335**, etc.). By degrees Light whittled away the fingerboard and multiplied the gadgets for raising the pitch of strings by a semitone, these including simple ring-stops turned to grip the string, and the more complicated 'ditals' (so called by analogy with 'pedal') whereby a rod with a hole in it through which the string passes is moved in and out by sprung levers connected to a thumb button lower down. As with harp pedals the ditals can be locked in the 'on' position. Earlier models of harp-lute have straight neck and full fingerboards (**335**), next with an extra small fingerboard for the highest strings (**336**). The first *dital harp*, or *British harp-lute*, has a complex neck, perforated by an irregularly shaped hole (**337**). In the later dital harp the neck curves without a hole (**338**). The instrument could be slung as a guitar or played upright on the lap or a table, and in the late designs the left hand, besides actuating the ditals, can assist the right in playing on the strings.

The *harp Ventura* (**339**), patented by A. B. Ventura, London, 1828, incorporates *fourchette* mechanism taken from the Érard harp (**402**). The outline of the body is more rounded and the soundhole in front is square. As on the Light instruments small residual fingerboards serve to give a few extra high notes with economy of space. In a Danish *harpinella*, by Marstrand, Copenhagen, 1818, there are ditals but no finger-boards, truly a kind of chromatic lyre, as also Pfeiffer's *harpe ditale*, Paris, *c.* 1830 (**340**), which in shape distantly recalls the asymmetric lyres of Ancient Egypt; it has fourchettes actuated by levers on the cross-piece.

14 Banjo

Use of a simple stringed instrument by the Negroes in the New World is alluded to in the late seventeenth century (in Jamaica) and in the eighteenth (in the United States, with the name *banshaw* or *banjar*), but there seems to be no clear description of it before the early nineteenth century, during which the instrument spread among the American white population. It is said to have been introduced to England about the mid-century by the Christy Minstrels.

Illustrations: Banjo

341   Banjo. *c.* 1840. *London, Victoria and Albert Museum., 226–1882.* Pear-shaped hoop of pine with a closed back in which is a small ivory-bushed soundhole. Tacked vellum. Figure-of-eight head. Five strings including the short thumb string, this tuned at a small pegbox dovetailed into the right side of the neck. *Length* 99 cm. *Diameter of hoop* 34. *Depth* 9 cm.

342   Banjo. American, *c.* 1840. *London, Reuben Greene Coll.* Open back. Tacked vellum. Wavy neck. Five strings. *Length* 90 cm. *Diameter* 26 cm.

343, 344   Banjo. Fred Mather, New York, 1860. *Washington, Smithson. Instit., 207, 888.* Open back. Early rod tensioning. Machine head. Five strings.

345   Banjo. English, *c.* 1860–70. *Brighton, Museum.* Tunbridge ware decoration. Open back. Eight tensioning rods. Seven strings, two of the long strings being of wire. *Length* 86 cm. *Diameter* 30.5 cm.

346   Banjo. English, *c.* 1860. *London, Reuben Greene Coll.* Closed back and hollow neck. Vellum tensioned with wood screws. Machine head. Seven strings. *Length* 91 cm. *Diameter* 30 cm.

347   Banjo. Paul Bellevue da Silva, ? London. Dated 1889. *London, Reuben Greene Coll.* Open back. Rod tensioning. Seven strings. *Length* 94 cm. *Diameter* 31 cm.

348   Banjolin. American, late nineteenth century. *Ann Arbor, Univ. of Michigan, 1139B.* Mandolin-banjo. Fretted fingerboard. Four double courses of metal. *Length* 56.6 cm.

The vellum belly is stretched over the wooden hoop, at first with brass tacks (**341, 342**). Later the vellum is lapped onto a wooden hoop which is drawn down against the main hoop by wood screws (**346**), or by threaded tensioning rods (**343**). The neck is prolonged to traverse the main hoop beneath the vellum, this extension being termed the perch-pole. Though the back is typically left open, closed backs of many designs are found, leading eventually to the various metal sound-reflectors of modern banjos. The normal number of strings is five, one of which, the 'thumb string', is pegged to the bass side of the neck and has about two-thirds of the length of the others; it is tuned to a high G (or whatever the dominant may actually be) and gives this note only, both melodically and in various kinds of gay rhythmic ornamentation. Seven-stringed banjos (**345–7**) were popular in England during the last third of the nineteenth century; six strings are rarer. Frets and metal strings were not employed on the banjo until plectrum styles of playing came in, in America from the 1880s. The zither banjo of the end of the century is a fretted banjo, usually with five full-length metal strings tuned by machines (six machines often being in fact provided).

The vellum belly has been tested with other kinds of instrument, as guitars, even violins (a German example at New York, Metropol. Mus., 2292), but most successfully in the mandolin-banjo or *banjolin* (**348**), made in most countries.

15 Zithers

Among the Western instruments which have a neck-less soundbox with strings running from side to side, a distinct group, and one of intriguingly mysterious origin, is presented by those which have a fretted fingerboard for certain of the strings, laid along the long axis of the soundboard, usually down one side but sometimes down the centre line.[1] Among them, the Austro–German or Alpine series, from primitive forms up to the concert zither of modern times, will be looked at first.

Illustrations: Zithers

349   Scheitholt. Waszlberger, Hallein, 1763. *Salzburg, Mus. Carolino Augusteum, 81, Geir. 1*. Rectangular. Two rosettes of soundholes. Three melody strings and nine accompanying, tuned by wrest pins. Diatonic frets. *Length 66·5 cm.*

350   Kratz-zither. Franz Kren, Munich, first half of nineteenth century. *Berlin, Instit. f. Musikforschung, 2253*. Salzburg form. Diatonic frets and 11 strings. *Length 46 cm. Depth 4 cm.*

351   Kratz-zither. Josef Mayr, Halle, first half of nineteenth century. *Ann Arbor, Univ. of Michigan, 1147*. Bird head. Four 'octave' strings on further side. *Length 53·5 cm.*

352   Kratz-zither. Munich, first half of nineteenth century. *Berlin, Instit. f. Musikforschung, 554*. Mittenwald form. Overlapping edges. Pin bridge. Diatonic frets. Three metal and seven gut strings. *Length 53·5 cm. Depth 5 cm.*

353   Zither. Franz Kren, Munich. *Berlin, Instit. f. Musikforschung, 2246*. Guitar form. Pin bridge. Partly chromatic frets. Four plus ten gut strings. *Length 55 cm. Depth 7 cm.*

354   Concert zither. Georg Tiefenbrunner, Munich, 1845. *Brussels, Conserv. royal, 1516*. 'Helm' head. Four melody strings, 13 accompanying and 14 basses, of metal and overspun silk. Position dots.

355   Harp zither. Bavarian, nineteenth century. *Berlin, Instit. f. Musikforschung, 2248*.

356   Triple zither. Austrian Alps, nineteenth century. *Salzburg, Museo Carolino Augusteum, 149, Geir. 29*. 'Drillingszither' including central three-string set for bowing. The other sets each include three plus 19 strings. The back and soundboard are common to all three sets. *Length 88 cm. Depth 5 cm.*

357   Concert zither. Georg Tiefenbrunner, Munich, second half of nineteenth century. *London, Reuben Greene Coll*. Complete outfit in case. Pair of plectra resting on the damper stick.

358   Psalmodikon. Swedish, first half of nineteenth century. *Copenhagen, Musikhist. Mus., 445*. Chromatic frets. One string. Also eight sympathetic strings tuned at the wider end of the soundbox.

359   Épinette des Vosges. French, nineteenth century. *London, Horniman Mus., 15.10.48/10*. Marquetry belly and sides. Brass wire frets. Two plus three wire strings. *Length 60 cm. Depth 2·5 cm.*

360   Nordische Balk. Dutch, nineteenth century. *The Hague, Gemeentemus*. Wooden frets. Four strings.

361   Hummel. Swedish, nineteenth century. *Stockholm, Musikhist. Mus., 275*. Raised central soundboard with rose. F-holes at sides. Diatonic frets. Six plus seven strings.

[1] In large classificatory schemes, 'fretted zither' is a preferred general term for these instruments, since 'zither' has been purloined to embrace every kind of instrument with neck-less soundbox, including psalteries, etc, which are here dealt with in a following section. The word *zither* is an old German equivalent (seventeenth century or earlier) of 'cittern', and has retained this meaning in the *Waldzither* or folk cittern noticed earlier, p. 42. It was given to the Alpine fretted zither in the eighteenth century, when these were first built with cittern-like curves (in full, *Gebirgezither*, etc).

362   Appalachian dulcimer. United States, late nineteenth century. *New York, Metropol. Mus. of Art, 98.4.988.* Raised central fret-board. Four heart-shaped soundholes. Three strings.

363   Kentucky bowed dulcimer. George Dougherty, Grider, Kentucky, third quarter of nineteenth century. *Washington, Smithsonian Instit., 324,973.* Pine. Four plus four strings of metal. Hickory bow.

364   Bowed zither. Max Amberger, Munich, 1867. *London, Victoria and Albert Mus., 641–1869.* Petzmayer model. Three strings, machine head. Ivory stud position marks. *Length 46 cm.*

365   Bowed zither (*Streichmelodeon*). F. Sprenger, Nuremburg, after 1879. *Boston, Mus. of Fine Arts, 293.* Three ivory feet on back. Twenty-nine brass frets. Five strings, the first two steel, the others of overspun silk. *Length 61 cm. Depth 3·5 cm.*

366   Bowed zither, 'Trumpet zither'. Gennerich, Munich, second half of nineteenth century. *London, Reuben Greene Coll.* Three feet. Hollow neck communicating with brass trumpet bell. Four metal strings. *Length excl. trumpet 62 cm.*

Alpine Zithers

The South German and Swiss *Scheitholt* exemplifies a primitive European zither. It is a farmhouse musical instrument, traced to the fifteenth century though it may be considerably older, possibly a development from the medieval monochord. The earliest specimens, of the seventeenth and eighteenth centuries, have a rectangular soundbox (**349**) and from three strings upwards, normally of wire. The instrument is placed on a table or on the lap with the fretted side nearest. The strings are tuned on the left and run to hitch pins on the right. One string, or a pair, runs over the diatonic row of frets against which it is stopped by the left hand, either with the fingers or with a short metal or wooden stick. The further strings are open strings, tuned, like the drones of a hurdy-gurdy or bagpipe, to basic musical intervals as octave and fifth, or to a major chord. The right hand, with a plectrum, can sweep all the strings at once to back the melody with a rhythmic drone sound. During the second half of the eighteenth century makers started to enlarge the soundbox volume by adding a cittern-like bulge on the far side (**350**) or by complete rounding of the right-hand end (**352**), the resulting models becoming known as 'Salzburg form' and 'Mittenwald form' respectively from the chief towns of the localities where they were introduced. They are still played to some extent in the old swept manner (*Kratz-zither*, or *Scheitholt-zither*), though as touring performers brought the zither to the notice of city and court audiences in the first part of the nineteenth century technical developments were introduced, notably by the Austrian J. Petzmayer around 1830. These included chromatic fretting and numerous accompaniment strings of gut and overspun silk. N. Weigel of Munich developed the modern cyclic way of tuning these strings (codified at a conference in 1877) and the playing style which involves differential use of the right-hand fingers to sound accompaniments of chords plus bass notes (*Schlag-zither*). A small plectrum is clipped onto the right thumb for striking the melody strings. By 1850 zithers had virtually their modern forms (**354, 357**) with body of rosewood veneered on pine, open soundhole, spiked ball feet and some 29 frets. There are five melody strings (providing for playing in thirds and so on) tuned by enclosed machines, and up to 29 accompaniment and bass strings tuned by wrest pins. The Munich makers have made both Salzburg and Mittenwald forms, also 'guitar' (**353**), 'lyre' and 'harp' forms, the last allowing some increased length in the bass strings (**355**). The *Elegie-zither* by Tiefenbrunner, 1850, is a large model tuned an octave lower than the ordinary *prim* ('prime', i.e. normal-pitch) zither.

Double zithers, dating from the late eighteenth-century *Kratz* forms onwards, include combined *prim* and smaller zithers built in one beside each other; two zithers back to back; two zithers built in a staggered way for duet playing. A triple zither is shown (**356**).

German bowed zithers. These are likewise placed flat on a table and have spiked feet to hold them in position. They differ from the preceding instruments in shape, being designed for sounding with a violin bow or special bow. There are three or four wire strings running over a central fret-board, and no accompanying strings. The first type (**364**) is due to Petzmayer, 1823, with a heart-shaped body bowed at the pointed end. At first it had three strings tuned by wrest pins. Late forms may have four strings in violin tuning and machine head. Other types are mostly four-stringed in fancy 'violin' forms, with vaulted belly, tailpiece, nickel-silver frets and machine head. Some of the body shapes look as if inspired by Renaissance paintings, as in the case of Leopold Breits' *Streichmelodeon*, Brun, 1856 (**365**). In the later nineteenth-century 'trumpet zither', the soundbox communicates through a hollow neck with a trumpet bell at the head (**366**). These bowed zithers are strung in the reverse way from a violin, the deepest string being located in zither fashion, i.e. to the far side as the instrument lies on the table with its head to the left. (For the *philomele*, see p. 16.)

Other Fretted Zithers

The *monochord*, employed in the Middle Ages for demonstrating musical intervals, could be described as a zither in its simplest form: a string stretched over a long rectangular soundbox bearing a calibrated rule, and either plucked or bowed. Such monochords have been made up to modern times for laboratory work and for use in determining musical pitch in field research in primitive music. A nineteenth-century bowed monochord is the Swedish *psalmodikon* (**358**) introduced by the educationist Dillner, 1829, for playing psalms in churches and schools, in which it remained in use until its replacement by the harmonium some 40 years later. The bow of a nyckelharpa (**158**) was preferred (Norlind). The form of the soundbox varies from a simple rectangular shape to models imitating the shape of the violin, etc. The gut string runs over frets placed down the centre line, and some examples, as the one shown, have wire sympathetic strings, in this case placed above the soundbox.

Only a few of the other regional zithers can be shown here (for full accounts see Panum, Norlind, and of the American zithers or 'dulcimers', Seeger). The *épinette des Vosges* (**359**) is the smallest, familiar to collectors through prettily inlaid instruments made in the last century in Valdajol and other places not far from Mirecourt of violin-making fame. They have a pegbox (as have most of the folk zithers of North-west Europe), two metal melody strings and three drones. Zithers of the Low Countries, no longer played, include the *bûche de Flandres* (example at Paris) and the Dutch *nordische balk* (**360**), both larger than the preceding, from about 84 to 114 cm in length, and sometimes with a bulge on the right of the further side. Examples are scarce. The Norwegian *langeleik*, still played, has traditional forms, some going back at least to the eighteenth century, either straight-sided or, in the Valdres model, with the sides slightly out-curved and often a pegbox at each end. Here there are eight strings. The older examples of the Swedish *hummel* are much like the preceding, but late in the eighteenth century the soundbox began to be enlarged with bulges, the frets carried on a raised central platform, and the tuning changed to wrest pins (**361**).

The best-known American form, the *Appalachian dulcimer*, has been traced to the late seventeenth century, though without settling the question of which particular European nationality introduced it. The typical shape (**362**) has both sides curved in two gentle bouts, and frets carried on a raised platform communicating internally with the soundbox, as in Sweden. There is one melody string with two or three drones. Another form is the straight-sided, wrest-pin tuned *Pennsylvania zitter*, of which a series of specimens is preserved in the Museum of the Bucks County Historical Society, Doylestown, Pennsylvania (see Seeger). Some of these were played with a bow, as was the Kentucky bowed dulcimer (**363**).

16 Psalteries and Dulcimers

Several types of instrument having strings stretched across a flat soundbox, all struck 'open', there being no frets, include psalteries, dulcimers and various upright or 'harp' psalteries, along with miscellaneous further instruments like the wind-sounded Aeolian harps.

Illustrations

367   Dulcimer. French, seventeenth century. *Paris, Conserv.* Ebony, carved and gilt, with front side in three bays. Nineteen courses.

368   Dulcimer. German, early eighteenth century. *Brunswick, Städt. Mus., 16, 102.* With left-hand extension and box for spare strings. In painted case.

369   Dulcimer (*Hackbrett*). Appenzell, Switzerland, late eighteenth century. *Basel, Hist. Mus., 1927.284.* With one beater.

370   Dulcimer. Antonio Battaglia, Milan, 1766. *Berlin, Instit. f. Musikforschung, 2148.* Gilt decoration. Strings in triple and quadruple courses. Inscribed *Questo strumento si dice Cariliune. Length 77 cm. Depth 7 cm.*

371   Gusli. Russian, Cheremiss, nineteenth century. *Brussels, Conserv. royal, 1485.* Pine, with gut strings in single courses.

372   Two Kanteles. Finnish. The smaller, eighteenth century. *Oxford, Pitt Rivers Mus., 131.D.10.* From farmhouse near Joensuu, Karelia. Nine strings. The larger, Westermark, 1893. *Oxford, Pitt Rivers Mus., 131.D.14.* Sixteen strings.

373   Autoharp (*Akkord-zither*). German, nineteenth century. *Ann Arbor, Univ. of Michigan, 1162.* Twenty-four metal strings, six chord levers. Chart of notes with Italian names. *Length 49 cm. Depth 7·8 cm.*

374   Regent zither. United States, late nineteenth century. *Ann Arbor, Univ. of Michigan, 1160.* Twenty-four strings in three groups. Chords on printed label. *Length 38 cm. Depth 8 cm.*

375   Violin-zither. Hopf, Germany, late nineteenth century. *London, Kneller Hall. Hopf's Jubelklänge.* 'Harp' model. Ball feet. Five seven-stringed chords, and two sets of nine strings.

376   Bell harp. English, first half of eighteenth century. *London, Horniman Mus., 29–212.* Simcock model. Sixteen triple courses of wire strings passing to hitch pins concealed behind the two sliding panels which form the front of the instrument. Back left rough. *Length 57 cm. Depth 3·7 cm.*

377   Bell harp. R. Cook & Co (London), nineteenth century. *Oxford, Pitt Rivers Mus., dd.YMCA.1919. Fairy Bells.* Sixteen strings, with note names.

378   Table harp. ? German or Danish, late eighteenth century. *Copenhagen, Claudius Coll., 14(493).* Twenty-one gut strings on the side shown, 24 steel on the other. *Height 79·5 cm. Depth of soundbox 9 cm.*

379, 380   Arpanetta (*Spitzharfe*). German, early eighteenth century. *Nuremberg, German. Nationalmus., Rück Coll. Height 77 cm.*

381   Aeolian harp. French, eighteenth century. *Paris, Conserv., E.1527, C.1436.* Three-sided, on legged stand and with suspension ring at top. Six strings on each face, pegged alternately top and bottom. *Height* of soundbox 98 cm.

382   Aeolian harp. London, nineteenth century. *Brussels, Conserv. royal, 2514. Auto musician, Inventor R. W. Keith late Longman & Herron, London.* Model for sash window. Twelve strings. With cover.

The psaltery of the later Middle Ages and early Renaissance consisted of a flat soundbox with slanting or incurved sides between which were ranged numerous courses of strings; whether the latter were of metal, or of gut as in an existing Arab parent form, *qanun*, is uncertain. The psaltery was usually played with the back of the soundbox resting against the player's body, longest side uppermost, and the strings were struck with a pair of quill plectra. No specimen survives, though various elementary instruments of a basically similar nature are known from fairly recent times (one being illustrated in Galpin, 1910, Pl. XI). The Mariiski *gusli* of Russia is an existing species which comes close to the ancient psaltery, though in this case the longest side of the instrument is placed lowermost, resting on the lap (**371**). The gut strings, plucked with the fingers, pass over low bridges glued to the pine soundboard, which extends for some distance to the (player's) right of a shorter, hollowed-out soundbox affixed behind, the whole construction being remarkably light. The ordinary Russian *gusli*, the Finnish *kantele*, is a smaller instrument with a wing-shaped soundbox placed flat on the lap. Old examples (**372**) are carved from one piece open at the back. The metal strings are attached to a cross bar on the right. Both types of gusli have been variously modernized from the late years of the last century.

Dulcimer. Apart from such regional survivals as the big gusli, the early type of psaltery was superseded during the fifteenth century by the harpsichord, its keyboard version in which the handling of a chromatic compass presents no problem; the psaltery itself must be presumed to have had a diatonic tuning, like the folk survivors and like most harps. The sixteenth century, however, saw the development of an improved type on which, by an ingenious arrangement of bridges, a partly, even wholly, chromatic compass can be covered without difficulty so long as the instrument is placed flat and is played in the Persian style with a pair of beaters. In English literature this has generally been described as a *dulcimer* (**367–70**). The soundbox is trapeze shaped, stoutly built in order to bear the strain of heavily tensioned metal strings running in from some 19 to 28 multiple courses—from triple to sextuple, often amounting to over 100 wires in all. The instrument is generally placed on a table or stand, and can be played in its painted case with the lid open. The oblique sides are thick planks, that on the player's right holding the iron or steel wrest pins for tuning and the other the hitch pins (thus the reverse of zithers). The soundboard has two inset roses. Upon it rest two long bridges of a high balustrade form, often of a divided or flexible construction which can take up irregularities that may develop in the soundboard; one form of the bridge is a row of individual turned balusters surmounted by a flexible brass rod. The basic system of stringing is as follows, starting with the shortest course. This passes through an opening in the right-hand bridge without touching and bears upon the left-hand bridge which is so placed that it divides all courses which rest upon it in the length ratio 2:3, corresponding to the musical interval of a perfect fifth. This first course might thus be tuned to give a G and a C. The second course bears upon the right-hand bridge (which is placed close to the wrest plank) and passes through an opening in the other straight to its hitch pins. It is typically tuned to a note pitched a sixth or seventh below the lower note of the preceding course, in our example e.g. E. The third and fourth courses repeat the same pattern one degree lower and so on up to the long strings in the front, chromatic notes being incorporated where desired (see specimen tuning on p. 71). A 20-course dulcimer can thus supply 30 notes. Three zones for striking are where the shorter and longer sections of the odd-numbered courses, and the whole lengths of the even-numbered, respectively lie uppermost as they incline up to the bridge concerned. Some examples have a widened hitch plank or an added frame on the left side to allow for longer bass courses than usual (**368**).

The beaters are very light, of wood or split cane, and in some late dulcimers like the Hungarian concert *cimbalom*, padded with wool. Their length is approximately 25–30 cm. Alternatively the instrument can be played psaltery-wise with plectra, though since the design is less well adapted for this, it has been rarer. Spain retained a preference for plectra; an example made in Barcelona in 1779 (Brussels, 1486), with 25 quintuple and sextuple courses, has with it three finger-plectra with small quill points, 2·3 cm long, held in metal rings to be clipped to the fingers in the manner of an Arab *qanun* or German zither player.

The dulcimer was a fairly popular domestic instrument from the sixteenth century to the eighteenth. Handsome examples are preserved from the seventeenth century onwards, those of the Battaglia family in Milan (**370**) and Berti in Florence being rated among the finest. As a folk instrument, the Swiss *Hackbrett* ('chopping board', **369**) recorded before 1500, is still sometimes heard, and likewise the plainly decorated dulcimers of English street music, very popular in Victorian times. The dulcimer is much played in Rumania (*tsambal*) and Greece (*santouri*). The large cimbalom of the gypsy orchestras standing on legs was developed by Schunda, Budapest, towards the end of the last century.

Fretless zithers. Several designs of these were brought out by German manufacturers in the second half of the nineteenth century, intended chiefly for chord playing with a minimum of musical knowledge. Many are still in manufacture. They have neither frets nor fingerboard, and can be played either on a table or lyre-wise on the left arm. Among them the *Autoharp* (**373**) has felted levers each of which, when pressed down on the metal strings, silences those not required by the particular chord named on the face of the lever. A melody can meanwhile be played on the exposed sections of the strings; although some strings are silenced by the chord lever in operation, this hardly matters so long as the harmonizations are kept very basic. Printed paper slips sometimes show how given tunes are to be played. In other types (**374, 375**) the strings are grouped to sound basic chords. There may be further strings for melody, but the main purpose is chords to support the voice, and in models with some eight strings per chord, the chords swept with the fingers can ring with powerful volume and a tone-quality between harpsichord and harp. Small levers may be provided for changing major chords to minor, by lowering the third degree in the chord.

String drum. A Pyrenean folk instrument (*tambourin à cordes, t. de Béarne*) with long narrow soundbox some 75 cm or more in length, often with wavy edges (**413**). Six thickish gut strings are tuned to octaves and fifths. The instrument is slung vertically by a strap and the strings are beaten with a short drumstick held in the right hand in accompaniment to a three-holed pipe played by the left. Specimens date back to the eighteenth century, though the instrument can be traced to the Middle Ages.

Bell harps have metal strings arranged vertically inside an open-ended soundbox, the front side of which ends short of the upper end of the instrument to leave a space where the strings can be plucked with the fingers. The instrument is gripped near the top between the two thumbs and swung to and fro whilst playing in order to produce an undulating sound reminiscent of the Aeolian harp. The first known model, Simcock's *bell harp* or *English harp* (**376**), *c.* 1700, is wedge-shaped, with a front composed of two pine panels which can be slid out for attention to the fastening of the strings to the slanting bridges screwed to the back plate. There are up to 24 triple and quadruple courses, tuned by wrest pins along the top. Some examples are provided with a projecting lug on each side to help holding and swinging. A simpler type made in France and England in the nineteenth century and sometimes used by street entertainers has a narrow rectangular soundbox (**377**) and from eight to 16 wire strings. (It is sometimes stated that bell harps were swung between the fingers and plucked with the thumbs, but on no type does this appear to be practicable.)

Arpanetta (Spitzharfe). A domestic table harp very popular in the second half of the seventeenth century and first half of the next, chiefly in Germany and the Netherlands (**379–80**) though French and Italian examples occur. The pointed soundbox is stood upright with the shorter strings nearest the player, as on a harp. There is a soundboard on each side and sometimes an internal partition board reaching nearly to the top, apparently to serve as a 'false back' to each soundboard (rather than as a strength member). The soundboards have paper roses and are usually painted with flowers and homely scenes on a bright-coloured ground. The total height from the supporting feet to the top of the carved finial at the peak may exceed 150 cm, though most instruments are smaller, down to around 70 cm.

The wire strings are tuned by wrest pins along the bottom. The strings on the right-hand side (which, as in Continental harps, is the 'treble' side) may number 60 or more courses comprising double courses tuned diatonically and a set of single strings for the sharps, these lying closer to the soundboard. Each set has its own wooden bridge, glued to the soundboard. The left-hand side has fewer strings, usually tuned chromatically and descending a few notes lower than those on the right side. The strings were struck with the fingernails or with plectra worn on the fingers. An example with perhaps the earliest date is by Kindermann, Nuremberg, 1621 (Berlin Collection). Most dates are pre-1730.

The arpanetta has sometimes been classed as a 'harp-psaltery' along with other species seen in medieval and later pictures and also made exceptionally up to the nineteenth century. These generally differ from the arpanetta in being tuned along the top, e.g. the perhaps Danish instrument shown (**378**). Another instance is Edward Light's *diplokithara*, *c.* 1800 (illustrated in Galpin, 1910, Pl. XIII).

Aeolian harps are wire or gut-strung soundboxes designed for hanging or standing in situations where the strings will be set in vibration by the wind. They were made in most countries from the seventeenth century to the nineteenth. Shapes vary. Some are rectangular and strung on one side, sometimes with an adjustable shutter for focusing the wind; a model for placing horizontally in a sash window is shown (**382**). Others are half-round or three-sided, placed upright and with strings on each face (**381**).

17 Harps

The three principal structural members of a harp are: (1) The body or soundbox, including the sound-board or belly pierced down the centre line with a row of holes in which the lower ends of the strings are held by grooved ebony pins or less commonly by toggles. (2) The neck or 'harmonic curve', along which the upper ends of the strings are wound on metal tuning pins which pass through the neck and are tuned on the further side by separate tuning key; the dip in the neck serves to secure good proportionate length and even tension of strings through the different octaves of the compass. (3) The post or, as usually termed if it is straight, pillar, which completes the three-sided structure of the harp as evolved in Europe in the Middle Ages, possibly first in Ireland or England in the eleventh century, though the evidence for this is by no means conclusive and certain precedents are suggested by, for instance, some harps of Central Asia and Siberia (illustrated in Vertov et al, *Atlas*), forming possible links with the harps of Antiquity.

In traditional Irish and Welsh practice the harp was rested against the left shoulder, and this was also the general medieval practice. The left hand here plays the treble while the right plays mainly on the longer strings. On the Continent, from the Renaissance onwards, possibly under the influence of keyboard instruments, the opposite has prevailed, the harp being held against the right shoulder, etc, and so it is with the pedal harps of the modern era. A 'simple' harp is one which has a single row of strings, tuned diatonically, without provision for changing the pitch of any string save by re-tuning. Such provision is obtained in an elementary way in hook harps and by more elaborate means in pedal harps. Some other types of harp have two or three parallel rows of strings in order to supply a chromatic or partly chromatic compass without the aid of mechanical devices.

Illustrations: Harps

383   Gaelic harp. Fifteenth century. *Edinburgh, Nat. Museum of Antiquities of Scotland.* The Lamont harp. Body including belly hollowed in one piece, with added back. Four soundholes. String holes in belly shod with brass. Thirty-two strings. *Height* 81 cm.

384   Irish harp. Built 1702. *Dublin, Arthur Guinness & Co (Dublin) Ltd.* The Downhill harp, instrument of Denis Hempson (1697–1807). Alder throughout. Early alterations and later repairs.

385   Irish harp. Eighteenth century. *Dublin, Nat. Mus. of Ireland, 121–1945.* The Sirr Harp, long associated with the O'Neill family. High-headed. Body willow with pine back. Alder neck. Finial in form of a goshawk and banded with metal. Brass reinforcing strip for the pin holes in the belly. Thirty-six metal strings. *Height* (post) 143 cm.

386   Harp. ? German, sixteenth century. *Nuremberg, German. Nationalmus., MI.59.* Twenty-six strings. *Height* (post) 101 cm.

387   Harp. German, seventeenth century. *Berlin, Instit. f. Musikforschung, 21.* Sycamore body with two iron feet. Six rosettes. Post with carved volute and crowned female head. Nuts below tuning pins. Thirty-six strings. *Height* 143 cm.

388   Double-strung harp. Italian, probably early seventeenth century. *Brussels, Conserv. royal, 1504.* Body of five staves. Thirty strings on left, 23 on right, with 'bray' pins in belly. *Height* 151 cm.

389   Harp. German, 1739. *Brussels, Conserv. royal, 1497.* Inscribed dedicatory date *1739*. Head carved with figure of King David between two lions. Ten rosettes. Thirty-three strings. Two hooks added. *Height* 124 cm.

390   Small harp. Welsh, eighteenth century. *London, R. Coll. of Music, 290.* Strung with wire. Tuned on left. *Height* 96 cm.

391   Triple harp. Bassett Jones, Cardiff, 1838. *London, R. Coll. of Music, 295.* Gilt decoration and scroll. Tuned on right. *Height* 203 cm.

392, 393   Triple harp. Italian, early seventeenth century. *Bologna, Museo Civico.* Body of nine staves. Four rosettes. Curved post with carved female figure. Ninety-four strings (32, 31, 31). *Height* 193 cm.

394   Triple harp. David Evans, London, 1736. *London, Victoria and Albert Mus., 1740–1869.* With 34, 29 and 25 strings, tuned on left. *Height* 190 cm.

395   Hook harp. Italian, eighteenth century. *Ann Arbor, Univ. of Michigan, 1003.* Body inlaid with ivory. Six rosettes. Carved and gilt female head. Thirty-seven strings and 23 hooks. *Height* (post) 144 cm.

396   Hook harp. Tyrolean, eighteenth century. *New York, Metropol. Mus. of Art. 1712.* Six rosettes. Thirty-two strings and 21 hooks *Height* 127 cm.

397   Pedal harp. Sebastian Lang, Bavaria, 1755. *Nuremberg, German. Nationalmus., Rück Coll.* Single action similar to French *crochets. Height* 135·5 cm.

398   Pedal harp. H. Naderman, after 1785. *London, Victoria and Albert Mus., 425–1884.* Back of five staves of oak and sycamore. Neck and pillar of birch. Rear view, showing pedal-operated shutters. *Height* 168 cm.

399   Pedal harp. H. Naderman, Paris, *c.* 1780. *Paris, Conserv., C293.* One of two made for Marie Antoinette. Sumptuously decorated, with painted belly and garlanded pillar. Thirty-six strings. Single action by *crochets. Height* 160 cm.

400   Pedal harp. H. Naderman. (Same instrument as **398**). Close view of single-action *crochet* mechanism.

401   Pedal harp. G. Cousineau, Paris, *c.* 1770. *London, R. Coll. of Music, 199.* Close view of 'Grecian' head and single action by *béquilles.*

402   Pedal harp. Sebastien Érard, Paris, 1786. *London, Reuben Greene Coll.* Inscribed *No 158.* Close view of head and single action by *fourchettes.*

403   Pedal harp. S. & P. Érard, London, 1858. *London, Victoria and Albert Mus., W.48–1931.* Close view of 'Gothic' head and double action. (The harp has five hinged traps actuated by eighth pedal, and total height 270 cm.)

404   Cross-strung harp. ? French, *c.* 1800. *London, Victoria and Albert Mus., 830–1884.* Sides of back apparently made from a normal French harp of the period. Two cross-posts and necks. Forty strings to each neck. *Height* 174 cm. Posts 74 cm apart at their bases.

405   Cross-strung 'chromatic harp'. Pleyel, Paris, end of nineteenth century. *Brussels, Conserv. royal.* Système Lyon. Single pillar. *Height* 188 cm.

406   Portable harp. John Egan, Dublin, *c.* 1820. *London, Horniman Mus., 289.* Round back with six slots and open base. Body and belly painted green with gilt flowers. Seven levers on the post, with bone knobs lettered with note names. Single action by *fourchettes.* Thirty gut strings, tuned on the right. Adjustable iron leg withdrawn inside body. *Height* 91 cm.

407   Cross-strung 'chromatic harp'. H. Greenway, Brooklyn, New York. after 1895. *New York, Metropol. Mus., 1235.* Maple body. Double soundboard with gilt scroll-work. Two pillars crossing at a boss in gilt gesso. Forty-five strings on left, and 33 on right. *Height* 168 cm.

408   Double-strung harp. Italian, late sixteenth century. *Modena, Galleria Estense.* Decorated with miniatures painted in gold, red and blue in Ferrara style by Giulio Marescotti, 1587. One-piece back. Flat curved post. Twenty-eight strings in principal row. Ten (or 11) additional strings mounted on left side of treble, and 11 on right side of bass. *Height* 150 cm.

Irish harp. Last played at the beginning of the nineteenth century, this retained an ancient and distinctive construction of the body from a single piece, often willow, hollowed out to form the sides and belly, soundholes being cut in the latter. The back is a separate piece, often pine. The build is thick-walled and massive, the heavy neck often shod with brass plates. The strings, of brass, are held in the belly with toggles. Early examples of 'Gaelic harps' (two fifteenth–sixteenth century examples at Edinburgh (**383**) having descended from Scottish families) keep much of the small size of the common medieval harp, which was 60 cm or less in height and played on a stool. Subsequently the harps become larger (**384**), approaching 150 cm in high-headed instruments of the eighteenth century, in which greater length is allowed for the bass strings (**385**; the succession of types and sizes is pointed out by Rimmer, *GM*, XVII, 1964). The Irish harp was principally if not entirely a professional instrument, played by itinerant harpers, many of whom, as has so often been the case in professional music in the old civilizations, were blind. The Irish amateur harp of the nineteenth century is noticed later (**406**).

Continental simple harps. The European Renaissance harp, the light and graceful instrument depicted in paintings of the fifteenth century, survives in a small ivory specimen in the Louvre, Paris. The harp shown here (**386**), though later, illustrates the form more typically. The soundbox is quite shallow, in some instances with back and sides carved in one piece, though also with separate back and sides, as becomes commoner with the larger harps made from the seventeenth century onwards. In these,

Fig 8 Harp 'bray' pin

alternatively, the body may be 'coopered', with five or more staves. The belly, of pine, has open soundholes or rosettes of holes. The neck is frequently carved with one or more peaks or crests (**389**) and a carved figure may surmount the slender post which, by the eighteenth century, is more often straight than curved in the old manner. Pointed iron feet (**387**) allow the harp to stand without support. From 30 to 36 gut strings give a diatonic compass up to five octaves. Some examples are provided with angular pins or 'brays' for the lower ends of the strings (Fig 8), intended to impart a vibrant quality to the sound.

During the eighteenth century this simple harp became more and more a folk instrument for light music and dances, played especially in the Alpine regions and Bohemia; also in Spain, from which the simple harp had earlier been implanted in Latin America where it survives in the large, locally-developed forms made today. The European instruments are rarely signed, having no doubt been made by local woodworkers—not that they are any the worse musical instruments for that.

Double- and triple-strung harps. From the latter part of the sixteenth century, in order to blend the unique sonority of the harp to polyphonic ensemble music, means were sought to make the instrument chromatic, or at least partially so, by mounting parallel rows of strings. Italy appears to have been the initial scene of these experiments, the general schemes of which can be understood from the diagrams below: the primary diatonic row is represented by circles and the additional row by dots, as if looking down onto the string holes in the belly with the shortest string on the right of each diagram.

```
                              . . . . . .
  1                       O O O O O O O O   (etc)   O O O O O O O O
                                                     . . . . . .

                            . . . .
  2                       O O O O O O O O   (etc)   O O O O O O O O
                                                   . . . . . .

                          O O O O O O O              O O O O O O O O
  3                        . . . . .        (etc)   . . . . . . .
                          O O O O O O O O            O O O O O O O
```

The player's right hand (treble) is chiefly concerned with the strings which are uppermost in each diagram and the left with the lower. Diagrams 1 and 2 show *double-strung harps*. In the first, illustrated by a very pretty harp in the Este Collection (**408**), ten (but holes in the belly for 11) extra strings are mounted on the left of the trebles of the primary row and similarly 11 strings on the right of the bass. These auxiliary strings were presumably tuned to scales which contained the needed extra sharps or flats and were plucked by the left and right hands respectively, leaving these hands otherwise clear for their traditional occupation with bass and treble in the primary scale. The auxiliary rows are, however, staggered vis-à-vis the primary row, so that, for example, sharps in the treble can also be taken by reaching through with the right fingers. In Diagram 2, the three rows are condensed into two by switching the primary scale from the left to the right at some mid-point of the compass. A double-strung harp from the former Correr Collection would have been so tuned (though some accounts, e.g. Talbot, indicate merely parallel primary and auxiliary rows, which seems hardly practicable). The left-hand row of this harp is continued in the bass for an octave beyond the other, the lowest octave thus being diatonic only, as in theorbos and contemporary keyboard instruments with 'short octave' in the bass. This specimen (**388**) is provided with 'brays', mentioned above.

Diagram 3 is of the very much more successful *triple harp*, in which the primary row is duplicated and an auxiliary row with the sharps and flats sandwiched between. Here the player can use both hands over the full primary scale just as on the simple harp, while either hand can reach through for any sharp. The neck is twice stepped to accommodate the three rows of tuning pins. Mersenne describes the triple harp as a Neapolitan invention, and an early Italian example (**392, 393**) has recently been discussed by Rimmer, *GSJ*, XVIII, 1965. By about 1630 the triple harp was a soloist's instrument known in England, and by the end of the century it was being adopted by the Welsh harpers in Wales and London. Welsh triple harps exist from the eighteenth century (**394**) and nineteenth (**391**), all of them high-headed, the body usually of nine staves and the neck connected to the body by a curved bracket. Stringing on the left of the neck was traditional in Wales, but exceptions occur, as **391**, won as a prize by John Thomas, Queen Victoria's harper, in 1838. Nowhere else has preserved the triple harp, which in Wales took precedence over an older simple harp of which several examples from the eighteenth and nineteenth centuries are preserved in the National Museum of Wales. A small-size simple harp (**390**) would have been made either for a child or for playing while standing or marching in processions. *Cross-strung* double harps are noticed below, p. 68.

Hook harps. These are simple harps with the addition of 'hooks', generally of stout wire, fixed in the neck on the left side below the tuning pins (**395, 396**). A hook is turned manually to nip its string and so raise its pitch by a semitone (Fig 9). Often only certain strings are so provided, e.g. if the harp is tuned to the scale of C, the F and C strings alone may have hooks. To turn a hook whilst playing involves the movement of the left hand away from the strings and even so only sharpens a note in one octave of the compass. Thus the hook harp, though useful in light music, is scarcely a chromatic harp in a concert sense. It has been traced back to the second half of the seventeenth century in the Tyrol and in Bavaria—regions that have

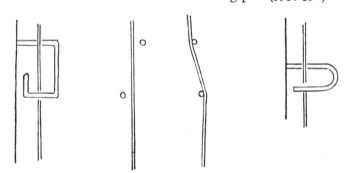

Fig 9 Diagram of hook harp action (a second shape of hook on right)

preserved the strongest harp-playing tradition in Europe—and most examples are from the neighbourhood of the Alps, some made after 1850. At least two Welsh examples exist, one having hooks in the form of brass rings.

Pedal harp. The pedals, normally seven, are housed in a low pedestal at the base of the harp. Each, through a linkage of rods and cranks concealed inside the hollow pillar and deep neck, turns the semitone-stopping mechanism for a given note simultaneously in every octave of the compass. The idea is said to have originated in Bavaria, following the hook harp, of which it is a direct development, by some 50 years. Contemporary sources variously credit it to Hochbrucker, Donauwörth, *c*. 1720, Vetter, Nuremberg and others. Some harp music of the period confirms its appearance by that date (Rimmer, *Proc. R. Mus. Assoc.*, 1964). A German hook harp in the Brussels Collection (1507) bears traces of a single pedal which at one time worked the hooks for C and F. Hochbrucker is said to have employed five pedals, but no example of his is known. One of the earliest extant Bavarian pedal harps must be that by Lang (**397**), with seven pedals, though by this date, 1755, the idea was already receiving the attention of the Paris harp makers who in due course perfected the pedal harp. J. H. Naderman began his work *c.* 1740, using what the French termed *crochets*. These are right-angled hooks which are moved by the pedal horizontally inwards and outwards, pulling the string against a fixed nut immediately below it (**400**). On release of the pedal the hooks are returned outwards by concealed springs. The harp by Lang employs a similar mechanism. The French version is fully described in Diderot's *Encyclopédie* in 1767, with seven pedals and, as still today, the C strings coloured red and the F strings blue, to assist the player. Improvements and elaborations of ornament led to the sumptuous Naderman 'Grecian' harps of the 1780s and after (**399**), including the 1785 model worked out jointly with the player Krumpholtz, with pedal-operated shutters placed in the soundholes at the back (**398**) for echo effects, etc. The *crochet* mechanism was also used in Paris by Cousineau, Holtzman, and by Renault & Chatelain. Similarities in the decoration, both painting and carving, suggest the activities of special workshops in this branch of work.

The second Parisian mechanism is Cousineau's 'crutch' system (*à béquilles*) though the date of the invention does not appear to have been recorded. For each string (except, as in most pedal harps, the longest) there are two small crutch-ended levers, placed one above the other on opposite sides of the string (**401**). The pedal turns one of them clockwise, the other anticlockwise, to nip the string in a firmer, more controlled manner than the *crochets*, which also suffered from the disadvantage (a) of pulling the strings out of their vertical alignment and (b) of allowing them sometimes to buzz against the metal.

The third mechanism, essentially that which is used today, is Sebastien Érard's system of *fourchettes*. For each string there is a small brass disc from which project two pins (**402**). The pedal rotates the disc so that the string is nipped by the pins. Érard, already well known as a harpsichord maker, was making this harp mechanism in Paris in 1786. Then he fled the Revolution and patented his invention in London in 1794. In 1810 he patented the double action (**403**). This provides a second row of *fourchette* discs placed below the first row in order to raise the string by a whole tone. Each pedal can here be depressed to two notches, the upper bringing into action the semitone discs and the lower the whole-tone. In fact, the pedal turns the lower disc, which is linked to the upper via a bell-crank in such a way that on the second notch of the pedal the lower disc is turned without conferring any appreciable further rotation to the upper disc. With double action the harp can be played in every tonality, which was not possible with single action unless, as Cousineau had attempted in the 1780s, extra pedals were provided to actuate a whole-tone mechanism independently. In the matter of decoration for the salon, the 'Gothic' model (**403**) was introduced by Érard's nephew, Pierre, in 1836, and is still familiar to concert goers.

John Egan's 'Portable Irish Harp' (**406**) was introduced in Dublin, *c.* 1819, to foster an amateur interest in Irish harping. It is a small single-action harp with gut strings and *fourchette* mechanism actuated manually by seven levers located along the post. The latter is curved, preserving a ghost of the form of the old Irish harps, and the instrument is similarly tuned on the left. It is usually painted green. Egan also advertised a double-action model. Later in the century simplified instruments were built, keeping roughly to Egan's overall design but without the mechanism, being simply hook harps with brass blades fixed in the neck for raising the pitch of each string independently. Such harps ('Celtic harp', etc) are still in manufacture.

Cross-strung harps are double-strung harps in which the two sets of strings are arranged in planes which cross one another at some point, so that every string is directly available to either hand, whether above or below the point where the strings cross. The idea appears in the eighteenth century, e.g. in a small example in the Brussels Collection which has two sets of strings running from the belly up to opposite sides of the neck, this being supported by two slanting posts which meet at the top. A later example (**404**) has two divergent necks supported by two posts crossed in an X. Its body was apparently made by splitting a normal soundbox and spacing out the two halves to provide a separate soundbox for each set of strings. Further designs followed during the nineteenth century leading to Pleyel's *harpe chromatique*, Paris, 1894, designed by G. Lyon (**405**). This employs a single pillar, but the neck is wide enough to allow crossing of the strings. Greenway's New York design, from about the same time, has crossed pillars (**407**). Neither gained more than fleeting successes against the well-established pedal harp.

18 Specimen Tunings of Stringed Instruments

The tunings shown are not a historical survey, being intended merely to provide some specimen data should it be desired to tune an old instrument which is in a condition to be tuned. In most instances tunings have been variable in one way or another. In such cases a frequent tuning is given as being broadly representative, but where the variation is considerable the tuning is followed by 'etc'. (With instruments that are played alone or alone with the voice the overall pitch of the tuning is not necessarily absolute, i.e. the tuning is a pattern of intervals that may be set at any convenient chosen pitch.) A slanting dotted line between two notes indicates intervening strings tuned in diatonic sequence. Double courses are indicated by single notes in most cases of the fretted instruments.

II Woodwind Instruments

II Woodwind Instruments

'Woodwind' is a term introduced in the last century to denote one section of a symphony orchestra, but 'woodwind instruments' may be employed in a wider sense to take in all pipes in which the covering and uncovering of holes by movements of the fingers constitutes the primary means of making the notes of the scales. The material of the pipe may be ivory, metal, glass, etc, though for most types the traditional material has been wood and makers generally served their apprenticeships as wood turners.

The means of sound-production are essentially two. (1) By blowing a jet of air onto a sharp edge provided by the instrument, as in recorders and flutes (and also in certain non-tubular instruments like the ocarina and again in the non-fingerhole panpipe). (2) By causing the airstream to set in vibration a 'reed' made from natural cane cultivated for reed-making purposes in the South of France and elsewhere, as in the case of crumhorns, shawms, oboes, clarinets, bagpipes, etc, spoken of generically as 'reed instruments' (briefly classified on p. 92). A reed, fragile and perishable, is rarely found with an old specimen of these. A 'single reed', tied or clipped to the wooden mouthpiece of an old clarinet, stands a slightly better chance of survival than the 'double reed' of an oboe or bassoon, which is removed from the instrument after playing and kept in a separate box holding several such reeds, very seldom handed down to posterity, and if it has been, probably empty. Modern reeds are apt to be unsuitable for old designs of reed instruments, though often added to museum specimens for appearance's sake.

There have also been pipes which are fingered as other pipes but are sounded like brass instruments, namely by vibration of the player's lips across a mouthpiece cup. Such are the old cornett and the serpent, and whether to class them for descriptive purposes with the woodwind or with the brass is a moot point. They are here described after the reed instruments (662–91).

Up to the second quarter of the nineteenth century the favourite material for the smaller woodwind was boxwood (often stained dark brown) and for the larger, maple, pear, etc. Ebony and ivory were the chief alternatives to box before rosewood, followed by other tropical woods (cocus, and blackwood or 'grenadilla'), became progressively more employed as the nineteenth century went on, not however totally to supplant box, which was still used, e.g. in France, for cheap clarinets and fifes, up to the 1914 war. In construction, the instruments are bored and turned either in one piece, or in a number of separate sections known as 'joints', fitted together by tenon and socket. The older, one-piece construction (still met in folk and oriental instruments) prevailed in European woodwind-making up to the middle of the seventeenth century. Jointed work as a regular procedure, even for the smallest kinds of instrument, came in with the revolution in woodwind practice which occurred during the third quarter of the seventeenth century, when Lully in Paris was forming the basis of the modern orchestra and his associates the first genuine military bands since the Middle Ages. Then were introduced new bores for flutes;

also new species of instrument, notably the oboe, followed in *c.* 1700 by the clarinet, while old species like crumhorns, shawms and cornetts dropped, or began to drop, out of use. In most cases the joints of the new models are turned with thickenings over the sockets, often mounted with a ring of ivory, silver or horn, whence these 'Baroque' woodwind instruments (as they are often described by modern makers and writers) gain an ornamental appearance which makes a sharp contrast with the plain, though nonetheless purposeful and well-finished lines of the one-piece 'Renaissance' instruments. The wooden tenons of the joints are lapped with waxed thread, though sometimes in the earlier period one finds an unlapped tenon.

The general practice since the time of these new developments up to the present has been for makers to stamp their names on the front of at least one joint of an instrument. With the indispensable help of Langwill's *Index of Wind-instrument Makers* an idea of the date of a specimen should then easily be formed. During the one-piece period, however, name stamps are rare. Instead one may find letters (initials?) or abbreviated names (e.g. *HIER.S*) or various signs, particularly a plume formed by two ! disposed in a **V**. Ganassi (*Fontegara*, 1535) includes three tables of special fingerings for recorders 'da maestri novi', headed by sketches of instruments bearing in turn the marks *B*, *A* and a trefoil. He does not say that these are the marks of particular makers, though 'da maestri novi' rather implies that this is what they are, and probably Venetian. Each of these marks is matched among extant specimens which could well be of Venetian make, while a recorder with trefoil mark is actually dated 1535 (Salzburg Museum). Whether the plume mark is also Venetian is more open to question. It occurs on instruments singly, or as two together, also as three (two above one); among specimens with three plumes are cornetts surviving in England (Norwich Museums, and the pair at Christ Church, Oxford, which were bought new in London in 1604). It remains for further research to prove that among instruments with plume mark there are specimens which *could not* have been built in Venice and exported to foreign countries.

An unmarked specimen of the jointed era can usually be approximately placed and dated by stylistic evidence, and above all by the number and form of its keys and key mounts. In this matter, however, the multifarious developments of keywork from the 1770s onwards make the woodwind a complicated subject which can be reviewed only cursorily in the present illustrations. To avoid repetition later a few general aspects of keywork will be summarized here. Keys are metal levers, brass or silver until nickel-silver came into use for this purpose in about the 1830s. The end of the key which is pressed by the finger is the 'touch'; the end which covers a hole may be called the 'flap'. Keys have two principal functions. One is to close an open hole located where the hand in its playing position could not otherwise reach it. This is an 'open' key, sprung to uncover the hole when at rest. It is the earliest type of key, first evidenced early in the fifteenth century on the tenor shawm, and shown in its typical Renaissance form in **527**, where it will be seen to comprise two levers, the longer one with the touch tilting the flap. The touch is here fishtailed for use by whichever hand the performer preferred to place lowermost— a provision which endured in a few cases until after the eighteenth century. Up to four open keys were employed among the early recorders, shawms, etc, chiefly on the larger instruments with the purpose of extending the compass diatonically downwards (**414, 531–4,** two of the keys being on the back, worked by the lower thumb).

The other main function of a key is that of uncovering a hole which is normally required to remain closed. These 'closed' keys, strongly sprung to close the hole and requiring only a single lever, occur very rarely before the jointed models, an exception being with the bagpipe *musette* (**497**) which had them by Mersenne's time. Their main purpose has been the provision of sharps and flats which players of the day judged to be imperfectly obtainable by the ancient expedients of cross-fingering and (less commonly) half-covering.

As to the form of keys, the common type of the late seventeenth to early nineteenth centuries has a round or square flap turning on a wire pin inserted through a socket moulding or other turned boss in the wood or ivory—either an annular boss or 'ring' (Fig 10a), or a similar boss cut away to leave a 'block' (Fig 10b). Such keys remained in frequent use even after the mid nineteenth century, though by then improved patterns had come into use. An early metal key-mount is a 'saddle' screwed to the joint and traversed by a threaded pin on which the key turns (Fig 10b). Developed from the Renaissance key-mount, it appears early in the eighteenth century on the bassoon, and was often used in the first half of the nineteenth on the small instruments, sometimes together with the mounts in the wood just described.

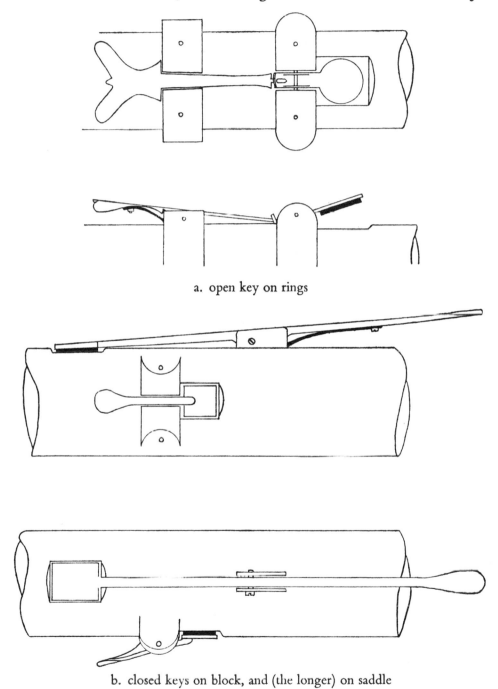

a. open key on rings

b. closed keys on block, and (the longer) on saddle
Fig 10

Far-reaching improvements of the early nineteenth century followed two innovations: cup-shaped flaps for holding stuffed pads (ascribed to Ivan Muller in his clarinet of *c.* 1810); and pillar mounts (used by Laurent, Paris, from 1807 in his glass flutes, **476**). Stuffed pads and pillar mounts are still in regular use

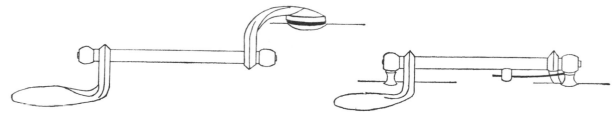

Fig 11 Key on pillar-mount, with needle spring

today, together with a development of the 1830s by which the touch branches from one end of a long pillar-mounted axle (a 'barrel') and the flap from the other end (Fig 11); when both are placed on the same side of the axle an open key is possible without the old need for a separately-pivoted flap. Long

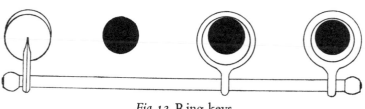

Fig 12 Ring keys

axles are also needed with 'ring keys', perfected by Boehm in 1832 (**486** and Fig 12). Here a metal ring branches from the axle to encircle a fingerhole round which the wood is cut away to allow the ring to sink flush with the hole. The ring is in most cases sprung to rise. The finger lowers it in the same motion as covering the hole, thereby simultaneously closing a key flap which is fixed for a specific purpose at some other point along the same axle, or to another axle mechanically linked with the first. For springing the keywork, the old flat springs placed under a key lever (Fig 10) are still in use though largely superseded by the needle spring held in a pillar, attributed to A. Buffet, Paris, *c.* 1840 (Fig 11).

The fingerholes in the front of an instrument are conventionally numbered from the highest, nearest the blowing end, downwards. Basically there are three for each hand, often plus a seventh, for the little finger of the lower hand—which, having in most cases also to take the weight of the instrument, is normally the right hand. When any of the primary six holes are covered not directly by the finger but by an open key, as some may be in large instruments on account of the limited stretch of the hand (or in late systems through special requirements of the design and mechanism), they are generally termed 'covered holes'. When all the holes are so provided with open keys—whether lever keys, or 'plates' on long axles—the instrument is said to have 'covered action', a familiar example being the modern flute and saxophone. A thumbhole is for the thumb of the uppermost hand unless otherwise stated.

The 'pitch' of an instrument can be considered in one sense to mean its nominal tonality, which defines its pitch relatively to that of other-sized instruments of the same kind. It is stated when needed by the name of the note sounded when the seven front holes are covered. If this note is an F, the instrument is said to be 'in F'. With clarinets, it is stated in terms of the *upper* register (since the low register sounds an octave plus a fifth lower). With flutes which have only six holes, a seventh, which would give a note a whole tone lower than the six, has to be imagined: a six-hole flute with lowest note D is thus said to be 'in C'. This method of reckoning brings all flutes into line with other woodwind, and must be regarded as having superseded a traditional English way of giving flute and fife pitch in terms of the six-finger note (though the latter will sometimes be added in parenthesis, this note often being stamped on English small flutes up to *c.* 1840 and cf. **463**).

Pitch can also be deduced by length measurement, representative figures for which will be found in the notes to the illustrations or in the adjoining text. Lengths do not correspond between similarly pitched instruments of different families owing to the differing physical properties of the various kinds of pipe. Also, for a given type of instrument of a given pitch, one meets variations in length through differences in makers' models or through past fluctuations in tuning pitch, sometimes making it very difficult to place a specimen when two possibilities for its pitch lie a semitone apart. Historical probability may be a guide, but sometimes different probabilities lie very close in respect of time and place.

1 Flageolets, Recorders

The well-known principle of these is that the upper end of the tube is closed by a wooden plug which is shaved flat down one side to leave a narrow windway inside the wall of the pipe; the wind emerges from this to cross a rectangular aperture in the pipe, strike a sharp edge and set up an eddy frequency. The aperture and edge may be termed the 'voicing'. (The word 'fipple', sometimes used, seems more correctly to denote the beak-like upper end of the pipe which the player takes in the lips.) For a generic name for these instruments when required, *flageolet*, surviving form of the medieval French *flageol*, is suitable, distinguishing the group from the cross-blown flutes.

Illustrations: Pipe and Tabor, Recorder

409   Galoubet and tambourin. France, Provence, nineteenth century. *Brussels, Conserv. royal, 2284.* Deep cord-tensioned drum, approx 71 cm long and 30 cm diameter. Pipe and drumstick attached. One-piece pipe. *Length c.* 31 cm.

410   Pipe and tabor. England, Oxfordshire, nineteenth century. *Washington, Lib. of Congress, Dayton Miller 722 A and B.* Pipe said to have been played for Morris dances for 40 years by Thomas Humphries (d. 1886). Ebony pipe, bound with string. *Length* 30·9 cm. Tabor, with snare, laced with cotton tape. *Diameter* 21·5 cm.

411   Flaviol and tamboril. Barcelona, late nineteenth century. *Barcelona, Mus. de musica, 306 and 401.* Ivory-mounted pipe, four holes in front, two behind, no keys. Rod-tensioned drum, snare on rear head.

412   Tabor pipe. Cahusac, London, beginning of nineteenth century. *Washington, Lib. of Congress, Dayton Miller 1266.* Ivory. *Length* 30·6 cm.

413   Chirula and tambourin à cordes. France, Béarne, eighteenth/nineteenth century. *London, R. Coll. of Music, 74 and 213.* The string drum, with inset roses, is painted green with gilt foliage and an inscription which reads *Le 1. Avril. 1754.* Also a painted shield above a scene of red lions, with female bearers and surmounted by a crown. Six gut strings run from wooden pegs under metal loops to hitch studs at the base. *Length* 80 cm. *Depth* 7 cm. Boxwood pipe, probably of later date. Stick missing.

414   Great bass recorder. *Antwerp, Vleeshuis Museum.* Trefoil mark. Attributed on evidence from Charles Burney's *Present State . . . in Germany*, 1773, to Caspar Rauch von Schrattenbach, Hamburg (?), first half of sixteenth century. Restored with new cap, barrel, crook and three keys (one on back). *Length* 262 cm.

415–17   Three recorders, treble, tenor and bass, sixteenth century. *Frankfurt, Hist. Mus., Epstein 116, 118, 120.* Stamped *HD.* Box. *Lengths* 40·5, 59·5, 90 cm.

418   Recorder case, holding the preceding three instruments and others similar. Sixteenth century. *Frankfurt, Hist. Mus., Epstein 120b.* Marked *HD PM.* Wood. Holds 11 recorders.

419   Treble recorder. J. C. Denner, Nuremberg, 1682. *Eisenach, Bachhaus, Buhle 115.* Two joints.

420   Quint-bass recorder. Sixteenth century. *Brussels, Conserv. royal, 188.* Box. Brass crook and one key. Double plume-mark. *Length* without crook 125 cm. *Pitch* (modern) D flat. From the former Hanseatic Consulate, Antwerp.

421   Tenor recorder. German, seventeenth century. *Leipzig, K.-M.-Univ., 1134.* One brass key. *Pitch* (modern) B.

422   Tenor recorder. Sixteenth century. *Frankfurt, Hist. Mus., Epstein 114.* Stamped *FF PM.* Rounded top. Without duplicate seventh hole. From the former Barfüsserkirche. *Length* 55·5 cm.

423   Set of two treble and two descant recorders, in case. Schlegel, Basel, mid-eighteenth century. *Paris, Conserv., E.683, C.392.* Ivory. *Length* treble 48 cm, descant 25 cm.

424   Bass recorder, J. C. Denner, Nuremberg, early eighteenth century. *Berlin, Instit. f. Musikforschung, 92.* Box. Three joints. *Length* 103 cm.

425-7   Columnar recorder (bass). Late sixteenth century (? French). *Paris, Conserv., E.127, C.410.* Box, brass mounted. Four keys. *Height* 94 cm.

428, 429   Columnar recorder (tenor). As above. *Paris, Conserv., E.691, C.409.* Companion piece to the preceding. *Pitch* F. *Height* 73 cm.

430   Tenor and bass recorders. J. Hotteterre 'le Romain', Paris, early eighteenth century. *Paris, Conserv., E.590, C.402 and E.589, C.413.*

431   Treble recorder. P. J. Bressan, London, first half of eighteenth century. *Washington, Lib. of Congress, Dayton Miller 127.* Box, ivory mounted. *Length* 50·3 cm.

432   Descant recorder. Lorenz Walch, Berchtesgaden, mid nineteenth century. *Washington, Lib. of Congress, Dayton Miller 663.* Light wood, horn mounted. *Pitch* C. *Length* 34 cm.

Flageolets, Pitch Pipes, Ocarinas

433   Bird pipe. Lecler, Paris, first half of eighteenth century. *Paris, Conserv., E.119, C.375.* Long cap. Box. *Length* 23·4 cm; sounding length 12·3 cm. *End bore* 0·3 cm.

434   Bird pipe. Martin, Paris, 1827–40. *Washington, Lib. of Congress, Dayton Miller 668.* Short cap. Box, horn mounts. *Length* 16·5 cm.

435   Picco pipe. London, second half of nineteenth century. *London, Horniman Mus., Carse 237.* Marked *Improved, London, A 1 G 2.* Box. *Length* 9 cm.

436   French flageolet. Naust, Paris, early nineteenth century. *Washington, Lib. of Congress, Dayton Miller 624.* Short cap. Ebony, ivory mounts. *Length* 20 cm.

437   French flageolet. Goodlad & Co., London, 1830–7. *Washington, Lib. of Congress, Dayton Miller 1191.* Long cap. Ebony, ivory mounts. Three silver keys. *Length* 34 cm.

438   French flageolet. Buffet Crampon & Cie., Paris, late nineteenth century or early twentieth. *Washington, Lib. of Congress, Dayton Miller 570.* Long cap. Cocus, silver mounted, pearl mouthpiece. 'Boehm system' with silver keys and rings. *Length* 41·8 cm.

439   French triple flageolet. David, Dijon, eighteenth century. *Paris, Conserv., E.644, C.385.* Box. Flageolet in centre, drone on each side. *Length* 35 cm.

440   Flûte d'accord. Anciuti, Milan, pre-1740. *London, Kneller Hall, 21.* Box. *Length* 25 cm.

441   Pitch pipe. English, eighteenth century. *Birmingham, School of Music.* From Salisbury Cathedral Choristers' School. Square pipe and plunger. Shown with the calibrated plunger removed.

442   Pitch pipe. ? English, early nineteenth century. *Washington, Lib. of Congress, Dayton Miller 812.* Ivory mounted. Telescopic, one plunger within the other. *Length* 32·7 cm.

443   Set of ocarinas. Zach, Vienna, late nineteenth century. *London, Reuben Greene Coll.* Brown earthenware, with curved mouthpieces. In leather case. Marked *Terzett.*

444   Ocarina. German. *London, Horniman Mus., 15.10.48/227.* Blue and white Meissen ware.

445   English flageolet. T. J. Weygandt, Philadelphia, c. 1840. *Washington, Lib. of Congress, Dayton Miller 407.* Box, ivory mounted. Seven holes and thumb hole. One brass key. *Length* 39·5 cm.

446   Double flageolet. Bainbridge, London, early nineteenth century. *Brighton, Museum.* One-piece body of box, ivory mounted. There are two tuning holes in head under silver covers. Shutter for right-hand pipe worked by thumb. *Length* c. 41 cm.

447   Double flageolet. Eisenbrandt, Baltimore, 1810–57. *Washington, Lib. of Congress, Dayton Miller 698.* Ebony, silver mounted. Right pipe with five holes and four keys; left with seven holes and four keys. *Length* 48 cm.

448   Double flageolet. Hastrick, London, 1835–55. *Washington, Lib. of Congress, Dayton Miller 514.* Box, ivory mounted, silver keys. Right pipe, four holes, six keys; left, six holes, seven keys. *Length* 52·3 cm.

449   Double flute-flageolet. Bainbridge, London, 1819. *Washington, Lib. of Congress, Dayton Miller 911.* Box, ivory mounted, silver keys. Right-hand pipe, three holes, four keys and shutter operated by the lips; left, five holes and five keys. *Length* 60 cm.

450 Triple flageolet. Bainbridge, London, *c.* 1820. *Washington, Lib. of Congress, Dayton Miller 721.* Box, ivory mounted, silver keys. Right-hand pipe, five holes, four keys; left, seven holes, four keys; bass pipe, four keys. *Length* 62 cm. (Shown from right side.)

Pipe and Tabor

This one-man musical outfit comprises a pipe and a drum, making use of a pipe which can be played with one hand, in fact a three-holed flageolet with two fingerholes in front and a thumbhole higher up the pipe on the back (**412**). The voicing is relatively narrow, giving good notes in the overblown registers at the expense of the fundamentals, which are not employed in the technique. The voicing edge is often shod with metal. The scale begins with four notes in second harmonics, continued upwards by third and higher harmonics as far as one needs. The pipe is held and played with the left hand while the right holds the drumstick—the traditional manner since the thirteenth century, when in dance and military music the beat of the drum was presumably felt to precede in importance the tune of the pipe. The drum is suspended in various ways from the player's body.

Through the fifteenth and sixteenth centuries the pipe and tabor was not uncommonly played together with other instruments, stringed and wind, and most courts possessed a set among their musical instruments. No representative set from that era seems to have survived, however. A bass tabor pipe with a brass crook (Brussels, 1022) is all that remains of an Italian late sixteenth-century set of different-sized pipes for performance in consort, as indicated, e.g. in a Paris inventory of 1551 (Lesure, *GSJ*, VII, 22). This practice has been preserved, or possibly reintroduced, by players in the Basque cities of Spain. Other tabor pipes in collections are mostly eighteenth- and nineteenth-century folk instruments from England, South France, North Spain, the Balearic Islands, and (introduced from Spain) Mexico. Superior pipes of ivory (**412**) built around 1800 show that the pipe and tabor was then still being played for dancing in middle-class homes in England, where it survived in villages for Morris dancing up to the beginning of the present century (**410**); several English tabors in collections still have the remains of their brightly coloured Morris ribbons attached. English pipes usually have separate head and body joints while the similar-sized Provençal pipe, *galoubet*, is generally in one piece (**409**). The pipe used in Catalonia (**411**) differs from others in having the holes of a French flageolet (p. 84), though still played with one hand.

The size and shape of the tabor varies considerably according to regional tradition. Three characteristic types are illustrated (**409–11**). The Basque tabor is of medium proportions. The Pyrenean variant with gut strings instead of drum-skin (**413**) is mentioned on p. 62.

Recorders

Historically the recorder appears to be a fifteenth-century or perhaps late fourteenth-century development of the medieval *flageol* for use in chamber music. With seven fingerholes plus thumbhole, and aided by a relatively wide voicing, it commands a colourful fundamental register with a compass of a ninth, which, extended by three or four notes in the overblown register, suffices for the rendering of a typical part in Renaissance polyphonic music; the higher part of the upper register is unstable and unequal in quality as compared with flageolets in general.

The earlier or 'Renaissance' type of recorder built in one piece is known by many specimens of the second half of the sixteenth century and the first half of the seventeenth, the Vienna Collection alone possessing 34 instruments of all sizes. One-piece recorders are not tunable, and anyway, as inventories bear out, a large musical establishment of the period might require two or more sets of recorders built to agree with the playing pitch of different organs and other wind instruments with which they might be musically combined. This can make it difficult to decide whether an example is built as a descant, treble or tenor of a set. One may consider as a basis some overall lengths of recorders given by Praetorius: descant 32 cm, treble 42 cm, tenor 63·5 cm, bass 93 cm, etc. The three examples shown from the Frankfurt *Stadtpfeifferei* (**415–17**) come fairly close to this. So do many of the Vienna specimens from the old Catajo Collection, Padua, though among these are others of intermediate sizes, probably matching up in higher-tuned sets. In the small collection at Verona Cathedral a difference of a whole tone is apparent between two contemporary and otherwise similar bass recorders.

The large sizes have an added wooden cap fitted over the top end of the pipe. It has a blowing slot cut in it or else a hole to take a brass crook (**417, 420**). Under the cap the wooden plug which shapes the windway may be substantially cut away on the opposite side from the windway to leave a rough-hewn chamber evidently intended for a sponge for soaking up condensed moisture. In these older recorders the bore contracts gently throughout. In the smaller sizes the seventh fingerhole is normally offset to the right and (but not always) duplicated on the left to suit the little finger of 'left-handers' (**415**). In large sizes the seventh hole is covered by an open key partially concealed inside a removable barrel perforated with air holes in rosettes (**417, 420**). A tenor recorder may have this key instead of the more usual offset hole (**421**). The compass of the largest recorders was sometimes extended downwards, with from one to three extra open keys. No example of this has survived complete, but the great bass at Antwerp has recently been restored with the missing parts (**414**; it is illustrated before restoration in Hunt, Plate V). This is the largest extant recorder, other great basses measuring between 165 and 183 cm. 'Quint basses', around 120 cm in length (**420**), are pitched a fifth below the usual bass of the period and have provided the prototypes for the modern 'great bass' in C.

Little variation is found in the modelling of these early recorders. There is a round-topped instrument at Vienna (C.159) equal in size to the example shown (**422**) though with a different mark. A dated recorder by J. C. Denner, the celebrated Nuremberg *Flötenmacher* (**419**), may be set beside several other woodwind specimens in which a jointed construction occurs, yet not in the decisive manner evinced by the fully-fledged 'Baroque' woodwind. A freak design is the columnar recorder, apparently referred to in a Stuttgart court inventory of 1589 as '10 *Collonen*' of brown wood '*so Antonius Cousseau gemacht*'. Two extant examples in the Paris Collection (**425–9**), with a third at Brussels (189, height 52 cm, with one key), constitute a set of bass, tenor and treble. The bore runs down the boxwood column and back again. Engraved brass lattices conceal the voicing and the four keys, two of which are operated by thumb buttons. Doors of similar lattice cover the thumbhole when the instrument stands idle, looking very decorative.

The Baroque jointed recorder was possibly created by Jean Hotteterre the elder, Paris, *c.* 1650. Of the three joints, the head, with a rich moulding over the socket, is cylindrical or very slightly tapered in bore, the body compensating for this with a steeper taper than that of the earlier instruments. The separate head joint allows extension of the instrument for tuning, and the separate foot joint, with the seventh hole, can be turned to the position which suits the player's little finger and thus the need for duplication of the hole is done away with. When a key is needed for the seventh hole it is exposed. The bass recorder is again capped and it is blown through a brass crook. In some English, French and Dutch basses the foot joint is built with a bulbous end for holding a wooden supporting peg. This is inserted into the terminal orifice, the acoustic vent being a hole in the side (**430**). Among Baroque sets of recorders, the Chester quartet (Grosvenor Museum) by Bressan is well known; Bressan, who came over from France, *c.* 1683 and worked in London until *c.* 1731 (Halfpenny, *GSJ*, XII, 1959), and the two Stanesbys, father and son, were the best-known English makers of the first half of the eighteenth century (**431**), contemporary with the Hotteterre grandson in Paris (**430**). A case of ivory recorders by Schlegel (**423**) dating from perhaps after 1750 shows a set suitable for duets or trio sonatas, using either two descants or two trebles as preferred. Many elaborately carved and decorated examples exist of the eighteenth-century treble recorder, musically the important Baroque size and the one for which Bach and Handel wrote solo music and obbligati. After the mid-century recorder making declined, though some good English examples of *c.* 1800 exist, e.g. by Goulding, London, with flute-like foot joint (London, V. & A., 285-1882). A later instrument from the Walch dynasty in Berchtesgaden, Bavaria, illustrates the continuance of the recorder, if only as a child's toy, almost to the eve of the modern revival (**432**).

Other Flageolets

Picco pipe (**435**). Picco, a blind Sardinian shepherd, won international celebrity about the middle of the nineteenth century as a concert soloist on this three-holed 'pastoral tibia' of his own making. He eventually became a member of the Saint Cecilia Academy of Rome. The pipe, which recalls certain Iron Age bone pipes (e.g. from Malham, *GSJ*, V, 1952), can be closed at the end to obtain extra notes and was copied under the name Picco pipe by several flute makers up to near the end of the century as a musical plaything.

Bird pipes and French flageolets. The French flageolet is characterized by having four holes in front and two behind, thus amounting to two plus a thumbhole for each hand. The arrangement, attested from the sixteenth century though no doubt known earlier, is particularly suited to very small pipes on which the breadth of a man's finger might make six front holes difficult to manage. It is therefore the usual arrangement in the bird pipes made from the seventeenth century to the nineteenth for inducing cage birds to sing (**433, 434**). Bird pipes and French flageolets are usually made in one joint, often with a removable cap. The cap is either short (**436**) or else quite long, nearly as long as the pipe itself (**437**). Such long caps are often provided with a small ivory or bone mouthpiece and give a comfortable distance between hands and face whilst playing. One of the smallest bird pipes must be an unsigned boxwood instrument at Paris (C.371), only 11 cm long, with lowest note A, fifth space above the treble stave, though quite soft and pleasant in tone, like other well-made bird pipes.

The ordinary French flageolets of the eighteenth and nineteenth centuries are stouter in build and stronger in sound, having been much played for dance music. The bore is slightly tapered, and in the nineteenth century keys were generally provided for improving the semitones (**437**), leading eventually to 'Boehm system' models by Buffet, Paris, and other French makers (**438**). A curious eighteenth-century compound flageolet is a French design in which the pipe is fixed between two hole-less unison drone pipes, all three being sounded simultaneously from one mouthpiece (**439**).

Flûte d'accord: a species of double recorder with two bores drilled in a single piece of wood (**440**), built on the Continent from the second half of the seventeenth century to the early nineteenth. Among the earliest is a Bavarian example by G. Walch, 1662 (Amsterdam, Rijksmuseum). The instrument is from *c.* 25-35 cm long, and the voicing of the right-hand pipe is placed lower down than that of the other so that the two are pitched a third apart. The two rows of holes are placed close together, the sizes and slantings of the holes being gauged so that simultaneous fingering of the two pipes produces a diatonic scale in thirds. Most are of box, though Anciuti, Milan, made ivory examples, as he did of most woodwind instruments. (Another one-piece double flageolet common in collections is the *dvoinice*, a folk instrument of Yugoslavia, which is still made; the wood is cut away between the lower parts of the pipes, which usually diverge at a slight angle and have four and three burnt-out holes respectively.)

English flageolets. This expression has been taken as applying either to flageolets in general which have six holes in front, or, more correctly, to the ingenious and pretty instruments introduced near the beginning of the nineteenth century by William Bainbridge, London, and made by him (succeeded *c.* 1835 by Hastrick) and from *c.* 1826 by his pupil J. Simpson, also of London, and by several makers in America. They include single flageolets (445), some with the same holes as a recorder, several types of double flageolets, and also triple. A characteristic feature is the insertion of ivory studs between the holes to guide the novice's fingers; also the marking of note names beside holes and keys, though these features are not invariably present. As with the case of Edward Light's harp-lutes of the same era, to go through the Bainbridge series in detail cannot be attempted here, for continual small modifications appeared, especially with the double flageolets. These last are intended principally for playing melodies in thirds and sixths. The first pattern is that which is described in a British patent of 1806 in the name of Thomas Scott. The two bores are in a single length of box, circular in cross-section and tapered towards the foot (446). Otherwise the double flageolets have two separately turned pipes held in a common head joint furnished with a small bone mouthpiece (447, 448). Basically, the right-hand pipe sounds the accompaniment to the left. One or either of the pipes can be silenced by a pivoted shutter which occludes the voicing. The silver keys are mounted on blocks. In some examples a blind block is present, possibly for subsequent addition of a key or shutter if desired. Several of Bainbridge's patents are occupied with longer flageolets held in the manner of a flute, e.g. in 1819 for a 'double flute-flageolet' (449) on which the right hand, on the nearer pipe, can accompany the other pipe. The triple flageolet, dating from the late 1820s, is similar to the ordinary type of double flageolet with the addition of a short wide boxwood cylinder mounted at the back (450). This is closed below and provided with a tuning plunger and keys for giving bass notes on the ocarina principle. A wooden leg is supplied for propping the instrument while playing.

Pottery whistles and ocarina. Among small painted earthenware whistles made in many parts of Europe as toys and carnival whistles two kinds predominate: the water whistle, to be half filled with water which causes the note to chirrup; and the bird whistle in the form of a hen or other bird, with a fingerhole in the breast for changing the note. Both kinds have a primitive flageolet voicing of baked clay. The ocarina, said to have been introduced by G. Donati, Budrio (Italy), *c.* 1860, is an elongated whistle of the second kind, with a torpedo shape which gives room for a series of fingerholes for playing more or less like a flute. Two examples illustrate the early spread of the ocarina outside Italy (443, 444).

Panpipes

Though not flageolets, these will be noticed here for convenience. A panpipe normally consists of a row of canes, stopped at their bottom ends and graduated in length to give a diatonic scale when blown across their upper ends. This ancient pastoral instrument and trade call has occasionally been introduced to Western musical circles. Two finely mounted French eighteenth-century specimens (452, 453) must have been made for enjoyment in *fêtes champêtres* or use in stage productions based on classical pastoral themes. The simply made English example (451) is one of a set of panpipes of different sizes played by a militia ensemble of the early nineteenth century, reflecting a vogue for 'Pandeans', touring groups of panpipers who gave concert performances (*Grove*, 5th edn., 'Panpipe').

Illustrations: Panpipes

451   Panpipe. English, early nineteenth century. *Halifax, Bankfield Museum.* One instrument from a pair of sets used by the Halifax local Militia. Cane pipes bound with red baize.

452   Panpipe. French, eighteenth century. *Paris, Conserv., E.111, C.455.* Twenty-three cane tubes mounted with ivory and horn, with horn frame and silver bolts. Scale of C. *Outside length* of longest pipe, 21 cm.

453   Panpipe. French, eighteenth century. *Paris, Conserv., E.110, C.454.* Carved ebony frame. *Length* of longest pipe, 22·5 cm.

2 Flutes

'Flute' is understood here in the modern musician's sense of a transverse flute with mouth-hole in the side of the head of the tube. Just above this mouth-hole, at a distance about equal to the radius of the bore, the tube is closed by a stopper, usually of cork. In playing, the controlled aperture of the player's lips together with the far edge of the mouth-hole form a voicing analogous to that made by the windway and sharp edge of the recorder, but flexible, admitting a great range in compass and loudness. Flutes were known in Europe in the thirteenth century but little is recorded of their use until the end of the fifteenth, when flute consorts similar to recorder consorts had begun to be built. The Swiss partnership of flute (fife) and side drum for dance and military music, more vigorous than the old pipe and tabor, further added to the popularity of the flute during the sixteenth century. 'Fife' denotes a flute, usually small, intended for playing with the drum, though the term has grown obsolete following changes in military music during the second half of the nineteenth century.

Illustrations: Flutes

454 Flute. C. Rafi, Lyons, first half of sixteenth century. *Brussels, Conserv. royal, 1066.* Box. *Length* 72 cm. *Bore* 1·85 cm.

455 Flute. Italian, sixteenth century. *Brussels, Conserv. royal, 1064.* Double plume mark. Box. *Length* 66·5 cm. *Bore* 1·8 cm.

456 Descant flute. Italian, sixteenth century. *Brussels, Conserv. royal, 1062.* Box. *Length* 40 cm. *Bore* 0·95 cm.

457 Bass flute. ? Flemish, sixteenth century. *Brussels, Conserv. royal, 2695.* Marked *H. VITS*. Two joints. *Length* 95 cm. *Bore* 2·5 cm.

458 Flute. Italian (?), seventeenth century. *Vienna, Kunsthist. Mus., C.187.* Marked on main joint (unclear) *LIBSILV*. Box. Three joints. *Length* 60 cm. *Bore* 1·7 cm.

459 Fife. W. Crosby, Boston, Mass., *c.* 1850–74. *Washington, Lib. of Congress, Dayton Miller 944.* Rosewood, engraved silver mounts. *Pitch* A flat. *Length* 44·5 cm.

460 Fife. Cotton, London, late eighteenth century. *London, Horniman Mus., Carse 14e.* Box, brass mounted. In two joints. One brass key. With regimental marks. *Pitch* A flat.

461 Fife. Thibouville Frères, Ivry (France), mid nineteenth century. *Washington, Lib. of Congress, Dayton Miller 603.* Dark wood, silver mounted. Silver key. Thumbhole. Two slinging holes. *Length* 35·6 cm.

462 Fife. T. Prowse, London, *c.* 1816–36. *Washington, Lib. of Congress, Dayton Miller 856.* Pearwood, long brass ferrules. In two joints. Four brass keys. *Pitch* A flat. *Length* 39 cm.

463 Fife (*fifre Bernois*). Charles Felchlin, Berne, Switzerland, mid nineteenth century. *Geneva, Mus. d'Art et d'Histoire, 9390.* Box, ivory mounted. In three joints. One square key. Marked D.

464 E flat piccolo. H. F. Meyer, Hanover, mid nineteenth century. *Washington, Lib. of Congress, Dayton Miller 924.* Cocus or blackwood, silver mounted, with ivory head. Six keys. *Length* 25·7 cm.

465 Fife with metal case. Jacob Streulli, Horgen (Switzerland), *c.* 1850. *Washington, Lib. of Congress, Dayton Miller 869.* Box, brass mounted. *Length* 36·5 cm.

466 Flute. Hotteterre, Paris, early eighteenth century. *Berlin, Instit. f. Musikforschung, 2670.* Also stamped with anchor. Stained box, ivory mounts. Three joints. Brass key. *Length* 70·5 cm.

467 Flute. Naust, Paris, early eighteenth century. *Paris, Conserv., E.710, C.444.* Stained box, ivory mounts. Three joints. Straight foot. *Length* 76 cm.

468 Flute. Bressan, London, *c.* 1720. *London, Victoria and Albert Mus., 452–1898.* Ebony inlaid with silver, silver mounts. Four joints. Square key.

469 Flute. Bizey, Paris, m¡d eighteenth century. *Paris, Conserv., E.598, C.439.* Ivory. Four joints. *Length* 62 cm.

470 F Flute. Scherer, ? Paris, *c.* 1770. *Paris, Coll. G. Thibault.* Ivory, in four joints. *Length* 52·4 cm.

471 Flute. Quantz, Potsdam, *c.* 1750. *Washington, Lib. of Congress, Dayton Miller 916.* Once the property of Frederick the Great (see Gilliam and Lichtenwanger, *Checklist*). Ebony, ivory mounts. In four joints, with five additional upper joints. Two silver keys (E flat, D sharp). *Length,* with the different upper joints, 63·6–67·2 cm.

472 Pair of flutes. Thomas Lot, Paris, third quarter of eighteenth century. *London, Horniman Mus., Carse 263.* Gold key of upper flute bears crown and cipher said to be that of Louis XV. Satin wood, ivory mounts. In four joints, with four additional upper joints. Lower flute has silver key and similar extra joints. In sharkskin case, silver mounted.

473 Walking-stick flute. Lambert, Paris, eighteenth century. *Washington, Lib. of Congress, Dayton Miller 908.* Light wood with a key of the same. *Length* 89 cm.

474 Bass flute. Wigley & MacGregor, London, 1811–16. *Brussels, Conserv. royal, 1070.* Reversed head. Box, ivory mounted. *Length c.* 101 cm.

475 Flute. Potter senior, London, 1777. *London, Horniman Mus., Carse 193.* Box, ivory mounts. Six square silver keys (three on foot, and F, G sharp and B flat on body joints).

476 Flute. Claude Laurent, Paris, 1807. *Washington, Lib. of Congress, Dayton Miller 1051.* Fluted glass, silver mounts. Four silver keys on pillars. *Length* 62 cm.

477 Flute. Louis Drouet, London, *c.* 1818. *Luton Museum, FL/21.* Ivory, silver mounts. Eight round silver keys. *Length* 67·5 cm.

478 Flute. Clementi, London, *c.* 1830. *Cobham, Morley-Pegge Coll.* Nicholson's Improved model. Rosewood. Silver mounts, eight saltspoon keys. *Length* 66·2 cm.

479 Flute. Jacques Nonon, Paris, first half of nineteenth century. *Cobham, Morley-Pegge Coll.* Tulou model. Rosewood. Eleven silver keys.

480 Flute. Abel Siccama, London, *c.* 1850. *Washington, Lib. of Congress, Dayton Miller 133.* Cocus, silver mounts. Twelve keys. *Length* 64·3 cm.

481 Flute. Pentenrieder, Munich, 1837–47. *Washington, Lib. of Congress, Dayton Miller 1038.* Stained box, ivory mounts. Ten silver keys including two crescent keys. *Length* 68 cm.

482 Flute. Rudall & Rose, London, 1830–7. *Washington, Lib. of Congress, Dayton Miller 440.* Cocus, silver mounts. Thirteen keys. B flat foot. *Length* 74·5 cm.

483 Flute. F. Schauffler & J. Leukhardt, Boston, 1851–7. *Washington, Lib. of Congress, Dayton Miller 119.* Cocus, silver mounted. Foot to low A. Thirteen keys. *Length* 78·5 cm.

484 Burghley bass flute. Burghley, London, *c.* 1845. *London, Bate Coll.* Reversed head. Flute has five wooden keys. *Length* of flute 89 cm (head).

485 Albisiphone (bass flute in C). Abelardo Albisi, Milan, *c.* 1891. *Washington, Lib. of Congress, Dayton Miller 232.* Silver. *Length* of flute 98 cm.

486 Flute. Theobald Boehm, Munich, after 1832. *London, Horniman Mus., Carse 11a.* Marked *Th. Boehm à Munich.* System of 1832. Conical bore.

487 Flute. Cornelius Ward, London, *c.* 1842. *Washington, Lib. of Congress, Dayton Miller 572.* Ward's patent. Rosewood, silver mounted. *Length* 65·3 cm.

488 Flute. A. G. Badger & Co., New York, 1860–8. *Washington, Lib. of Congress, Dayton Miller 1248.* Rosewood, silver mounts. Conical Boehm system with Dorus G sharp. *Length* 67 cm.

489 Giorgi flute. Joseph Wallis & Sons, London, *c.* 1888. *Washington, Lib. of Congress, Dayton Miller 481.* Ebonite. Eight holes. Three silver keys. *Length* 52 cm.

490 Flute. Rudall & Rose, London, *c.* 1850–4. *Washington, Lib. of Congress, Dayton Miller 1236.* Marked *Th. Boehm München, Rudall & Rose Patentees . . .* Cylindrical. Silver. Rings and open G sharp. Rack-and-pinion head tuning. *Length* 65 cm.

491 Flute. Theobald Boehm, Munich, 1848. *Washington, Lib. of Congress, Dayton Miller 1237.* Boehm's No 14 of this model. Silver. *Length* 70·6 cm.

492 Flute. Louis Lot. Paris, *c.* 1860. *Washington, Lib. of Congress, Dayton Miller 91.* Cocus and silver. Perforated plates. Dorus G sharp. B foot. *Length* 70·3 cm.

493 Flute. Rudall Carte & Co., London, 1896. *Washington, Lib. of Congress, Dayton Miller 4.* Ebonite and silver. Made for Dayton C. Miller. Boehm system (Rockstro's model) with extra keys by Dayton Miller. *Length* 68 cm. Alternative foot joint to B flat.

494 Piccolo. Rudall Carte & Co., London, late nineteenth century. *Coll. of the late Charles Overy, Knighton, Wilts.* Silver. '1867' system.

495 Piccolo. George W. Haynes, New York, 1888. *Washington, Lib. of Congress, Dayton Miller 448.* Cocus and silver. Boehm system. Sharp and flat pitch heads. *Lengths* 30·4, 31·3 cm.

496 Bass flute in F. George W. Haynes, Los Angeles, 1898. *Washington, Lib. of Congress, Dayton Miller 118.* Tube of Mexican silver dollars and lip plate of a 20-dollar gold piece. Boehm system. Closed G sharp. Drawn tone holes. *Length* 95·4 cm.

Older Cylindrical Flutes

The Renaissance flute is a plain cylindrical boxwood pipe with six fingerholes and no thumbhole (no normal Western flute has a thumbhole before the 1830s). It has no key and no head cap. There are three principal sizes (455-7) corresponding to the treble, tenor and bass recorders of the sixteenth century, though again dimensions vary owing to differing tuning-pitch requirements. The middle size, then nominally 'tenor' (455), corresponds with the ordinary flute of later periods with lowest note middle D of the piano. Some specimens, also of the bass flute, date from the first half of the sixteenth century, including instruments by Claude Rafi, Lyons, 1515-53 (454; see Lesure, *GSJ*, VII, 1954, p. 30). The Verona Collection, containing original wind instruments of the Verona Philharmonic Academy, includes six Rafi flutes of the tenor size (62 cm long), adding to the evidence of a Lyons international trade in woodwind instruments at that early date, which extended also to South Germany in competition with the products of Venice and the German towns. The small treble flute, *c.* 40 cm, is scarcer (456) All these flutes are made in one piece save for specimens of the bass which have a separate head joint (457). A rare three-jointed example of the old cylindrical flute (458) possibly antedates the advent of the conical jointed flute of the second half of the seventeenth century.

Fife. The Swiss infantry fife was coming into use in France and England at the beginning of the sixteenth century. In Italy, a 1543 inventory of the Verona Academy (Turrini, 26) still gives the German name, *Phayfer 5 da sonar da Campo.* The instrument was built on the same lines as the above flutes, perhaps with rather smaller bore, and in length between the treble and tenor flute: Praetorius shows the *Schweitzerpfeife* 56 cm long. Examples must be very rare—if any exist at all—of fifes earlier than the mid eighteenth century, by which time they are of a smaller kind (*c.* 36 cm or a little more) which remained in use thenceforth. The cylindrical bore is kept and the one-piece tube is shod with a long brass ferrule at each end (459, 465). Two-jointed fifes also occur (460), and metal fifes and fifes with one key. The pitch is B flat or C. Though military fife calls were generally going out by the end of the nineteenth century, the later models with a pair of slinging holes close to the lower end (461) remained in manufacture in France and Germany until recently—a last survival of the Renaissance cylindrical flute (though cylindrical flutes are common among folk instruments, notably in South-east Europe).

Conical Flutes

The second known type of European flute is the jointed flute with cylindrical head joint, tapered body, and a foot joint which may be either. As in later flutes the end of the head is mounted with a cap, of ivory or silver, this cap often being pierced to receive a threaded ivory rod by which the position of the stopper can be adjusted. The early type is the classic one-keyed flute. Its place of origin is thought on present evidence to have been Paris, in the third quarter of the seventeenth century. Up to about 1730 it was built in three joints with rounded foot (466), later straight (467). The mouldings are large, and that of the foot carries the key, a closed key for E flat. The next model is four-jointed (468, 469, 472), with lightened construction and shorter head. The body is divided into an upper and a lower joint, the upper being generally supplied in from three to six alternative sizes for tuning the flute to the playing pitch required. A reason for this provision is the better cross-fingering on the one-keyed flute when tuned in this manner rather than simply by pulling out the head joint as one does with later flutes. The second key visible on a flute (471) by Joachim Quantz, Frederick the Great's flute master and a leading musician of his day, is for giving the fractionally sharper note he wanted for D sharp. It was little copied.

One-keyed flutes continued to be made through the nineteenth century as low-priced models. The eighteenth-century mouth-hole is small and round; in the nineteenth it is larger and often oval, and sometimes the hole in an older instrument was later widened. One-keyed small flutes and piccolos are mentioned later (p. 90). Flutes pitched a third (E flat) or a fourth (F) above the ordinary were made from around 1730, the earlier examples being in F (470). Later in the eighteenth century a one-keyed E flat flute ('F flute' in contemporary English sources), *c.* 54 cm long, was being made for bands, being suited to the flat tonalities preferred by bands based on clarinets. Most specimens of this flute are, however, of the first half of the nineteenth century, as are also those of the one-keyed low A flat flute ('B flat tenor flute') measuring *c.* 75 to 77 cm. The *flûte d'amour* in A (*c.* 73 cm) was commoner on the Continent. When built to a low tuning pitch it may be difficult to distinguish from the above-mentioned low A flat band flute, though this is principally English.

Bass flutes of the eighteenth century include an example by J. Beuker which may be pre-1750 (Paris Conservatoire, E.248, C.453). It is in C, straight-built, with covered holes for both ring-fingers, each lever having a fishtailed touch to allow for 'left-handed' playing (with the flute pointing to the left). A later pattern has a 'reversed' head (with U-bend) which reduces overall length and brings the hands closer to the body. An example by Delusse, Paris (Paris Conservatoire, E.1079, C.1108), may be late eighteenth-century; it is again one-keyed and it has three covered-hole levers. An identical model was patented in London in 1810 by Malcolm MacGregor, and a number of examples survive marked Wigley & MacGregor (474), some having additional closed keys. The reversed head of these bass flutes is either with parallel bores in one flat piece of wood, or with two separate parallel joints connected by a metal U-bend as shown.

Additional keys. Apart from Quantz's idiosyncratic D sharp key mentioned above, the first additional key to the flute after the original E flat key was an open key for a low C sharp, the foot joint being lengthened accordingly. This was known as an experimental feature as far back as *c.* 1720, but no flute having these two foot keys and no other keys seems to have survived. Closed keys on the body joints were introduced by London makers, an early instance being a six-keyed flute by Gedney, 1769 (Champion Coll., illustrated in Baines, *Woodwind Instruments*, Pl. XXVI). A flute by Richard Potter, 1777 (475), has the same equipment, viz. closed keys for B flat, G sharp and F and a foot joint extended to low C natural. Potter later invented the keys with pewter flaps, 1785, which remained not uncommon for the foot keys through much of the nineteenth century.

By 1800 an up-to-date concert flute had seven or eight keys: four or five on the conical body joints and three on the C foot (477). This was the basic model up to the adoption of Boehm flutes and long after continued to be made as a 'simple-system' flute, usually with a metal tuning slide incorporated in the head joint (another feature which first appears at the end of the eighteenth century). It is commonly referred to as an eight-keyed flute. A few of its countless designs are illustrated. The flute by Laurent (476) is one of his earliest in glass and is with a foot joint for D only, unlike most of his instruments.

In London a model with enlarged second, fourth and fifth fingerholes for increased tonal power was brought out by T. Prowse, 1822, following the ideas of the soloist Nicholson (**478**). A later flute by Nonon, Paris (**479**), shows improvement due to another soloist, Tulou, including long axles derived from Boehm's flutes. In Germany and Austria the conical flute based on the eight-keyed system lasted as a professional instrument into the last quarter of the century, often with a foot joint extended to give notes below the usual low C, a practice occasionally followed elsewhere (**482**); in Vienna, Koch made foot joints descending—not very satisfactorily—to the low G. In the later German-style instruments various trill keys and alternative touches are usually added to the basically eight-keyed system (**483**), often still mounted on blocks and giving a cumbersome, ill-thought-out appearance in marked contrast to the scientific neatness and economy of Boehm's models. A rare specimen (**481**) shows crescent-shaped touches, ascribed to the Swiss inventor Gordon, *c.* 1831, in pursuit of a reformed fingering system contemporary with Boehm's first system with rings (**486**). The crescents are here to perfect the whole-tone trills on F sharp and G sharp.

Small conical flutes. Three-jointed one-key piccolos were made in the late eighteenth century, also a small A flat flute for bands. The latter (*c.* 36–38 cm) is the prototype of that which later became the lead instrument of civilian flute bands, and their military equivalent, the corps of drums, which grew up around the mid nineteenth century. Extra harmony, if required, is provided by the E flat and low A flat flutes noticed earlier (p. 89) and a sopranino voice is usually supplied by an E flat (**464**) or D flat piccolo. From *c.* 1860 the instruments are of blackwood rather than of box, with from one to six nickel-silver keys. By this period, the low A flat flute functions as a bass ('B flat bass flute' in England) and usually has a reversed head of nickel-silver. An unusual transitional model, half fife, is shown (**462**), also a well-made Swiss one-keyed flute in high C (piccolo pitch) illustrating the adoption of the conical and jointed small flute by the homeland of the cylindrical fife (**463**).

Walking-stick flutes (**473**) and recorders (*czakan*) were popular mainly in Germany and Austria through the first half of the nineteenth century, along with walking-stick violins, sticks incorporating clarinet at one end and piccolo at the other, and so on. The experimental *Burghley flute*, a light-weight all-wooden flute, London, *c.* 1845, is illustrated by a reversed-head bass (**484**). The *Giorgi flute*, 1888, made in ebonite by Wallis, London (**489**), is held like a recorder; the mouth-hole is situated in the top end of the cylindrical tube, this end being shaped to give the feel of a normal flute when put to the lips. Made with or without keys, the instrument works quite well; typologically it may be compared to the ancient 'vertical flutes' found elsewhere, from the Balkans (*kaval*) to Japan. About the same time, *c.* 1889, Wünnenberg, Cologne, designed other flutes to be played in recorder attitude, though in these the head is a short one of normal transverse kind, connected to the downwards-held flute by a curved metal section; cf also Albisi's bass flute (**485**).

Boehm Flutes

Theobald Boehm (1794–1881), apprenticed goldsmith and professional flutist of Munich and the king of the nineteenth-century woodwind engineers, produced his new conical flute in 1832 (**486**). By rearrangement of the holes and provision of an open key for the left thumb, and through ring keys on long axles, the entire chromatic scale lies directly under the fingers, scientifically tuned and even in strength. Boehm put the two main axles on opposite sides of the flute, but makers of his model in London (Rudall & Rose) and Paris (Godfroy) soon put them both on the near side. To avoid the salient unfamiliarity, to the conventional player of the time, of Boehm's open key for G sharp, many makers, particularly in Paris, fitted the compound key of Dorus, fingered as a closed key (**488**). An independent series owing much to Boehm is that of Cornelius Ward, London, from 1852 (**487**); Ward's pull-wires for closing the foot keys are distinctive.

In 1847, after some 13 years devoted to other work, Boehm, now aged 54, brought out his cylindrical flute with a roughly parabolic head-joint bore, in all essentials the flute universally played today. Silver was his preferred material for the tube. A trial version keeps the rings of his conical flute (**490**) but the final hole-widths became too large for the fingers to cover, and padded plates replaced the rings (**491**). A subsequent addition is Briccialdi's second thumb lever for an alternative fingering of B flat (London, 1849). Again French makers reversed Boehm's open G sharp key, first by Dorus key, later by a simple closed key, though elsewhere the open key remained much in use after the end of the century. Perforated plates, with ring-shaped pads, were introduced in Paris by Louis Lot (**492**) and remain a French preference. In London, A. Siccama is one who combined Boehm's cylindrical bore with the old system or small modifications of it (**480**). Rudall Carte's '1867' model offers, up to a point, alternative fingering in the old way and the Boehm way, as illustrated by a piccolo (**494**), with the two round thumb-plates characteristic of the model. Boehm-system piccolos, incidentally, generally kept a conical bore until indeed quite recently (**495**). Rockstro's flute is simply a Boehm flute with extra trill devices (**493**). Much of the value of an individual Boehm flute depends upon the quality of the head joint, and often a particularly good head joint will be found to have been transferred to a newer instrument.

A bass flute in F (**496**), by one of the celebrated Haynes family of American flute makers, is pitched a tone lower than the normal *alto flute* in G which Boehm himself devised *c.* 1854. Boehm also built a full bass flute in C, of metal in straight form (Bate Collection) but rather tiring to hold. A reversed or coiled or T-shaped head later became usual with these largest flutes, as those by Albisi, Milan, the earliest of which may have shortly preceded the turn of the century (**485**).

3 Bagpipes

Western reed instruments may be placed in four classes according to type of bore and reed:
  (1) Cylindrical bore, double reed (crumhorn, racket, etc).
  (2) Conical bore, double reed (shawm, oboe, etc).
  (3) Cylindrical bore, single reed (chalumeau, clarinet).
  (4) Conical bore, single reed (saxophone, tarogato).
'Conical' bore denotes one which expands from the blowing end to the other, or at least through the first part of the tube length. A cylindrical bore very often leads to a terminal expansion or bell. In the following sections reed instruments are noticed for the most part in the above order, and bagpipes, in which the four classes of pipe are variously combined in a single instrument, similarly, with respect to the chanter. The distinctions made in this grouping are not entirely academic. Admittedly in their more ancient manifestations the different specifications may not lead to such sharply contrasted sound-qualities as are heard between cultivated opposites like oboe and clarinet, but on the whole the tone of a cylindrical instrument, from which the even-numbered overtones are absent or weak, is closed and humming compared with the more open and declamatory sound of a conical bore of corresponding pitch. One can thus compare the crumhorn and the shawm, both of the same epoch. Both these are sounded by a double reed, but the type of reed is a minor determinant of sound-quality so long as the quality of the reed is good. Both oboe and bassoon can be played with a single-reed mouthpiece without very noticeable change from the tone ordinarily produced with a double reed. Such interchanges of reed form are, however, very rare; each type of instrument is in normal practice firmly associated with its accepted type of reed, which is therefore counted a major typological factor along with bore profile.

Illustrations: Bagpipes

497   Musette. French, eighteenth century. *London, Royal Coll. of Music, 192*. Ivory chanters and shuttle drone. Bellows. *External length* of chanter 26 cm.

498   Cornemuse. French, eighteenth century. *New York, Metropol. Mus. of Art, 865*. Ivory pipes, the chanter with silver key. Bag cover of silk tapestry bordered with gold and silver lace. *Length* of chanter 25·5 cm.

499   Gaita gallega. Spanish (Galicia), nineteenth century. *London, Horniman Mus., 16.2.59/1*. Boxwood pipes, including small drone with stopper. Red-brown velvet bag cover.

500   Cornemuse. French (said to be from Normandy), nineteenth century. *London, R. Coll. of Music, 139*. Boxwood chanter. Drones and stocks decorated with pewter. *External length* of chanter 55 cm, of bass drone 108 cm.

501   Small-pipe. Northumberland, *c.* 1770–80. *Ryton-on-Tyne, Cocks Coll*. Open keyless chanter of ivory and three ivory drones. Bellows.

502   Small-pipe. Northumberland, *c.* 1850. *Ryton-on-Tyne, Cocks Coll*. Eight-keyed closed ivory chanter and four drones. Bellows.

503   Union pipe. Kenna, Dublin and Mullingar, 1768–94. *Ryton-on-Tyne, Cocks Coll*. Keyless double chanter. Three drones, one regulator. Bellows.

504   Union pipe. Coyne, Dublin, *c.* 1850. *Dublin, Nat. Museum of Ireland, 484–93*. Keyed chanter, three drones, three regulators including 'differential' bass regulator. Bellows.

505   Lowland pipe. Scottish, late eighteenth century. *Ryton-on-Tyne, Cocks Coll*. Three drones. Bellows.

506   Scottish union-pipe. Scottish, ? late eighteenth century. *Oxford, Pitt Rivers Mus., Balfour 113, 1921.* Boxwood pipes. Chanter in two joints, brass mounted. Three drones, the bass drone being looped, and four-keyed regulator. Bellows. *Total length* of chanter 50 cm.

507   Dudy. Bohemian, ? eighteenth century. *Oxford, Pitt Rivers Mus., Balfour 129, 1906.* Sewn bag of goatskin, the hair on the outside. Chanter and drone with brass-mounted bells of cowhorn. Drone with right-angled upper joints and middle joint with doubled-back bore. Bellows.

508   Zampogna. Italian, nineteenth century. *Oxford, Pitt Rivers Mus., Balfour 124.* Bag of a whole sheepskin. Small and large drones to the rear. Larger chanter with brass key in barrel and screw-off bell.

509   Ciaramella. Italian, nineteenth century. *Brussels, Conserv. royal, 954.* Wood, in one piece. *Length* 47 cm. With reed.

510   Highland bagpipe. Scottish, *c.* 1850. *Ryton-on-Tyne, Cocks Coll.* Presentation set. Three drones in separate stocks.

511   Chanter of bagpipe. Thuringia, Germany, eighteenth century. *Hamburg, Mus. f. Hamburg. Geschichte, 1924.208a.* Wooden bell, brass mounted, the rim decorated with hunting scenes and arms of Saxony.

Into the bag of a bagpipe, which is of a whole animal skin or sewn from leather, are tied two or more tubular wooden sockets termed stocks, which hold the various pipes. These pipes include: the leather-valved blowpipe (Fig 13a) through which the bag is filled with air from the lungs or from bellows strapped to the body and the right arm; the chanter, which is the fingerhole pipe on which the melodies are played; and, though not in every species, the drone (or drones), without fingerholes and sounding a single note continuously. Chanter and drones are provided with reeds, fed by the air expelled from the bag by the pressure of the arm upon it. Drones are normally made in two or three joints connected by long tenons, extendable for tuning the drone note to the chanter. With the various bores, reeds and arrangements of these pipes, bagpipes make a typologically complex group, numbering some 30 distinct European regional kinds (with others in Asia and North Africa) whose historical interrelationships are for the most part quite unknown, even though many similarities between one species and another are recognizable. Only a few can be illustrated here, these being mostly, like the wind instruments in other sections, of the kinds which have been constructed by professional town craftsmen. (For a fuller survey, see W. A. Cocks, 'Bagpipe', *Grove*, 5th edn; also Baines, *Bagpipes*, 1960.)

Cylindrical chanter with double reed. Bagpipes thus provided are led by the French *musette* of which many seventeenth- or eighteenth-century examples have been preserved thanks to the grace of their design and construction resulting from the fashion for the instrument in prosperous circles of those times. The pipes are of ivory (**497**) or ebony, the chanter having seven closed keys of silver and (as in most West European bagpipes) seven holes in front and a thumbhole higher up on the back. The bell is removable. Attached to this chanter is an auxiliary chanter (*petit chalumeau*), flat in shape with a flask-like outline, and with a narrow bore which is blind, not reaching to the bottom. It has no finger-holes, but six closed keys, three on each side, which can be opened by little finger and thumb to give notes above the range of the main chanter; until one of these keys is opened the *petit chalumeau* remains silent. It is said to have been added to the musette by Jean Hotteterre in the mid seventeenth century. The drone is of the 'shuttle' form: an ivory or ebony cylinder is pierced with numerous parallel bores connected to make four separate windways of different tube lengths, each of which is a drone provided with its own double reed inserted into a socket in the top of the shuttle. Each drone vents through a slot in the side and is tuned, or if desired, silenced, by an external slider valve of ivory and leather. Three of these drones were used at a time, the remaining one being a substitute for one of the others when playing in a different key. The bag is sewn from sheepskin and is enclosed in a silk cover.

The Northumbrian and Scottish *Small-pipes* appeared in the late seventeenth century, apparently derived from the musette. In their old forms, chanters resemble the main chanter of the musette, though without keys (**501**). A few early Northumbrian examples even have the shuttle drone. The Scottish Small-pipe was mouth-blown and it kept the simple form of chanter even when it was occasionally made in the mid nineteenth century (e.g. an example by Thos Glen, Edinburgh, in the Pitt Rivers Museum; Baines, Pl. XIII). Towards the end of the eighteenth century the chanter of the bellows-blown Northumbrian Small-pipe was stopped at the bottom, making possible silences between notes (by closing all the fingerholes) and keys were added up to the number of nine (**502**), later sometimes more. There are four separate drone pipes held in a common stock, each sounded by a single reed of the ancient form used everywhere in Europe save in Italy for bagpipe drones, made by cutting a tongue in the side of a short tube of cane. Each drone can be silenced when required by means of a sliding stopper at the bottom, the vent being in the side of the pipe.

Conical chanter with double reed is met on most of the traditional bagpipes of Western Europe, combined with cylindrical drones sounded with single reeds of the kind just noticed. The French *cornemuse* is variable, ranging from small craft-made instruments, often as finely made as a musette though with a simple chanter and plain drone (**498**), to larger, sometimes very large, exclusively peasant varieties often decorated with lead or pewter inlay (**500**). A common French feature is a small drone placed beside the chanter, sharing the same stock, which is flat in shape. The bass drone, if present, is held in a separate stock. The bagpipe of Brittany, belongs on the other hand to a Hispano–Scottish group, being in its traditional form a half-size equivalent of the bagpipe of North-west Spain typified by the *gaita gallega* (**499**). This last has a keyless chanter of boxwood and three-jointed bass drone with bulbous cavity in the bell. The specimen illustrated also has a small treble drone which can be silenced by a wooden stopper. The *Highland bagpipe* of Scotland (**510**) is fundamentally much the same, though the number of drones was increased to three in the eighteenth century, each drone being held in a separate stock. The Scottish *Lowland Pipe* is an indoor variety of the eighteenth and nineteenth centuries (rare after *c.* 1850), with narrower-bore chanter, drones in a common stock, and bellows (**505**).

The bagpipe of Ireland, *Union-pipe* (sometimes in modern times Irished as Uileann pipe), is an eighteenth-century development of an earlier bellows-blown pipe about which little is recorded. The chanter is a long one so that its end can be stopped on the player's knee, both for staccato effects and for making the pipe jump to a higher register. It has keys. Some sets have a double chanter, with the two bores fingered in unison (**503**). The large drone stock holds three narrow-bore drones, the deepest being looped to save length, and also from one to four stopped pipes termed 'regulators', each provided with a row of closed keys. By opening these keys with the wrist of the right hand whilst playing, chords can be sounded in accompaniment to the melody of the chanter. In the second half of the eighteenth century there was one regulator only (**503**). Later and up to today three have been usual. A deep-pitched 'differential' bass regulator of complicated design is fitted to some sets of the second half of the last century (**504**; the working of this regulator is fully described by Bessarabov, p. 91). A Scottish variant of the late eighteenth century has been described by Cocks as a 'hybrid Union pipe'. It resembles the early one-regulator Union pipe but has a keyless chanter with vent-hole, and this cannot be stopped on the knee (**506**).

A once important peasant and popular bagpipe of Northern Europe disappeared by the end of the

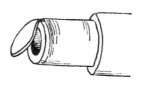

Fig 13a A bagpipe blowpipe, with leather valve

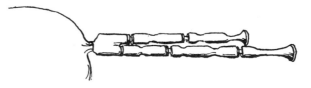

b. Sketch of drones of extinct North European bagpipe

eighteenth century apparently without leaving a single specimen. This is of the kind which is well known in the paintings of Dürer, Breughel, the seventeenth-century Dutch masters and others. The chanter appears to be of a normal conical kind, but a distinguishing feature is the pair of cylindrical drones, one about a third or half the length of the other, mounted together in a common drone stock (Fig 13b).

The Italian bagpipe, *zampogna*, is unique, having a chanter for each hand, the two being played in harmony; the smaller one has four fingerholes, thumbhole, and vent-holes; the larger has three finger-holes and a brass key encased in a perforated wooden barrel as in the old shawms (**508**). The bores have a crudely executed conicity and the flared bells are usually bulbous internally. In the same stock as the chanters are two rather short cylindrical drones of different sizes. All four pipes have double reeds of a characteristically long, narrow shape. Some sets are very large, with the longer chanter measuring *c*. 150 cm and sounding notes as low as the bottom F of the bass voice. The zampogna usually accompanies a small shawm-like pipe named *piffaro* or *ciaramella* (**509**) similar in appearance to the smaller chanter but with seven fingerholes and sometimes a thumbhole. Specimens of this have sometimes been mistaken for early shawms.

Cylindrical chanter with single reed is characteristic of Central and East Europe. The drones are single-reeded as in the West. There are two principal forms with single chanter. One includes the Polish *koza* and Bohemian *dudy* (**507, 511**) and was formerly played in the Slav-populated parts of Germany (sixteenth-century examples formerly at Berlin and Nuremberg). The elaborate up-turned bells of cowhorn and brass are notable features, also the right-angled bass drone which rests on the player's shoulder and hangs down behind, though not all instruments have this. The other is the Bulgarian and Macedonian *gajda*, with a narrow end to the chanter carved from horn in the form of an obtuse angle

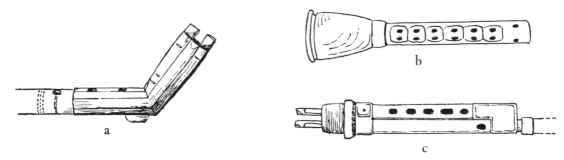

Fig 14 Some East European chanters: a. Bulgarian *gajda*; b. Dalmatian *diple*; c. Hungarian *duda*

with two small terminal prongs (Fig 14a). Among the types with a double chanter having two parallel bores in a single piece of wood, that which prevails in Slovakia, Hungary, Slovenia and Rumania, is distinguished by the single fingerhole in one of the bores (Fig 14c), low down by the bell (which is often a small bell of cowhorn). This one-hole bore, fingered by the lower little finger, supplies an auxiliary drone oscillating on two notes a fourth apart. Bagpipes with no separate drone, and with a double chanter having similar holes in the twin bores (or six in one and two in the other) are of the *diple* type from Dalmatia and Bosnia (Fig 14b). The wood is usually dished at each pair of holes.

Conical chanter with single reed is, as also with the bagless woodwind, the rarest combination, exemplified by a Bulgarian variety (Baines, 89).

4 Crumhorn, Racket, etc

Bagless instruments with cylindrical bore and double reed are now extinct in the West, though through the sixteenth and seventeenth centuries they were represented by a number of species which for convenience may be dealt with together.

Illustrations: Crumhorn, etc

512 Six crumhorns. German, sixteenth or early seventeenth century. *Berlin, Instit. f. Musikforschung, 668–673.* Boxwood. From left to right: bass with one brass key, tenor, descant, two trebles, tenor. *Heights* 81, 61·5, 33·5, 38, 40, 58 cm.

513 Set of six crumhorns in original case. Italian, second half of sixteenth century. *Brussels, Conserv. royal, 610–615.* Said to have been made for Duke Alfonso II of Este (reigned 1559–97). Boxwood. From top to bottom, 615, bass with two brass keys and two sliders; 614, bass with one key; 613, tenor; 612, tenor; 611, treble; 610, tenor. All with single plume mark. Wooden case lined with black, white and pink striped cloth and with four lidded compartments.

514 Bass tartöld. German, sixteenth century. *Vienna, Kunsthist. Mus., A.223.* One of a set of five (bass, two tenors, two trebles). Dragon-shaped casing of brass painted green, red and gold, with open jaws containing swaying iron tongue. The detachable coiled crook (the dragon's tail) with 50 cm of tube leads to a long coil of 160 cm of cylindrical brass tube of width 1·5 cm, with seven holes leading to the outside of the case and a thumbhole similarly.

515, 516 Great bass sordone (*Sordun*). ? Italian, sixteenth century. *Vienna, Kunsthist. Mus., A.229.* Boxwood column containing two parallel cylindrical bores of diameter *c.* 1 cm connected by a cross bore at the base. Removable wooden cap at each end of the column. Six holes and thumbhole. Six brass keys with fishtailed touches, mounted in wooden casings. *Height* 114·5 cm.

517 Racket. Tyrol, *c.* 1650. *Leipzig, K.-M.-Univ. 1414.* With arms of Carl von Schurf, Tyrol (b. 1613). Ivory solid cylinder 18 cm high, drilled with nine parallel bores interconnected. Eleven fingerholes and six others. With ivory pirouette.

518 Racket. W. Wyne, Nymegen, Holland, *c.* 1700. *Berlin, Instit. f. Musikforschung, 64.* Boxwood body, height 21 cm, diam 11 cm, containing brass pipes. Coiled crook and small bassoon-like bell.

519 Bass crumhorn: the largest of those in **513**. *Brussels, Conserv. royal, 615.*

520 Crumhorn (?). Said to be Italian. *Brussels, Conserv. royal, 1970.* Leather covered.

521, 522 Tenor Rauschpfeife. German, late sixteenth or early seventeenth century. *Berlin, Instit. f. Musikforschung, 666.* Marked *HC.* Maple with conical bore. *Total length* 53·5 cm.

523 Great-bass capped shawm (*Rauschpfeife?*). Sixteenth century. *Prague, Nat. Mus.* Cap missing. Six holes and thumbhole. Brass key. *Length c.* 112 cm.

Crumhorn

A technical compromise between on the one hand taking the reed directly in the lips and, on the other, feeding it from an inflated bag (bagpipe), is to enclose the reed in a cap with a hole at the top for blowing into as in a recorder. Passing over primitive forms of reed cap found among hornpipes, a professionally turned and exactly fitted wooden cap appears towards the end of the fifteenth century in the crumhorn, a hook-shaped pipe with a narrow cylindrical bore from about 0·38–0·85 cm in diameter according to the pitch and size of the instrument, and gently evased to an oval orifice at the upturned end (**512, 513**). In all but two of the 35 or so surviving crumhorns (from which various replicas have been built) the bore is pierced throughout the boxwood pipe which is afterwards bent round with the aid of heat. In one of the sixteenth-century specimens at Vienna (A.214), however, the curved part is a separate joint which was first bent in a sharp U, then cut with a blind bore down each leg of the U; the bottoms of these two drillings are connected by a transverse drilling straight through the base of the U, its openings to the exterior being closed by removable wooden plugs. An example in the Morley-Pegge Collection obtained in Paris has a body of softer wood than the customary boxwood, shaped in two longitudinal halves glued together and covered with leather.

Into the top of the bore of a crumhorn is placed a short brass tube or 'staple', carrying a double reed the size of a bassoon reed or larger. The instrument is completed by a long boxwood cap which covers the reed and has a hole in the top for blowing into, exactly as in the *Rauschpfeife* illustrated (**522**). To hold the cap well, the body is fitted with a separate turned moulding and tenon which in certain specimens has been lost. For lengths of bore the splendid Brussels set (**513**) may be referred to: (without the brass staple) treble, approx 39·5 cm, tenor (of which the set contains three) 58·5 cm; one-key bass 81·3 cm; two-key bass with sliders 92 cm (**519**). A unique great bass crumhorn is in the Prague Collection. The crumhorn holes are seven plus a thumbhole as in the recorder, though considerably smaller, and there is a vent hole further down save in the case of the bass with sliders. The latter are situated at two points along the inside of the curve. Each is a narrow rectangular brass plate with a length of *c.* 2 cm, lying flush with the surface of the pipe in a recess cut for it and kept in place by a brass bridge (Fig 15). By its attached knob the plate may be slid along the recess to uncover a hole in the pipe. The setting of the two sliders determines the lowest note of the instrument as obtained by closing both keys.

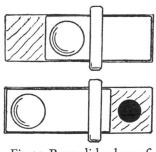

Fig 15 Brass slider key of crumhorn

Throughout the sixteenth century and the first third of the next, a set of crumhorns provided a pleasant consort of easily-maintained reed instruments with a cheerful nasal tone but restricted in compass, since the crumhorn, like most bagpipes, has no upper register. It is associated mainly with Germany and Italy, the commonest Italian name having apparently been *cornamusa*.[1] A small mystery is the occurrence of a French name *cromorne* in documents relating to the Grand Écurie of Louis XIV in the latter part of the seventeenth century, mentioned here because this French term has been identified by some

[1] Doubt over the interpretation of this word in sixteenth-century Italian usage seems removed by a list of an outfit of instruments recommended to Pier Luigi Farnese for the court of Parma in 1546:

Primo di trombetta a tute le sorte che si possa sonare trombeta

Poi in musica di tromboni sei

Poi di pifari sei

Poi di corneti sei

Poi di cornemuse sei

Poi di flauti sei

Poi di pifari ala alemana sei

Poi de viole de brazo sei. (N. Pelicelli, 'Musicisti in Parma nei secoli xv–xvi', *Note D'Archivio per la storia musicale*, Rome, IX, 42.) The translation of the terms following the *tromboni* must be shawms, cornetts, crumhorns, recorders, flutes, violins. A Verona inventory of three years earlier (Turrini, 26) lists the crumhorns under the other Italian name *piva* and the four preserved at Verona are probably the remains of this set of five.

authorities with an uncouth species of leather-covered hook-shaped instrument of which several collections possess a specimen (**520**). The tube is *c.* 6 cm thick, with wide and more or less cylindrical bore. The holes are cut down one side, with the seventh hole in line with the others but duplicated to one side— as in a figure in Diderot from which perhaps the species originated. There is no thumbhole. The intended nature of the sounding apparatus inserted into the domed top end is uncertain.

Straight Pipes with Reed Cap

An ill-lit corner in the picture of sixteenth-century reed instruments is that which is occupied by further capped instruments made in consorts but lacking both the distinctive form of the crumhorn and contemporary description precise enough to clarify their typology and nomenclature. Such instruments include *Rauschpfeifen*, named as such in a 'Burgundian band' in Burgkmair's 'Maximilian's Triumphs' of 1512; *Schreierpfeifen*, named from 1541 and rather inadequately described by Praetorius; and other kinds, likewise chiefly in German sources. The main question is whether their bores, or their respective bores, were cylindrical or conical. Only the latter is known among surviving consort pipes of the period with straight build and played with reed caps. These include a set of six at Berlin (**521, 522**) and a longer set at Prague (**523**). They expand gently rather like a *cornemuse* (French bagpipe) chanter and have a thumbhole as in those chanters and in the crumhorn, suggesting a nine-note compass without overblow. Their overall lengths range from 42 cm, the smallest of the Berlin set, to 129·5 cm, the largest of those at Prague as it is now restored with a cap. Curt Sachs provisionally labelled the Berlin instruments, which were obtained from the Wenzelskirche, Naumberg, *Rauschpfeifen*. It also became fairly common practice from the seventeenth century onwards to fit a cap to a bagpipe chanter for playing it without the bag. The French *hautbois de Poitou* described by Mersenne is one example and the bagpipe practice chanter used today in Scotland and Spain (Galicia) makes another, while the crumhorn and *Rauschpfeife* may have themselves originated through this practice.

Racket, Sordone

The *racket*[1] contains a number of short parallel bores connected in series to make up a total windway of a metre or more, providing a deep compass in a compact fashion. Of the early form, of the last quarter of the sixteenth century onwards, three authentic specimens survive (**517**, at Leipzig, and a pair at Vienna). The bores here are made in a solid ivory cylinder 12–18 cm long, like the shuttle drone of a musette. The cross cavities through which the end of one bore connects with the end of the next are closed with wooden inserts. Fingerholes open to the side of the cylinder to be manipulated by the two hands, which are held level with each other, and the last bore, with terminal orifice at the bottom, has vent-holes for tuning the bottom note. At the top a metal tube carries a bassoon-like reed partially enclosed by an ivory pirouette. An early mention of the instrument is in the 1577 inventory of the Graz music room of the Archduke Karl of Styria (Schlosser; p. 19), and a coloured illustration in the Hans Mielich Codex (Munich, Staatsbibl. Mus., MS A., Bd. 2, p. 187) shows a racket being played in the Bavarian *Hofkapelle* directed by Orlando Lassus some years earlier.

[1] Curt Sachs held that name should correctly be *Ranket*, from an old German adjective meaning 'to and fro'. The shape of the instrument, however, compared with illustrations in contemporary works on pyrotechnics, suggests that the instrument was named after a rocket (*Raquete*).

From towards the end of the seventeenth century and into the beginning of the eighteenth further rackets were built, apparently as curiosities and including examples by known woodwind makers like J. C. Denner (Vienna Coll.) and W. Wyne (**518**). In these the windway is composed of interconnected brass tubes enclosed in a hollow wooden cylinder. The exit point is in the centre of the top, with a miniature bassoon-like bell. The entry, reached by a coiled brass crook, is near the edge of the top. A large specimen at Paris (C.497) with cylinder 30 cm long, is marked ROZET and has three brass keys.

Tartöld. The 1596 inventory of the music room of the Archduke Ferdinand at Schloss Ambras contains an entry *In ainem fueteral 5 tartöld, wie drackhen geformiert* (Schlosser, 11). The actual instruments are preserved with the case at Vienna (A. 219–223) and are unique. The brass tube makes one continuous coil, enclosed within a painted brass sheath representing a dragon (**514**). The looped brass crook would have carried a double reed similar to that of a racket. Schlosser suggests that the name may be the word *Kortholt*, a German equivalent of the French *courtaut* (below), influenced by the Italian *torto*.

Sordun (or Italian *sordone*). Another instrument of which unique examples, numbering four, come from Schloss Ambras and are preserved at Vienna (A. 226–229). One of these is shown (**515, 516**). The instrument is described by Praetorius, who shows a less elaborately constructed form of it, and something similar to it is described by Mersenne under the name *courtaut*. The narrow cylindrical windway runs down and up inside a wooden column. The double reed is affixed to a brass crook (missing in the Vienna specimens) inserted into the side towards the top, and the terminal orifice is likewise near the top, on the opposite side. Like the racket the sordone seems to have been played mainly in small ensembles of mixed instruments. So sometimes was the crumhorn. It is interesting to note that remote and quaint as these Renaissance cylindrical-bore double-reed instruments may now appear, modern musicians engaged in reviving music from the late fifteenth century to the late sixteenth have found a genuine need for instruments of these kinds, for blending with instruments of better-known types.

5 Shawms, Oboes, Bassoons

In this major series of double-reed instruments the reed is carried on a conical metal tube which is inserted into the narrow end of the conical bore of the instrument (though this bore rarely has the lines of a true cone before designs of the modern era). The metal tube is generally termed a 'staple' if short, or if long a 'crook', this last being usually curved or coiled. For the oboe—and also for bagpipes which employ a double reed—the shaped and folded strip of cane forming the twin blades of the reed is bound to a short staple *c.* 2–4 cm long, which is then wound with thread or lapped with cork for insertion into the socket in the top end of the instrument. The fold of the cane is cut through to separate the tips of the blades, which remain tied to their staple until worn out and replaced with fresh cane. With shawms and bassoons the preparation of the reed is similar save that the cane is bound over a temporary mandrel which reproduces the form of the tip of the separate staple or crook belonging to the instrument. With shawms a characteristic feature is the round wooden *pirouette* (Fig 16, a, b) which is placed on the staple—in some cases permanently secured to it—the reed being placed above it. The player's lips are rested lightly against the surface of the pirouette for the sake of strong blowing, with the most free vibration of the reed that is possible without losing lip control over the pitch—the first requisite of the shawm, an open-air band instrument, being great volume of sound. An English word for pirouette is 'flue', given in the Talbot manuscript, but the French word (from Mersenne) is generally accepted. In old specimens of shawms, bassoons, etc, original staples or crooks are usually missing and the older museum replacements tend to be inappropriate.

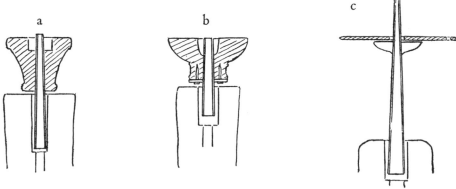

Fig 16 a and b. Treble shawm pirouettes (a. reconstruction by Mahillon; b. with **526**). c. Corresponding Asiatic and North African assembly

Shawms

The European shawm[1] is a thirteenth-century importation from Arab military and open-air music. A close resemblance in many particulars between sixteenth- or early seventeenth-century Western shawms

[1] The word 'shawm' is a Jacobean form of the older English 'shalmele', 'shalmuse', etc (from French *chalemelle*, *chalumeaux*). The German word is *Schalmey* and the Italian *piffaro*. The French equivalent from the sixteenth century, *hautbois*, later passed to the oboe; Italian (and later English) *oboe* and pre-nineteenth-century English 'hoboy' are phonetic derivatives of the French. The other German name *Pommer*, commonly used to denote the larger shawms, from tenor upwards, derives from fifteenth-century French *bombarde* (German *pumhart*, etc), the original name of the tenor shawm.

and Arab and Turkish shawms made up to the present day indicates how little the former can have changed since they first arrived to lead European band music; but some of the differences should be pointed out as a precaution against misidentification of a recent oriental shawm (or Balkan *zurla*, which is similar) for an ancient European treble shawm. In the first place the Eastern instruments have a thumb-hole intermediate in location between the highest two fingerholes; the true Western shawm has no thumbhole. Secondly the tube is usually bored almost cylindrically, while a removable two-pronged component lines and narrows the upper part of the bore—though an Indian species has an expanding bore throughout as in the West. Thirdly, the oriental reed is placed on a conical metal staple 5 cm or more long, and to this is soldered a wide metal disc, or else a round metal plate for supporting a loose disc of bone, etc (Fig 16c), against which the oriental player rests the lips; in the West this is replaced by the wooden pirouette already mentioned.

Illustrations: Shawms

524   Tenor shawm (*Altpommer*). German, sixteenth century. *Berlin, Instit. f. Musikforschung, 646.* Boxwood, in one piece. One brass key in barrel. *Length* 75 cm.

525   Treble shawm. ? Spanish, sixteenth century. *Brussels, Conserv. royal, 2324.* Marked *Melchor/R.S.* with crown. Boxwood, in one piece. Four vent holes. Pirouette is a restoration. *Length* 66 cm.

526   Treble shawm. ? Catalan, seventeenth-eighteenth century, *Barcelona, Mus. de Musica, 608.* Carved on bell a shield over crossed keys and crooks. Boxwood, in one piece. One vent-hole. *Length* 64 cm. With original boxwood pirouette, width 4·3 cm, length 2·3 cm, nailed to round brass plate which is soldered to the brass staple (Fig 16b).

527, 528   Tenor shawm. Close view of **524** showing barrel removed and in position.

529   Bass shawm. German, seventeenth century. *Brussels, Conserv. royal, 986.* Marked *G. Strehl.* Dark-stained maple. In two joints, the upper being 48·5 cm long with 5 cm long tenon. Four brass keys. *Length* 210·5 cm.

530–4   Five shawms. German, sixteenth–seventeenth century. *Berlin, Instit. f. Musikforschung, from left to right,* 646, 290, 643, 642, 289. From the Wenzelskirche, Naumberg (Prussia), save for 289 and 290 which are from the Marienkirche, Danzig. From left to right: Tenor shawm (*Altpommer*), one key, *length* 75 cm; Tenor shawm (*Altpommer*), four keys *length* 92 cm; Basset shawm (*Tenorpommer*), marked *CR* with trefoil, four keys, *length* 130·5 cm; Great-bass shawm (*Grossbass Pommer*), four keys, covered fourth hole, *length* 271·5 cm; Bass shawm (*Basspommer*), marked *CR* with trefoil, in two joints, four keys, *length* 185·5 cm. Crooks missing in *532, 534.*

535   Treble shawm. R. Haka, Amsterdam, late seventeenth century. *Amsterdam, Rijksmuseum.* Brass mounted. No key. *Length* 62·3 cm. (Barrel removed to show vent-hole beneath.)

536   Tenor shawm. German, late seventeenth century. *Leipzig, K.-M.-Univ., 1305.* One key.

537   Tenor shawm. German, late seventeenth century. *Salzburg, Mus. Carolino Augusteum, 248.* Plum, brass mounted. No key. Long pirouette. *Length* 75 cm.

538   Treble shawm. J. Denner, Nuremberg, c. 1700. *Frankfurt, Hist. Mus., 437; Epstein 136.* Two joints. One key on rings. *Length* 57 cm.

539   Shawm or oboe. French (?), late seventeenth century or later. *Brussels, Conserv. royal, 972.* Box, in three joints. One brass key and two sets of vent-holes in bell. *Length* 62·5 cm. *Bore* at tenons approx. 1·5, 2.8 cm.

540   Shawm or oboe. R. Haka, Amsterdam, late seventeenth century. *Amsterdam, Rijksmuseum, 11430.81.* Ebony, in three joints, silver mounted. One silver key. No vent-holes. Thumbhole, higher than first fingerhole. Recessed top end, with remains of a brass staple which is probably not original. *Length* 52·5 cm. *Bore* at tenons, approx. 1·4, 2·3 cm. (Upper joint turned in photograph.)

541   Basse de musette. Swiss, eighteenth century. *Berne, Hist. Mus.* Stamped on key touch *I.IR.* Maple, in three joints. One brass key and four covered holes on rings and blocks. Coiled brass crook with wooden pirouette. *Length* without crook 104 cm.

542   Tenor shawm (*tenora*). ? Barcelona, second half of nineteenth century. *Barcelona, Mus. de Musica, 63.* Once owned by Pep Ventura. Box, in three joints, brass mounted. Brass bell. Brass keys. Pirouette absent. *Length c. 85* cm.

543   Musette (*bombarde*). French, eighteenth or nineteenth century. *Paris, Conserv., E.1180, C.1110.* Boxwood. Key in barrel. Thumbhole.

544   Musette (*Schalmei*). L. Walch, Berchtesgaden, mid nineteenth century. *Salzburg, Mus. Carolino Augusteum, 251.* Cherry, in two joints. No key. Six holes. *Length 51* cm.

545   Musette (*dulzaina*). Probably French, late nineteenth century. *Barcelona, Mus. de Musica, 786.* From Salamanca Province, Spain. Box. Eight brass keys.

546   Eunuch flute. French, c. 1800. *Oxford, Pitt Rivers Mus., Balfour dd.1939, 469.* Wood.

547   Treble shawm (*tiple*). Catroi, Barcelona, late nineteenth century. *Barcelona, Mus. de Musica, 379.* Jinjolero wood, in three joints with bone mounts. Brass keys. Wooden pirouette. *Length c. 58·5* cm.

A set of shawms from *c.* 1540, when the bass had come into use, to the decline of the shawm band in the last quarter of the seventeenth century, could include instruments from treble to great bass (**530–4**); a smaller size was known in Germany but was unimportant. The treble is normally keyless (**525**) with four vent-holes near the bell. Some specimens have a fishtailed open key enclosed in a removable barrel, though this is more characteristic of the tenor (in German nomenclature *Alt*, **524**). Basses and some tenors have two keys in front with overlapping touches for the little finger, and two keys behind for the lower thumb, with plain touches. The great bass was built in two joints and may have one or more covered holes. Some ordinary basses are also in two joints (**529**), and all the large sizes were provided with brass crooks. With a crook the pirouette was generally dispensed with, though Praetorious shows a pirouette fitted onto the right-angled crook of the basset shawm (German *basset* or *tenor*, **532**). A striking feature of these older shawms is the thickness of the wood, especially at the top end; in the treble shawm the outside diameter of the pipe near the top end may be 3 cm, though the bore inside is but little wider than that of an early oboe. At the bottom end the pipe flares out much as in a trumpet. A late treble of the early pattern is by J. C. Denner (Frankfurt Museum), inscribed with the name of a Frankfurt town bandsman.

By the end of the seventeenth century a lighter type of shawm built in two joints (**535–7**) appeared in the Netherlands and Germany. Talbot, who gives valuable particulars of shawms at this period, names it *Deutsche Schalmey* (the old type being called by him 'English hautbois or waits'—the latter term from its use by town bands and the former in distinction from the 'French hautbois', i.e. oboe). This late shawm was apparently made for military music reflecting the recent development of the French military band of oboes. Makers include Haka (d. 1709) of Amsterdam, and Schlegel, Basel. There is often no key but merely a vent-hole (**535**) under the elegant barrel, though the tenor generally has one key; a Haka tenor (Rijksmuseum) has oboe-like turnery at the top. There are also some small specimens down to 46 cm in length. Again a pirouette was used (**537**), and the trumpet-like bell flare generally has a scalloped brass rim, sometimes found also on the earlier shawms.

Some unusual instruments appear to show an increasingly strong influence of oboe-making upon the shawm in its last days in Northern Europe. A two-jointed treble by the younger Denner (**538**) has the key mounted on rings in oboe style, though the body is of the ancient thick-walled kind; like the Denner shawm mentioned above, this was once owned by a civil bandsman. A curious, barely placeable instrument by Haka (**540**) in three joints has the top joint modelled in the same style as an oboe by Rijkel, also of Amsterdam, *c.* 1695 (illustrated in Bate, *The Oboe*, Plate II); the linear dimensions are oboe-like but the bore is wide, while the thumbhole is a most peculiar feature (possibly for some reason added later). Another wide-bore one-keyed specimen (**539**) is unsigned. It may be an early type of oboe, though more likely a well-made French 'folk oboe' of later date, similar to rustic versions of the classic French oboe which were still played for dancing recently in the Ariége district, and of which an interesting example is exhibited in the Museum at Arles.

The shawm lasted as a folk instrument in parts of Bohemia and Hungary into the nineteenth century and is still met in a debased form on the Adriatic island of Krk. The true band shawm survives uniquely in the sardana bands of Catalonia and of Roussillon (France), made in two sizes known as *tiple* ('treble') and *tenora*—the accompanying noun *chirimia* (Spanish for 'shawm') having passed out of use. With the development of these bands by Pep Ventura (b. 1818) keywork of a simple French oboe type was added to the formerly keyless instruments (**526**) and the tenor was lengthened by a brass bell (**542**). The tiple is pitched in F (**547**) and the tenora a fifth lower. Their approximate lengths excluding pirouettes are 58–60 and 84–88 cm respectively. A prominent folk instrument of North-central Spain is the *dulzaina* (or *pito*), which is properly a small wide-bore instrument of local design, with wide metal staple upon which a double reed in placed without pirouette. The bell is scarcely flared and there is simple keywork (illustrated in the hands of a player in Baines, *Woodwind Instruments*, Pl. XVIII). The present illustration (**545**) is of an instrument which has often done duty for the dulzaina, namely the pipe which French manufacturers have made since about the middle of the last century under the name *musette*, historically the separated chanter of the former bagpipe of the same name. It is made in box or blackwood, often with the bell slightly bulbous and with one or more keys. Some of the earlier examples have a reed cap. A genuine folk species, *bombarde*, has been preserved in Brittany to accompany the local bagpipe. Often it used to be prettily made in boxwood, with separate bell, a key enclosed in a barrel (in the Vannes variety), and in some instances a thumbhole (**543**). In Germany small instruments described as *Schalmei*, roughly corresponding to the French commercial musette, have been manufactured through the nineteenth century up to modern times, with or without a key (**544**), now as a plaything, though formerly no doubt for sale as a folk instrument.

Basse de musette. This large and distinctive instrument (**541**) was built in Switzerland in the eighteenth century, apparently for use in churches. The name has been coined by historians in the lack of knowledge of the correct native description, though examples of the instrument are not uncommon in collections. Most have the unexplained mark *I.IR* on the key touch; in one instance (Basel, Hist. Mus., 77, from a nearby monastery) *D.H. I.IR. 1777*. The jointed body has wide conical bore and four of the six large, widely spaced fingerholes are covered by open keys. The reed is placed on a coiled brass crook, and among six examples at Berne, several have a wooden pirouette, as shown.

The **Eunuch flute** may be interpolated here (**546**), being a kind of mock shawm and sometimes mistaken for a true wind instrument. It is merely a thing for humming tunes into, with a membrane (e.g. onion skin) for adding a buzzing quality. The membrane is attached over the upper end of the tube (which is often of brass or iron) inside the perforated bulb, and the mouth is applied to the hole in the pipe below the bulb (Mersenne).

Oboes

The oboe differs from the treble shawm principally in the relative narrowness of its dimensions and consequent refinement of the sound. The fingerholes are narrower, especially those for the upper hand, and so is the reed, which is made on its own staple, like the double reed of a bagpipe and blown without pirouette. It was most likely introduced in France shortly before 1660, probably by Jean Hotteterre and his associate musicians and makers of the *Grand Écurie* (see Joseph Marx, *GSJ*, IV, 1951). The oboe quickly reached other countries and before the end of the century had become the leading reed instrument of cultivated music, chamber, orchestral and military band.

Illustrations: Oboes, Cors anglais, etc

548 Oboe. ? Dutch, late seventeenth century. *London, Victoria and Albert Mus., 808–1869.* The original maker's name barely visible, partly erased and overstamped *W. Beukers* (early eighteenth century). Ivory mounted and carved in relief with foliage patterns and, on the bell, two scenes of musicians and dancers (see Halfpenny, *GSJ*, X, 1957). Three keys. *Length* 57 cm.

549 Oboe. H. Richters, ? Dutch, *c.* 1700. *Washington, Lib. of Congress, Dayton Miller 158.* Ebony, with engraved ivory mounts. Three silver keys. *Length* 56·8 cm. *Bore* at lower tenon 1·65 cm.

550 Oboe. Nicholas Hotteterre, Paris, last quarter of seventeenth century. *Brussels, Conserv. royal, 2320.* The bell is an early eighteenth-century replacement marked *Debey*. Boxwood. Three keys.

551 Oboe. Thos. Stanesby (senior), London, early eighteenth century. *London, Horniman Mus., Carse 232.* Stained boxwood, ivory mounted. Three keys. *Length* 59·5 cm.

552 Oboe. Kusder, London, *c.* 1760–80. *London, Horniman Mus., Carse 258.* Straight topped model. Stained box, ivory mounted. Two keys. *Length* 58·5 cm.

553 Oboe. Cahusac, London, late eighteenth century. *London, Kneller Hall, 56.* Box, ivory mounted. Two keys.

554 Oboe. J. G. Liebel, Adorf (Germany), 1798. *Washington, Lib. of Congress, Dayton Miller 42.* Box. Three brass keys. Two alternative top joints. *Length* 56–57·5 cm.

555 Oboe d'amore. P. Wolraupier, first half of eighteenth century. *Brussels, Conserv. royal, 970.* Box, horn mounted. Bulbous bell. Three brass keys. *Length* 61 cm.

556 Oboe d'amore (*grand hautbois*). Bizey, Paris, mid eighteenth century. *Boston, Mus. of Fine Arts, 138.* Box, ivory mounted. Bell with internal flange. Brass crook. Two silver keys. *Length* 61·7 cm.

557 Great bass oboe in F. French, second half of eighteenth century. *New York, Metropolitan Mus. of Art 2351.* Stained wood. Two square keys. Brass crook. *Length* 180 cm.

558 Pair of oboi da caccia. ? Italian, first half of eighteenth century. *Bologna, Museo Civico.* Wood painted light brown, with turned upper end, the rest shaped octagonally. Separate bell, flared, without internal flange and with two vent-holes. Three brass keys, the C key round, the E flat keys wedge-shaped. Brass crook possibly original. *Tube length* without crook 80·5 cm.

559 Oboe da caccia or cor anglais. J. G. Bauer, Vienna, mid eighteenth century. *Berlin, Instit. f. Musikforschung, 581.* Octagonally shaped body made in two longitudinal halves and leather covered. Flared bell. Two keys.

560 Cor anglais. Bimboni, Florence, second half of eighteenth century. *Author's collection.* Two boxwood joints bent after boring and covered with black leather with gilt tooling. Horn mounts. Bulbous bell with two vent-holes. Two brass keys on blocks. Crook missing. *Tube length* 75 cm.

561 Tenor oboe. J. C. Denner, Nuremberg, *c.* 1700. *Leipzig, K.-M.-Univ., 1547.* Two square keys. *Length* 80 cm. Crook missing.

562 Tenor oboe. Martin Lot, Paris, second half of eighteenth century. *London, R. Coll. of Music, 76.* Box, ivory mounted. Bulbous bell with one vent-hole. Three keys, the C key round, the E flat keys square. Curved crook. *Length* without crook 81 cm.

563 Tenor oboe. T. Collier, London, *c.* 1770. *Glasgow, Art Gallery and Museums.* Stained box, ivory mounted, in two joints. Narrow bell. Two square brass keys. Angular crook. *Length* without crook 76 cm.

564 Bass oboe in C. J. C. Denner, Nuremberg, *c.* 1700. *Nuremberg, German. Nationalmus., MI.94.* Two keys. *Length* 98·5 cm. Crook missing.

565 Oboe. Delusse, Paris, *c.* 1810–20. *London, Bate Coll.* Cedar. Four silver keys, including F sharp and low B. *Length* 57 cm.

566 Oboe. W. Milhouse, London, *c.* 1820. *London, Bate Coll.* Box, ivory mounted. Two silver keys, also a long C sharp key for left little finger stamped *W. Parke Inventor.* *Length* 57 cm.

567 Oboe. Goodlad & Co., London, *c.* 1830. *London, Kneller Hall, 61.* Ebony, ivory mounted. Bell with internal flange. Eight silver keys on blocks and rings.

568, 569 Oboe. H. Grenser, Dresden, possibly pre-1813. *Geneva, Mus. d'Art et d'Histoire.* Box, ivory mounted. Two extra top joints. Nine keys (square except for the octave key). Low B key missing.

570 Oboe. Uhlmann, Vienna, *c.* 1840. *London, Bate Coll.* Box, mounted with nickel-silver. Extendable top socket for tuning. Sixteen keys on blocks and rings. *Length* 55 cm.

571 Oboe. G. Triébert, Paris, *c.* 1830. *Cobham, Morley-Pegge Coll.* Stained box, ivory mounted. Nine flat keys, to low B, most mounted on saddles. *Length* 56 cm.

572 Oboe. Tabard, Lyons, *c.* 1840. *Luton Mus., O/5.* Brod model. Twelve keys on pillars, to low B flat.

573 Oboe. L. A. Buffet, Paris, *c.* 1850. *London, Bate Coll.* 'Boehm system'. Rosewood and nickel-silver. *Length* 54 cm.

574 Oboe. A. Morton, London, *c.* 1872. *London, Bate Coll.* 'Military model' with thumb-plate action. Blackwood. *Length* 54 cm.

575 Oboe. F. Triébert, Paris, *c.* 1870. *London, Bate Coll.* Blackwood. Full Barret system of 1862. *Length* 57 cm.

576 Oboe. Meyer, Hanover, *c.* 1870. *London, Bate Coll.* Blackwood. Fifteen keys. *Length* 57·5 cm.

577 Cor anglais. Grundmann, Dresden, 1791. *Liverpool, Rushworth & Dreaper Coll.* Angular form. Box, in four joints including horn-mounted knee-joint. Bell with bulbous internal shape and one vent-hole. Two brass keys. Brass crook.

578 Cor anglais. C. Golde, Dresden, *c.* 1840. *London, R. Coll. of Music, 82.* Curved form. The two curved joints covered with leather and ivory mounted. Bulbous bell. Eleven round brass keys on brass saddles. Lowest note C. Crook not original.

579 Cor anglais. Stephan Koch, Vienna, *c.* 1820. *Leipzig, K.-M.-Univ., 1349.* Angular form. Eleven round brass keys on blocks, to low B.

580 Bass oboe (*hautbois baryton*). G. Triébert, Paris, 1825. *London, R. Coll. of Music. 79.* Box, ivory mounted. Seven keys on pillars. Butt joint and raised bell.

581 Bass oboe. Unsigned, ? Paris, late nineteenth century. *London, Horniman Mus., Carse 303.* Cocus, Nickel-silver keys (to low B). Upturned bell. *Length* without crook 101 cm.

582 Cor anglais. G. Triébert, Paris, *c.* 1830. *Cobham, Morley-Pegge Coll.* Partly curved form. Curved leather-covered top joint leads to a short ivory-mounted straight connecting joint, and thence to straight lower joint. Ten brass keys on blocks.

583 Cor anglais. Henry Brod, Paris, pre-1839. *London, Bate Coll.* 'Cor anglais moderne'. Cocus, with nickel-silver keys on pillars. *Length* without crook *c.* 81 cm.

584 Bass oboe. Charles Bizey, Paris, pre-1750. *Paris, Conserv., C.494.* Lower joint connected to a butt from which rises a flared bell lying against the back of the instrument. Raised fingerholes. Two brass keys. Brass crook. *Height* 83 cm.

An oboe normally consists of three joints, top, lower and bell. Average bore dimensions are 0·5 cm or less where the conical bore begins at the bottom of the reed socket, 1·1 cm at the tenon in the middle and 1·6 cm at the lower tenon. Usually in the earlier instruments, and also in some of the nineteenth century, the bore dimensions at the upper end of lower joint and bell are slightly greater than those of the respective tenon ends, giving a stepped profile; and the bell ends with an internal flange. Some early oboes are richly ornamented (**548, 549**). The nationality of the maker of the second of these two examples is unknown, though the concentration of his oboes in Dutch collections points to Holland. Up to *c.* 1750, at the height of its period as the unchallenged leader of the woodwind, and in some cases later, the oboe carried duplicate closed keys for E flat, one placed on either side of the fishtailed open key for C. A French instrument by one of the Hotteterre family (**550**) and an English by the elder Stanesby (**551**) show the earlier form of top-end baluster. The twin third hole is for a low register G sharp by uncovering one of the holes, and the twin fourth hole similarly gives a better-tuned low F sharp than the normal cross-fingering. A later model with straight-topped top joint (**552**) is peculiar to England through the second half of the eighteenth century and its bell may lack the internal flange. By this time the classic model with onion-shaped baluster was coming in in Germany and France and began to replace the straight-topped model in England in the last quarter of the century (**553, 554**; for the succession of early oboe types in England, see Halfpenny, *GSJ*, II, 1949). Provision of alternative top joints for tuning dates mainly from *c.* 1790–1820, but is less common with oboes than with flutes. Old cases for oboes are rare, the instrument having generally been carried about in a wash-leather bag. The *oboe d'amore* is an eighteenth-century German variety pitched in A (the ordinary oboe being a minor third higher) built from *c.* 1720 to *c.* 1774—a specimen by Grundmann of Dresden bearing this last date (Berlin, 2957). A short brass crook, slightly curved, is inserted into the top end of the body, which is but little longer than that of an oboe and has a bulbous bell (**555**). A prominent maker was J. H. Eichentopf, by whom both three-key (duplicated closed key) and two-key examples survive. Eichentopf, who made wind instruments of most kinds, was a Leipzig contemporary of J. S. Bach, whose obbligati for the oboe d'amore have warranted the instrument's revival in modern times. A unique French instrument with plain bell (**556**) corresponds with the oboe d'amore in pitch and was perhaps inspired by it.

Nineteenth-century oboes. Towards the end of the eighteenth century additional keywork was fitted by the Dresden makers Grundmann and Grenser in some of their oboes, though it was not generally found to be needed at that time. Even up to *c.* 1820 the additions by most makers are restricted (**565, 566**). A Grenser oboe with nine keys (**568**), if made by the firm before the death of Heinrich Grenser in 1813, is well in advance in this respect. Further progress of the oboe in Germany and Austria is illustrated by **570** and **576**, Meyer's including the brille or 'spectacle' key comprising two rings on the lower joint for correction of the tuning of F sharp—a device taken from earlier French designs of *c.* 1840. A typical English oboe before the mid-century importation of French models also retains classical features and even still has C as its lowest note (**567**). The central evolution of the modern oboe took place in France, mainly in the Triébert workshop in Paris. Guillaume Triébert came to Paris from Hesse, Germany, as an apprentice in 1804. He set up on his own in 1810 and died in 1848, succeeded by his son Frédéric (d. 1878), whose creative work was continued by François Lorée while the firm itself passed to Gautrot (bought up in 1884 by Couesnon). Oboes by the elder Triébert are not radically different from contemporary German instruments as regards keywork, though the build and finish are exceptionally fine (**571**). An important influence on the future Triébert work was that of Henri Brod (d. 1839), who used pillar mounts and took the compass down to B flat—more, probably, for the good acoustic effect of the lengthened bell than for the sake of this actual note (**572**). By 1840 the Triéberts had adopted pillars, re-designed the key touches, and added the brille and the 'half-hole plate' for the first finger. This is virtually the 'simple-system' oboe still recently in manufacture as a beginner's instrument. An oboe by Morton (**574**) illustrates the English adoption of Triébert models. It includes the thumb-plate action for C and B flat devised by F. Triébert in 1849. In the most complex of the examples shown (**575**) Triébert has incorporated both thumb-plate and right-hand action for these notes, as well as automatic octave keys, etc, ideas partly due to the player Barret in 1862. The Boehm-system oboe, patented by Buffet and Klosé, Paris, 1844 (**573**), is at once distinguishable from the regular series by the three lower-joint rings in close position. Though still advertised after the turn of the century, players in general found something unsatisfactory with its tone. No design of oboe with Boehm-system fingering has yet won more than local or fleeting popularity, though in time one may succeed. (For a full account of the French development of the oboe, see Bate, *The Oboe.*)

Tenor and Bass Oboes, Cors Anglais

Tenor oboes and cors anglais are pitched in F, a fifth lower than the oboe. Basses are usually in C, a fourth lower still. The tenor oboe appeared concurrently with the oboe to take the tenor part in four-part military music of the late seventeenth and early eighteenth centuries, a bassoon taking the bass. It is straight bodied, with a right-angled or curved brass crook. As with the oboe itself, many Dutch and German instruments figure among the early specimens, some closely reproducing the form and ornamental turnery of the contemporary oboe (**561**), though variations may be found in the bell. An early eighteenth-century Dutch tenor by Wyne (Amsterdam, Rijksmuseum) has an outwardly flared bell containing a bulbous cavity (cf **577**). Some others, as by Rottenburgh of Brussels (Brussels, 180, 2618) and by M. Lot, Paris (**562**), have a completely bulbous bell, the origin and purpose of which—and on the cor anglais too—have been much argued about. English tenors from Stanesby junior (Victoria and Albert Museum) onwards are plainly and economically built in two joints, the lower of which includes the bell, which is almost without a flare (**563**). Some *bass oboes* were built from J. C. Denner (**564**) onwards reproducing the forms of the tenor and owing their existence no doubt to then recent memories of the bass shawm; their musical use is not described. Two French examples are known of a larger 'great bass' oboe (or in modern terminology 'contrabass'), one by Delusse (Paris Conservatoire) said to have been played experimentally in the Paris Opera in 1784. It is 215 cm long, excluding crook, with covered holes as on the *basse de musette*, and five keys, three of them on the back (octave key, G Sharp, and open low B possibly added later). The other (**557**) is unsigned and has the conventional two keys of the period.

Oboe da caccia or **cor anglais.** The first named, associated notably with Bach's works up to *c.* 1740, denoted some instrument of tenor oboe pitch. It is a reasonable assumption that it was of a curved form with flared bell, as seen in an early pair of instruments preserved at Bologna (**558**). Shortly after the mid-century the name *corno inglese* begins to occur in Viennese compositions and two curved instruments of about that time made in Vienna by J. G. Bauer survive. One of these (**559**), though two-keyed, resembles the Bologna pair in its octagonal pipe and flared bell. The other, in the Paris Collection, is three-keyed, with round pipe and a squat bulbous bell. Both are made in the old 'cornett' manner from two longitudinal halves hollowed out, glued together and covered with leather. Presumably these are both early cors anglais. A rather later Italian example with two keys (**560**) illustrates a commoner construction of the curved cor anglais which with subsequent additions to the keywork (**578**) was built on the Continent until late in the nineteenth century. The joints are here first bored. Next, wedges are cut from the side which is to be on the inside of the curve of the joint. The wood is then bent, the cuts are glued and their angles filled with wooden gussets to allow shaping to the finished curve. Finally the joints are leather-covered. An angular form of cor anglais with two straight joints connected by a knee joint dates from the late eighteenth century (**577**) and was built especially in Vienna (**579**) until well after 1850.

The straight tenor was re-invented in Paris by Brod in 1839 under the name *cor anglais moderne* (**583**). Triébert adopted it from *c.* 1860 in place of the earlier curved models, or models with curved top joint combined with a straight lower joint which is evidently an original construction and not a replacement (**582**).

Other bass oboes. An instrument by Bizey (**584**) initiates a line of French bass oboes in C in which length is saved by turning up the lower end. A bassoon-like butt contains the reversal of the tube, as again in Triébert's *hautbois baryton* of *c.* 1823 onwards (**580**). Some of the latter have the bulbous bell in brass. In 1889 Lorée brought out a model which is nearly straight, the bell alone being turned up (as in the unsigned example shown, **581**).

Bassoons and Curtals

The structural feature of bassoons is the doubled-back conical tube which brings the bell above or at least level with the crook socket. The sixteenth-century instruments or curtals[1] are made in one piece. Jointed construction was variously developed through the seventeenth century, the modern build in four joints dating from the second half of the century.

Illustrations: Curtals, Bassoons

585 Great curtal (*Doppelfagott*). Italian, sixteenth century. *Vienna, Kunsthist. Mus., C.199.* Marked *HIER.S.* Ornamental moulding carved half-way up the body. Two fishtailed keys. *Height* 131·7 cm.

586 Descant curtal. ? Spanish, sixteenth or seventeenth century. *Brussels, Conserv. royal, 2329.* Marked *Melchor R.S.* Maple, brass-mounted. Two exposed brass keys on saddles, one in front, the other on the back with touch for the lower thumb. Two thumbholes. *Height* 43 cm.

587 Curtal (*gedächt Chorist-fagott*). German, sixteenth–seventeenth century. *Berlin, Instit. f. Musikforschung, 655.* Marked *LR.* Two keys. Pepperpot bell. *Length* 87·5 cm.

588 Curtal (*gedächt Chorist-fagott*). J. C. Denner, Nuremberg, late seventeenth century. *Leipzig, K.-M.-Univ., 1360.* Covered bell with perforations below. Two brass keys. (Rear view).

589 Curtal (*Chorist-fagott*). German, sixteenth century. *Hamburg, Mus. f. Hamburg. Geschichte, 1928.389.* Box, brass-mounted. Separate bell. Two brass keys. *Height* 104 cm.

590 Curtal (*Chorist-fagott*). ? Italian, seventeenth century. *Vienna, Kunsthist. Mus., C.201.* In three joints. Two keys (the thumb key missing). *Height* 105 cm.

591 Bassoon. J. C. Denner, Nuremberg, late seventeenth century. *Berlin, Instit. f. Musikforschung, 2970.* Three brass keys on rings and blocks. *Height* 126·5 cm.

592 Bassoon. German, early eighteenth century. *Basel, Hist. Mus., 1904.311.* Pear. Four square brass keys. (Some flaps missing.) *Height* 123 cm. (Rear view).

593 Bassoon. Dutch or Flemish, 1730. *Brussels, Conserv. royal, 997.* Engraved on butt ring *G. de Bruijn. 1730* (perhaps the owner). Left-handed. Four brass keys on brass saddles.

594, 595 Bassoon. Dondeine, ? French, *c.* 1720. *London, Bate Coll.* Four round keys on saddles.

596, 597 Fagottino. Martin Lot, Paris, *c.* 1780. *London, Bate Coll.* Five round keys on saddles. *Height* 64 cm.

598 Fagottino. H. Grenser, Dresden, beginning of nineteenth century. *Berlin, Instit. f. Musikforschung, 2973.* Six ivory keys including little-finger low E flat. *Height* 65 cm.

599 Bassoon. F. G. Kirst, Potsdam, late eighteenth century. *Hamburg, Mus. f. Hamburg. Geschichte, 1928.387.* Six brass keys on saddles. Vent-hole in bell and brass bell ring. (Long joint turned in photograph to show keys.) *Height* 123 cm.

600 Bassoon. H. Grenser, Dresden, beginning of nineteenth century. *Amsterdam, Rijksmus., NM.10616.* Nine ivory keys and ivory-bushed low C hole.

601 Bassoon. Proser, London, 1777. *London, Horniman Mus., Carse 318.* Four brass keys on saddles. *Height* 124 cm.

602 Bassoon. Goulding & Co., London, *c.* 1800. *London, Horniman Mus., Carse 125.* Six keys on saddles. With clarinet-type mouthpiece. *Height* 123 cm. (Rear view).

603 Tenoroon. Savary jeune, Paris, *c.* 1840. *London, Bate Coll.* Maple. Fifteen cup keys on saddles. *Height* 97 cm.

[1] *Curtal*: English equivalent of German *Dulzian*, name of the early one-piece bassoon, though 'curtal' was retained in military usage for some years to denote the jointed bassoon after this had come in. The Italian name *fagotto* and French *basson* cover both types, as also German *Fagott* (in the older period an alternative word to *Dulzian*).

604 Bassoon. J. Ziegler, Vienna, mid nineteenth century. *Leipzig, K.-M.-Univ., 1392.* Twelve keys sunk in grooves in the wood. Viennese flared bell. (Rear view.)

605 Bassoon. Stengel, Bayreuth, *c. 1830. Hamburg, mus. f. Hamburg. Geschichte, 1926, 411.* Flamed maple. Sixteen flat brass keys on flush saddles. *Height* 131 cm. (Rear view.)

606 Bassoon. Heckel, Biebrich-am-Rhein, *c. 1870–80. London, Horniman Mus., Carse 212.* Seventeen keys. *Height* 127 cm.

607 Bassoon. A. Lecomte, Paris, *c. 1889. Ann Arbor, Univ. of Michigan, Stearns 682.* Brass, nickel plated. Seventeen keys. *Height* 135 cm.

608 Bassoon. Prudent, Paris, *c. 1810. Neuchâtel, Switzerland, Kunst. u. Hist. Museum.* Six gilt keys with open-work touches in fan pattern, on interior saddles. *Length* 126 cm. (Rear view.)

609 Bassoon. R. J. Bilton, London, *c. 1840. London, Bate Coll.* Fourteen keys on saddles. Closed B key on bell. Military outfit including music card-holder in wooden case lined with green baize.

610 Double bassoon. Thos. Stanesby, junior, London, 1739. *Dublin, National Mus. of Ireland.* Maple. Four keys on saddles. *Height* 254 cm. (Shown with the long joint turned.)

611, 612 Double bassoon. Caspar Tauber, Vienna, early nineteenth century. *Yale, Philip Young Coll.* Maple. Six keys (F key missing). *Height* 166 cm.

613 Bassoon. H. J. Haseneier, Coblenz, *c. 1850. London, F. Rendell.* Covered action. *Height c.* 115 cm.

614 Bassoon. Triébert, Paris, *c. 1855. Brussels, Conserv. royal, 3119.* Marzoli-Boehm system. (Rear view.)

615 Double bassoon. French, *c. 1885. London, Bate Coll.* Marked *Lafleur, London* (importer from France). Probably by Gautrot, Paris. Rosewood, in six joints. Each butt composed of two separate tubes fastened together. Raised holes for right hand. Twelve nickel-silver keys and half-hole plate. Lowest note C. *Height* 205 cm.

616 Double bassoon. Heckel, Biebrich-am-Rhein, *c. 1879. London, Bate Coll.* Marked *Stritter.* Maple. Covered action, Lowest note C. *Height* 149 cm.

617 Double bassoon ('semi-contra bassoon'). J. Samme, London, 1854. *London, R. Coll. of Music, 91.* Eight cup keys on saddles. Pin hole in crook. Open C hole. Pitched a fourth below ordinary bassoon. *Height* 163 cm.

Curtals

The curtal is probably an Italian product of the second quarter of the sixteenth century. An early mention is in 1546, when the Verona Academy bought a *fagotto* and a *dolzana* from a soldier (Turrini, 44); the meaning of the terms is none too clear at this date, but one of them must have denoted a curtal. By the last quarter of the century the instrument was known as far as England (Hengrave Hall inventories, 1574). The long, flat billet of maple, pear, box, etc, is bored from the bottom upwards along one side, and from the top downwards, for the wider part of the conical windway, on the other side. The two bores are connected at the bottom by a cut-away chamber closed by a plug of wood (in later practice, cork). The wider bore ends with a short flare of variable form, and into the adjacent narrower bore is inserted a brass crook on which the double reed is placed. The six fingerholes lead across to the narrower bore and the two thumbholes lead to the wider. There is an open key on the front for the little finger and on the back an open key for the lower thumb. The keys are usually encased in brass covers screwed to the wood. A late example at Salzburg, by W. Kress (first half of the eighteenth century), has five square keys, but this is exceptional. The fishtailed touch for the little-finger key allows the instrument to be played with either hand lowermost, though specimens designed expressly for left-handers have the bell to the left of the crook socket as seen from the fingerhole side (585).

The most valuable curtal in music was the bass or *Chorist-fagott* (in England 'double curtal'). This (589) corresponds to bassoon pitch and stands around 100 cm high (±15 cm, the late examples generally the longest). A *gedächt* or 'covered' curtal is muted by some form of pepperpot bell-cap (**587, 588**). The *Doppelfagott* (contemporary English term unknown) is described as a fourth or fifth deeper (**585**). Small sizes are the rarest; some examples marked *Melchor*, from the former Barbieri Collection in Madrid and now at Brussels (2327–9), measure 65 cm ('single curtal', Spanish *bajoncito*, a fifth above the *Chorist*), 51 cm (a fourth above), and 43 cm (a ninth above, **586**). With them, but unsigned, is the smallest extant curtal (2330), 34·2 cm tall, a twelfth above the Chorist.

Though one-piece construction persisted in normal practice to the last days of the curtal, at least three jointed specimens survive, and Trichet (Bordeaux, *c.* 1640) writes that the larger sizes of *basson* could be taken apart in two pieces 'pour la commodité' (ed. Lesure, p. 91). A two-jointed *Chorist-fagott* at Vienna (C.200) takes apart half way up with an elliptical tenon on the lower piece which contains both bores. The three-jointed example in the same collection (**590**) has the separate butt, wing and long joints of the later bassoon, the butt being of the length needed to accommodate the D key for the lower thumb.

Bassoons, Double Bassoons

The bassoon built as today in four joints—wing, butt, long joint and bell—may be assumed to date from the same time as the original oboe, which, in its early form, it matched functionally and also decoratively. The assumption is supported by a painting, 'The Bassoon-player', ascribed to H. Hals (d. 1669) at Aachen (reproduced by Langwill, *Index*, 39). Here are seen the handsome oboe-like mouldings over the crook socket and the socket at the base of the bell, characteristic of bassoons dating from the last quarter of the seventeenth century (**591, 592**). Three specimens are by J. C. Denner, with three open keys, the minimum number that the bassoon can have, since a third key above the two normally possessed by a curtal is required to sound a low B flat through the new bell joint. The two keys on the back are both entrusted to the upper thumb, one key being placed above the thumbhole and the other below it, both on the long joint. The keys are mounted in rings and blocks in the wood, as again in some of the early four-keyed instruments with a closed key for A flat corresponding to the E flat key on the oboe (**592, 594**). Four keys remained standard well into the last quarter of the eighteenth century, the bassoon meanwhile becoming more plainly built and having the keys mounted on brass saddles. The surviving bassoon of Stanesby junior, dated 1747 (illustrated in Galpin, Pl. 34, and now in the collection of the Rev C. Sharpe, Guildford), is practically of the normal English build for the rest of the century (as **601**). From *c.* 1790 English makers began to make a bell of slightly flared form, as in **602**, this specimen being fitted with the clarinet-type mouthpiece of ebony (or ivory) which was used by some players, probably provincial bandsmen, during the first quarter of the nineteenth century instead of the correct double reed. A fifth key (closed key for low E flat) came in from *c.* 1780 (**608**), followed later in the century by a sixth (**602**, etc) and from *c.* 1800 by further keys, mostly on the wing (**600**). In German bassoons, especially the highly regarded instruments of A. and H. Grenser, the keys are often of ivory.

Many small bassoons were built in the eighteenth century. Most of these are *fagottini*, pitched an octave above the ordinary and *c.* 64–68 cm tall (**596–8**); a late seventeenth-century three-keyed example by J. C. Denner is in the Boston Collection (146). An intermediate size, *tenoroon*, was much made in England in the second half of the century, though less commonly on the Continent until the early nineteenth century (**603**). Its pitch is usually a fourth above the bassoon, though examples a fifth higher (French *basson-quinte*) occur. A rare eighteenth-century musical score demanding these small bassoons is by Trost (see Hedlund, *GSJ*, XI, 1958).

Later bassoons. Further additions of keys to traditional models led in England to forms like that of

Bilton (**609**) and in France to the once celebrated models of Savary, Paris (**603**), of flamed sycamore, the keys still of brass, much copied later in the nineteenth century in England and by Mahillon in Belgium; the modern French bassoon by Buffet-Crampon shows the ultimate stage in the development of this traditional model. In Austria too a traditional model was developed with extra keywork, often along with a flared bell (**604**). Flared metal bells also appear sporadically in most countries during the first part of the century, followed in Paris by bassoons entirely of metal (**607**) initiated by a Sax design of 1842. In Germany the bassoon was substantially redesigned by Carl Almenraeder, Mainz, from 1820, in order to stabilize notes which tend to be weak or insecure on the traditional models. A fine early Almenraeder bassoon, stamped with the name of B. Schott who sold the instruments, is in the Horniman Museum, Carse 52. A Stengel example (**605**) shows a trace of the improvements, the main work on which was continued by Almenraeder's assistant, J. A. Heckel and Heckel's descendants (**606**), to produce the modern German bassoon.

Eccentric mid nineteenth-century designs include an efficient covered-hole model by Haseneier, Coblenz (**613**), and the over-complicated 'Boehm system' bassoon of Triébert and Marzoli, Paris, *c.* 1855 (**614**). (For detailed accounts of these systems from Almenraeder to the 'Boehm', see Langwill, 1965, in which there is also a full history of the contrabassoon.)

Contrabassoon (double bassoon). This, standing an octave lower than the bassoon, seems to have been first built by Stanesby junior, London, 1739 (**610**). Though with a tube-length of seven and a half metres, it keeps the form of a four-keyed bassoon save for a long brass pipe between crook and wing, and it works fairly well. Scaled-up bassoon models are also found in a few specimens of intermediate pitch, as by Grenser, a fifth below the bassoon (Brussels, 1000), and later by Samme, London, 1854, a fourth below (**617**). The next true contrabassoons after Stanesby are Austrian and German of the last quarter of the eighteenth century, in which overall height is saved by incorporation of a second butt joint placed at the top, and by limitation of the downwards compass to C or D (**611, 612**). Models like this continued to be made until late in the nineteenth century, in France also (**615**, with joined parallel tubes instead of butt joints). A more efficient instrument and more compact is Haseneier's *Kontrabassophon*, 1849 (**660**), though the wide bore and widely spaced holes of large diameter (recalling Streitwolf's bass horn, **691**) give sonorous results which are really those of a new kind of instrument. Copies were made in London by Morton (London, R. Coll. of Music, 287, dated 1875). The modern contrabassoon was worked out by Heckel, 1877–9, some early examples stamped with the name of Stritter, a Heckel workman (**616**). As in the Kontrabassophon the windway, after the crook, is led through a metal joint and then three wooden joints connected by wooden bows.

6 Clarinets

Clarinets have a cylindrical bore, approximately 14–15 cm wide in the common B flat clarinet, leading to a terminal expansion which usually begins just above the flared bell. Over the oblong opening in the side of the beak-like mouthpiece a cane blade, the 'single reed', is secured with string, or with a metal 'ligature' tightened by two screws. It is a curious thing that there is no positive record of this simple and effective type of mouthpiece and reed, perfectly suited to cylindrical bores of medium size, before its appearance *c.* 1700 on the clarinet, the invention of which is attributed to J. C. Denner, Nuremberg (d. 1707). Certain arrangements akin to it occur in folk instruments, but there is no proof that they are earlier. Even the ancient kind of single reed made by cutting a tongue in the side of a tube of cane, though much employed in bagpipes, does not appear in a European concert instrument until the end of the seventeenth century, though this is understandable since this reed offers little scope for lip-controlled playing; the instrument here in question is the *chalumeau* or Mock trumpet (see Dart, *GSJ*, VI, 1953), sold at first in *c.* 1695 as a musical toy, but redesigned in the eighteenth century using a mouthpiece with tied-on reed as in the clarinet and also probably due to Denner. The chalumeau, scored for in a number of eighteenth-century operas, is about half the length of the early clarinet, and is described as late as 1795 (Reynvaan), keyless, or with one or two keys near the top end. Specimens are extremely rare (**620**), though instruments much like it are made in Czechoslovakia as folk instruments.

Illustrations: Clarinets

618   Clarinet. J. C. Denner, Nuremberg, *c.* 1700. *Munich, Bayer. Nationalmus., 136.* Boxwood, in three joints. Two square brass keys (one behind). *Pitch D. Bore* 13 mm, slightly tapering to lower end. *Length* 48 cm. (Double hole in foot joint not visible in photograph.)

619   Clarinet. Klenig (? German), early eighteenth century. *Stockholm, Musikhist. Mus., 141.* Similar to the preceding, but with pear-shaped barrel.

620   Chalumeau. Stuehnwal (? German), *c.* 1700. *Munich, Bayer. Nationalmus.* Box, in two joints. Two brass keys. Twinned seventh hole. *Length* 22·3 cm.

621   Clarinet. J. Denner, Nuremberg, *c.* 1730. *Nuremberg, German. Nationalmus., MI.149.* Box, in four joints including mouthpiece. Two brass keys. *Pitch D. Length c.* 52 cm. (Shown on larger scale.)

622   Clarinet. G. Walch, Berchtesgaden, *c.* 1730. *Salzburg, Mus. Carolino Augusteum, 250, Geir. 211.* Plum, in four joints. Three keys including open B key. *Length* 52 cm. (Rear view.)

623   Clarinet. Kusder, London, *c.* 1770. *Ilford, Halfpenny Coll.* Box, in four joints. Five keys. *Length* 68 cm.

624   Clarinette d'amour. F. Lehner, Germany, *c.* 1760. *Brunswick, Städt. Mus., Ck.112, Schröder 104.* Four keys. Brass crook. *Length* without crook 75 cm.

625   Clarinet d'amour. Venera, Turin, *c.* 1780. *London, Bate Coll.* Stained wood in four joints, horn mounted. Five square keys. Brass crook and boxwood mouthpiece. Two vent-holes in bell neck. *Pitch G. Length* excluding mouthpiece 75 cm.

626   Clarinet. Baumann, Paris, early nineteenth century. *Cobham, Morley-Pegge Coll.* Box, ivory mounted. Five square keys, including extendable long keys for use with 'A' lower joint. *Pitch* B flat and A (shown in B flat).

627   Clarinet. W. Milhouse, London, *c.* 1810. *Brighton, Museum.* Box, ivory mounted. Six square keys. *Pitch C. Length* 59·5 cm.

628   Clarinet. Griesbacher, Vienna, late eighteenth century. *Leipzig, K.-M.-Univ., 1484.* Box, horn mounted. Five square keys; the long keys with extendable touches. *Pitch* B flat and A (shown in A).

629 Clarinet. Asa Hopkins, Litchfield, Conn., *c.* 1825. *Washington, Smithsonian Instit., 1825–37.* Box, ivory mounted. Five square keys. *Pitch* C. *Length* including mouthpiece 60 cm.

630 Clarinet. H. Grenser. Dresden, *c.* 1800. *Berlin, Instit. f. Musikforschung, 83.* Box, ivory mounted. Eight square keys. *Pitch* B flat. *Length* 64 cm.

631 Clarinet. Stengel, Bayreuth, *c.* 1840. *Leipzig, K.-M.-Univ., 1495.* Box, ivory mounted. Twelve square keys. Ivory mouthpiece.

632 Clarinet. Thos. Key, London, 1834. *London, Bate Coll.* Ebony, silver mounted. Thirteen flat round silver keys on blocks, the long keys with rollers. *Pitch* B flat. *Length* 66 cm.

633 Clarinet. F. Lefèvre, Paris, *c.* 1840. *London, Bate Coll.* Box, ivory mounted. Twelve cup keys on pillars mounted on brass plates. *Pitch* C. *Length* 59 cm.

634 Clarinet. German, late nineteenth century. *London, Bate Coll.* German system. Blackwood. *Pitch* E flat. *Length* 43·5 cm without mouthpiece.

635 Clarinet. Thos. Key & Co. London, *c.* 1856. *London, Bate Coll.* Brass, silver-plated. Thirteen keys. Mouthpiece locking-ring. *Pitch* B flat. *Length* 67 cm.

636 Clarinet. E. J. Albert, Brussels, *c.* 1875. *London, Bate Coll.* Clinton system. Box, later stained. *Pitch* B flat, *Length* 67 cm.

637 Clarinet. Louis Auguste Buffet, Paris, 1844. *London, Bate Coll.* Boehm system, as made for Klosé. Box, with brass keywork on pillars. *Pitch* C. *Length* 58 cm.

638 Clarinet. Eugène Albert, Brussels, *c.* 1865. *London, Bate Coll.* Solo instrument of Henry Lazarus. Cocus, with nickel-silver keys. Albert system with patent C sharp, rollers, and extra trill key. *Pitch* B flat.

639 Alto clarinet. A. Knockenhauer, Berlin, 1856. *New York, Metropol. Mus. of Art, Crosby Brown 2126.* Box, ivory mounted. Curved wooden barrel. Thirteen square keys on blocks. *Pitch* F. *Length* 85 cm.

640 Alto clarinet. Key, London, *c.* 1840. *Luton Museum, C/16.* Stained box, ivory mounted. Curved brass crook. Thirteen flat keys, ten on blocks, three on saddles. *Pitch* F. *Length* 94 cm.

Basset Horns

641 Basset horn. Mayrhofer, Passau, *c.* 1770. *Hamburg, Mus. f. Hamburg. Geschichte, 1927.159.* Marked in cartouche on the 'box' *Ant: et Mich: Mayrhofer. Inven. & Elabor. Passavii.* Sickle form. Boxwood, in two longitudinal halves joined, shaped octagonally and covered with brown leather. Brass mounts. Sixth fingerhole is twinned. Seven brass square keys on saddles, one of them giving low C; low D is lacking. E flat key on left of fishtailed C key (for left-handed player). Circular brass bell inscribed with the fox of Passau. Barrel missing. *Bore* at top end *c.* 1·3 cm.

642 Basset horn. August Grenser, Dresden, 1784. *Stockholm, Musikhist. Mus., 553.* Straight form with box. Boxwood, horn mounted. Brass crook and bell. Eight square keys.

643 Basset horn. A. or H. Grenser, Dresden, 1793. *The Hague, Gemeentemus.* Angular form. Box, ivory mounted. Eight keys.

644 Basset horn. Probably Viennese, *c.* 1780. *Nuremberg, German. Nationalmus., Rück Coll., MIR.465.* Marked *A.S.* Sickle form, octagonally shaped, with wooden bell. Eight square keys.

645 Basset horn. G. Glezl (German), *c.* 1800. *Munich, Bayer. Nationalmus., 111.* Right-angled form. Boxwood, horn mounted. Eight round and square keys. Brass bell.

646 Basset horn. Braun, Mannheim, *c.* 1845. *Leipzig, K.-M.-Univ., 1537.* Straight form without 'box' and with right-angled bell with side orifice. Ivory mounted. Seventeen square keys on blocks and rings.

Bass Clarinets

647   Bass clarinet. H. Grenser, Dresden, 1793. *Stockholm, Musikhist. Mus., 1957.58.28.* In bassoon shape, with two thumbholes, three keys and speaker key on the back. Bore 40 per cent conical. *Pitch* B flat (lowest note sounds A flat). *Height* 79 cm.

648   Bass clarinet (*glicibarifono*). Catterino Catterini, Padua, after 1838. *London, Bate Coll.* Two bores in one piece of box, brass mounted. Brass crook, wooden bell. Twenty-four keys on saddles, including the dished plates of the covered action. *Pitch* B flat. *Height* 83 cm.

649   Bass clarinet. Nicola Papalini, Padua, c. 1815. *Boston, Mus. of Fine Arts, 119.* Body of pear, in two halves in zig-zag form fastened together with iron pins. Horn mounts. Separate wooden crook, also made in two halves, and barrel and bell (with vent-hole). Nine holes in front and two thumbholes. Five keys on blocks, two of them on the back. *Pitch* C. *Height* 68 cm. *Bore* 20 mm.

650   Bass clarinet. Adolphe Sax, Paris, 1845. *The Hague, Gemeentemus.* Maple, brass mounted. Brass crook and bell. Thirteen keys and two speaker keys. Covered action. *Height* 133 cm.

651   Contrabass clarinet (*Bathyphon*). Wieprecht & Skorra, Berlin, after 1839. *Berlin, Instit. f. Musikforschung, 2904.* Two maple tubes with short butt below. Brass crook and bell. Covered action with long axles on pillars. *Pitch* C. *Height* 99·5 cm.

652   Bass clarinet. A. Buffet jeune, Paris, c. 1860. *Ann Arbor, Univ. of Michigan, Stearns 635.* Cocus, with brass crook, bottom bow and bell. The bore of the longer tube slightly conical. Covered action in brass. *Height* 68 cm.

653   Contrabass clarinet. Fontaine Besson, Paris, after 1889. *London, Bate Coll.* Model of 1889. Three maple tubes. Nickel-silver crook, bows and bell. Albert system. *Pitch* E flat. *Height* 113 cm.

It now seems generally agreed that instruments of the type illustrated by **618, 619** may be taken to represent Denner's initial, or at any rate early, overblowing design of single-reed instrument, i.e. clarinet. They are in three joints including the recorder-like foot joint, and have two closed keys near the upper end, one of which, for the thumb, is opened to make the pipe overblow to a second register at a twelfth above the fundamentals and in unison with the scale of the contemporary trumpet (*clarino*), whence the new instrument's name.

More recognizably a clarinet is a two-keyed form with an oboe-like bell, dating from c. 1720 and including an example by J. Denner, possibly the son who died in 1735 (**621**). Some others are by Flemish and Dutch makers. This is assumed to be the form in which the clarinet was introduced to France and England around 1740. A few specimens which may date from c. 1730 onwards have also an open key closed by the lower thumb to give, through a lengthened bell joint, the note B which links the two registers and is imperfectly available on the two-keyed clarinet (**622**). After the mid-century, perhaps during the 1760s, the instrument was advanced to the classic five-keyed stage (**623**), with two long keys (one of them closed) for the left little finger, and a closed E flat key for the other little finger (the clarinet by this time being played always with the right hand lowermost). Examples with only four keys are rare, one by A. Grenser being dated 1777 (Leipzig, 1472), though four keys are found in several specimens of the *clarinette d'amour* (**624**), a deeper instrument with curved brass crook or curved wooden barrel, and with a bulbous bell (**625**) or a flared bell with bulbous interior.

Five-keyed clarinets may have up to six joints including the mouthpiece. The upper half of the instrument then as now comprises mouthpiece, the short joint known as the 'barrel', and the main left-hand joint. In many specimens pre-1780 mouthpiece and barrel are made as one. In the lower half, if it also has three joints, the first takes in only the three main right-hand holes, the second the little finger hole and keys, while the third is the bell. With a B flat clarinet, the first of these could be supplied in an alternative longer version which switched the clarinet into A, the long keys on the next joint then preferably having extendible touches (**626, 628**). On some eighteenth-century clarinets this last joint and the bell are made in one. Otherwise, as generally in the nineteenth century and today, the first and second sections are made as one. Six-keyed clarinets appeared towards the end of the eighteenth century, the sixth key in England being a long trill key on the upper joint (**627**), but on the Continent sometimes a G sharp key, near the bottom of this joint. Eight keys are already found in some German instruments of the beginning of the nineteenth century (**630**) and advanced models of *c.* 1810 had 11 and, by 1820, 13 or more. Yet five- and six-keyed boxwood clarinets remained popular for some time (**629**) and indeed were still made as cheap instruments at the end of the nineteenth century. A few examples illustrate characteristic 12–13 keyed clarinets of different countries in the first half of the century (**631–3**), though the mechanical development of the clarinet during the nineteenth century, pressed especially by the severe demands on the instrument in military-band music, is too diversified to be covered in any detail here (for a full account, see Rendall). By 1840 Boehm's flute mechanism had suggested the brille rings on the lower joint; also the Klosé-Buffet 'Boehm system' clarinet of 1844 (**637**), the prevailing system today. Opposed to this last are various elaborations of the 13-key system by Albert, Brussels (**638**, and with later English additions, **636**), and by German makers leading to the Oehler system (**634**). The last example also illustrates the relative size of the small E flat clarinet (*c.* 49 cm complete) built from the early nineteenth century for use above the ordinary clarinets in bands. A slightly earlier variety, little made after *c.* 1830, is in F, *c.* 44 cm. A later pitch (from *c.* 1840) is the high A flat clarinet, *c.* 37 cm long.

The *alto clarinet* in F or E flat, dating from *c.* 1820, resembles the *clarinette d'amour* in being a large-sized clarinet with curved crook or barrel, though it has a flared bell of normal design and was meant for bands (**639, 640**). In most later models of the nineteenth century the bell is of metal and turned upwards.

Basset Horn and Bass Clarinet

The basset horn is mainly a German instrument, similar in pitch to the alto clarinet but earlier in date and extended in downwards compass by two whole tones to its low C. Its invention is attributed to Mayrhofer, Passau, on the strength of the inscription on one of the sickle-shaped instruments shown (**641**). The other, also with an octagonal tube (**644**), is marked with initials which tempt one to imagine it to have belonged to Mozart's friend and clarinet soloist Anton Stadler. Inside the flat piece above the bell, commonly called the 'box', the windway passes through three parallel channels, so that the overall length is hardly more than it would have been without the extended compass. The bell is usually of brass, often of a flattened shape which can be placed between the knees. From *c.* 1780 the sickle form became superseded by models which dispense with curved joints. (1) With two straight joints meeting in a right angle (**645**), of which an example dated 1782, by Rosmeisel, Graslitz, is in the Prague Collection. (2) With two joints meeting in an obtuse angle (**643**), with an example by Grundmann dated 1787 (Hamburg Coll.). (3) Straight form, with a 'box' (**642**). (4) Straight form without 'box' and with a globular or cylindrical bell which points either backwards or forwards (**646**), apparently with no dated example. The basset horn was much built in Germany up to *c.* 1830, after 1800 largely for wind bands and most commonly in the obtuse-angled form, no. (2) above. In the second half of the nineteenth century the instrument was built in straight models, the best for playing seated, without 'box' and with or without an up-turned bell of wood or metal.

An early *bass clarinet*, pitched an octave below the ordinary clarinet, is that of H. Grenser, 1793 (**647**), built in a bassoon form. A type which, however, may be considerably older (though there are no contemporary descriptions of it) has a straight bore passing down a flat plank of wood which enlarges in depth downwards, allowing deep oblique drilling of the lower fingerholes; it has a brass crook and up-turned bell, and Rendall, who illustrates one of the three known specimens, none of which is signed, places it as early as *c.* 1750 (*The Clarinet*, Pl. VIIa). Two bass clarinets of the early nineteenth century are by North Italian makers who, curiously, are not known by wind instruments of any other type: Papalini's freakish construction of *c.* 1810 of which several specimens are known (**649**), and Catterini's *glicibarifono* of *c.* 1838 in a form recalling that of the old curtal (**648**). A second German model in bassoon form is by Streitwolf, 1828, shortly after which, in 1839, Wieprecht, the celebrated Berlin bandmaster, designed a contrabass clarinet, *Bathyphon* (**651**). Meanwhile in France various models appeared in the early decades of the century leading to those of Buffet, at first in a bassoon shape (**652**), later straight with up-turned bell. Of greater import for the future, however, was the straight model of Adolphe Sax, Brussels, 1838, first made with downwards bell (**650**). Sax also designed a contrabass which has not survived, though a number of examples remain of the later model of Besson, Paris, 1889, made both in E flat (**653**) and in the full contrabass pitch of B flat, two octaves below the clarinet. Other designs have followed in the present century.

7 Saxophone and Other Late Reed Instruments

Illustrations

654 Alto fagotto. Wood & Ivy, late George Wood, London, *c. 1835. London, Victoria and Albert Mus., 47–1884.* Stained wood in four joints. Seven brass keys on saddles. Brass crook. *Height 54·6* cm. (Rear view.)

655 Tarogato. Stowasser, Budapest, late nineteenth century. *London, Kneller Hall, 67.* Cocus, five rings. Automatic octave keys. Mouthpiece beside on left.

656 Tenor sarrusophone. Gautrot Marquet. Paris, after 1856. *Author's Coll.* Imported by Distin. Brass. *Height 71* cm.

657 Baritone sarrusophone. Gautrot Marquet, Paris, after 1856. *Paris, Conserv., C.1128.* Brass, silver plated. *Height 88* cm.

658 Soprano saxophone. Adolphe Sax, Paris, *c. 1855. London, Horniman Mus., Carse 83.* Brass, silver plated. *Length 54* cm.

659 Tenor saxophone. C. Mahillon & Co., Brussels, late nineteenth century. *From the maker's catalogue.* Brass, nickel plated. Simple system. *Height c. 82* cm.

660 Kontrabassophon. H. J. Haseneier, Coblenz, after 1849. *Leipzig, K.-M.-Univ., 1601.* Wood, brass keys. *Height c. 125* cm (see p. 111). (Rear view.)

661 Contrebasse à anche. C. Mahillon & Co., Brussels, *c. 1870. London, Kneller Hall.* Brass. *Height 104* cm.

Of fresh types of reed instrument that appeared during the nineteenth century the major success has proved to be the saxophone, the only important wind instrument which combines conical bore with single-reed mouthpiece. This mouthpiece is not unlike that of a clarinet, while the bore is a large one, capable of delivering sound up to great strength. The tube is brass and the wide holes are controlled wholly by covered action. Adolphe Sax (1814–94) began work on his invention shortly before his move in 1842 from Brussels to Paris where he patented it in 1846. An original set of four saxophones exhibited by Sax in 1849 (Paris Conservatoire, 553–6) was unfortunately lost during the last war. The instrument was almost immediately introduced into French army bands, other countries following this valuable departure by degrees, America among the first; the Gilmore band had four saxophones by the 1870s. To distinguish the different saxophones, the soprano is normally straight (**658**), those bent in the shape of the alto being fancy models of the present century. The smaller sopranino is very rare. From alto downwards the instruments have detachable crooks and upturned bells. The alto (standing height *c.* 63–67 cm) has a crook with a single bend. The tenor (*c.* 82 cm) has a return bend in the crook (**659**), likewise a smaller tenor in C (*c.* 72 cm) which occurs most as the 'C melody' (i.e. non-transposing) saxophone fairly popular around the 1920s. The baritone (*c.* 103 cm) has a loop in the upper end of the tube and the bass (*c.* 134 cm) a longer loop. The original keywork was developed in several minor respects during the last third of the nineteenth century by Lecomte and other Paris manufacturers, and the bell first lengthened for a low B flat in 1887, but even so saxophones descending only to B natural and with two separate octave keys lasted well into the present century.

The *Alto fagotto* (**654**) is George Wood's (London) version, *c.* 1830, of a small bassoon-like *Caledonica* invented by W. Miekle of Lanarkshire (illustrated in Langwill, *Index*, 81). The single-reed mouthpiece is Wood's replacement of the inventor's double reed. The instrument met small success. The *Tarogato* (**655**) is a straight conical pipe in wood with wide saxophone-like bore, vent-holes in the bell, and a clarinet-like mouthpiece which is inserted into the top end. Invented by Schunda, Budapest, at some time in the 1890s as a national instrument to replace an obsolete shawm of the same name, it has since become a popular folk instrument in Rumania. (An almost identical instrument by J. Thibouville-Lamy, Paris, belongs to the 1920s.) An *Octavin*, by Adler, Markneukirchen, 1890, has a conical bore wholly contained in a short bassoon-like butt, with metal bell protruding sideways from the top next to a socket for a tarogato-like mouthpiece (Carse, Pl. IX).

The success of the saxophone in French bands suggested to Sarrus, a bandmaster, the idea of a corresponding family of brass-tube double-reed instruments, *Sarrusophones*, 1856, first made by Gautrot, Paris (**656, 657**). The considerable quantity, in all pitches, that survive, some stamped with the names of foreign importers, shows the interest the instrument aroused in certain band circles for the rest of the century, though only the contrabass has enjoyed much use since. What most acted against their success were no doubt the problems of double-reed making and replacement. The soprano is straight, like a kind of brass oboe. The others are in roughly bassoon-shape, the alto being given a respectable overall length by a 12 cm loop of dummy tubing beyond the lower bend. The tenor and the baritone are illustrated. The bass is around 90 cm tall and the full contrabass in B flat 132 cm with a coiled crook. There is also a smaller contrabass in E flat. (The *Rothphone*, by Roth, Milan, is a kind of sarrusophone in saxophone shape; its date of appearance seems unrecorded.) Often confused with the sarrusophone is the *Contrebasse à anche* ('reed contrabass', **661**). This is a development from a *Tritonikon* or *Universal Kontrabass* brought out by Schöllnast, Bratislava, as early as 1839. As made by Mahillon in Brussels (1868) and others from the last third of the century, it consists of a wide-bore conical brass tube in two loops, sounded with a large double reed. The action comprises entirely closed keys, one opened at a time for each note of the chromatic scale, save for an open key in the bell. For some time, and into the present century, it proved fairly successful in large military bands.

8 Cornetts, Serpents

Small horns of cowhorn or wood, sounded in the ordinary manner of horns but pierced with fingerholes down one side, seem to have been fairly extensively employed as musical instruments in the earlier part of the Middle Ages and have lasted up to the present as folk instruments, particularly in Russia and Scandinavia (670). The cornett and the serpent are two specialized post-medieval manifestations of this fingerhole horn. The cornett[1] was perfected during the fifteenth century and ranked high among professional wind instruments through the next two centuries. The serpent appeared at the end of the sixteenth century but came into wide use only towards the end of the eighteenth and was generally obsolescent after 1850.

Illustrations

662   Cornettino. German, 1518. *Author's Coll.* Plum (?), leather covered, silver mounted. Centre mount engraved with the date *1518*; bottom mount with *IIIK* between arrows. *Length* 42 cm. Ex-Galpin Collection. Mouthpiece not original.

663   Cornett. ? Italian, sixteenth century. *Vienna, Kunsthist. Mus., A. 241.* Plume mark. The left-handed instrument of a pair. Leather covered. *Length* 58 cm. With original mouthpiece of horn, *total length* 3 cm, *width* 1·4 cm.

664   Cornett. Late sixteenth century. *Stockholm, Musikhist. Mus., 549.* Ivory, silver mounted.

665   Cornett. ? Italian, seventeenth century. *Paris, Conserv., 0083, C.683.* Double curve. Leather covered. *Length* 59 cm.

666   Cornett. ? Italian, sixteenth or seventeenth century. *Paris, Conserv., E.581, C.624.* Serpentine. Viper's head with the lower orifice of the tube in the chin. *Length* 60 cm.

667   Mute cornett. Italian, sixteenth century. *Vienna, Kunsthist. Mus., A.236.* Double plume mark. Boxwood. *Length* 66·5 cm.

668   Mute cornett. ? French, seventeenth century. *Geneva, Mus. d'Art et d'Histoire.* Box, in two joints, gilt mounts.

669   Straight cornett. Hetsch, Urach, nineteenth century. *Nuremberg, German. Nationalmus., Rück Coll., MIR.34.* Box, in three joints, horn mounted. One brass closed key on saddle, for the upper little finger. Signature accompanied by the letter *A*. Mouthpiece is modern.

670   Folk cornett (*tuohitorvi*). Finnish (recent). *Miss W. N. Bartlett, Dartington Hall, Devon.* Wound with birch bark. Thumbhole on back. *Length* 68 cm.

671   Cornett. Italian, ? seventeenth century. *Ann Arbor, Univ. of Michigan, Stearns 829.* Tobacco-pipe shape. Leather covered. Bone top with horn mouthpiece. No thumbhole. *Height* 44 cm. *Greatest width* 6 cm.

672   Tenor cornett. German, sixteenth century. *Brunswick, Städt. Mus., 66.* Double plume mark. No key. *Length* 88·5 cm.

673   Tenor cornett. French, ? sixteenth century. *Lisbon, Conserv. nacional.* Marked *Bavoux et Poïseau.* Mostly round. One key.

674   Serpent. Belgian, eighteenth or nineteenth century. *Brussels, Conserv. royal, 2447.* Mouthpiece missing.

675   Serpent. Spanish, eighteenth or early nineteenth century. *Barcelona, Mus. de Musica, 60.* Unusual form.

---

[1] Or cornet, the old spelling with double 't' having been revived by Galpin (1910) to distinguish the instrument from the modern brass instrument of the same name. Italian *cornetto*, French *cornet à bouquin*, German *Zink*.

676 Tenor cornett. French, sixteenth century. *Paris, Conserv., 0087.* Serpentine. Dragon or viper's head bell with orifice in chin. One key. *Length* 100 cm.

677 Bass cornett. Italian, sixteenth century. *Paris, Conserv., C.636.* Serpentine. Four keys, of which two on the back for the thumb act closest to the bottom end. Top end damaged. *Length c.* 100 cm.

678 Bass cornett. Italian, sixteenth–seventeenth century. *Paris, Conserv., C.634.* Octagonal. Left-handed. No key. Sixth hole offset to left. Bell in the form of a horned serpent's or dragon's head.

679 Serpent. German, early nineteenth century. *Nuremberg, German. Nationalmus., Rück Coll., MIR. 46.* Three brass keys. German form of crook. Right hand over tube. *Height* 81 cm.

680 Serpent. Thomas Key, London, *c.* 1810. *Oxford, Pitt Rivers Mus.* From Band of Oxfordshire Militia. Three brass keys on saddles. Right hand under tube.

681 Serpent militaire. French, early nineteenth century. *London, R. Coll. of Music, 195.* Partly straightened form. Four keys (one missing). *Height* 105 cm.

682 Serpent. Thomas Key, London, *c.* 1840. *Cardiff. Nat. Museum of Wales.* Brass. Covered action.

683 Serpent. Embach, Amsterdam, *c.* 1825. *Leipzig, K.-M.-Univ., 1586.* Embach's compact model. Covered action. *Height* 53 cm.

684 Bass horn. French, early nineteenth century. *London, Horniman Mus., Carse 292.* Form resembling Frichot's *basse-trompette* of 1806. Four turned joints of pear, dark-stained, with brass mounts. Three brass keys on saddles. Crook in two joints. Ivory-bushed holes. *Height* 75 cm.

685 Bass horn. English, *c.* 1800. *Cobham, Morley-Pegge Coll.* Brass. Three brass keys.

686 Serpent Forveille. Forveille, Paris, *c.* 1825. *Cobham, Morley-Pegge Coll.* Leather covered. Brass crook and upper joint. Three brass keys. *Height* 94 cm.

687 Contra-bass-horn. J. B. Coëffet, Chaumont-en-Vexin (France), *c.* 1840. *Leipzig, K.-M.-Univ., 1599.* Leather covered. Brass bell and crook. Six brass keys. *Height c.* 93 cm.

688 Russian bassoon. Hirschbrunner, Sumiswald (Switzerland), *c.* 1820. *Hamburg, Mus. f. Hamburg. Geschichte, 1922.70.* Maple, brass mounted. Painted dragon bell. Three brass keys on saddles. *Height* 123·5 cm.

689 Russian bassoon. Swiss, *c.* 1820. *Zürich, Schweitz. Landesmus.* Dragon bell. Two keys.

690 Russian bassoon. F. Tabard, Lyons, *c.* 1830. *Leipzig, K.-M.-Univ., 1591.* Painted dragon bell. Covered holes. *Height* 112 cm.

691 Chromatic bass horn. Streitwolf, Göttingen, *c.* 1825. *The Hague, Gemeentemus.* Brass keys on saddles with covered action on axles over raised holes. Brass bell. *Height* 126 cm. (Rear view.)

The ordinary curved treble cornett (**663**) is about 56–64 cm long. The conical bore is carved in two lengths of wood (pear, plum, etc) which are glued together and shaped to an octagonal section save in the upper part, which is usually carved in a diamond pattern (possibly a memory of some ancient binding of plaited work). The pipe ends without bell flare. Six fingerholes are cut in one of the facets which comes uppermost when the pipe is laid flat on a bench, and a thumbhole is cut on the opposite facet higher up the pipe. The curve of the instrument eases the stretch for the lower hand, curved cornetts being intended for either right- or left-handed playing according to the curve-direction of the facet chosen for the location of the fingerholes. The pipe is finally covered with black leather, cut through to open up the holes already drilled in the wood. Ivory cornetts are of course left uncovered (**664**). In the narrow end of the pipe is a mouthpiece socket, reinforced with a brass ferrule over which there may be a silver mount. The mouthpiece being a separate piece, few original examples are preserved; it is a small cup mouthpiece usually turned from horn, with a sharp rim (**663**).

Sixteenth-seventeenth-century examples of the curved treble cornett are fairly numerous (60 at least, probably more), among them some of slightly deeper pitch which should perhaps be termed altos. There are variant shapes (**665, 671**) and the bottom end is sometimes carved in the form of a wolf's or serpent's head (**666**)—a feature seen in pictures of cornett-like instruments as far back as the eleventh century (Buhle). There are two particularly fine viper-belled cornetts at Verona, described as *a testa di bissa* (viper) in the 1569 inventory of the Accademia Filarmonica, which apparently bought them in 1544

(Turrini). A smaller size of cornett, *cornettino*, pitched a fourth or fifth above the treble, is very much rarer (**662**). Many facsimiles of curved cornetts of various sizes have been made over the last hundred years.

The *tenor cornet*, pitched a fifth lower than the treble, is also variable in design. Some specimens have a round section for all or part of the length and many have an open key to produce the low C of the tenor voice (**673**). The usual shape has a reverse curve with the fingerholes cut in the side which is in front as the instrument is played pointing downwards with the bottom end turned towards the audience (**672**). This eases the stretch for the fingers, though an unusual specimen at Paris with the holes placed along a side facet as in the treble cornet seems quite comfortable to handle (**676**). A very few larger cornetts exist, though contemporary sources do not specifically mention such. One, from the Correr Collection, is of approximately tenor pitch but has extended tube and four keys which take the compass down to the low G (**677**; and see Morley-Pegge, *GSJ*, XII, 1959). Another, also at Paris, is of a deeper pitch but has no keys; its viper mouth is particularly well carved (**678**).

Straight and mute cornetts. A straight cornett turned in boxwood, and without leather covering, is figured or described from Virdung (1511) to the late seventeenth century (Talbot). Specimens are rare; a good example is at Brussels (2451), with the double plume mark. Another, interesting for its late period and three-jointed construction, is **669**, one of a pair by Hetsch, a name which also occurs on a one-keyed flute (Langwill, *Index*); they have been ascribed to the second quarter of the nineteenth century, from which time dates the latest record of the cornett in active use, in the tower band at Stuttgart, 1840 (Kastner), i.e. a hundred years after it was extinct, as far as one knows, in other countries save for folk forms of Eastern Europe, especially Russia.

The fingerholes on cornetts have to be spaced rather widely apart to give clear notes, and a difficulty with the straight treble (there are no straight tenors) is the absence of any relief for the stretch of the lower fingers. The same holds for the *mute cornet* (**667**) though here advantage is taken of the lathe-turned pipe to cut the mouthpiece cup in the top end of the pipe itself. The cup is shallow, while the rounded throat and relative softness of the wooden walls take the edge off the sound, and the tone of the mute cornett is very sweet, that of the ordinary cornett being brighter. Mute cornetts expand in exterior diameter from *c.* 1·8–4 cm. A handsomely mounted specimen in two joints (**668**) may be of the late seventeenth century.

Serpents, Bass Horns

The serpent is pitched about an octave lower than the tenor cornett, from which it also differs in possessing a very much wider conical bore, giving free amplitude to the deeper frequencies. Again it is of wood, covered with leather, equally difficult to play well and equally effective when played well. It is stated in an eighteenth-century French work to have been invented *c.* 1590 by a canon of Auxerre, and it was certainly known in France at the beginning of the seventeenth century (see *Grove*, 5th edn, 'Serpent', by R. Morley-Pegge) in the form in which it remained in use as a church instrument up to late in the nineteenth century. This *serpent d'église* (**674**) is keyless, with six holes and no thumbhole, and was generally made in two halves like a cornett. The brass crook is turned in a right angle and the cup mouthpiece of roughly trombone size is of horn or sometimes ivory. The serpent was brought to England in the latter part of the seventeenth century to be used sporadically in bands and orchestras up to the third quarter of the eighteenth century, when the expansion of military bands created a new interest in the instrument, matched by a similar development in Germany.

The German military serpent kept the long French model with bends of fairly wide radius, but employed a crook with a double bend which brings the mouthpiece nearer the centre line of the instrument (**679**). There are models without keys (e.g. by W. Schmidt, Mainz, in the Brunswick museum) and with two or three keys as shown. They were held with both hands placed above their respective sections of the tube, thus keeping the basic sequence of finger movements in line with that of other woodwind instruments. The same holds with a curious keyless serpent in the Barcelona Collection (**675**), Spanish bands also having adopted the serpent and used it through much of the last century. In England the serpent was built in more compact shape with the upper bends of small radius, and the crook keeps the single bend of the traditional French instrument. The fingerholes are bushed with ivory (**680**). Keyless examples are known (e.g. by Thos. Key, Peterborough Museum) but most have from three keys upwards, arranged for playing with the right hand below the tube, palm upwards, so that the ring finger covers the fourth hole instead of the sixth, and so on. Some nineteenth-century English serpents have bodies built up in sections. Makers include well-known woodwind makers like Milhouse, Gerock, Bilton, and especially Key, who produced (1841 ?) a final design with all holes covered by brass keywork (**682**). By this time the serpent was largely displaced from bands by valved instruments, though it lasted in Festival orchestras up to 1870 (e.g. at Birmingham). Exceptional English serpents include examples with bodies of copper (London, Boosey & Hawkes Coll.) and a contra-serpent twice the size of the ordinary, made *c.* 1840 (Huddersfield, Tolson Museum; see Morley-Pegge, *GSJ*, XII, 1959).

The idea of straightening the serpent tube for more comfortable handling originated, like the instrument itself, in France. Piffault, Paris, *c.* 1806, effected it fairly neatly (**681**) and serpents in different partially straightened forms are found in collections (*serpent de cavalerie*, like a small wavy tuba, etc). In the later model of Embach, on the contrary, the bends are sharpened to produce a very compact and small instrument, held sideways (**683**). More important in band history are 'upright serpents' composed of two straight tubes placed parallel or slightly diverging, and connected at the bottom. Frichot, a French refugee, had produced the *bass horn* in England during the 1790s. It is of brass or copper (though a wooden example is in the Horniman Museum, Carse 284) with flared bell and fingerholes raised on short tubes (**685**) as has often been the practice when metal is substituted for the thicker-walled wood (e.g. metal clarinets and bassoons). The bass horn is also narrower in bore than a serpent and rather easier to manage, and it was played in English bands up to the 1830s, sometimes beside an ordinary serpent. After his return to France, Frichot invented a more compact design also of metal, the *basse-trompette*, 1806, illustrated in *Grove* ('Serpent') while a wooden version is shown here (**684**). The *serpent Forveille*, Paris, *c.* 1823, reverts to leather-covered wood. The first three holes, however, are in a detachable brass joint with the holes raised, and this carries the brass crook (**686**). A larger and later instrument of similar kind is a contra-bass-horn (**687**) by Coëffet, 1810, another French maker and inventor.

A number of upright serpents meanwhile appeared in Germany, generally known there as *Bass-horn*. One is a 'chromatic bass horn' by Streitwolf, Göttingen, 1820, with a metal bow joining the lower ends of two turned wooden tubes and with brass keys (**691**). There seems also to have been an all-metal model, another name of which was *Bombardone* (advertisement of Schott, Mainz, in *Cäcilia*, 1825). A design commoner on the Continent than any of the preceding (save perhaps for the *serpent Forveille* in Paris) is the *serpent basson* or *Russian bassoon* (also *serpent russe*, *Russische Bass-horn*, etc). Why 'Russian' is unexplained, but the instrument is very distinctive, being modelled on the bassoon, with three wooden joints, including wing and butt, and a brass bell characteristically—though not invariably—in the form of an open-jawed dragon's head with scaley skin painted in several colours and wagging tongue (**688, 689**). It has been thought to be derived from an invention of J. J. Régibo, Lille, announced in 1789, and was extensively played up to *c.* 1840, varying mainly in the arrangement of the three lower holes. Odd joints of these Russian bassoons are sometimes mistaken for bits of old bassoons, compared with which their proportions are thicker and shorter. A less common pattern (**690**) has the body built up solid, instead of having detachable wooden joints.

1 Lira da braccio. Giovanni d'Andrea, Verona, 1511. *Vienna, Kunsthistorisches Museum, Sammlung alter Musikinstrumente,*
C.94. **2–4** Lira da braccio. Giovanni Maria (dalla Corna) of Brescia, Venice, *c.* 1540 or earlier. *Oxford, Ashmolean Museum.*
5, 6 Lira da braccio. *London, Royal College of Music, 52.*

7

8

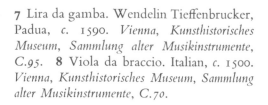

7 Lira da gamba. Wendelin Tieffenbrucker, Padua, *c.* 1590. *Vienna, Kunsthistorisches Museum, Sammlung alter Musikinstrumente, C.95.* 8 Viola da braccio. Italian, *c.* 1500. *Vienna, Kunsthistorisches Museum, Sammlung alter Musikinstrumente, C.70.*

9 Viola da braccio. Label printed in capitals, though in type of a later character than the date given, *Nicolaus Franciscus Constantini. 1508. Lisbon, Conservatório Nacional, 58.* 10 Lira da gamba ('lirone perfetto'). Unsigned. *Brussels, Conservatoire royal de Musique, 1444.*

9

10

11 Lira da gamba. Unsigned. Italian, ? 1659. *Leipzig, former Heyer Collection, 784.* **12** Large viola da braccio. *Brussels, Conservatoire royal de Musique, 1415.* **13, 14** Violin. Ventura Linarol, Venice, 1581. *Vienna, Kunsthistorisches Museum, Sammlung alter Musikinstrumente, C.96.* **15** Viola. Gasparo da Salò, 1561. *Oxford, Ashmolean Museum.* **16** Viola. Gasparoda Salò, Brescia, c. 1580. *Oxford, Ashmolean Museum.*

17–19 Violin. Andrea Amati, Cremona, 1564. Oxford, *Ashmolean Museum.* **20, 21** Viola. Andrea Amati, Cremona, 1574. Oxford, *Ashmolean Museum.* **22** Violin. Formerly ascribed to Gasparo da Salò, Brescia. *Bergen, Vestlandske Kunstindustri Museum.*

23, 24 Violin. Nicolò Amati, Cremona, 1680. *London, W. E. Hill & Sons.*   **25, 26** Violin. Antonio Stradivari, Cremona, 1683. *Oxford, Ashmolean Museum.*   **27, 28** Violin. Antonio Stradivari, Cremona, 1716. *Oxford, Ashmolean Museum.* **29** Violin bow. Italian, date d 1694. *London, W. E. Hill & Sons.*

30, 31 Violin. Jakob Stainer, Absom, 1688. *London, W. E. Hill & Sons.* **32, 33** Violin, Jan Boumeester, Amsterdam, 1683. *The Hague, Gemeentemuseum.* **34, 35** Viola. Antonio Stradivari, Cremona, 1690. *Florence, Istituto Luigi Cherubini, 5.* **36** Viola. Daniel Parker, London, 1715. *London, W. E. Hill & Sons.*

37 Viola pomposa. J. Chr. Hoffmann, Leipzig, 1720. *Brussels, Conservatoire royal de Musique, 1445.* **38, 39** Rebec. Probably Italian, 18th century. *Lisbon, Conservatório Nacional, 57.* **40** Rebec (*liritsa*). Dalmatian, 19th century. *London, Horniman Museum, 15.10.48/87.* **41** Walking-stick violin. Moritz Gläsel, Markneukirchen, 19th century. *Ann Arbor, University of Michigan, Stearns Collection, 1308.* **42** Kit. Dimanche Drouyn, Paris, 17th century. *London, Victoria and Albert Museum, 519–1872.* **43** Kit. Joachim Tielke, Hamburg, 1675. *London, W. E. Hill & Sons.* **44** Pochette d'amour. Battista, Genoa, 18th century. *London, Royal College of Music, 38.* **45** Kit. Gaspar Borbon, Brussels, 1686. *Brussels, Conservatoire royal de Musique, 2764.* **46** Kit. Unsigned. *Brussels, Conservatoire royal de Musique, 493.* **47** Miniature violin. Unsigned. *Brussels, Conservatoire royal de Musique, 2766.*

48 Practice violin (*Brettgeige*). Johann Schorn, Salzburg, 1695. *Berlin, Staatliches Institut für Musikforschung, Musikinstrumenten-Sammlung, 282.* **49** Mute violin. English, 19th century. *London, Royal College of Music, 43.* **50** Violino-harpa. Th. Zach. Vienna, 1873. *Brussels, Conservatoire royal de Musique, 1359.* **51** Contra-alto. J. B. Vuillaume, Paris, 1851. *Brussels, Conservatoire royal de Musique, 235.* **52, 53** Violoncello piccolo. Jakob Stainer, Absom, 17th century. *Haslemere, Dolmetsch Collection.* **54** Violoncello. Martin Kaiser, Venice, 1679. *Brussels, Conservatoire royal de Musique, 1441.* **55, 56** Violoncello. Antonio Stradivari, 1690. *Florence, Istituto Luigi Cherubini, 6.*

57 Double bass. Gottfried Tielke, (Königsberg), 1662. *Leipzig, Karl-Marx-Universität, Musikinstrumenten-Museum, 940.*
58 Double bass. Pietro Zenatto, Treviso, 1683. *Brussels, Conservatoire royal de Musique, 1437.* **59** Double bass. Barbieri Franscesco, Verona, 1697. *Lisbon, Conservatório Nacional, 90.*

60 Double bass. Carlo Giuseppe Testore, Milan, 1694. *London, in private ownership.* **61** Double bass. John Frederick Lott, London, first half of 19th century. *In private ownership.* **62, 63** Violone. Gio: Paolo Maggini, Brescia, early 17th century. *Haslemere, Dolmetsch Collection.* **64, 65** Violone. Ventura Linarol, Padua, 1585. *Vienna, Kunsthistorisches Museum, Sammlung alter Musikinstrumente, C.78.*

66 Husla (Wendish fiddle). 19th century. *Copenhagen, Musikhistorisk Museum, D.56.* **67, 68** Harding fiddle. Norwegian, 1841. *Oxford, Pitt Rivers Museum, 131.H.12.* **69** Violin. François Chanot, Paris, 1818. *Brussels, Conservatoire royal de Musique, 1332.* **70** Violin. Félix Savart, Paris, *c. 1819. Paris, Conservatoire de Musique, Musée instrumentale, C.19.* **71** Violin. Rigart Rubus, St Petersburg, 1850. *London, Royal Military School of Music, Kneller Hall, 195.* **72** Violin. Thomas Howell, Bristol, *c. 1835. London, Royal College of Music, 54.* **73** Philomele. German, second half of 19th century. *London, Horniman Museum, 15.10.48/30.* **74** Crwth (Welsh fiddle). Welsh, 18th century. *London, Victoria and Albert Museum, 175–1882.* **75** Crwth. Welsh, 18th century. *Warrington, Museum.*

76–9 Treble viol. Giovanni Maria (dalla Corna) of Brescia, Venice, *c.* 1540 or earlier. Oxford, *Ashmolean Museum.* **80–2** Bass viol. Hans Vohar (? Vienna, late 15th century or perhaps later). *Haslemere, Dolmetsch Collection.*

83 Tenor viol. Gasparo da Salò, Brescia, second half of 16th century. *Vienna, Kunsthistorisches Museum, Sammlung alter Musikinstrumente, C.72.* **84, 85** Bass viol. Gaspard Duiffoprugcar, Lyons, *c.* 1560. *The Hague, Gemeentemuseum.* **86** Bass viol. Battista Ciciliano, Venice, ? 16th century. *Brussels, Conservatoire royal de Musique, 1426.* **87** Tenor viol. Francesco Linarol, Venice, *c.* 1540. *Vienna, Kunsthistorisches Museum, Sammlung alter Musikinstrumente, C.71.*

88–90 Bass viol. Gasparo da Salò, Brescia. *Oxford, Ashmolean Museum.* 91, 92 Bass viol. Antonio and Geronimo Amati, Cremona, 1611. *Oxford, Ashmolean Museum.* 93 Bass viol. Venetian, 16th century. *Oxford, Ashmolean Museum.*

94–6 Lyra viol. John Rose, London, 1598. *Oxford, Ashmolean Museum.* **97** Bass viol. Ascribed to John Rose, London, late 16th century. *Oxford, Ashmolean Museum.* **98, 99** Bass viol. Henry Jaye, Southwark (London), 1619. *London, W. E. Hill & Sons.*

100 Bass viol. Richard Meares, London, 1677. *London, Victoria and Albert Museum, 170–1882.* **101, 102** Bass viol. Barak Norman, London 1697. *Berlin, Staatliches Institut für Musikforschung, Musikinstrumenten-Sammlung, 168.* **103, 104** Division viol. Barak Norman, London, 1712. *Haslemere, Dolmetsch Collection.* **105** Tenor viol. John Baker, 'Exon' (on label, but ? Oxford), 1660. *Haslemere, Dolmetsch Collection.*

106 Division viol. Ernst Busch, Nuremberg, 1644. *Leipzig, Karl-Marx-Universität, Musikinstrumenten-Museum, 808.* **107** Bass viol. Vicenzo Ruger, Cremona, 1702. *Berlin, Staatliches Institut für Musikforschung, Musikinstrumenten-Sammlung, 164.* **108** Bass viol. Jakob Stainer, Absom, 1655. *Haslemere, Dolmetsch Collection.* **109** Tenor viol. Johann Ulrich Eberle, Prague, 1749. *Leipzig, Karl-Marx-Universität, Musikinstrumenten-Museum, 796.* **110** Bass viol. Zenatto, Treviso, 1643. *Lisbon, Conservatório Nacional, 65.*

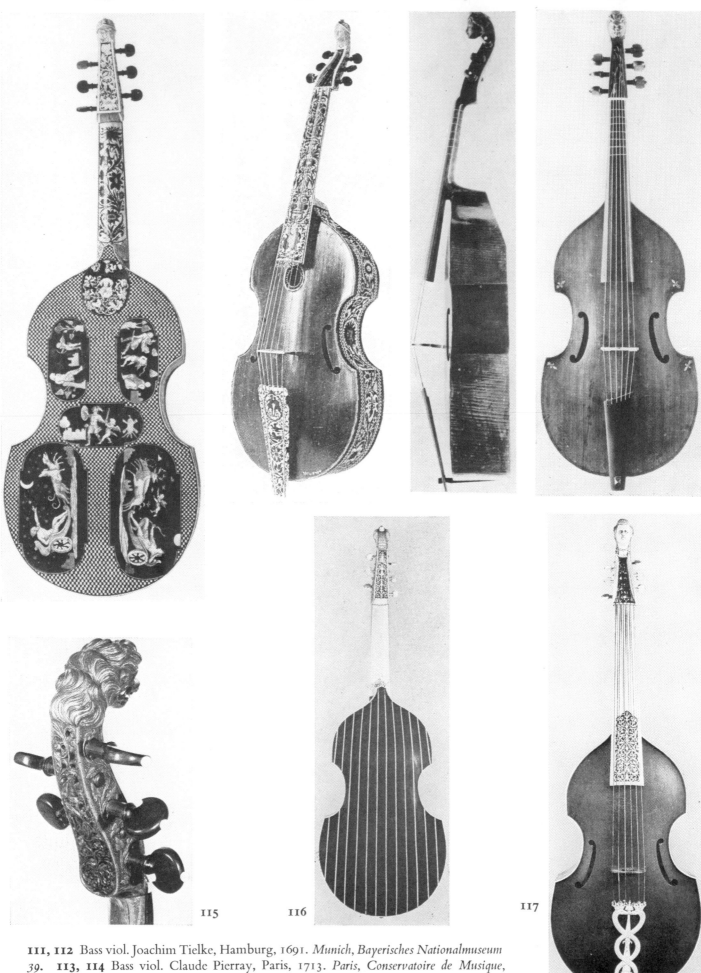

111, 112 Bass viol. Joachim Tielke, Hamburg, 1691. *Munich, Bayerisches Nationalmuseum 39.* **113, 114** Bass viol. Claude Pierray, Paris, 1713. *Paris, Conservatoire de Musique, Musée instrumentale, E.1006, C.173.* **115** Head of bass viol. Joachim Tielke, Hamburg, 1694. *Barcelona, Museo Municipál de Música, 693.* **116, 117** Bass viol. Joachim Tielke, Hamburg, 1701. *Brussels, Conservatoire royal de Musique, 229.*

118 Quinton. Nicolas Louis Gilbert, Metz, 1701. *Brussels, Conservatoire royal de Musique, 1396.* 119, 120 Pardessus de viole. Paul François Grosset, Paris, 1742. *Berlin, Staatliches Institut für Musikforschung, Musikinstrumenten-Sammlung, 4220.* 121, 122 Pardessus de viole. Louis Guersan, Paris, 1754. *Brussels, Conservatoire royal de Musique, 480.* 123, 124 Alto viol. Richard Duke, London, 1786. *Boston, Museum of Fine Arts, Leslie Lindsey Mason Collection, 277.* 125, 126 Viola d'amore. Caspar Stadler, Trabant (Munich), 1714. *Nuremberg, Germanisches Nationalmuseum, MI.208.*

127 Viola d'amore. J. B. Wassner, Passau, 1707. *Basel, Historisches Museum, 1956–431.* **128** Viola d'amore. Max Zacher, Breslau, 1733. *Berlin, Staatliches Institut für Musikforschung, Musikinstrumenten-Sammlung, 4526.* **129** Viola d'amore (Englisches Violett). Johann Paul Schorn, Salzburg, 1712. *Nuremberg, Germanisches Nationalmuseum, Rück Collection.* **130** Viola d'amore (Englishes Violett). J. U. Eberle, Prague, 1737. *London, Royal College of Music, 33.* **131** Bow of viola d'amore. Italian. *Brighton Museums, Spencer Collection.* **132** Viola d'amore. Probably French. *London, Victoria and Albert Museum, 157–1882.* **133** Violon d'amour. Salomon, Paris, 174–. *Brussels, Conservatoire royal de Musique, 481.* **134** Cither viol. John Perry, Dublin, 1767. *London, Victoria and Albert Museum, 156–1882.* **135** Cither viol. Stewart & Son (? London), 1828. *London, Reuben Greene Collection.*

136-8 Baryton. Jacques Sainprae, Berlin, first half of 18th century. *London, Victoria and Albert Museum, 1444–1870.* **139** Baryton. Joachim Tielke, Hamburg, 1686. *London, Victoria and Albert Museum, 115–1865.* **140** Bass viol (*viola bastarda*). Unsigned, German, second half of 17th century. *The Hague, Gemeentemuseum.* **141** Arpeggione. J. Georg Staufer, Vienna, 1824. *Leipzig, Karl-Marx-Universität, Musikinstrumenten-Museum, 609.*

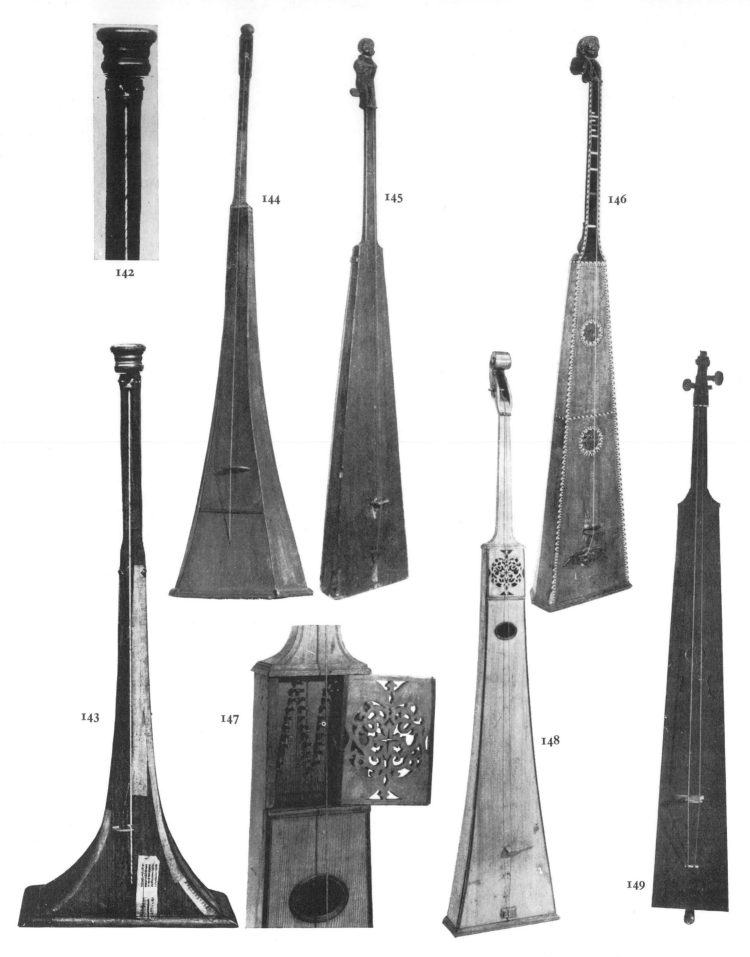

142, 143 Trumpet marine. German, 17th century. *Basel, Historisches Museum, 1876.21; Nef 151.* **144** Trumpet marine. Hornsteiner, Mittenwald, 1790. *Berlin, Staatliches Institut für Musikforschung, Musikinstrumenten-Sammlung, 158.* **145** Trumpet marine. German, 18th century. *London, Royal College of Music, 244.* **146** Trumpet marine. Renault, Paris, second half of 18th century. *London, Royal College of Music, 289.* **147, 148** Trumpet marine. ? German, c. 1700. *London, Victoria and Albert Museum, 174–1882.* **149** Trumpet marine. Italian, 18th century. *Lisbon, Conservatório Nacional, 100.*

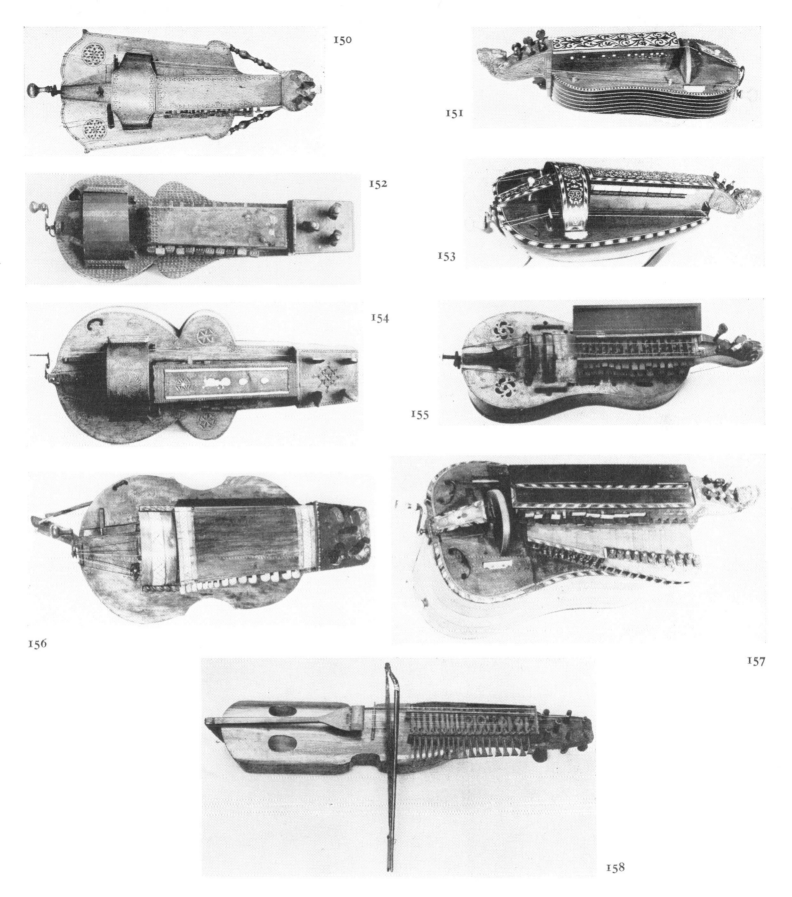

150 Hurdy-gurdy. French, 16th century. *Paris, Conservatoire de Musique, Musée instrumentale, E.2057.* **151** Hurdy-gurdy (*vielle en guitare*). French, 18th century. *London, Royal College of Music, 120.* **152** Hurdy-gurdy. German, 1787. *Hamburg, Museum für Hamburgische Geschichte, 1924, 223.* **153** Hurdy-gurdy (*vielle en luth*). Varquain, Paris, 1742. *London, Royal College of Music, 123.* **154** Hurdy-gurdy. German, 1714. *Hamburg, Museum für Hamburgische Geschichte, 1924, 222.* **155** Hurdy-gurdy. Quig, Ireland, late 18th or early 19th century. *Dublin, National Museum of Ireland.* **156** Hurdy-gurdy. Austrian, 17th or 18th century. *Salzburg, Museum Carolino Augusteum, 162, Geiringer 106.* **157** Organ hurdy-gurdy (*vielle organisée*). *London, Royal College of Music, 122.* **158** Keyed fiddle (*nyckelharpa*). Swedish, 19th century. *Stockholm, Musikhistoriska Museet, 2344.*

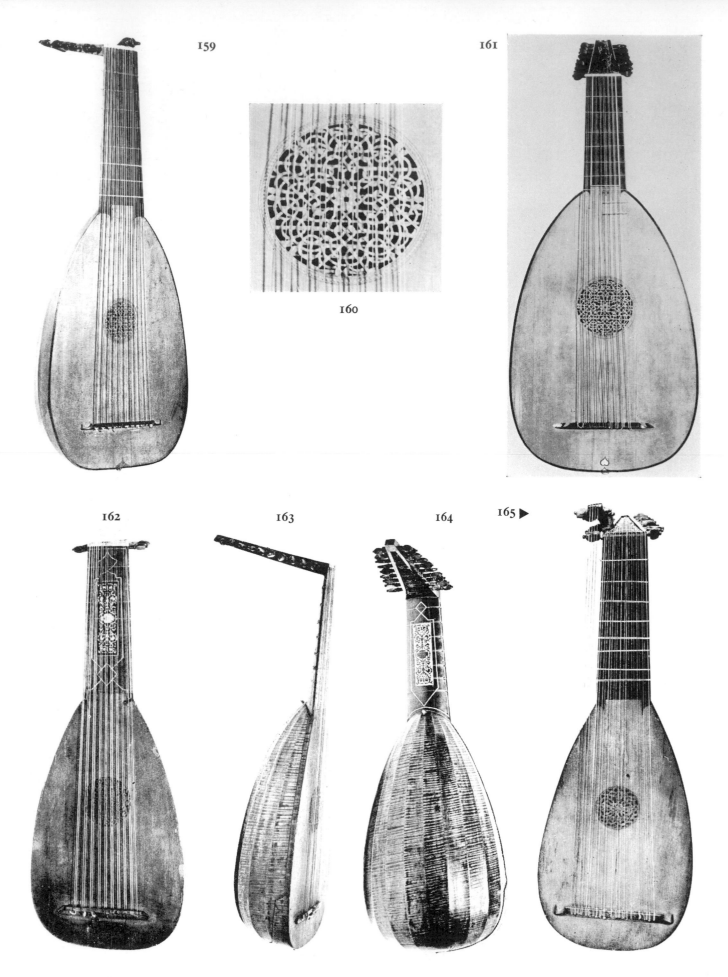

159 Lute. Laux Maler, Bologna, *c.* 1520. *Vienna, Kunsthistorisches Museum, Sammlung alter Musikinstrumente, C.32.* **160, 161** Lute. Michielle Harton, Padua, 1598. *Washington, Folger Shakespeare Library.* **162–4** Lute. Hans Frei, Bologna, *c.* 1550. *Warwick, Museum. Ex Halfpenny Collection.* **165** Lute. Gaspar Duiffoprugcar, Lyons, *c.* 1550. *Copenhagen, Claudius Collection, Musikhistorisk Museum, 91A.*

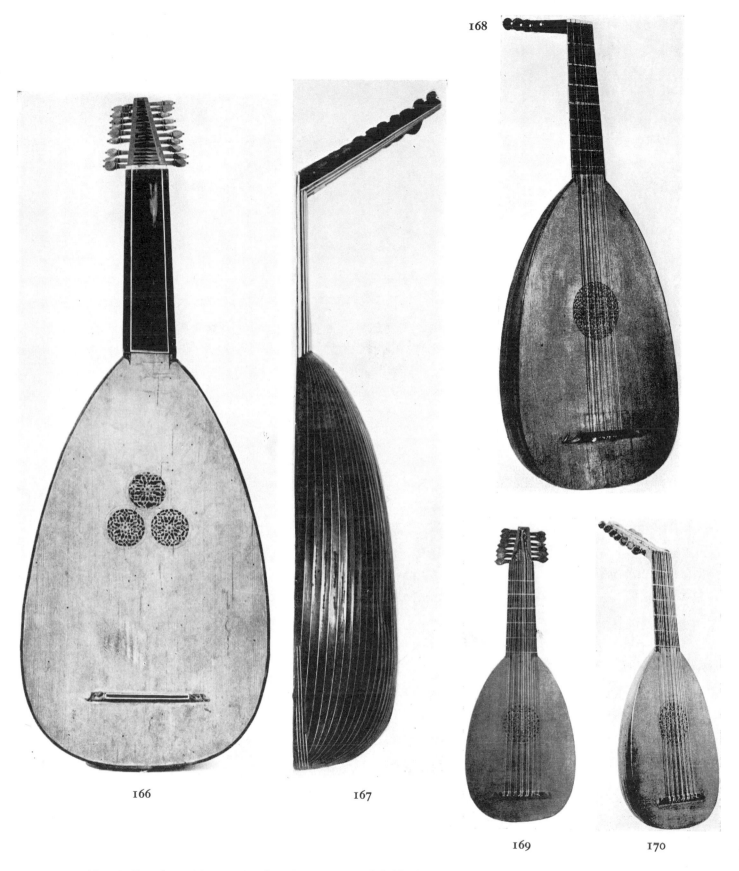

166   167   169   170

166, 167 Bass lute. Magnus Stegher, Venice, second half of 16th century. *Bologna, Museo Civico, 12.*
168 Lute. Wendelin Tieffenbrucker, Padua, 1582. *Vienna, Kunsthistorisches Museum, Sammlung alter Musikinstrumente, C.36.* **169, 170** Descant lute. Wendelin Tieffenbrucker, Padua. *Vienna, Kunsthistorisches Museum, Sammlung alter Musikinstrumente, C.39.*

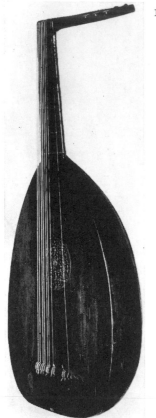

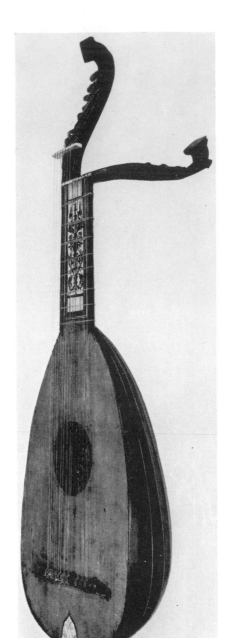

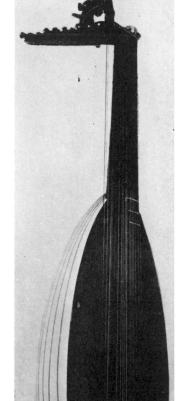

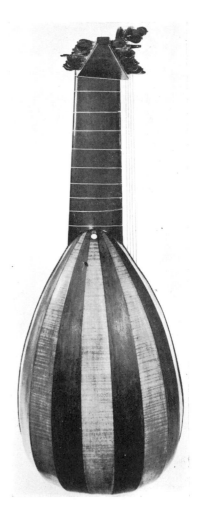

171 Treble lute. Giovanni Hieber, Venice, late 16th century. *Brussels, Conservatoire royal de Musique, 1561.* **172** Theorbo-lute. P. Massaini, Rome, 1570. *The Hague, Gemeentemuseum.* **173, 175** Theorbo-lute. Sebastian Schelle, Nuremberg, 1727. *Paris, Conservatoire de Musique, Musée instrumentale, E.233.* **174** Lute. Hans Burkholtzer, Füssen, 1596. *Vienna, Kunsthistorisches Museum, Sammlung alter Musikinstrumente, N.E.48.*

176–8 Small theorbo. Matteo Sellas, Venice, 1638. *Paris, Conservatoire de Musique, Musée instrumentale, E.1028, C.1052.* **179** Theorbo. Wendelin Tieffenbrucker, Padua, 1611. *Vienna, Kunsthistorisches Museum, Sammlung alter Musikinstrumente, C.47.*

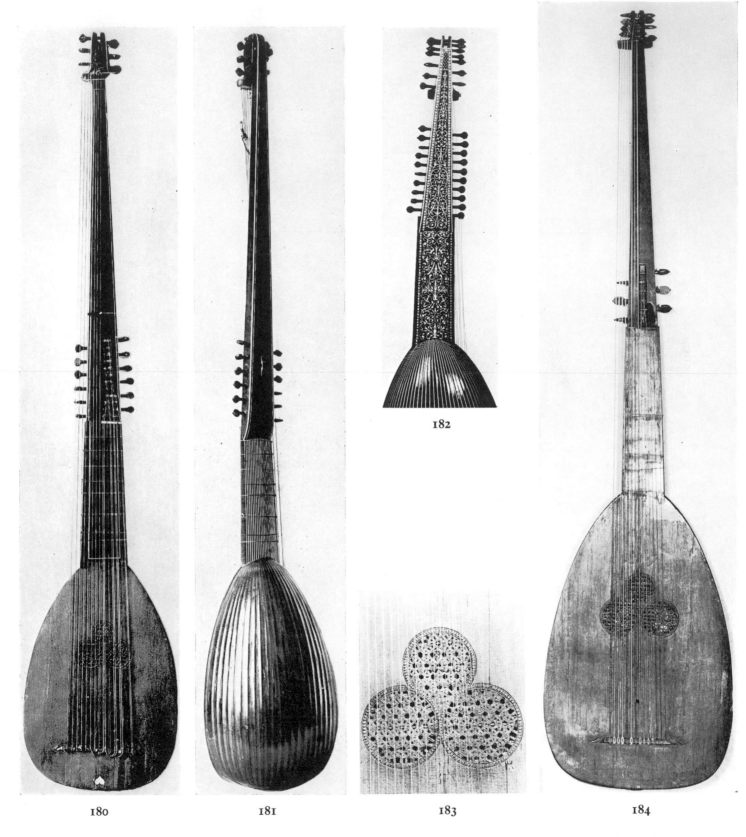

180, 181 Chitarrone. Magno Tieffenbrucker, Venice, second half of 16th century. *Vienna, Kunsthistorisches Museum, Sammlung alter Musikinstrumente, C.45.* **182** Theorbo, Magno Tieffenbrucker, Venice. *Barcelona, Museo Municipál de Música, 404.* **183** Rose of chitarrone. Matteo Buechenberg, Rome, 1614. *London, Victoria and Albert Museum, 190–1882.* **184** Chitarrone. Matteo Buechenberg, Rome, 1608. *Brussels, Conservatoire royal de Musique, 1570.*

185 Theorbo. Johann Christian Hoffman, Leipzig, 1717. *Berlin, Staatliches Institut für Musikforschung, Musikinstrumenten-Sammlung, 129.* 186 Theorbo. Matteo Sellas, Venice, first half of 17th century. *Brussels, Conservatoire royal de Musique, 1565.* 187 Theorbo. Jacob Heinrich Goldt, Hamburg, 1734. *London, Victoria and Albert Museum, 4274–1856.* 188 Angel lute. J. Chr. Fleischer. *Schwerin, Mecklenburgische Landesbibliothek.* 189, 190 Angel lute. Joachim Tielke, Hamburg, 1704. *Schwerin, Mecklenburgische Landesbibliothek.*

191

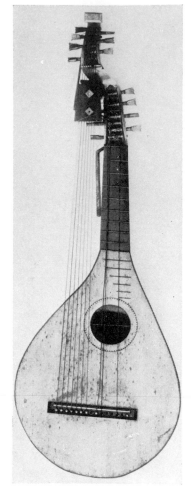

192

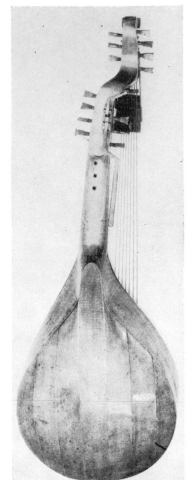

193

194

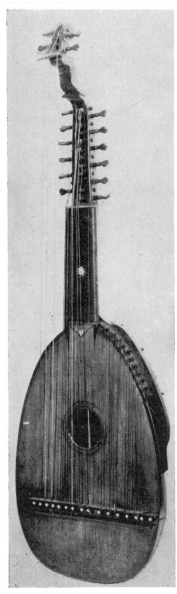

191 Cobsa. Moldavian, 19th century. *London, Horniman Museum, 28.4.56/238.* **192, 193** Swedish lute. Lorents Mollenberg, Stockholm, 1817. *London, Royal College of Music, 135.* **194** Lute. Mattias Griesser, Innsbruck, 1756. *Copenhagen, Claudius Collection, Musikhistorisk Museum, 99A.* **195** Russian theorbo. First half of 19th century. *London, Royal College of Music, 151.* **196** Russian bandura. *London, Royal College of Music, 286.*

195

196

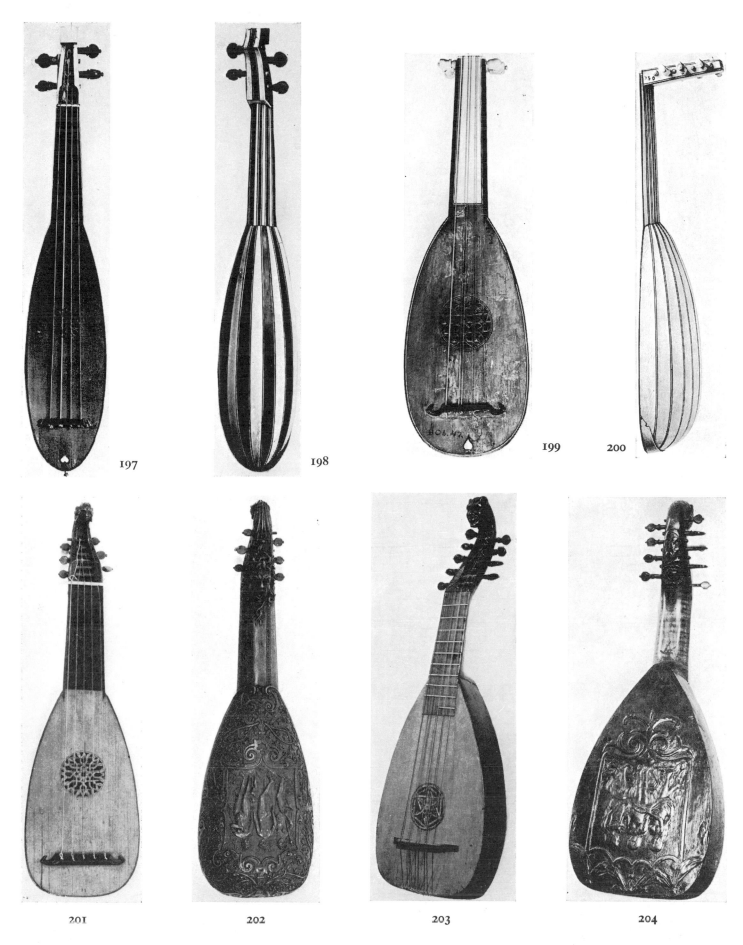

197, 198 Mandore. Italian, ? 16th century. *Vienna, Kunsthistorisches Museum, Sammlung alter Musikinstrumente, C.43.* 199, 200 Mandore. 16th or 17th century. *Copenhagen, Musikhistorisk Museum, 300.* 201, 202 Mandore. French, 17th century. *London, Victoria and Albert Museum, 219–1866.* 203, 204 Mandore. Jacques Dumesnil, Paris, mid 17th century. *Lisbon, Conservatório Nacional.*

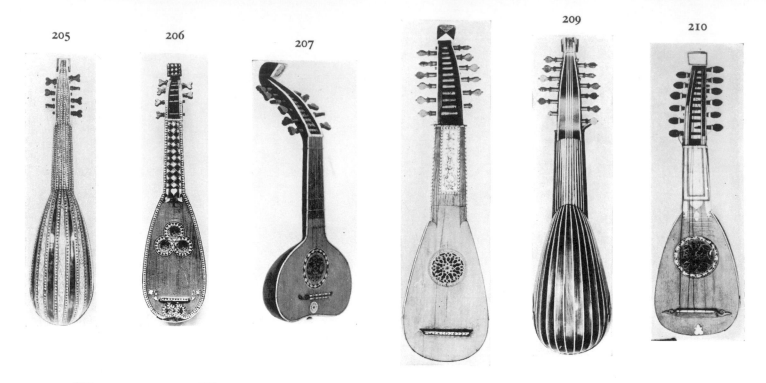

205 206 207 209 210

211 212

205, 206 Mandore. Pietro Antonio Gavelli, Perugia, 1690. *London, Victoria and Albert Museum, 504–1868.* 207 Mandore. Francesco Presbler, Milan, 1733. *London, Royal College of Music, 109.* 208, 209 Mandore. Giovanni Smorsone, Rome, 1714. *London, Royal College of Music, 201.* 210 Mandore (Milanese mandolin). Giuseppe Presbler, Milan, 1775. *London, Royal College of Music, 202.* 211, 212 Mandore. Joseph Gallina, Brescia, 17—. *London, Royal College of Music, 19.* 213 Mandore. J. N. Lambert, Paris, 1752 (last two figures unclear). *London, Victoria and Albert Museum, 503–1868.* 214 Mandore. David, Paris, 1786. *London, Royal College of Music, 165.* 215, 216 Mandolin. Antonio Vinaccia, Naples, 1772. *London, Victoria and Albert Museum, 10–1894.* 217 Mandolin. Petroni, Rome, 1865. *London, Victoria and Albert Museum, 924–1902.*

213 214

215

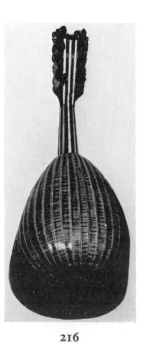

216 217

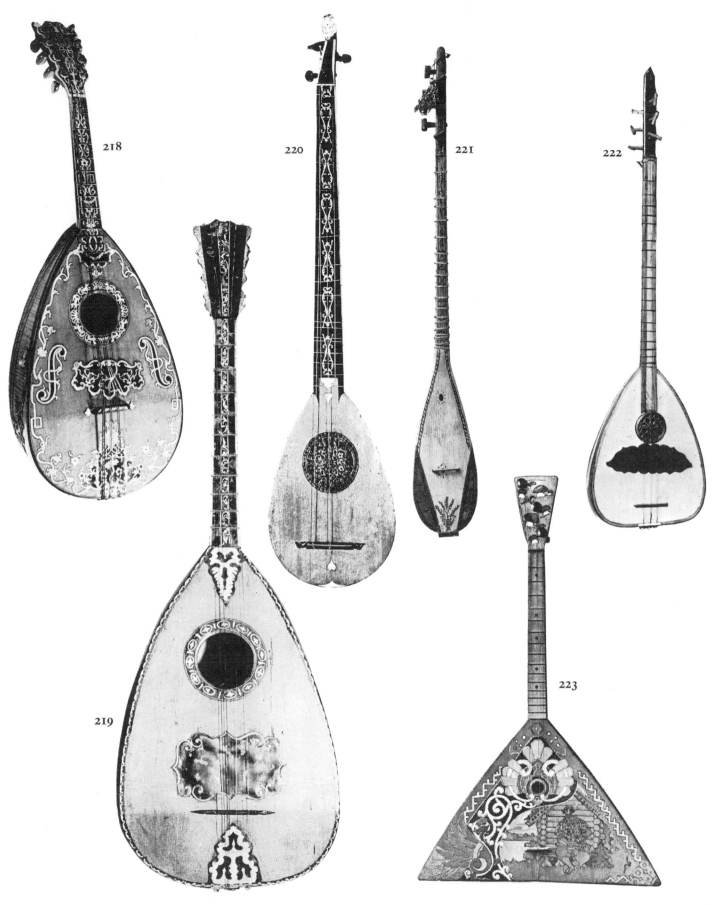

218 Mandola. Antonio Vinaccia, Naples, 1773. *London, W. E. Hill & Sons.* 219 Mandola. Gaetano Vinaccia, Naples, 1744. *Brussels, Conservatoire royal de Musique, 3182.* 220 Colascione. Italian, 17th century. *Brussels, Conservatoire royal de Musique, 1567.* 221 Bouzouki. Athens, 19th century. *Copenhagen, Musikhistorisk Museum, 317.* 222 Bouzouki (cavonto). Greek, late 19th century. *New York, Metropolitan Museum of Art, Crosby Brown Collection, 1018.* 223 Balalaika. Russian, 19th century. *Copenhagen, Musikhistorisk Museum, 319.*

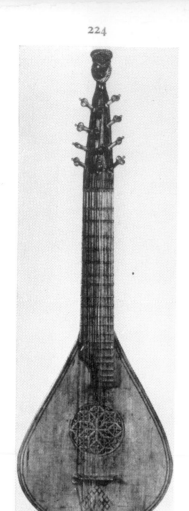

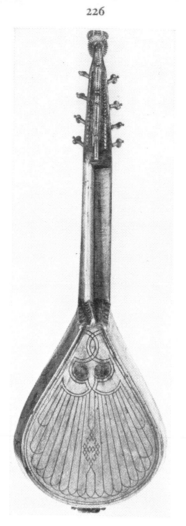

224–6 Cittern, Italian, *c.*1600. *Paris, Conservatoire de Musique, Musée instrumentale, E.543, C.250.* **227** Cittern. Italian, 1536. *Paris, Conservatoire de Musique, Musée instrumentale, E.1131, C.1054.* **228** Cittern. Girolamo de Virchis, Brescia, 1574. *Vienna, Kunsthistorisches Museum, Sammlung alter Musikinstrumente, A.61.* **229, 230** Cittern. Italian, 17th century. *Oxford, Ashmolean Museum.* **231** Cittern. ? Paduan, 16th or 17th century. *Vienna, Kunsthistorisches Museum, Sammlung alter Musikinstrumente, C.64.*

224

225

226

227

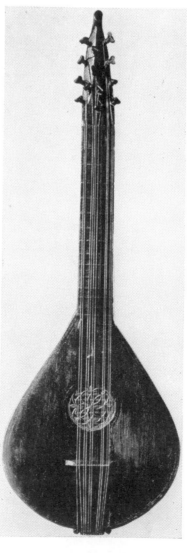

228

229

230

231

232

233

234

235

237

236

238

232-4 Cittern, Ascribed to Antonio Stradivari, Cremona, *c. 1700. Paris, Conservatoire de Musique, Musée instrumentale, E.1271, C.1055.* **235** Cittern. ? German, 1705. *Frankfurt-am-Main, Historisches Museum, Epstein, 51.* **236** Arch-cittern. Johann Gottfried Klemm. Radeberg, 1756. *The Hague, Gemeentemuseum.* **237** Arch-cittern. Andreas Ernst Kram, Nuremberg, 1768. *Berlin, Staatliches Institut für Musikforschung, Musikinstrumenten-Sammlung, 4080.* **238** Cittern (Wald-zither). Georg Nicol Köllmar, Krawinkel, 1816. *The Hague, Gemeentemuseum.*

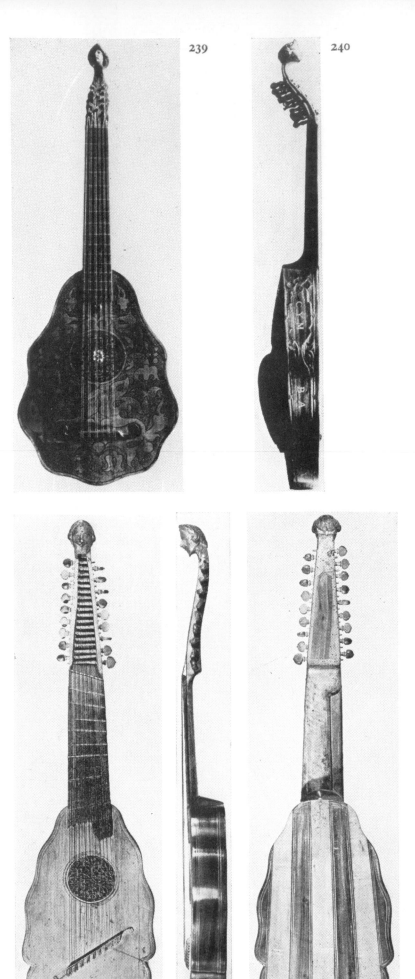

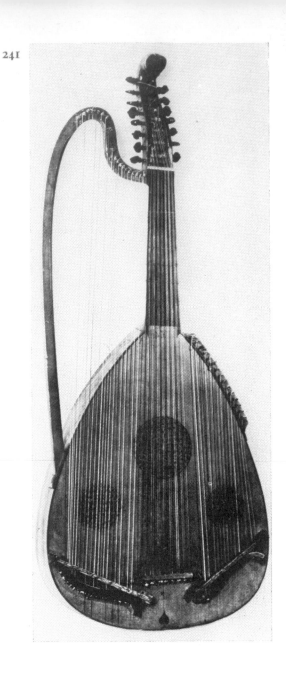

239, 240 Orpharion. John Rose, London, 1580. *Lord Tollemache, Helmingham Hall, Suffolk.* 241 Harp-cittern. Wendelin Tieffenbrucker, Padua, *c.* 1590. *Vienna, Kunsthistorisches Museum, Sammlung alter Musikinstrumente, C.67.* 242–4 Orpharion. Francis Palmer, London, 1617. *Copenhagen, Claudius Collection, Musikhistorisk Museum, 139 (23).*

245 Bell cittern. Joachim Tielke, Hamburg, c. 1700. *London, Victoria and Albert Museum, 1122–1869.* 246 Bell cittern. Joachim Tielke, Hamburg. *London, W. E. Hill & Sons.* 247 Bell cittern. Heinrich Kopp, Hamburg, 1702. *Berlin, Staatliches Institut für Musikforschung, Musikinstrumenten-Sammlung, 4798.* 248 Bell cittern. Michael Paiker, Copenhagen, 1739. *Copenhagen, Musikhistorisk Museum, 327.* 249 English guitar. John Preston, London, c. 1770. *Oxford, Ashmolean Museum.* 250 English guitar. Rudiman, Aberdeen, third quarter of 18th century. *London, Victoria and Albert Museum, 375–1882.* 251, 252 English guitar. John Zumpe, London, 1762. *Frankfurt-am-Main, Historisches Museum, Epstein 53.*

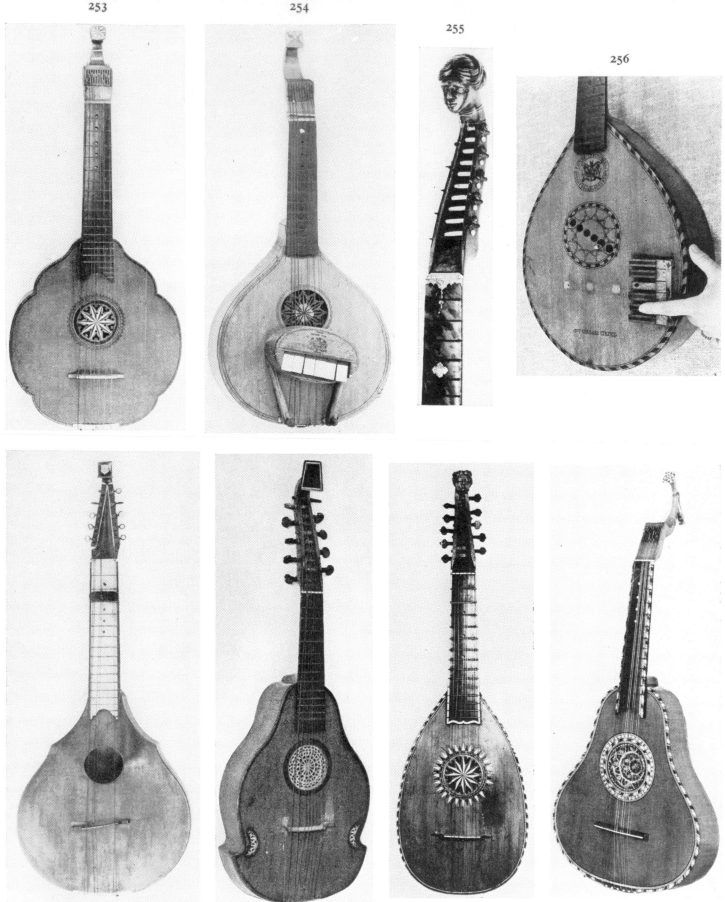

253 English guitar. Remerus Liessem, London, 1756. *London, Victoria and Albert Museum, 230–1882.* **254** English guitar. Frederick Hintz, London. *London, Victoria and Albert Museum, 37–1870.* **255** English guitar. J. C. Elschleger, England, third quarter of 18th century. *London, Royal College of Music, 21.* **256** English guitar. Claus & Co., London. *London, Victoria and Albert Museum.* **257** English guitar. William Gibson, Dublin, 1765. *London, Victoria and Albert Museum, W.17–1919.* **258** Norwegian cittern. Armund Hansen, Friederichshald, c. 1790. *Stockholm, Musikhistoriska Museet, 999.* **259** Cittern. Gérard J. Deleplanque, Lille, 1764. *Brussels, Conservatoire royal de Musique, 1525.* **260** Cittern. G. le Blond, Dunkirk, 1773. *Leipzig, Karl-Marx-Universität, Musikinstrumenten-Museum, 618.*

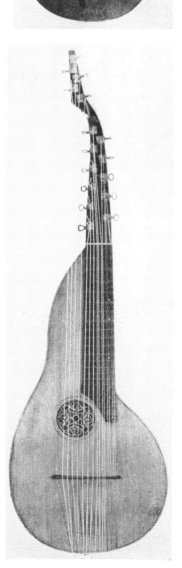

261 Arch-cittern. G. Deleplanque, Lille; keybox dated 1792. *Brussels, Conservatoire royal de Musique, 2916.* **262, 265** Arch-cittern. Renault, Paris, late 18th century. *Paris, Conservatoire de Musique, Musée instrumentale, C.260.* **263, 266, 267** Arch-cittern. Renault & Chatelain, Paris, 1787. *Paris, Conservatoire de Musique, Musée instrumentale, E.1662.* **264** Arch-cittern. Louis S. Laurent, Paris, 1775. *Brussels, Conservatoire royal de Musique, 252.*

268 Portuguese guitar. Jaco Vieira da Silva, Lisbon, 17—. *London, Victoria and Albert Museum, 208–1882.* **269** Portuguese guitar. Rosa & Caldeira, Lisbon, mid 19th century. *Brussels, Conservatoire royal de Musique, 2494.* **270** *Pandore en luth.* ? 18th century. *Brussels, Conservatoire royal de Musique, 1555.* **271–3** Bandurria. 18th century. *Paris, Conservatoire de Musique, Musée instrumentale, E.535, C.247.* **274** Bandurria. Late 19th century. *Brussels, Conservatoire royal de Musique, 3185.* **275** Treble guitar (*Cavaquinho*). Portuguese, 19th century. *London, Royal College of Music, 130.* **276** Rajão (guitar in form of a fish). Portuguese, 19th century. *London, Horniman Museum, 28.4.56/220.* **277** Guitar. Joze F. Coelho Lisbon, *c.* 1820. *London, Horniman Museum.*

278   279   280   283

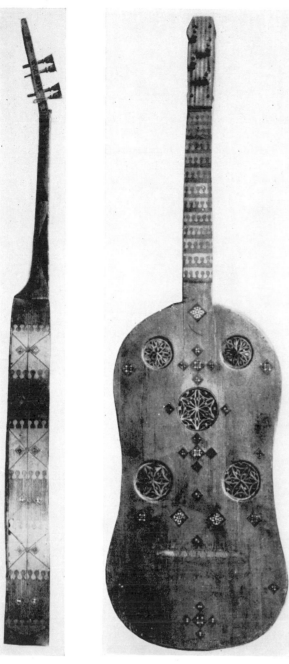
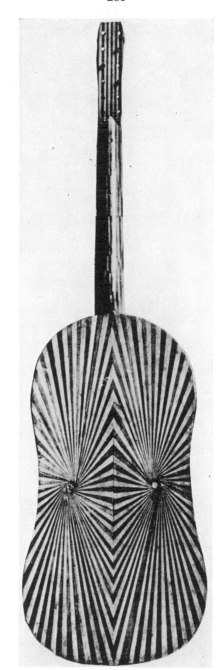

278–80 Vihuela. Spanish, 16th century. *Paris, Musée Jacquemart-André.* 281 Guitar. Giovanni Smit, Milan, 1646. *Vienna, Kunsthistorisches Museum, Sammlung alter Musikinstrumente, C.53.* 282 Guitar. Giovanni Smit, Milan, 1646. *Vienna, Kunsthistorisches Museum, Sammlung alter Musikinstrumente, C.52.* 283, 284 Guitar. Belchior Dias, 1581. *London, Royal College of Music, 171.*

281   282   284

285-7 Guitar. Matteo Sellas, Venice, c. 1630.
Brussels, Conservatoire royal de Musique, 550. **288,
289** Guitar. Giorgio Jungmann, Genoa, 1633. *Brussels,
Conservatoire royal de Musique, 3183.*

285

286

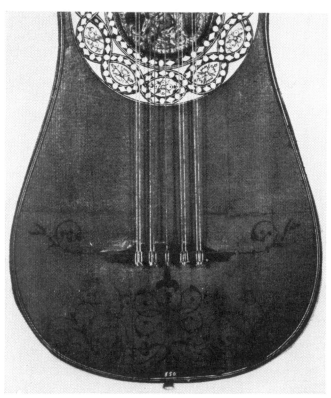

287

288

289

290 Guitar. René Voboam, Paris, 1641. *Oxford, Ashmolean Museum.* **291** Chitarra battente. Jakob Stadler, Munich, 1624. *London, W. E. Hill & Sons.* **292, 293** Guitar. Joachim Tielke, Hamburg, *c.* 1700. *London, Victoria and Albert Museum, 676–1872.* **294, 295** Chitarra battente. Italian, 17th or 18th century. *London, W. E. Hill & Sons.*

296 Guitar. Lamblin, Ghent, 1795. *Brussels, Conservatoire royal de Musique, 2909.* 297 Guitar. Thielemann, Berlin, 1814. *Berlin, Staatliches Institut für Musikforschung, Musikinstrumenten-Sammlung, 4676.* 298, 299 Guitar. Grobert, Mirecourt, first half of 19th century. *Paris, Conservatoire de Musique, Musée instrumentale, E.375, C.278.* 300 Guitar. José Pages, Cadiz, 1798. *London, Victoria and Albert Museum, 415–1905.* 301 Guitar. Gennaro Fabricatore, Naples, c. 1805. *London, Reuben Greene Collection.* 302 Guitar. Louis Panormo, London, c. 1820. *London, Reuben Greene Collection.* 303 Guitar. Harlot, Mirecourt, early 19th century. *Basel, Historisches Museum, 1897:28.*

304 Guitar. Louis Panormo, London, 1829. *Leipzig, Karl-Marx-Universität, Musikinstrumenten-Museum, 566.* **305, 306** Guitar. Antonio Torres, Almeria, 1859. *Barcelona, Museo Municipál de Música, 626.* **307** Guitar. Porcel, Barcelona, 1867. *Barcelona, Museo Municipál de Música, 445.* **308** Guitar. Martin & Coupa, New York City, c. 1835–50. *Washington, Smithsonian Institution, loaned by Walter Lipton.* **309** Guitar. O. F. Selling, Stockholm, c. 1835. *Stockholm, Musikhistoriska Museet, 1462.* **310** Guitar. Altimira, Barcelona, 184–. *London, Victoria and Albert Museum, W.15–1915.* **311** Guitar. G. Tiefenbrunner, Munich, mid 19th century. *Ann Arbor, University of Michigan, Stearns Collection, 1117.*

312 Lyre-guitar. J. G. Thielemann, Berlin, *c. 1800. Berlin, Staatliches Institut für Musikforschung, Musikinstrumenten-Sammlung,* 4677. **313, 314** French lyre. Charles, Marseilles, 1785. *Yale, University, Belle Skinner Collection.* **315** Lyre-guitar. Lupot, Orleans, 1778. *New York, Metropolitan Museum of Art, Crosby Brown Collection, 2590.* **316** Apollo lyre. Robert Wornum, London, before 1815. *London, Victoria and Albert Museum, 891–1875.* **317** French lyre. Boulan, Arras, 17—. *Brussels, Conservatoire royal de Musique, 3180.*

318 Arpi-guitare. Pacquet, Marseilles, 1784. *Brussels, Conservatoire royal de Musique, 3177.* **319** Guitar. Gennaro Fabricatore, Naples, 1817. *Brussels, Conservatoire royal de Musique, 1537.* **320, 321** Bissex. H. Naderman, Paris, 1773. *Paris, Conservatoire de Musique, Musée instrumentale, E.2372.* **322, 323** Guitare décacorde. Caron, Versailles, 1784. *Yale, University, Belle Skinner Collection.* **324** Guitar ('harp-guitar'). Jos. Beckhaus, Philadelphia, late 19th century. *New York, Metropolitan Museum of Art, Crosby Brown Collection, 1519.*

325 Guitar. Rafael Vallejo, Baza (Granada), 1789–92. *London, Victoria and Albert Museum, 389–1871.* **326** Double arch-guitar. Savains, Paris, *c.* 1783. *Brussels, Conservatoire royal de Musique, 1534.* **327** Harpolyre. J.-F. Salomon (Besançon; patent 1829). *Brussels, Conservatoire royal de Musique, 3176.* **328** Double harp-guitar. John Frederick Grosjean, London, *c.* 1840. *London, Victoria and Albert Museum, 201–1872.* **329** Bass guitar. Vissenaire, Lyon, 1825. *Leipzig, Karl-Marx-Universität, Musikinstrumenten-Sammlung, 597.* **330** Bass guitar. Lacôte, Paris, 182–. *Ann Arbor, University of Michigan, Stearns Collection, 1127.* **331** Bass guitar. (?) J. G. Schirzer, Vienna, *c.* 1865. *Copenhagen, Musikhistorisk Museum, 351, C.34.* **332** Harp-lute-guitar (harp-theorbo). Harley, London, early 19th century. *Oxford, Pitt Rivers Museum, Balfour 1939, 609.*

333 Harp-guitar. Levien, Paris, early 19th century. *New York, Metropolitan Museum of Art, Crosby Brown Collection, 1515.* **334** Harp-lute-guitar. Barry, London, *c. 1800. Brighton, Museums, Spencer Collection.* **335** Harp-lute. (Light), London, *c. 1810. London, Victoria and Albert Museum, 37–1873.* **336** Harp-lute. London, *c. 1815. London, Victoria and Albert Museum, 252–1882.* **337** British harp-lute. (Light), London, *c. 1816. London, Victoria and Albert Museum, W.33–1925.* **338** Dital harp. (Light), London, 1819. *Brighton, Museums, Spencer Collection.* **339** Harp Ventura. A. G. Ventura, London, after 1828. *London, Victoria and Albert Museum, 248–1882.* **340** *Harpe ditale.* Pfeiffer, Paris, *c. 1830. Brussels, Conservatoire royal de Musique, 248.*

341 Banjo. *c.* 1840. *London, Victoria and Albert Museum, 226–1882.* **342** Banjo. American, *c.* 1840. *London, Reuben Greene Collection.* **343, 344** Banjo. Fred Mather, New York, 1860. *Washington, Smithsonian Institution, 207,888.* **345** Banjo. English, *c.* 1860–70. *Brighton, Museums, Spencer Collection.* **346** Banjo. English, *c.* 1860. *London, Reuben Greene Collection.* **347** Banjo. Paul Bellevue da Silva, ? London. Dated 1889. *London, Reuben Greene Collection.* **348** Banjolin. American, late 19th century. *Ann Arbor, University of Michigan, Stearns Collection, 1139B.*

349 Scheitholt. Waszlberger, Hallein, 1763. *Salzburg, Museo Carolino Augusteum, 81, Geiringer 1.*

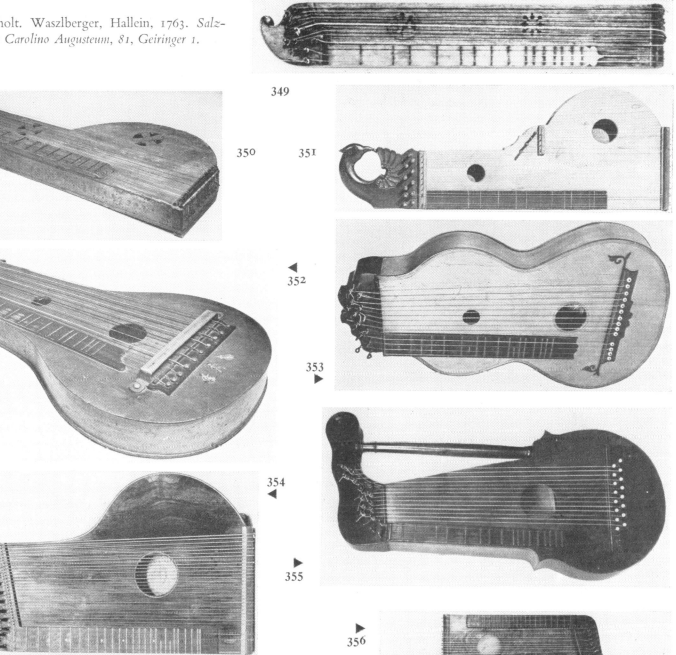

349

350   351

◄
352

353 ►

354
◄

355 ►

356 ►

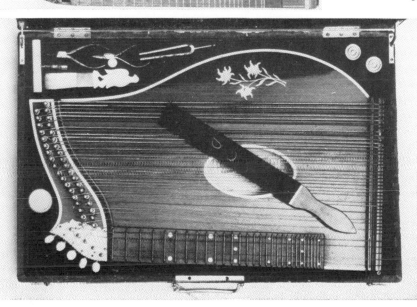

357

350 Kratz-zither. Franz Kren, Munich, first half of 19th century. *Berlin, Staatliches Institut für Musikforschung, Musikinstrumenten-Sammlung, 2253.* **351** Kratz-zither. Mayr, Salzburg, first half of 19th century. *Ann Arbor, University of Michigan, Stearns Collection, 1147.* **352** Kratz-zither. Munich, first half of 19th century. *Berlin, Staatliches Institut für Musikforschung, Musikinstrumenten-Sammlung, 554.* **353** Zither. Franz Kren, Munich. *Berlin, Staatliches Institut für Musikforschung, Musikinstrumenten-Sammlung, 2246.* **354** Concert zither. Georg Tiefenbrunner, Munich, 1845. *Brussels, Conservatoire royal de Musique, 1516.* **355** Harp zither. Bavarian, 19th century. *Berlin, Staatliches Institut für Musikforschung, Musikinstrumenten-Sammlung, 2248.* **356** Triple zither. Austrian Alps, 19th century. *Salzburg, Museum Carolino Augusteum, 149, Geiringer 29.* **357** Concert zither. Georg Tiefenbrunner, Munich, second half of 19th century. *London, Reuben Greene Collection.*

358 Psalmodikon. Swedish, first half of 19th century. *Copenhagen, Musikhistorisk Museum, 445.*

359 Épinette des Vosges. French, 19th century. *London, Horniman Museum, 15.10.48/10.*

360 Nordische Balk. Dutch, 19th century. *The Hague, Gemeentemuseum.*

361 Hummel. Swedish, 19th century. *Stockholm, Musikhistoriska Museet, 275.*

362 Appalachian dulcimer. United States, late 19th century. *New York, Metropolitan Museum of Art, Crosby Brown Collection, 98.4.988.*

363 Kentucky bowed dulcimer. George Dougherty, Grider, Kentucky, third quarter of 19th century. *Washington, Smithsonian Institution, 324,973.*

364 Bowed zither. Max Amberger, Munich, 1867. *London, Victoria and Albert Museum, 641-1869.*

365 Bowed zither (*Streichmelodeon*). F. Sprenger, Nuremburg, after 1879. *Boston, Museum of Fine Arts, Leslie Lindsey Mason Collection, 293.*

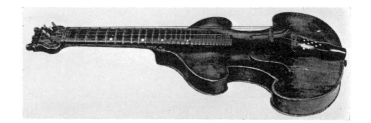

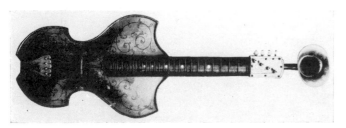

366 Bowed zither, 'Trumpet zither'. Gennerich, Munich, second half of 19th century. *London, Reuben Greene Collection.*

367 Dulcimer. French, 17th century. *Paris, Conservatoire de Musique, Musée instrumentale.*

368 Dulcimer. German, early 18th century. *Brunswick, Städtisches Museum, 16, 102.*

369 Dulcimer (*Hackbrett*). Appenzell, Switzerland, late 18th century. *Basel, Historisches Museum, 1927.284.*

370 Dulcimer. Antonio Battaglia, Milan, 1766. *Berlin, Staatliches Institut für Musikforschung, Musikinstrumenten-Sammlung, 2148.*

371

372

371 Gusli. Russian, Cheremiss, 19th century. *Brussels, Conservatoire royal de Musique, 1485.* 372 Two Kanteles. Finnish, the smaller, 18th century; the larger, Westermark, 1893. *Oxford, Pitt Rivers Museum, 131.D.10; 131.D.14.*

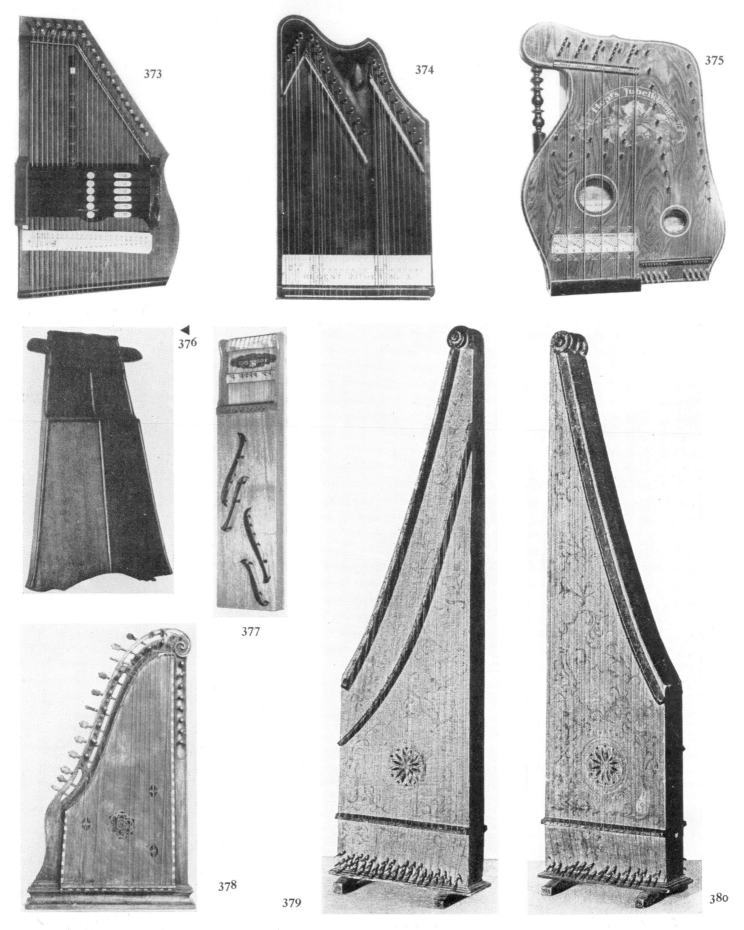

373 Autoharp (*Akkord-zither*). German, 19th century. *Ann Arbor, University of Michigan, Stearns Collection, 1162.* **374** Regent zither. United States, late 19th century. *Ann Arbor, University of Michigan, Stearns Collection, 1160.* **375** Violin-zither. Hopf, Germany, late 19th century. *London, Royal Military School of Music, Kneller Hall.* **376** Bell harp. English, first half of 18th century. *London, Horniman Museum, 29–212.* **377** Bell harp. R. Cook & Co. (London), 19th century. *Oxford, Pitt Rivers Museum, dd.YMCA.1919.* **378** Table harp. ? German or Danish, late 18th century. *Copenhagen, Claudius Collection, Musikhistorisk Museum, 14(493).* **379, 380** Arpanetta (*Spitzharfe*). German, early 18th century. *Nuremberg, Germanisches Nationalmuseum, Rück Collection.*

381 Aeolian harp. French, 18th century. *Paris, Conservatoire de Musique, Musée instru-mentale, E.1527, C.1436.* 382 Aeolian harp. London, 19th century. *Brussels, Conservatoire royal de Musique, 2514.* 383 Gaelic harp. 15th century. *Edinburgh, National Museum of Antiquities of Scotland.* 384 Irish harp. Built 1702. *Dublin, Arthur Guinness & Co. (Dublin) Ltd.* 385 Irish harp. 18th century. *Dublin, National Museum of Ireland, 121–1945.*

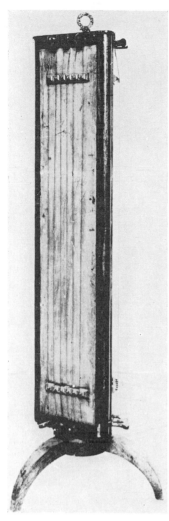

381

383

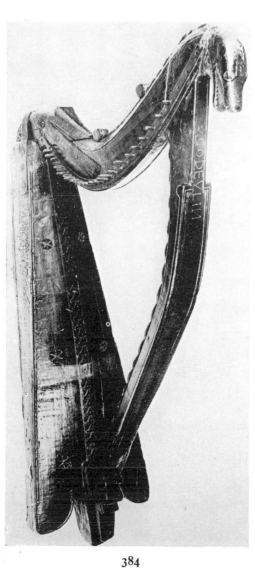

384

385

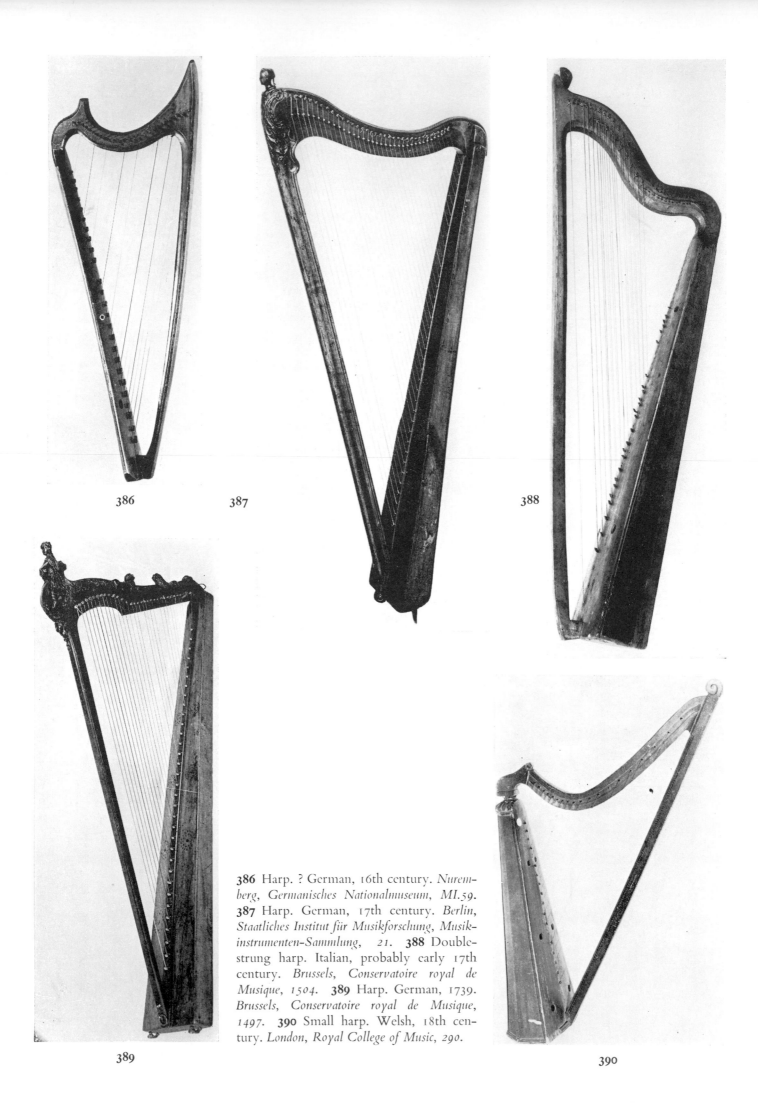

386

387

388

386 Harp. ? German, 16th century. *Nuremberg, Germanisches Nationalmuseum, MI.59.* **387** Harp. German, 17th century. *Berlin, Staatliches Institut für Musikforschung, Musikinstrumenten-Sammlung, 21.* **388** Double-strung harp. Italian, probably early 17th century. *Brussels, Conservatoire royal de Musique, 1504.* **389** Harp. German, 1739. *Brussels, Conservatoire royal de Musique, 1497.* **390** Small harp. Welsh, 18th century. *London, Royal College of Music, 290.*

389

390

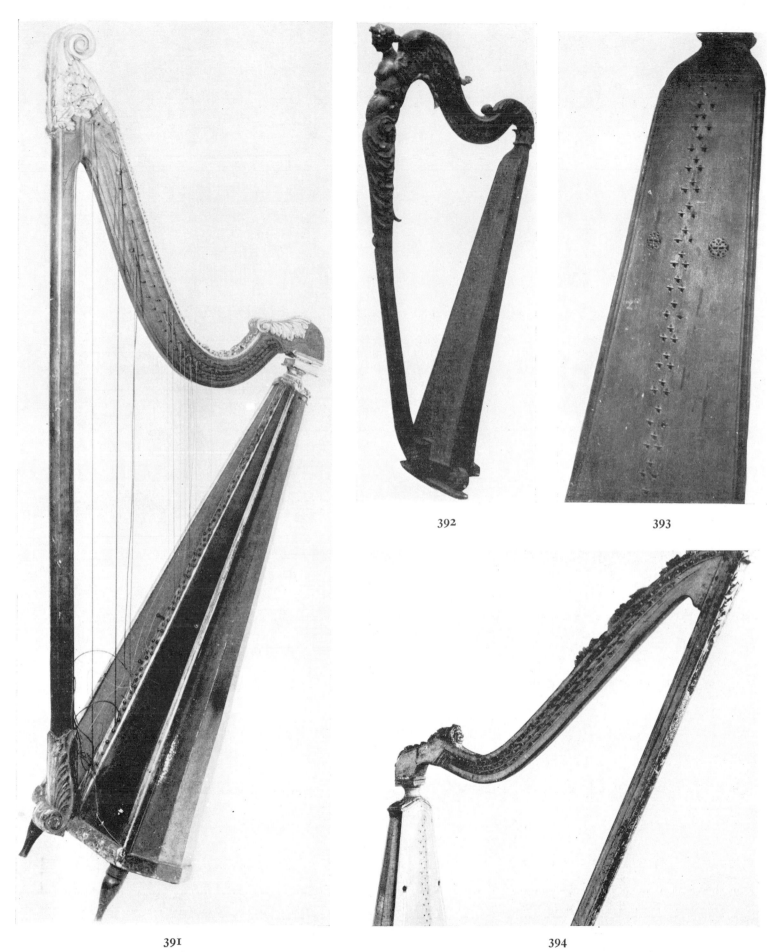

391 Triple harp. Bassett Jones, Cardiff, 1838. *London, Royal College of Music, 295.* **392, 393** Triple harp. Italian, early 17th century. *Bologna, Museo Civico.* **394** Triple harp. David Evans, London, 1736. *London, Victoria and Albert Museum, 1740–1869.*

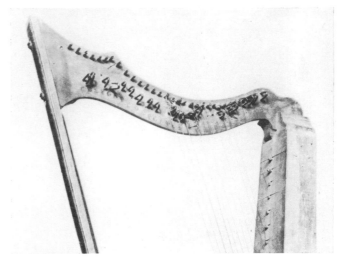

395 Hook harp. Italian, 18th century. *Ann Arbor, University of Michigan, Stearns Collection, 1003.* 396 Hook harp. Tyrolean, 18th century. *New York, Metropolitan Museum of Art, Crosby Brown Collection, 1712.* 397 Pedal harp. Sebastian Lang, Bavaria, 1755. *Nuremberg, Germanisches Nationalmuseum, Rück Collection.*

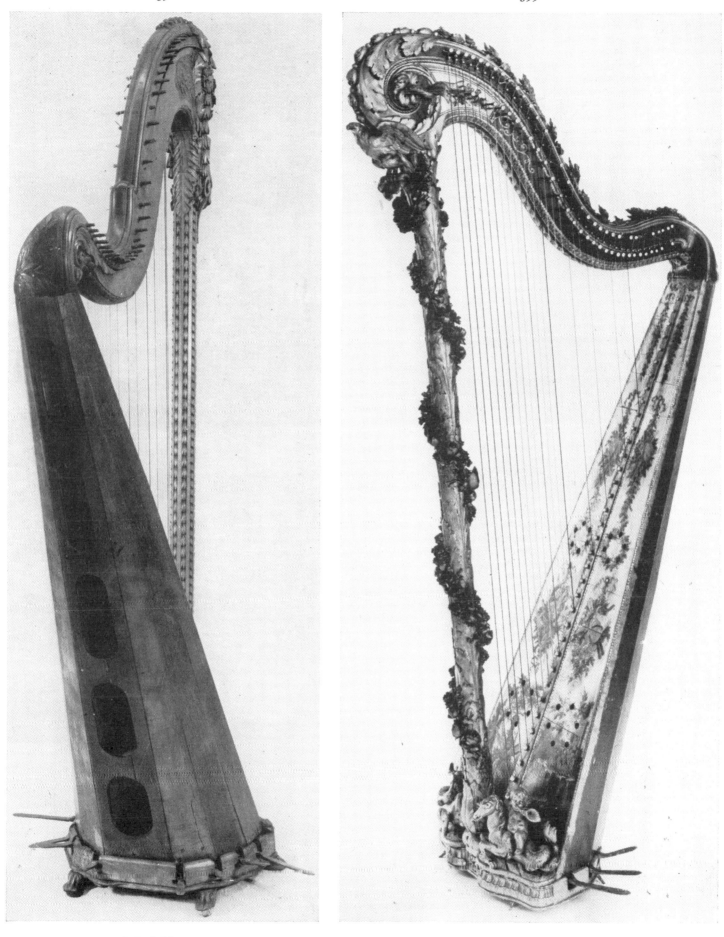

398 Pedal harp. H. Naderman, after 1785. *London, Victoria and Albert Museum, 425–1884*
399 Pedal harp. H. Naderman, Paris, *c.* 1780. *Paris, Conservatoire de Musique, Musée instrumentale, C.293*

400 Pedal harp. H. Naderman. (Same instrument as **398**).   **401** Pedal harp. G. Cousineau, Paris, *c.* 1770. *London, Royal College of Music, 199.*   **402** Pedal harp. Sebastien Érard, Paris, 1786. *London, Reuben Greene Collection.*   **403** Pedal harp. S. & P. Érard, London, 1858. *London, Victoria and Albert Museum, W.48–1931.*

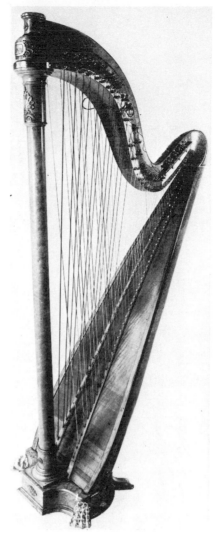

404

405

406

404 Cross-strung harp. ? French, *c.* 1800. *London, Victoria and Albert Museum, 830–1884.* 405 Cross-strung 'chromatic harp'. Pleyel, Paris, end of 19th century. *Brussels, Conservatoire royal de Musique.* 406 Portable harp. John Egan, Dublin, *c.* 1820. *London, Horniman Museum, 289.* 407 Cross-strung 'chromatic harp'. H. Greenway, Brooklyn, New York, after 1895. *New York, Metropolitan Museum of Art, Crosby Brown Collection, 1235.* 408 Double-strung harp. Italian, late 16th century. *Modena, Galleria Estense.*

407

408

409 Galoubet and tambourin. France, Provence, 19th century. *Brussels, Conservatoire royal de Musique, 2284.* **410** Pipe and tabor. England, Oxfordshire, 19th century. *Washington, Library of Congress, Dayton Miller Flute Collection, 722 A and B.* **411** Flaviol and tamboril. Barcelona, late 19th century. *Barcelona, Museo Municipál de Música, 306 and 401.* **412** Tabor Pipe. Cahusac, London, beginning of 19th century. *Washington, Library of Congress, Dayton Miller Flute Collection, 1266.* **413** Chirula and tambourin à cordes. France, Béarne, 18th/19th century. *London, Royal College of Music, 74 and 213.*

414 Great bass recorder. *Antwerp, Musée Vleeshuis.* **415–17** Three recorders, treble, tenor and bass, 16th century. *Frankfurt-am-Main, Historisches Museum, Epstein 116, 118, 120.* **418** Recorder case, holding the preceding three instruments and others similar. 16th century. *Frankfurt-am-Main, Historisches Museum, Epstein 120b.* **419** Treble recorder. J. C. Denner, Nuremberg, 1682. *Eisenach, Bachhaus, Buhle 115.* **420** Quint-bass recorder. 16th century. *Brussels, Conservatoire royale Musique, 188.* **421** Tenor recorder. German, 17th century. *Leipzig, Karl-Marx-Universität, Musikinstrumenten-Museum, 1134.* **422** Tenor recorder. 16th century. *Frankfurt-am-Main, Historisches Museum, Epstein 114.*

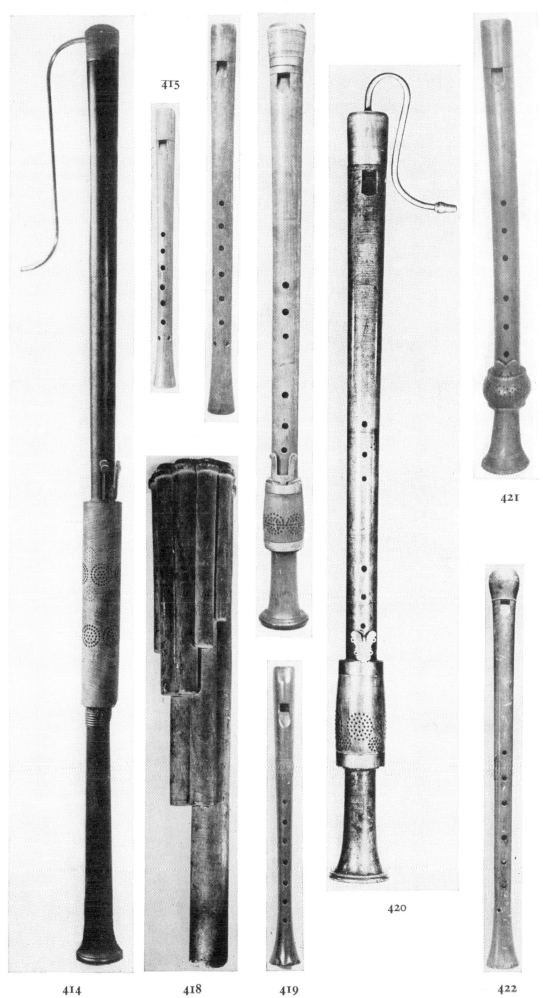

416   417

415

421

414   418   419   420   422

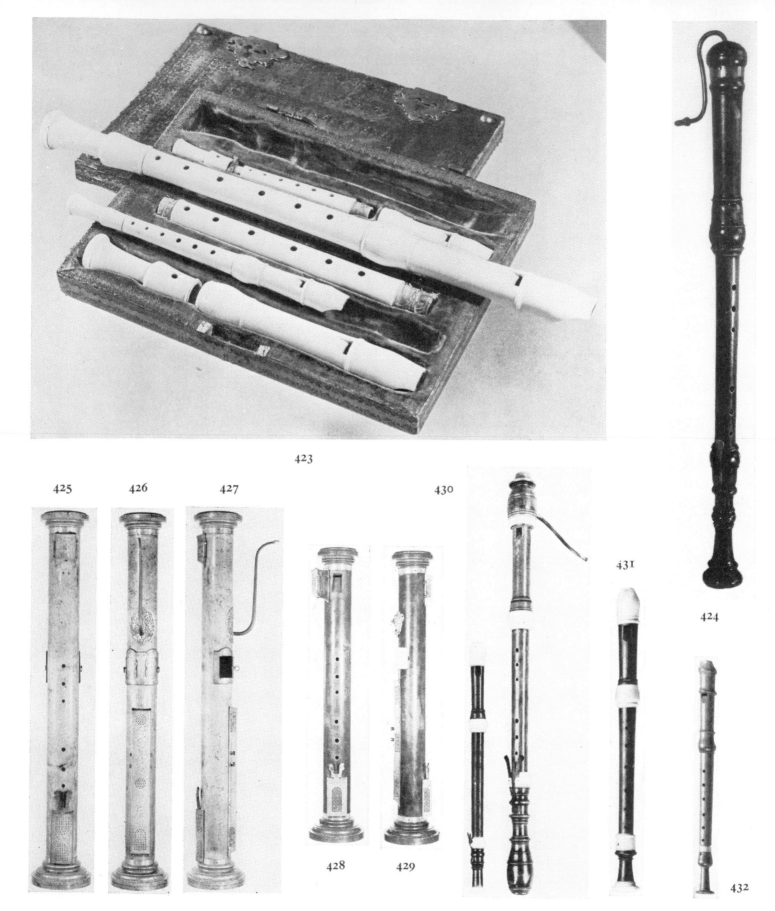

423 Set of two treble and two descant recorders, in case. Schlegel, Basel, mid 18th century. *Paris, Conservatoire de Musique, Musée instrumentale, E.683, C.392.* **424** Bass recorder. J. C. Denner, Nuremberg, early 18th century. *Berlin, Staatliches Institut für Musikforschung, Musikinstrumenten-Sammlung, 92.* **425-7** Columnar recorder (bass). Late 16th century (? French). *Paris, Conservatoire de Musique, Musée instrumentale, E.127, C.410.* **428, 429** Columnar recorder (tenor). As above. *Paris, Conservatoire de Musique, Musée instrumentale, E.691, C.409.* **430** Tenor and bass recorders. J. Hotteterre 'le Romain', Paris, early 18th century. *Paris, Conservatoire de Musique, Musée instrumentale, E.589, C.413.* **431** Treble recorder. P. J. Bressan, London, first half of 18th century. *Washington Library of Congress, Dayton Miller Flute Collection, 127.* **432** Descant recorder. Lorenz Walch, Berchtesgaden, mid 19th century. *Washington, Library of Congress, Dayton Miller Flute Collection, 663.*

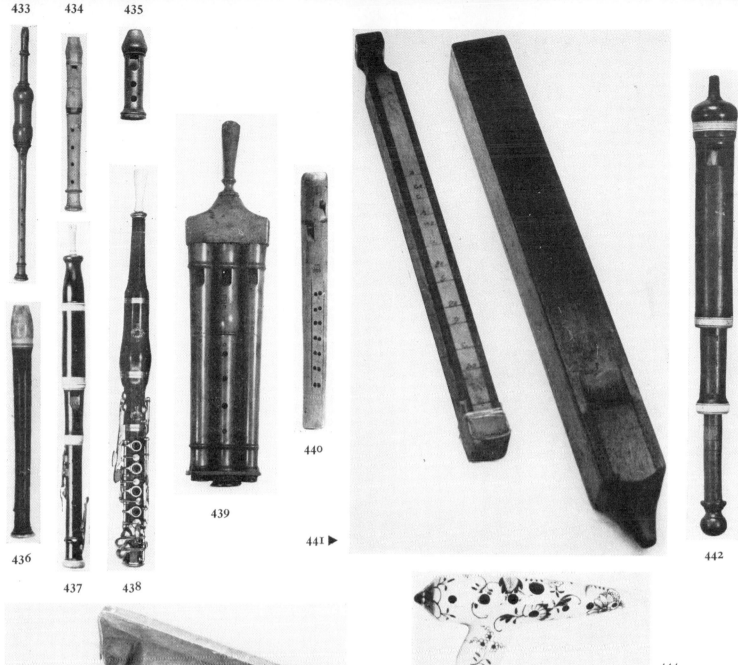

433 434 435

436 437 438 439 440 441 ▶ 442

444

443

433 Bird pipe. Lecler, Paris, first half of 18th century. *Paris, Conservatoire de Musique, Musée instrumentale, E.119, C.375.* 434 Bird pipe. Martin, Paris, 1827–40. *Washington, Library of Congress, Dayton Miller Flute Collection, 668.* 435 Picco pipe. London, second half of 19th century. *London, Horniman Museum, Carse 237.* 436 French flageolet. Naust, Paris, early 19th century. *Washington, Library of Congress, Dayton Miller Flute Collection, 624.* 437 French flageolet. Goodlad & Co., London, 1830–7. *Washington, Library of Congress, Dayton Miller Flute Collection, 1191.* 438 French flageolet. Buffet Crampon & Cie., Paris, late 19th century or early 20th. *Washington, Library of Congress, Dayton Miller Flute Collection, 570.* 439 French triple flageolet. David, Dijon, 18th century. *Paris, Conservatoire de Musique, Musée instrumentale, E.644, C.385.* 440 Flûte d'accord. Anciuti, Milan, pre-1740. *London, Royal Military School of Music, Kneller Hall, 21.* 441· Pitch pipe. English, 18th century. *Birmingham, School of Music.* 442 Pitch pipe. ? English, early 19th century. *Washington, Library of Congress, Dayton Miller Flute Collection, 812.* 443 Set of ocarinas. Zach, Vienna, late 19th century. *London, Reuben Greene Collection.* 444 Ocarina. German. *London, Horniman Museum, 15.10.48/227.*

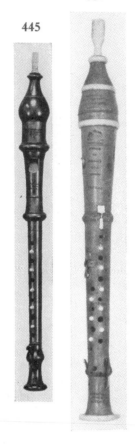

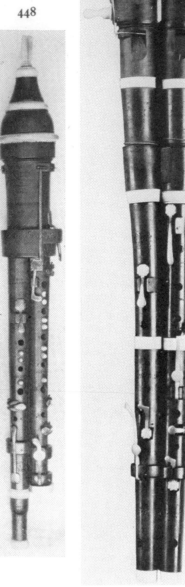

445 English flageolet. T. J. Weygandt, Philadelphia, c. 1840. *Washington, Library of Congress, Dayton Miller Flute Collection, 407.* **446** Double flageolet. Bainbridge, London, early 19th century. *Brighton, Museums, Spencer Collection.* **447** Double flageolet. Eisenbrandt, Baltimore, 1810–57. *Washington, Library of Congress, Dayton Miller Flute Collection, 698.* **448** Double flageolet. Hastrick, London, 1835–55. *Washington, Library of Congress, Dayton Miller Flute Collection, 514.* **449** Double flute-flageolet. Bainbridge, London, 1819. *Washington, Library of Congress, Dayton Miller Flute Collection, 911.* **450** Triple flageolet. Bainbridge, London, c. 1820. *Washington, Library of Congress, Dayton Miller Flute Collection, 721.* **451** Panpipe. English, early 19th century. *Halifax, Bankfield Museum.* **452** Panpipe. French, 18th century. *Paris, Conservatoire de Musique, Musée instrumentale, E.111, C.455.* **453** Panpipe. French, 18th century. *Paris, Conservatoire de Musique, Musée instrumentale, E.110, C.454.*

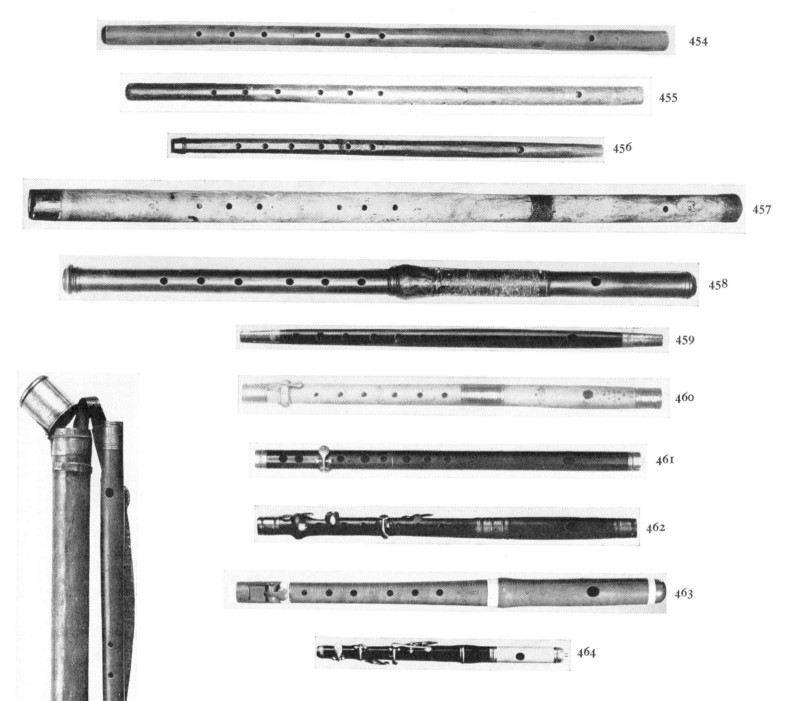

454 Flute. C. Rafi, Lyons, first half of 16th century. *Brussels, Conservatoire royal de Musique, 1066.* **455** Flute. Italian, 16th century. *Brussels, Conservatoire royal de Musique, 1064.* **456** Descant flute. Italian, 16th century. *Brussels, Conservatoire royal de Musique, 1062.* **457** Bass flute. ? Flemish, 16th century. *Brussels, Conservatoire royal de Musique, 2695.* **458** Flute. Italian (?), 17th century. *Vienna, Kunsthistorisches Museum, Sammlung alter Musikinstrumente, C.187.* **459** Fife. W. Crosby, Boston, Mass., *c.* 1850–74. *Washington, Library of Congress, Dayton Miller Flute Collection, 944.* **460** Fife. Cotton, London, late 18th century. *London, Horniman Museum, Carse 14e.* **461** Fife. Thibouville Frères, Ivry (France), mid 19th century. *Washington, Library of Congress, Dayton Miller Flute Collection, 603.* **462** Fife. T. Prowse, London, *c.* 1816–36. *Washington, Library of Congress, Dayton Miller Flute Collection, 856.* **463** Fife (*fifre Bernois*). Charles Felchlin, Berne, Switzerland, mid 19th century. *Geneva, Musée d'Art et d'Histoire, 9390.* **464** E flat piccolo. H. F. Meyer, Hanover, mid 19th century. *Washington, Library of Congress, Dayton Miller Flute Collection, 924.* **465** Fife with metal case. Jacob Streulli, Horgan (Switzerland), *c.* 1850. *Washington, Library of Congress, Dayton Miller Flute Collection, 869.*

465

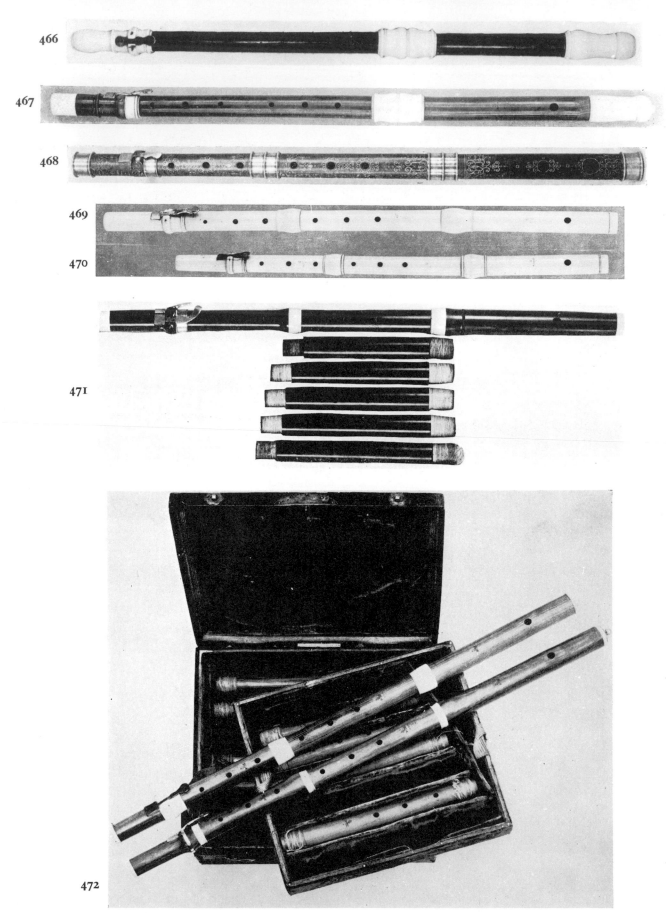

466 Flute. Hotteterre, Paris, early 18th century. *Berlin, Staatliches Institut für Musikforschung, Musikinstrumenten-Sammlung, 2670.*
467 Flute. Naust, Paris, early 18th century. *Paris, Conservatoire de Musique, Musée instrumentale, E.710, C.444.* **468** Flute. Bressan,
London, *c.* 1720. *London, Victoria and Albert Museum, 452–1898.* **469** Flute. Bizey, Paris, mid 18th century. *Paris, Conservatoire de
Musique, Musée instrumentale, E.598, C.439.* **470** F Flute. Scherer, ? Paris, *c.* 1770. *Paris, Collection G. Thibault.* **471** Flute. Quantz,
Potsdam, *c.* 1750. *Washington, Library of Congress, Dayton Miller Flute Collection, 916.* **472** Pair of flutes. Thomas Lot, Paris, third
quarter of 18th century. *London, Horniman Museum, Carse 263.*

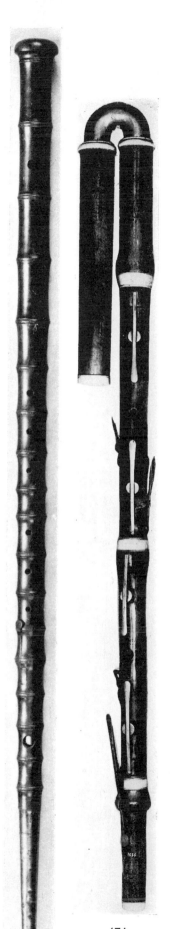

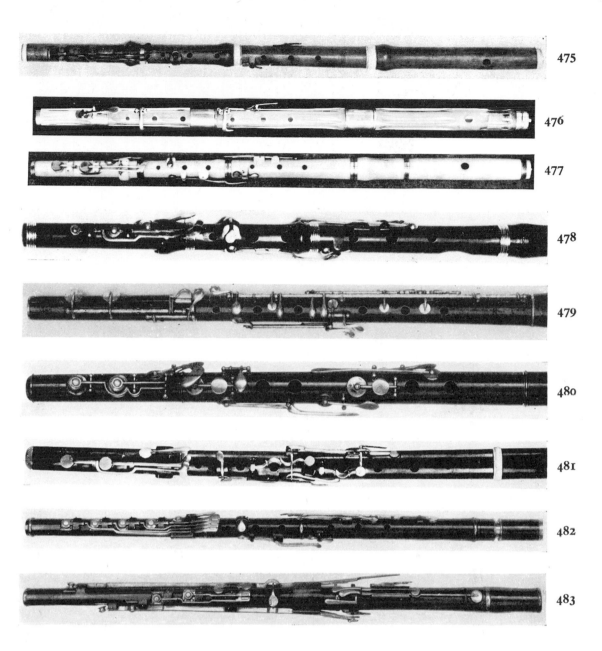

473 Walking-stick flute. Lambert, Paris, 18th century. *Washington, Library of Congress, Dayton Miller Flute Collection, 908.* **474** Bass flute. Wigley & MacGregor, London, 1811–16. *Brussels, Conservatoire royal de Musique, 1070.* **475** Flute. Potter senior, London, 1777. *London, Horniman Museum, Carse 193.* **476** Flute. Claude Laurent, Paris, 1807. *Washington, Library of Congress, Dayton Miller Flute Collection, 1051.* **477** Flute. Louis Drouet, London, c. 1818. *Luton Museum, Ridley Collection, FL/21.* **478** Flute. Clementi, London, c. 1830. *Cobham, Morley-Pegge Collection.* **479** Flute. Jacques Nonon, Paris, first half of 19th century. *Cobham, Morley-Pegge Collection.* **480** Flute. Abel Siccama, London, c. 1850. *Washington, Library of Congress, Dayton Miller Flute Collection, 133.* **481** Flute. Pentenrieder, Munich, 1837–47. *Washington, Library of Congress, Dayton Miller Flute Collection, 1038.* **482** Flute. Rudall & Rose, London, 1830–7. *Washington, Library of Congress, Dayton Miller Flute Collection, 440.* **483** Flute. F. Schauffler & J. Leukhardt, Boston, 1851–7. *Washington, Library of Congress, Dayton Miller Flute Collection, 119.*

484 Burghley bass flute. Burghley, London, *c. 1845. London, Philip Bate Collection.* **485** Albisiphone (bass flute in C). Abellardo Albisi, Milan, *c. 1891. No. 232.* **486** Flute. Theobald Boehm, Munich, after 1832. *London, Horniman Museum, Carse 11a.* **487** Flute. Cornelius Ward, London, *c. 1842. No. 572.* **488** Flute. A. G. Badger & Co., New York, 1860–8. *No. 1248.* **489** Giorgi flute. Joseph Wallis & Sons, London, *c. 1888. No. 481.* **490** Flute. Rudall & Rose, London, *c. 1850–4. No. 1236.* **491** Flute. Theobald Boehm, Munich, 1848. *No. 1237.* **492** Flute. Louis Lot, Paris, *c. 1860. No. 91.* **493** Flute. Rudall Carte & Co., London, 1896. *No. 4.* **494** Piccolo. Rudall Carte & Co., London, late 19th century. *Collection of the late Charles Overy, Knighton, Wilts.* **495** Piccolo. George W. Haynes, New York, 1888. *No. 448.* **496** Bass flute in F. George W. Haynes, Los Angeles, 1898. *No. 118.* All *Washington, Library of Congress, Dayton Miller Flute Collection,* except where otherwise shown.

497 Musette. French, 18th century. *London, Royal College of Music, 192.* 498 Cornemuse. French, 18th century. *New York, Metropolitan Museum of Art, Crosby Brown Collection, 865.* 499 Gaita gallega. Spanish (Galicia), 19th century. *London, Horniman Museum, 16.2.59/1.* 500 Cornemuse. French (said to be from Normandy), 19th century. *London, Royal College of Music, 139.* 501 Small-pipe. Northumberland, c. 1770–80. *Ryton-on-Tyne, William A. Cocks Collection.* 502 Small-pipe. Northumberland, c. 1850. *Ryton-on-Tyne, William A. Cocks Collection.*

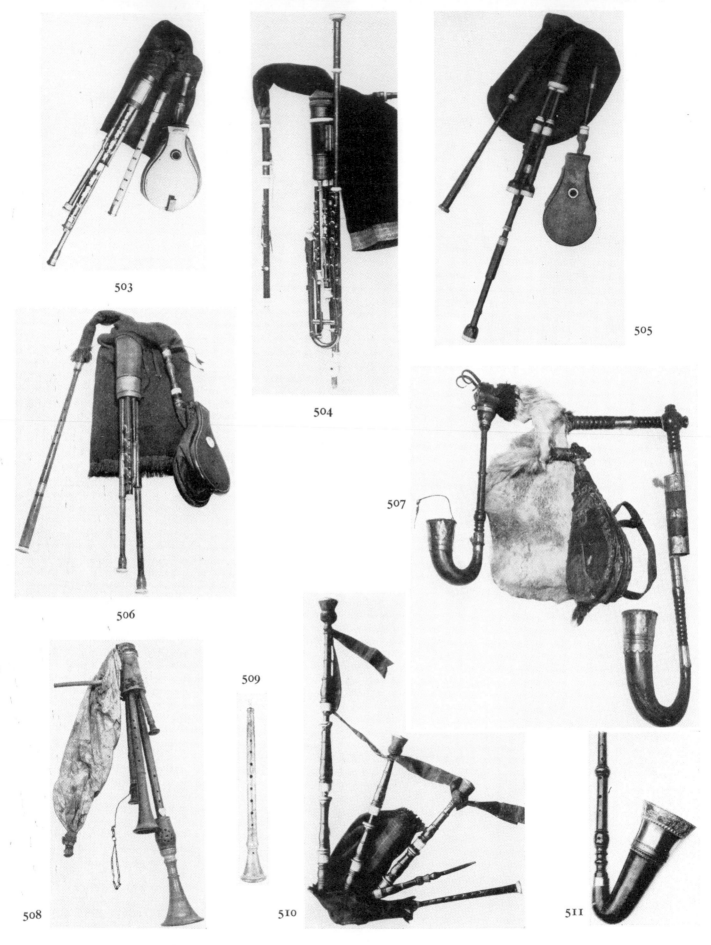

503 Union pipe. Kenna, Dublin and Mullingar, 1768–94. *Ryton-on-Tyne, William A. Cocks Collection.* **504** Union pipe. Coyne, Dublin, *c.* 1850. *Dublin, National Museum of Ireland, 484–93.* **505** Lowland pipe. Scottish, late 18th century. *Ryton-on-Tyne, William A. Cocks Collection.* **506** Scottish union pipe. Scottish, ? late 18th century. *Oxford, Pitt Rivers Museum, Balfour 113, 1921.* **507** Dudy. Bohemian, ? 18th century. *Oxford, Pitt Rivers Museum, Balfour 129, 1906.* **508** Zampogna. Italian, 19th century. *Oxford, Pitt Rivers Museum, Balfour 124.* **509** Ciaramella. Italian, 19th century. *Brussels, Conservatoire royal de Musique, 954.* **510** Highland bagpipe. Scottish, *c.* 1850. *Ryton-on-Tyne, William A. Cocks Collection.* **511** Chanter of bagpipe. Thuringia, Germany, 18th century. *Hamburg, Museum für Hamburgische Geschichte, 1924.208a.*

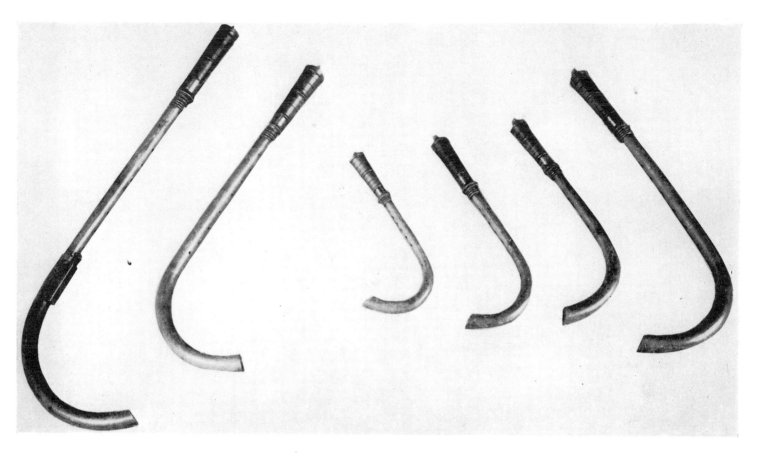

512 Six crumhorns. German, 16th or early 17th century
Berlin, Staatliches Institut für Musikforschung, Musikinstrumenten-Sammlung, 668–673.

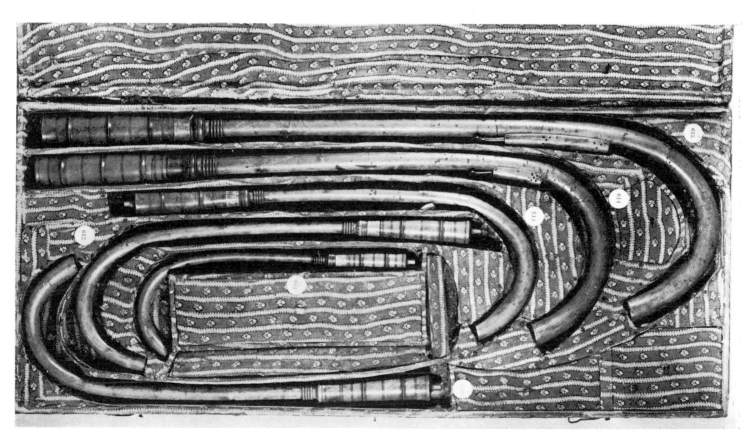

513 Set of six crumhorns in original case. Italian, second half of 16th century
Brussels, Conservatoire royal de Musique, 610–615.

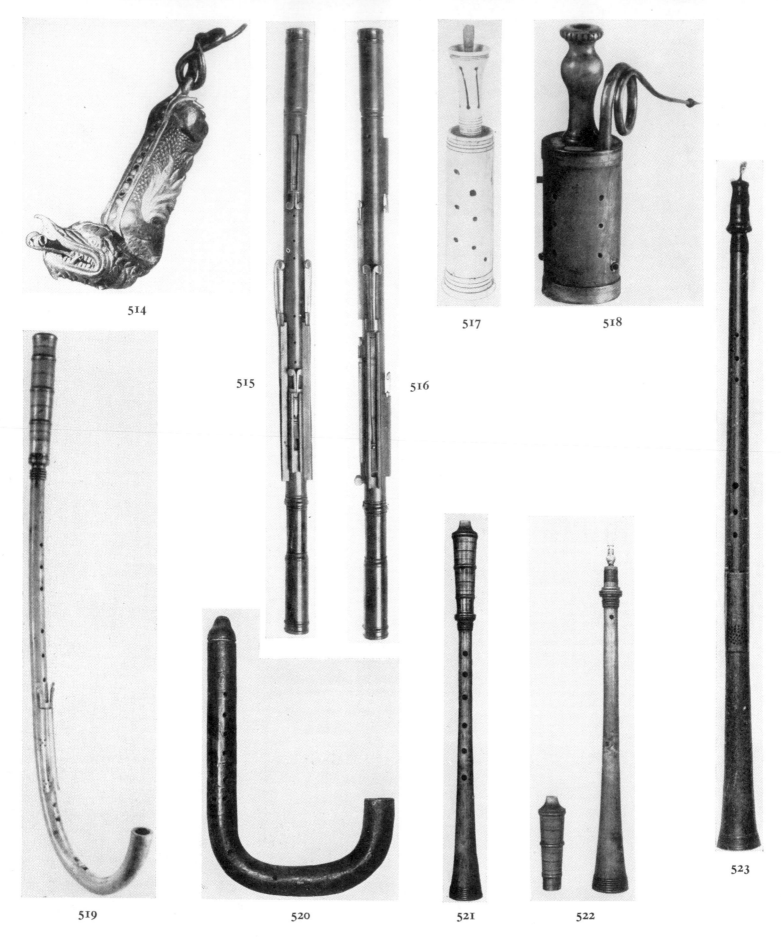

514 Bass tartöld. German, 16th century. *Vienna, Kunsthistorisches Museum, Sammlung alter Musikinstrumente, A.223.* **515, 516** Great bass sordone (*Sordun*). ? Italian, 16th century. *Vienna, Kunsthistorisches Museum, Sammlung alter Musikinstrumente, A.229.* **517** Racket. Tyrol, c. 1650. *Leipzig, Karl-Marx-Universität, Musikinstrumenten-Museum, 1414.* **518** Racket. W. Wyne, Nymegen, Holland, c. 1700. *Berlin, Staatliches Institut für Musikforschung, Musikinstrumenten-Sammlung, 64.* **519** Bass crumhorn, the largest of those in **513**. *Brussels, Conservatoire royal de Musique, 615.* **520** Crumhorn (?). Said to be Italian. *Brussels, Conservatoire royal de Musique, 1970.* **521, 522** Tenor *Rauschpfeife.* German, late 16th or early 17th century. *Berlin, Staatliches Institut für Musikforschung, Musikinstrumenten-Sammlung, 666.* **523** Great-bass capped shawm (*Rauschpfeife* ?). 16th century. *Prague, Narodni Museum.*

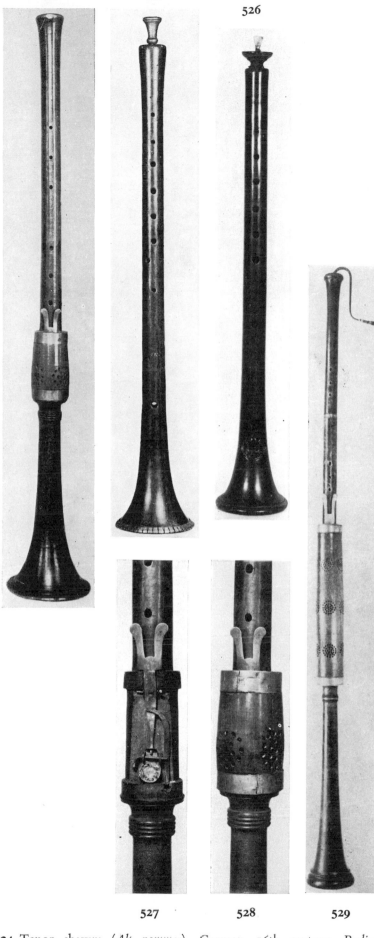

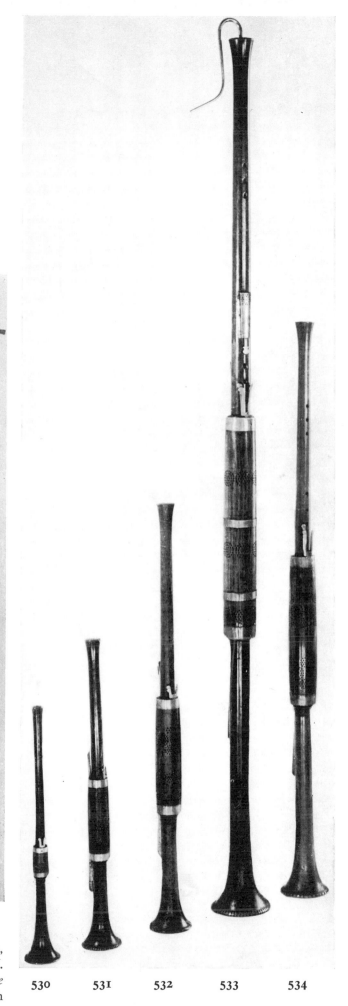

524 Tenor shawm (*Alt pommer*). German, 16th century. *Berlin, Staatliches Institut für Musikforschung, Musikinstrumenten-Sammlung, 646.* 525 Treble shawm. ? Spanish, 16th century. *Brussels, Conservatoire royal de Musique, 2324.* 526 Treble shawm. ? Catalan, 17th–18th century. *Barcelona, Museo Municipál de Música, 608.* 527, 528 Tenor shawm. Close view of 524 showing barrel removed and in position. 529 Bass shawm. German, 17th century. *Brussels, Conservatoire royal de Musique, 986.*

530–4 Five shawms. German, 16th–17th century. *Berlin, Staatliches Institut für Musikforschung, Musik-instrumenten-Sammlung, 646, 290, 643, 642, 289.*

535 Treble shawm. R. Haka, Amsterdam, late 17th century. *Amsterdam, Rijksmuseum.* 536 Tenor shawm. German, late 17th century. *Leipzig, Karl-Marx-Universität, Musikinstrumenten-Museum, 1305.* 537 Tenor shawm. German, late 17th century. *Salzburg, Museum Carolino Augusteum, 248.* 538 Treble shawm. J. Denner, Nuremberg, c. 1700. *Frankfurt-am-Main, Historisches Museum, 437; Epstein 136.* 539 Shawm or oboe. French (?), late 17th century or later. *Brussels, Conservatoire royal de Musique, 972.* 540 Shawm or oboe. R. Haka, Amsterdam, late 17th century. *Amsterdam, Rijksmuseum, 11430.81.* 541 Basse de musette. Swiss, 18th century. *Berne, Historical Museum.* 542 Tenor shawm (*tenora*). ? Barcelona, second half of 19th century. *Barcelona, Museo Municipál de Música, 63.* 543 Musette or *bombarde*. French, 18th or 19th century. *Paris, Conservatoire de Musique, Musée instrumentale, E.1180, C.1110.* 544 Musette or *Schalmei*. L. Walch, Berchtesgaden, mid 19th century. *Salzburg, Museum Carolino Augusteum, 251.* 545 Musette (*dulziana*). Probably French, late 19th century. *Barcelona, Museo Municipál de Música, 786.* 546 Eunuch flute. French, c. 1800. *Oxford, Pitt Rivers Museum, Balfour dd.1939, 469.* 547 Treble shawm (*tiple*). Catroi, Barcelona, late 19th century. *Barcelona, Museo Municipál de Música, 379.*

550   551   552   553   554

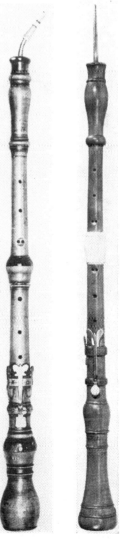

548 Oboe. ? Dutch, late 17th century. *London, Victoria and Albert Museum, 808–1869.* **549** Oboe. H. Richters. ? Dutch, c. 1700. *Washington, Library of Congress, Dayton Miller Flute Collection, 158.* **550** Oboe. Nicholas Hotteterre, Paris, last quarter of 17th century. *Brussels, Conservatoire royal de Musique, 2320.* **551** Oboe. Thos. Stanesby (senior), London, early 18th century. *London, Horniman Museum, Carse 232.* **552** Oboe. Kusder, London, c. 1760–80. *London, Horniman Museum, Carse 258.* **553** Oboe. Cahusac, London, late 18th century. *London, Royal Military School of Music, Kneller Hall, 56.* **554** Oboe. J. G. Liebel, Adorf (Germany), 1798. *Washington, Library of Congress, Dayton Miller Flute Collection, 42.* **555** Oboe d'amore. P. Wolraupier, first half of 18th century. *Brussels, Conservatoire royal de Musique, 970.* **556** Oboe d'amore (*grand hautbois*). Bizey, Paris, mid 18th century. *Boston, Museum of Fine Arts, Leslie Lindsey Mason Collection, 138.*

548   549

555   556

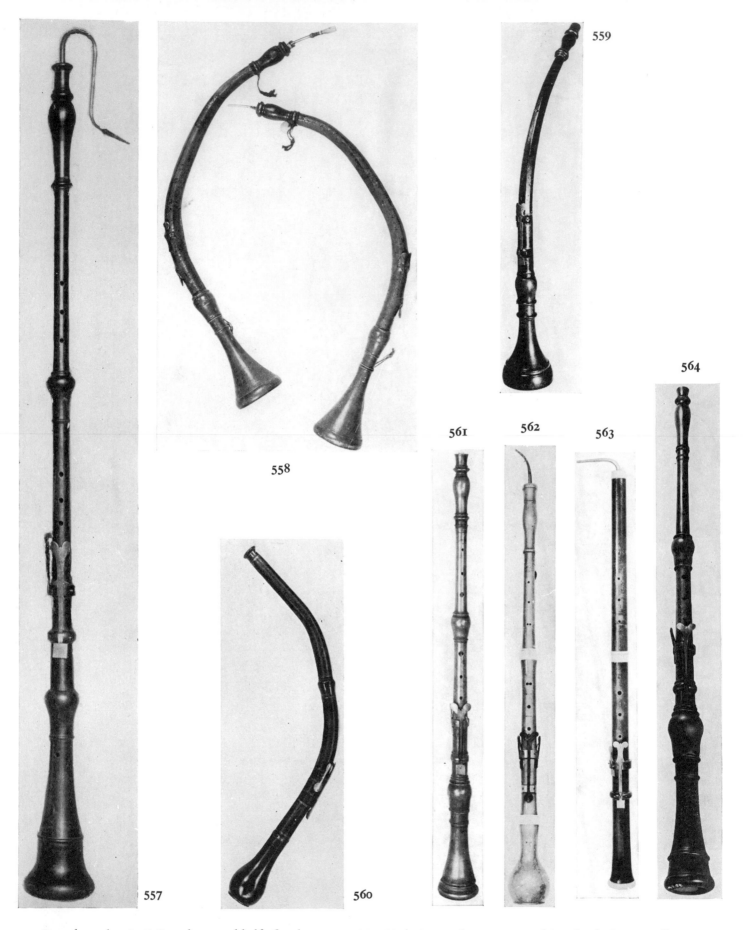

557 Great bass oboe in F. French, second half of 18th century. *New York, Metropolitan Museum of Art, Crosby Brown Collection, 2351.*
558 Pair of oboi da caccia. ? Italian, first half of 18th century. *Bologna, Museo Civico.* **559** Oboe da caccia or cor anglais. J. G. Bauer, Vienna, mid 18th century. *Berlin, Staatliches Institut für Musikforschung, Musikinstrumenten-Sammlung, 581.* **560** Cor anglais. Bimboni, Florence, second half of 18th century. *Author's collection.* **561** Tenor oboe. J. C. Denner, Nuremberg, *c.* 1700. *Leipzig, Karl-Marx-Universität, Musikinstrumenten-Museum, 1547.* **562** Tenor oboe. Martin Lot, Paris, second half of 18th century. *London, Royal College of Music, 76.* **563** Tenor oboe. T. Collier, London, *c.* 1770. *Glasgow, Art Gallery and Museums.* **564** Bass oboe in C. J. C. Denner, Nuremberg, *c.* 1700. *Nuremberg, Germanisches Nationalmuseum, MI.94.*

565 Oboe. Delusse, Paris, *c*. 1810–20. *London, Philip Bate Collection.* 566 Oboe. W. Milhouse, London, *c*. 1820. *London, Philip Bate Collection.* 567 Oboe. Goodlad & Co., London, *c*. 1830. *London, Royal Military School of Music, Kneller Hall, 61.* 568, 569 Oboe. H. Grenser, Dresden, possibly pre-1813. *Geneva, Musée d'Art et d'Histoire.* 570 Oboe. Uhlmann, Vienna, *c*. 1840. *London, Philip Bate Collection.* 571 Oboe. G. Triébert, Paris, *c*. 1830. *Cobham, Morley-Pegge Collection.* 572 Oboe. Tabard, Lyons, *c*. 1840. *Luton Museum, Ridley Collection, O/5.* 573 Oboe. L. A. Buffet, Paris, *c*. 1850. *London, Philip Bate Collection.* 574 Oboe. A. Morton, London, *c*. 1872. *London, Philip Bate Collection.* 575 Oboe. F. Triébert, Paris, *c*. 1870. *London, Philip Bate Collection.* 576 Oboe. Meyer, Hanover, *c*. 1870. *London, Philip Bate Collection.*

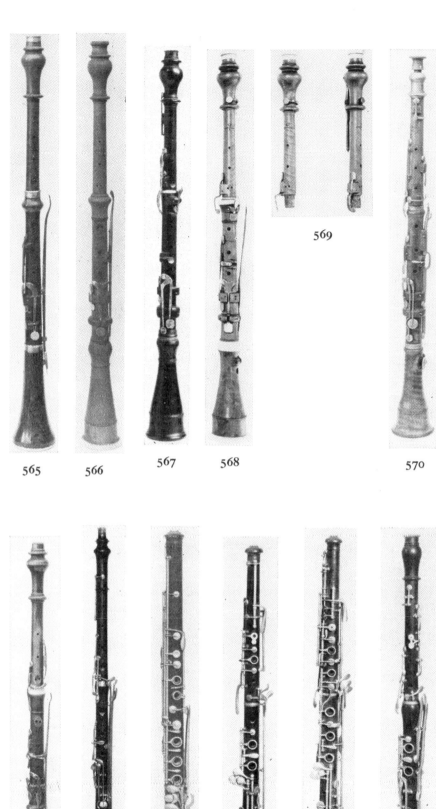

569

565   566   567   568   570

571   572   573   574   575   576

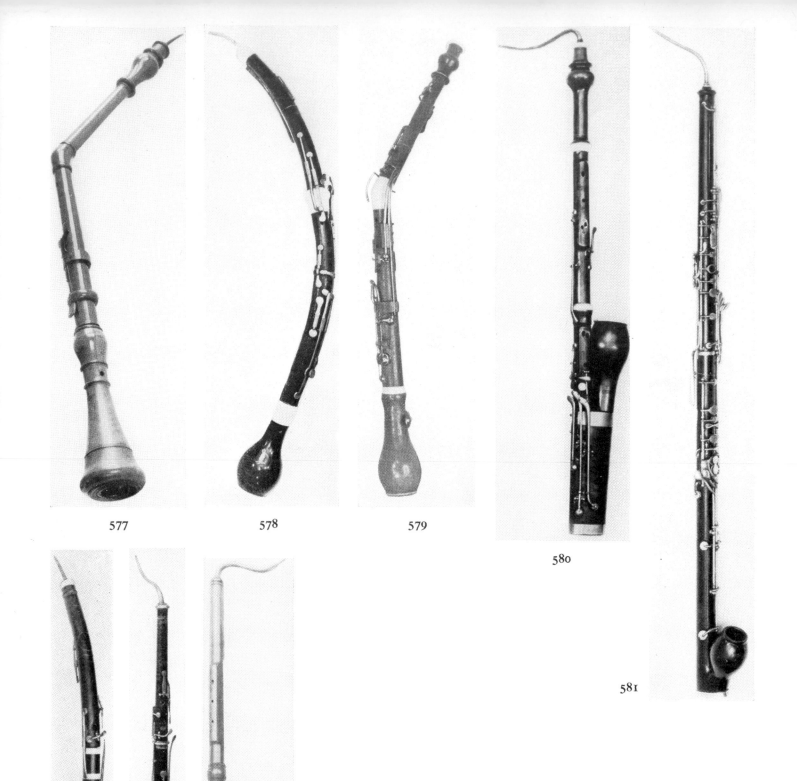

577 Cor anglais. Grundmann, Dresden, 1791. *Liverpool, Rushworth & Dreaper Collection.* 578 Cor anglais. C. Golde, Dresden, *c.* 1840. *London, Royal College of Music, 82.* 579 Cor anglais. Stephan Koch, Vienna, *c.* 1820. *Leipzig, Karl-Marx-Universität, Musikinstrumenten-Museum, 1349.* 580 Bass oboe (*hautbois baryton*). G. Triébert, Paris, 1825. *London, Royal College of Music, 79.* 581 Bass oboe. Unsigned, ? Paris, late 19th century. *London, Horniman Museum, Carse 303.* 582 Cor anglais. G. Triébert, Paris, *c.* 1830. *Cobham, Morley-Pegge Collection.* 583 Cor anglais. Henri Brod, Paris, pre-1839. *London, Philip Bate Collection.* 584 Bass oboe. Charles Bizey, Paris, pre-1750. *Paris, Conservatoire de Musique, Musée instrumentale, C.494.*

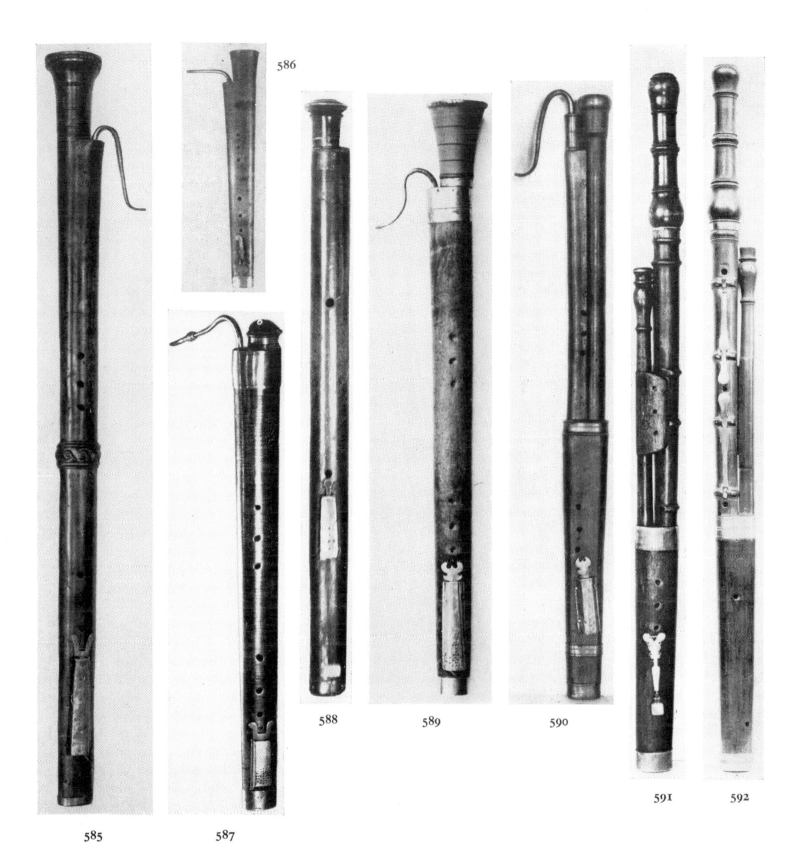

585 Great curtal (*Doppelfagott*). Italian, 16th century. *Vienna, Kunsthistorisches Museum, Sammlung alter Musikinstrumente, C.199.* **586** Descant curtal. ? Spanish, 16th or 17th century. *Brussels, Conservatoire royal de Musique, 2329.* **587** Curtal (*gedächt Chorist=fagott*). German, 16th–17th century. *Berlin, Staatliches Institut für Musikforschung, Musikinstrumenten-Sammlung, 655.* **588** Curtal (*gedächt Chorist=fagott*). J. C. Denner, Nuremberg, late 17th century. *Leipzig, Karl-Marx-Universität, Musikinstrumenten-Museum, 1360.* **589** Curtal (*Chorist-fagott*). German, 16th century. *Hamburg, Museum für Hamburgische Geschichte, 1928.389.* **590** Curtal (*Chorist-fagott*). ? Italian, 17th century. *Vienna, Kunsthistorisches Museum, Sammlung alter Musikinstrumente, C.201.* **591** Bassoon. J. C. Denner, Nuremberg, late 17th century. *Berlin, Staatliches Institut für Musikforschung, Musikinstrumenten-Sammlung, 2970.* **592** Bassoon. German, early 18th century. *Basel, Historisches Museum, 1904.311.*

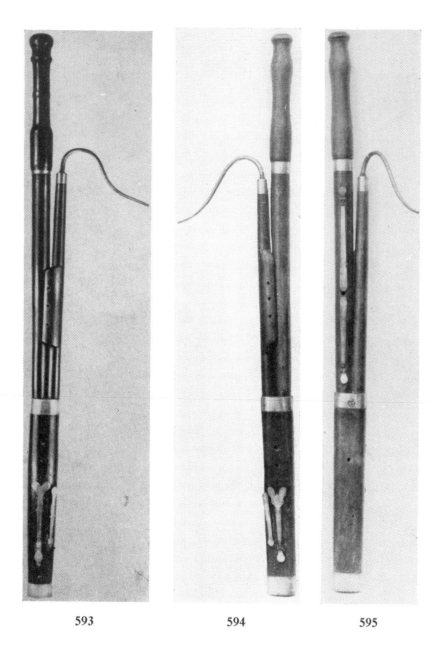

593   594   595

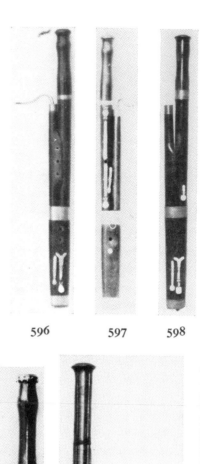

596   597   598

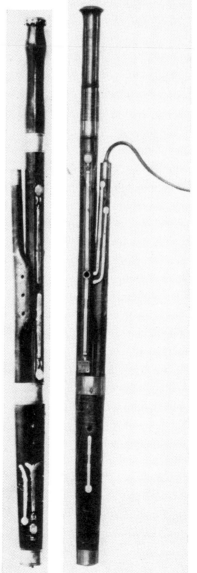

593 Bassoon. Dutch or Flemish, 1730. *Brussels, Conservatoire royal de Musique, 997.* **594, 595** Bassoon. Dondeine, ? French, c. 1720. *London, Philip Bate Collection.* **596, 597** Fagottino. Martin Lot, Paris, c. 1780. *London, Philip Bate Collection.* **598** Fagottino. H. Grenser, Dresden, beginning of 19th century. *Berlin, Staatliches Institut für Musikforschung, Musikinstrumenten-Sammlung, 2973.* **599** Bassoon. F. G. Kirst, Potsdam, late 18th century. *Hamburg, Museum für Hamburgische Geschichte, 1928.387.* **600** Bassoon. H. Grenser, Dresden, beginning of 19th century. *Amsterdam, Rijksmuseum, NM.10616.* **601** Bassoon. Proser, London, 1777. *London, Horniman Museum, Carse 318.*

599   600   601

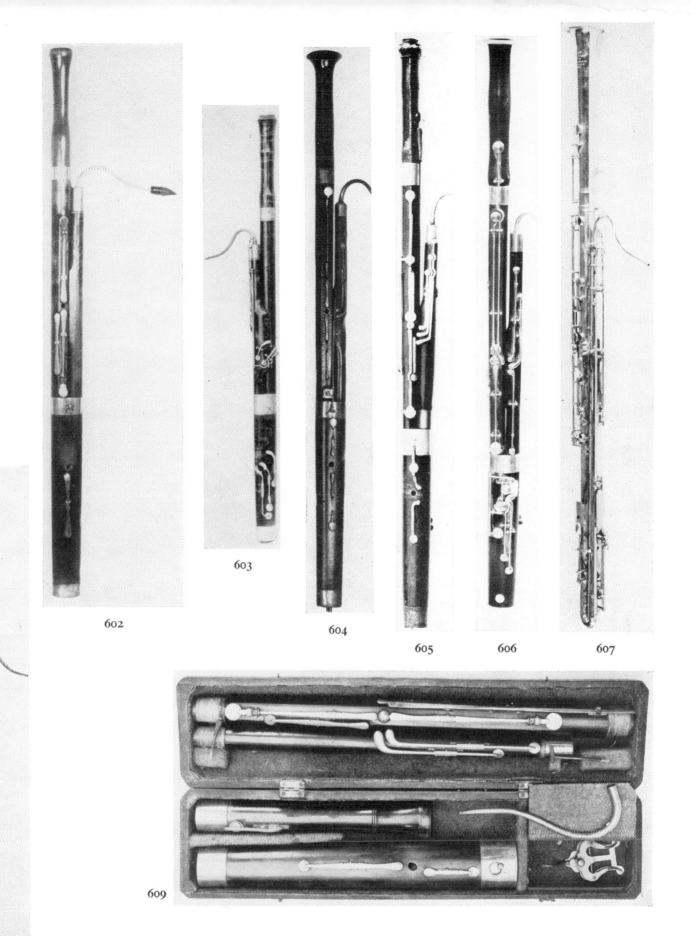

602 Bassoon. Goulding & Co., London, c. 1800. *London, Horniman Museum, Carse 125.* **603** Tenoroon. Savary jeune, Paris, c. 1840. *London, Philip Bate Collection.* **604** Bassoon. J. Ziegler, Vienna, mid 19th century. *Leipzig, Karl-Marx-Universität, Musikinstrumenten-Museum, 1392.* **605** Bassoon. Stengel, Bayreuth, c. 1830. *Hamburg, Museum für Hamburgische Geschichte, 1926.411.* **606** Bassoon. Heckel, Biebrich-am-Rhein, c. 1870–80. *London, Horniman Museum, Carse 212.* **607** Bassoon. A. Lecomte, Paris, c. 1889. *Ann Arbor, University of Michigan, Stearns Collection, 682.* **608** Bassoon. Prudent, Paris, c. 1810. *Neuchâtel, Switzerland, Kunst und Historisches Museum.* **609** Bassoon. R. J. Bilton, London, c. 1840. *London, Philip Bate Collection.*

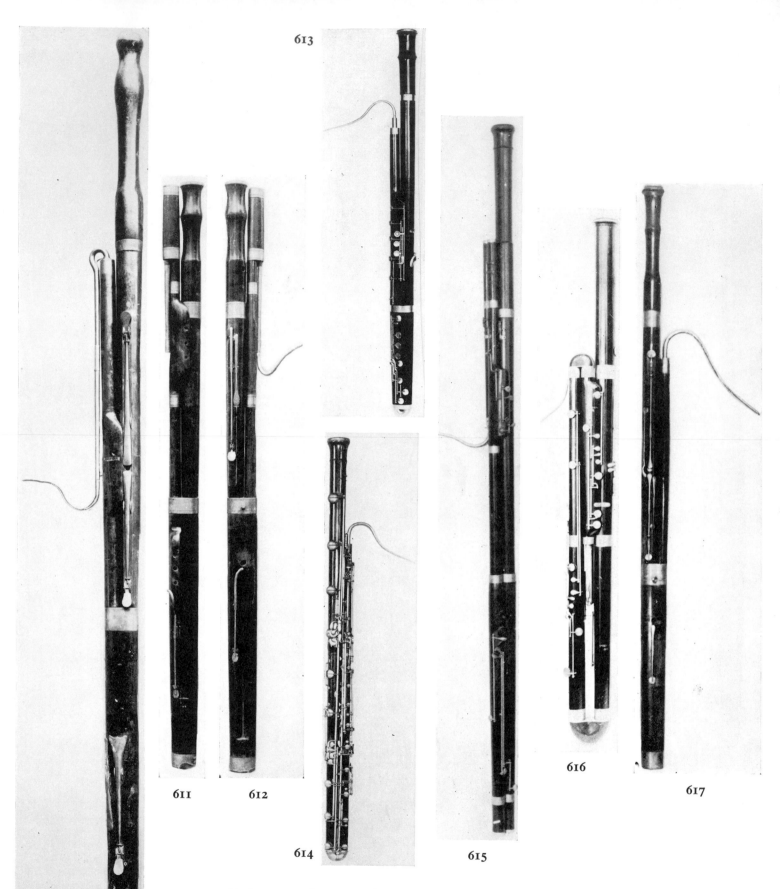

610 Double bassoon. Thos. Stanesby, junior, London, 1739. *Dublin, National Museum of Ireland.* **611, 612** Double bassoon. Caspar Tauber, Vienna, early 19th century. *Yale, Philip Young Collection.* **613** Bassoon. H. J. Haseneier, Coblenz, *c.* 1850. *London, F. Rendell, Esq.* **614** Bassoon. Triébert, Paris, *c.* 1855. *Brussels, Conservatoire royal de Musique, 3119.* **615** Double bassoon. French, *c.* 1885. *London, Philip Bate Collection.* **616** Double bassoon. Heckel, Biebrich-am-Rhein, *c.* 1879. *London, Philip Bate Collection.* **617** Double bassoon ('semi-contra bassoon'). J. Samme, London, 1854. *London, Royal College of Music, 91.*

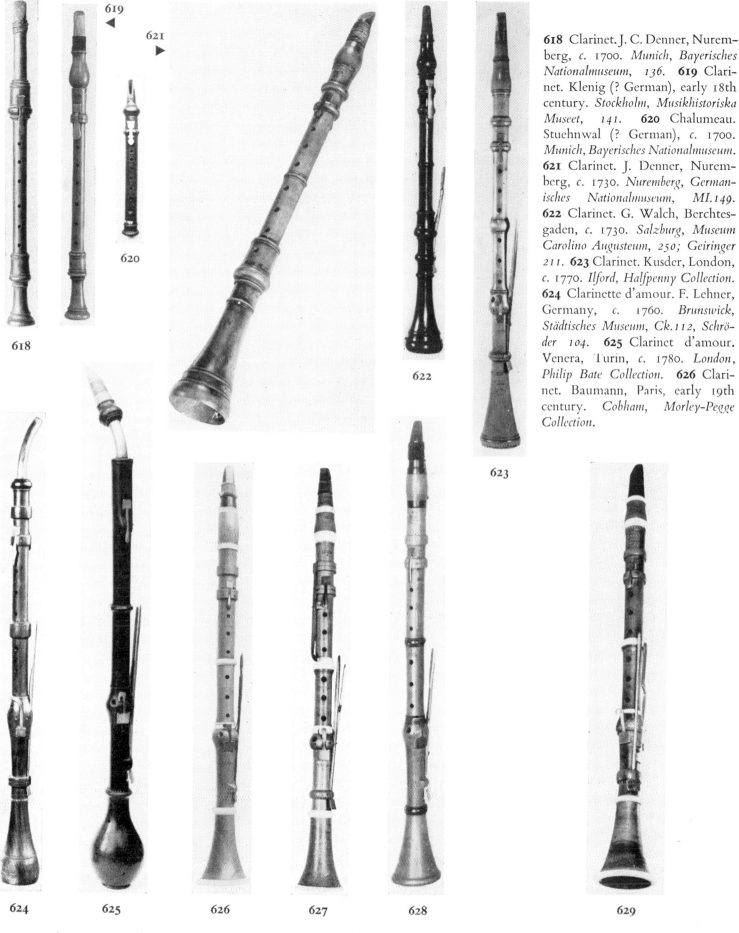

618

619

621

620

622

623

624 625 626 627 628 629

618 Clarinet. J. C. Denner, Nuremberg, c. 1700. *Munich, Bayerisches Nationalmuseum, 136.* **619** Clarinet. Klenig (? German), early 18th century. *Stockholm, Musikhistoriska Museet, 141.* **620** Chalumeau. Stuehnwal (? German), c. 1700. *Munich, Bayerisches Nationalmuseum.* **621** Clarinet. J. Denner, Nuremberg, c. 1730. *Nuremberg, Germanisches Nationalmuseum, MI.149.* **622** Clarinet. G. Walch, Berchtesgaden, c. 1730. *Salzburg, Museum Carolino Augusteum, 250; Geiringer 211.* **623** Clarinet. Kusder, London, c. 1770. *Ilford, Halfpenny Collection.* **624** Clarinette d'amour. F. Lehner, Germany, c. 1760. *Brunswick, Städtisches Museum, Ck.112, Schröder 104.* **625** Clarinet d'amour. Venera, Turin, c. 1780. *London, Philip Bate Collection.* **626** Clarinet. Baumann, Paris, early 19th century. *Cobham, Morley-Pegge Collection.*

627 Clarinet. W. Milhouse, London, c. 1810. *Brighton Museums, Spencer Collection.* **628** Clarinet. Griesbacher, Vienna, late 18th century. *Leipzig, Karl-Marx-Universität, Musikinstrumenten-Museum, 1484.* **629** Clarinet. Asa Hopkins, Litchfield, Conn., c. 1825. *Washington, Smithsonian Institution, 1825-37.*

630 Clarinet. H. Grenser, Dresden, c. 1800. *Berlin, Staatliches Institut für Musikforschung, Musikinstrumenten-Sammlung, 83.* **631** Clarinet. Stengel, Bayreuth, c. 1840. *Leipzig, Karl-Marx-Universität, Musikinstrumenten-Museum, 1495.* **632** Clarinet. Thos. Key, London, 1834. *London, Philip Bate Collection.* **633** Clarinet. F. Lefèvre, Paris, c. 1840. *London, Philip Bate Collection.* **634** Clarinet. German, late 19th century. *London, Philip Bate Collection.* **635** Clarinet. Thos. Key & Co., London, c. 1856. *London, Philip Bate Collection.* **636** Clarinet. E. J. Albert, Brussels, c. 1875. *London, Philip Bate Collection.* **637** Clarinet. Louis Auguste Buffet, Paris, 1844. *London, Philip Bate Collection.* **638** Clarinet. Eugène Albert, Brussels, c. 1865. *London, Philip Bate Collection.* **639** Alto clarinet. A. Knockenhauer, Berlin, 1856. *New York, Metropolitan Museum of Art, Crosby Brown Collection, 2126.* **640** Alto clarinet. Key, London, c. 1840. *Luton Museum, Ridley Collection, C/16.*

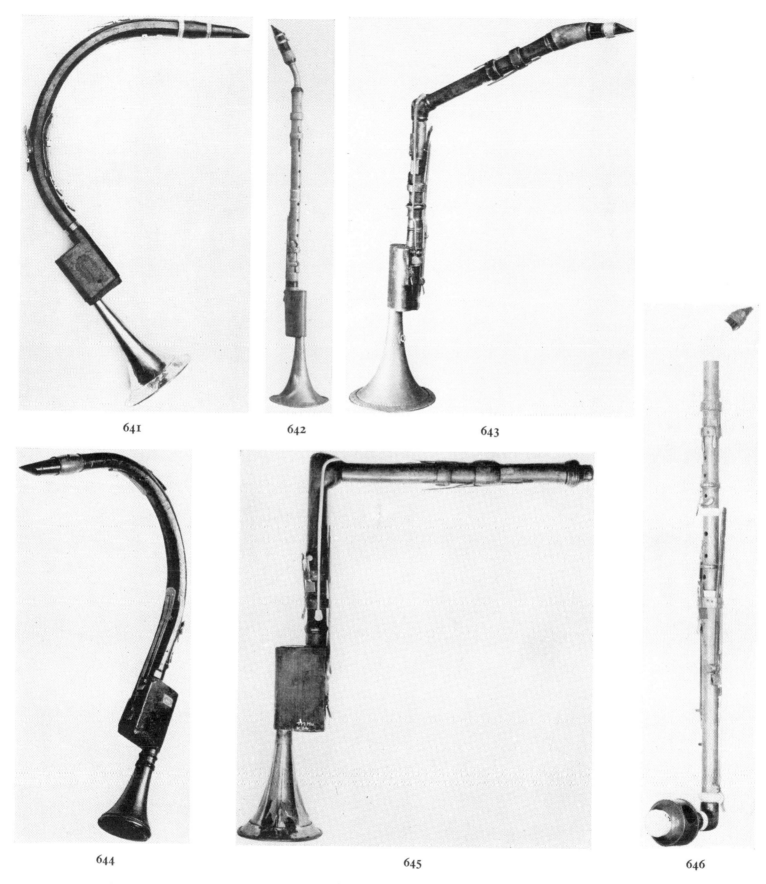

641 Basset horn. Mayrhofer, Passau, *c. 1770. Hamburg, Museum für Hamburgische Geschichte, 1927.159.* 642 Basset horn. August Grenser, Dresden, 1784. *Stockholm, Musikhistoriska Museet, 553.* 643 Basset horn. A. or H. Grenser, Dresden, 1793. *The Hague, Gemeentemuseum.* 644 Basset horn. Probably Viennese, *c. 1780. Nuremberg, Germanisches Nationalmuseum, Rück Collection, MIR.465.* 645 Basset horn. G. Glezl (German), *c. 1800. Munich, Bayerisches Nationalmuseum, 111.* 646 Basset horn. Braun, Mannheim, *c. 1845. Leipzig, Karl-Marx-Universität, Musikinstrumenten-Museum, 1537.*

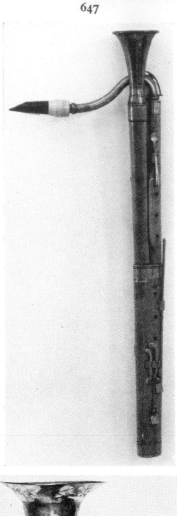

647

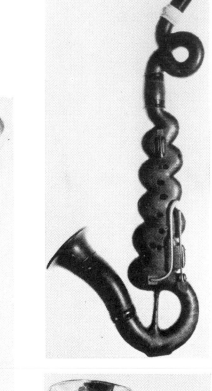

648

649

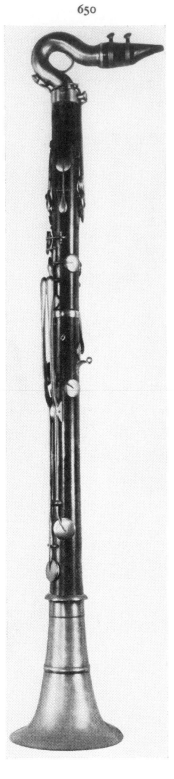

650

652

651

647 Bass clarinet. H. Grenser, Dresden, 1793. *Stockholm, Musikhistoriska Museum, 1957.58.28.* **648** Bass clarinet (*glicibarifono*). Catterino Catterini, Padua, after 1838. *London, Philip Bate Collection.* **649** Bass clarinet. Nicola Papalini, Padua, *c.* 1815. *Boston, Museum of Fine Arts, Leslie Lindsey Mason Collection, 119.* **650** Bass clarinet. Adolphe Sax, Paris, 1845. *The Hague, Gemeentemuseum.* **651** Contrabass clarinet (*Bathyphon*). Wieprecht & Skorra, Berlin, after 1839. *Berlin, Staatliches Institut für Musikforschung, Musikinstrumenten-Sammlung, 2904.* **652** Bass clarinet. A. Buffet jeune, Paris, *c.* 1860. *Ann Arbor, University of Michigan, Stearns Collection, 635.*

653 Contrabass clarinet. Fontaine Besson, Paris, after 1889. *London, Philip Bate Collection.* **654** Alto fagotto. Wood & Ivy, late George Wood. London, *c.* 1835. *London, Victoria and Albert Museum, 47–1884.* **655** Tarogato. Stowasser, Budapest, late 19th century. *London, Royal Military School of Music, Kneller Hall, 67.* **656** Tenor sarrusophone. Gautrot Marquet, Paris, after 1856. *Author's Collection.* **657** Baritone sarrusophone. Gautrot Marquet, Paris, after 1856. *Paris, Conservatoire de Musique, Musée instrumentale, C.1128.* **658** Soprano saxophone. Adolphe Sax, Paris, *c.* 1855. *London, Horniman Museum, Carse 83.* **659** Tenor saxophone. C. Mahillon & Co., Brussels, late 19th century. *From the maker's catalogue.* **660** Kontrabassophon. H. J. Haseneier, Coblenz, after 1849. *Leipzig, Karl-Marx-Universität, Musikinstrumenten-Museum, 1601.* **661** Contrebasse à anche. C. Mahillon & Co., Brussels, *c.* 1870. *London, Royal Military School of Music, Kneller Hall.*

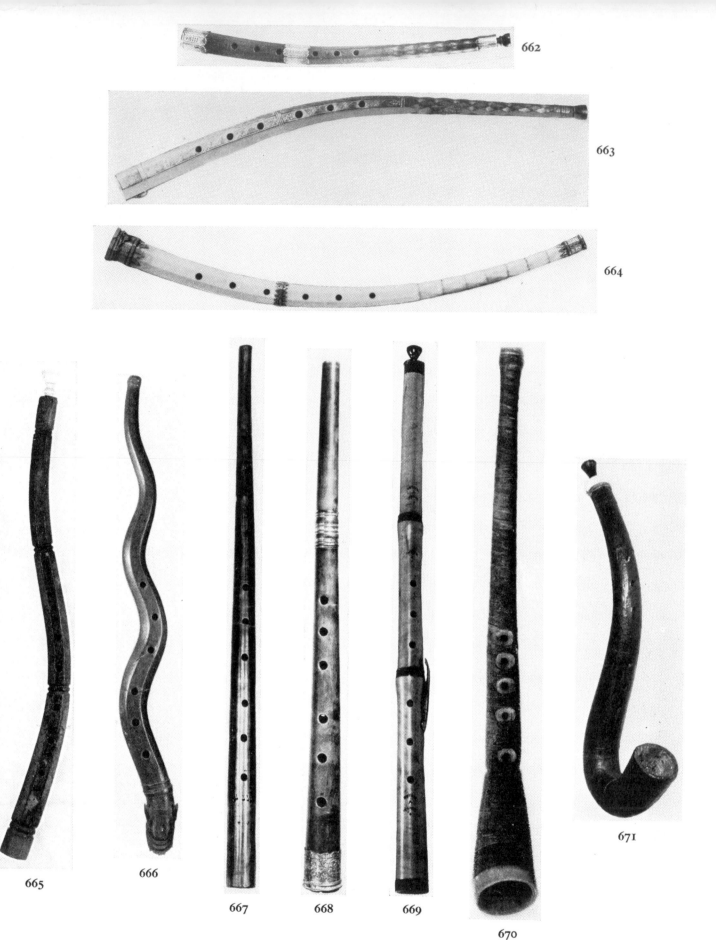

662 Cornettino. German, 1518. *Author's Collection.* 663 Cornett. ? Italian, 16th century. *Vienna, Kunsthistorisches Museum, Sammlung alter Musikinstrumente, A.241.* 664 Cornett. Late 16th century. *Stockholm, Musikhistoriska Museet, 549.* 665 Cornett. ? Italian, 17th century. *Paris, Conservatoire de Musique, Musée instrumentale, 0083, C.683.* 666 Cornett. ? Italian, 16th or 17th century. *Paris, Conservatoire de Musique, Musée instrumentale, E.581, C.624.* 667 Mute cornett. Italian, 16th century. *Vienna, Kunsthistorisches Museum, Sammlung alter Musikinstrumente, A.236.* 668 Mute cornett. ? French, 17th century. *Geneva, Musée d'Art et d'Histoire.* 669 Straight cornett. Hetsch, Urach, 19th century. *Nuremberg, Germanisches Nationalmuseum, Rück Collection, MIR.34.* 670 Folk cornett (*tuohitorvi*). Finnish (recent). *Miss W. N. Bartlett, Dartington Hall, Devon.* 671 Cornett. Italian, ? 17th century. *Ann Arbor, University of Michigan, Stearns Collection, 829.*

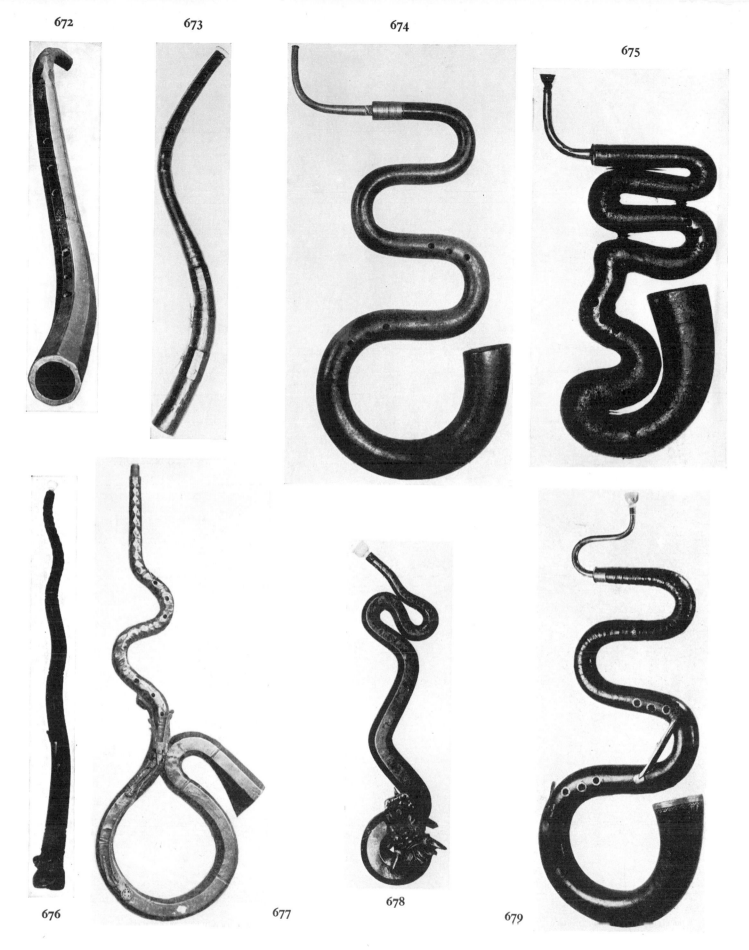

672 Tenor cornett. German, 16th century. *Brunswick, Städtisches Museum, 66.* 673 Tenor cornett. French, ? 16th century. *Lisbon, Conservatório Nacional.* 674 Serpent. Belgian, 18th or 19th century. *Brussels, Conservatoire royal de Musique, 2447.* 675 Serpent. Spanish, 18th or early 19th century. *Barcelona, Museo Municipál de Música, 60.* 676 Tenor cornett. French, 16th century. *Paris, Conservatoire de Musique, Musée instrumentale, 0087.* 677 Bass cornett. Italian, 16th century. *Paris, Conservatoire de Musique, Musée instrumentale, C.636.* 678 Bass cornett. Italian, 16th–17th century. *Paris, Conservatoire de Musique, Musée instrumentale, C.634.* 679 Serpent. German, early 19th century. *Nuremberg, Germanisches Nationalmuseum, Rück Collection, MIR. 46.*

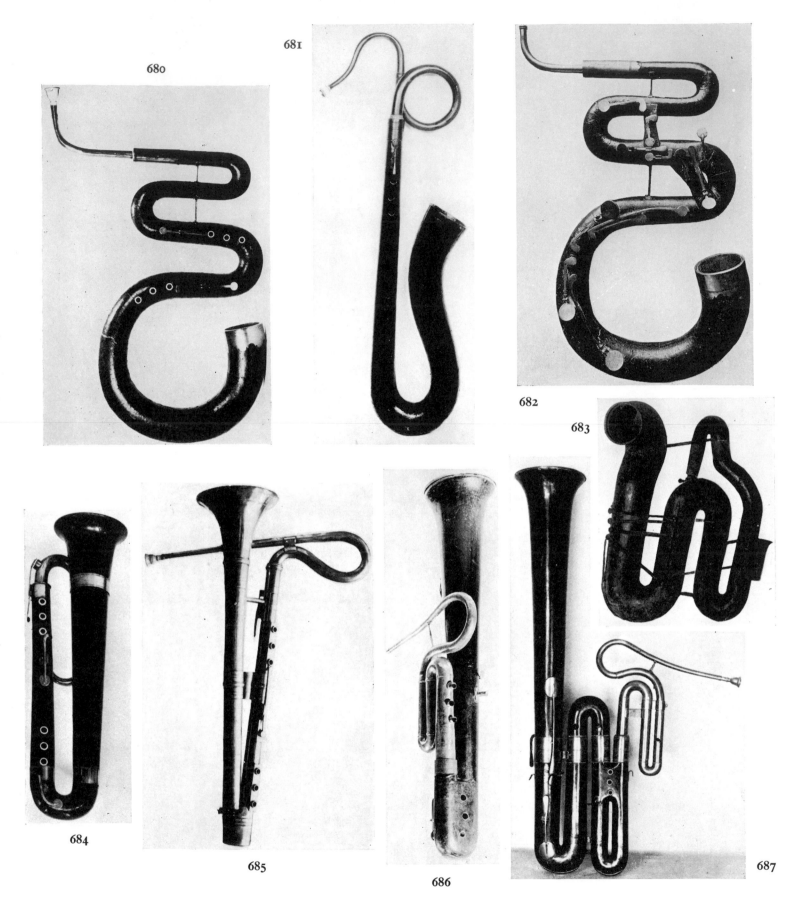

680 Serpent. Thomas Key, London, *c. 1810. Oxford, Pitt Rivers Museum.* **681** Serpent militaire. French, early 19th century. *London, Royal College of Music, 195.* **682** Serpent. Thomas Key, London, *c. 1840. Cardiff, National Museum of Wales.* **683** Serpent. Embach, Amsterdam, *c. 1825. Leipzig, Karl-Marx-Universität, Musikinstrumenten-Museum, 1586.* **684** Bass horn. French, early 19th century. *London, Horniman Museum, Carse 292.* **685** Bass horn. English, *c. 1800. Cobham, Morley-Pegge Collection.* **686** Serpent Forveille. Forveille, Paris, *c. 1825. Cobham, Morley-Pegge Collection.* **687** Contra-bass-horn. J. B. Coëffet, Chaumont-en-Vexin (France), *c. 1840. Leipzig, Karl-Marx-Universität, Musikinstrumenten-Museum, 1599.*

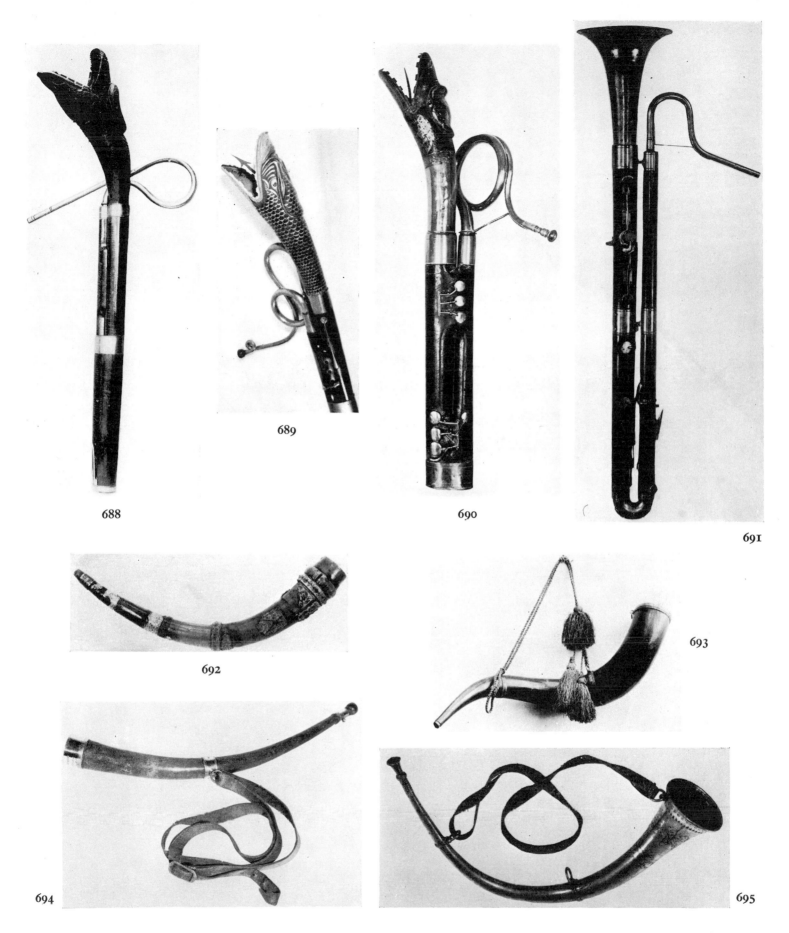

688 Russian bassoon. Hirschbrunner, Sumiswald (Switzerland), *c.* 1820. *Hamburg, Museum für Hamburgische Geschichte, 1922.70.*
689 Russian bassoon. Swiss, *c.* 1820. *Zürich, Schweitzerisches Landesmuseum.* 690 Russian bassoon. F. Tabard, Lyons, *c.* 1830.
Leipzig, Karl-Marx-Universität, Musikinstrumenten-Museum, 1591. 691 Chromatic bass horn. Streitwolf, Göttingen, *c.* 1825. *The*
Hague, Gemeentemuseum. 692 Hunting horn. Probably German, late 15th century. *London, Wallace Collection, 111.J.499.* 693
Hunting horn. French, 17th century. *Munich, Bayerisches Nationalmuseum, 227.* 694 Hunting horn. H. Grenser, Dresden, *c.* 1800.
Ann Arbor, University of Michigan, Stearns Collection, 785. 695 Hunting horn. Crétien, Vernon (Normandy). 17th century. *Paris,*
Conservatoire de Musique, Musée instrumentale, E.133, C.577.

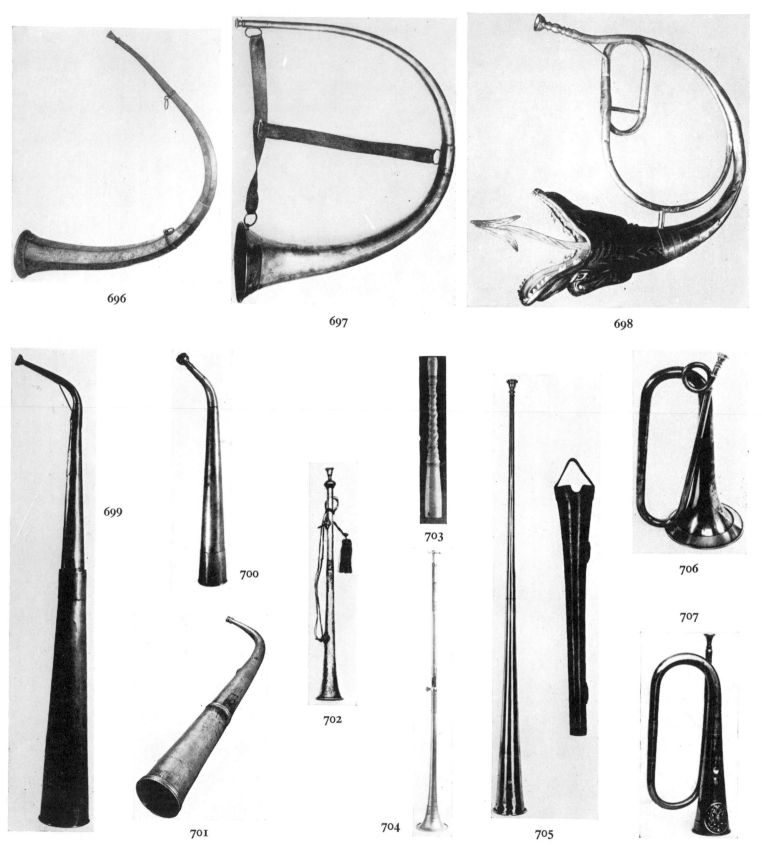

696 Hunting horn. Crétien, Vernon, 17th century. *Paris, Conservatoire de Musique, Musée instrumentale, E.792, C.576.* **697** Bugle horn. German, late 18th–early 19th century. *London, Royal College of Music, 137.* **698** Bugle horn. Hirsbrunner, Sumiswald (Switzerland), 1798. *Zürich, Schweizerisches Landesmuseum.* **699, 700** Two Russian horns. German, early 19th century. *Berlin, Institut für Musikforschung, Musikinstrumenten-Sammlung, 490, 495.* **701** Hunting horn. German, 1803. *Nuremberg, Germanisches Nationalmuseum, MI.374.* **702** Hunting horn. English, early 19th century. *London, Royal College of Music, 100.* **703** Hunting horn. French, 17th century. *Paris, Conservatoire de Musique, Musée instrumentale, E.296, C.566.* **704** Post horn. Mahillon, Brussels, late 19th century. *London, Royal Military School of Music, Kneller Hall.* **705** Coach horn. Köhler & Son, London, c. 1870. *Brighton, Museums, Spencer Collection.* **706** Bugle. Wigley, London, early 19th century. *Bradford, Bowling Hall Museum.* **707** Bugle. Russian, mid 19th century. *London, Horniman Museum, Carse 90.*

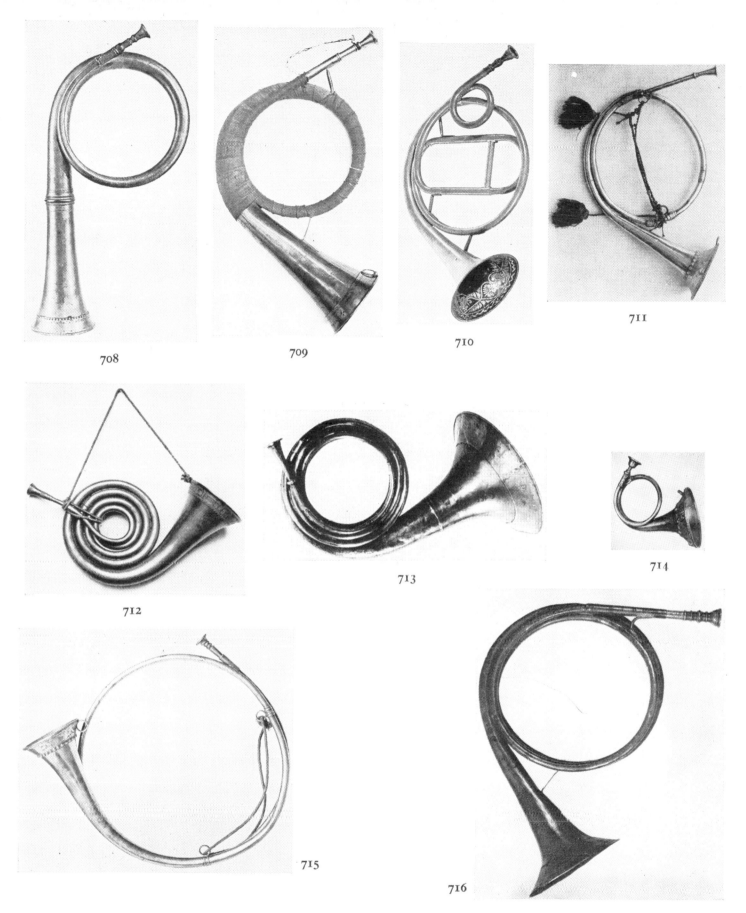

708 Horn. Jan Lechien, Antwerp, 1604. Replica. *Brussels, Conservatoire royal de Musique, 3145.* 709 Post horn. W. Schmidt, Halle, late 18th or early 19th century. *Berlin, Institut für Musikforschung, Musikinstrumenten-Sammlung, 4178.* 710 Post horn. Courtois frères, Paris, c. 1820. *Paris, Conservatoire de Musique, Musée instrumentale, C.606.* 711 Horn. Johann Wilhelm Haas, Nuremberg, 1682. *Basel, Historisches Museum, 1880.72.* 712 Horn. Dresden, c. 1570. *Dresden, Staatliche Historisches Museum.* 713 Horn. A. Buchswinder, Ellwangen, 1738. *Salzburg, Museum Carolino Augusteum, 225, Geiringer 155.* 714 Miniature horn. Haas, Nuremberg, first half of 18th century. *London, Wallace Collection, A.1334.* 715 Horn. Hieronymus Starck, Nuremberg, 1667. *Copenhagen, Claudius Collection, Musikhistorisk Museum, F.99.* 716 Horn (or Jägertrompete ?). Balthasar Fürst, Ellwangen, 1770. *Nuremberg, Germanisches Nationalmuseum, Rück Collection, MIR.122.*

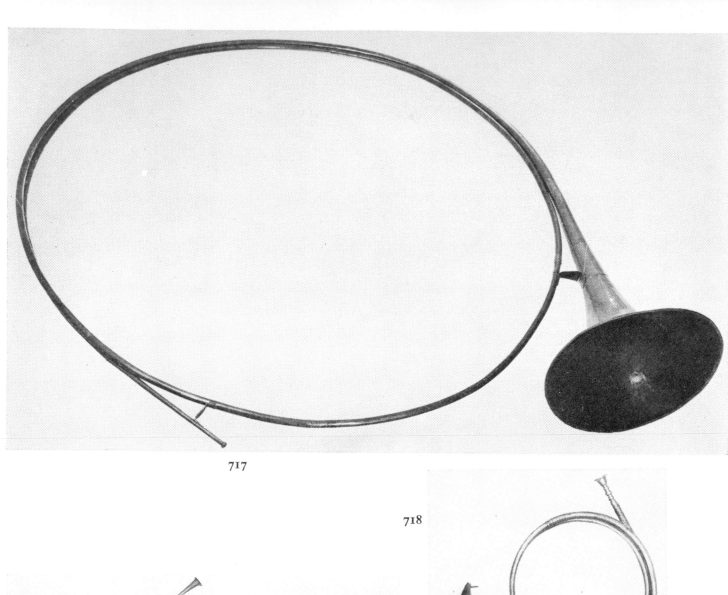

717

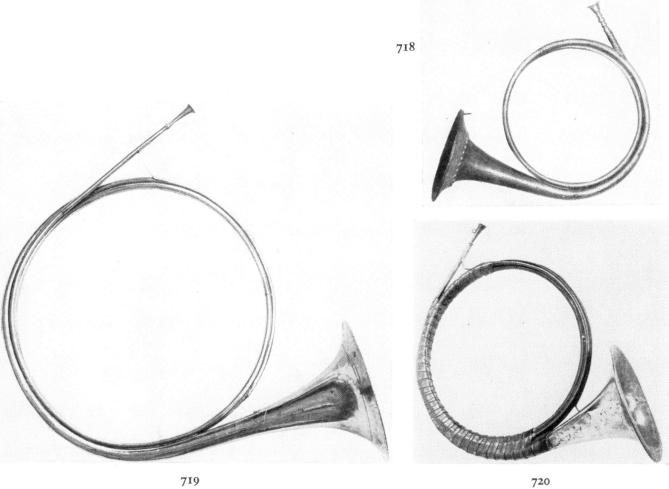

719   720

717 Horn. Crétien, Vernon, *c. 1700. Paris, Conservatoire de Musique, Musée instrumentale, C.578.* **718** Horn. Georg Friderich Steinmetz, Nuremberg, pre-1740. *Berlin, Institut für Musikforschung, Musikinstrumenten-Sammlung, 4187.* **719** Horn. Michael Leichamschneider, Vienna, 1718. *Basel, Historisches Museum, 1878.22.* **720** Horn. Nicolas Winkings, London, *c. 1750. Norwich Museums.*

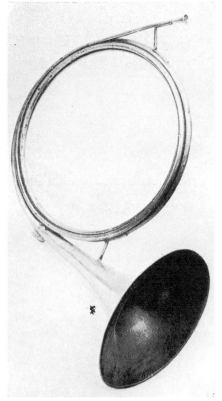

721

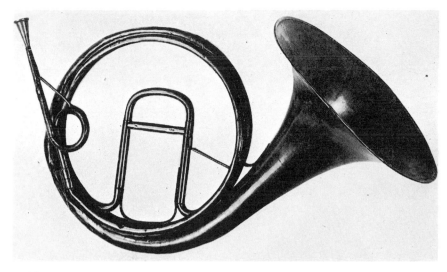

722

723

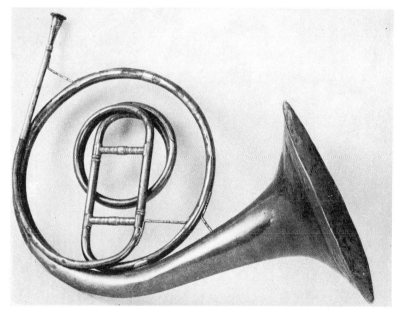

721 Horn. Carlin, Paris, *c.* 1755–60. *Cobham, Morley-Pegge Collection.* 722 Inventionshorn. J. G. Haltenhof, Hanau-am-Main, late 18th century. *The Hague, Gemeentemuseum, 773.* 723 Inventionshorn. C. Lobeit (? Bohemia, *c.* 1785). *Boston, Museum of Fine Arts, Leslie Lindsey Mason Collection, 193.* 724, 725 Pair of horns. George Henry Rodenbostel, London, late 18th century. *Gloucester, City Museum, F.1536, F.1537.*

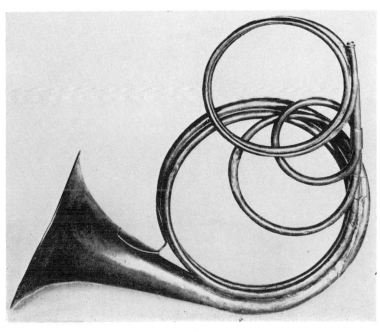

724

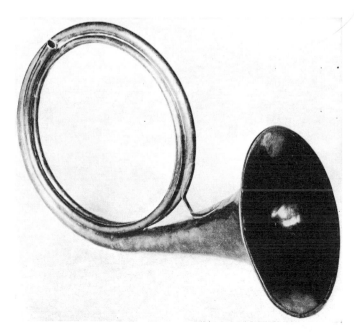

725

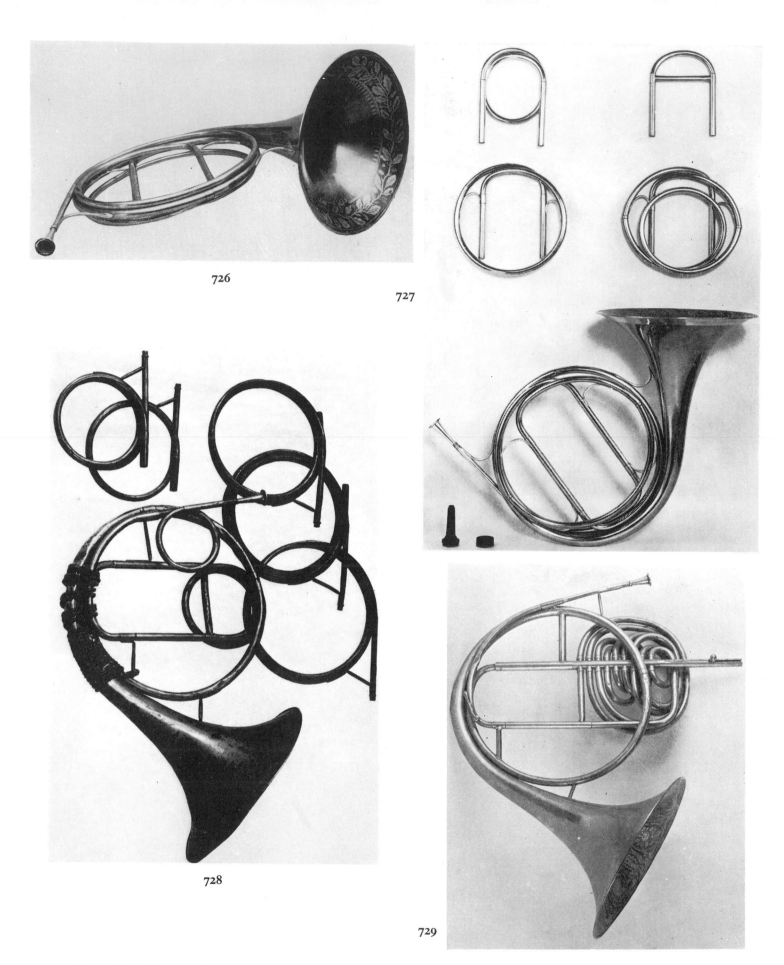

726, 727 Cor solo. Marcel-Auguste Raoux, Paris, *c.* 1826. *London, Victoria and Albert Museum, W.83–1926.* **728** Orchestra horn. Carl Gottlieb Schuster, Markneukirchen, *c.* 1800. *Nuremberg, Germanisches Nationalmuseum, Rück Collection, MIR.84.* **729** Omnitonic horn. Charles Sax, Brussels, 1833. *Boston, Museum of Fine Arts, Leslie Lindsey Mason Collection, 104.*

730 Straight trumpet. Hans Hainlein, Nuremberg, 1658. *Frankfurt-am-Main, Historisches Museum, 102.* **731** Trumpet. Philipp Schöller, Munich, mid 18th century. *London, Royal College of Music, 194.* **732** Trumpet. Harris, London, *c.* 1720. *Author's Collection.* **733** Trumpet mouthpiece. *Copenhagen, Musikhistorisk Museum.* **734** Trumpet mute. ? 18th century. *Basel, Historisches Museum, 1956.309.* **735** Box trumpet. Adam Puchswinder, Ellwangen, 1731. *Berlin, Institut für Musik-forschung, Musikinstrumenten-Sammlung, 298.*

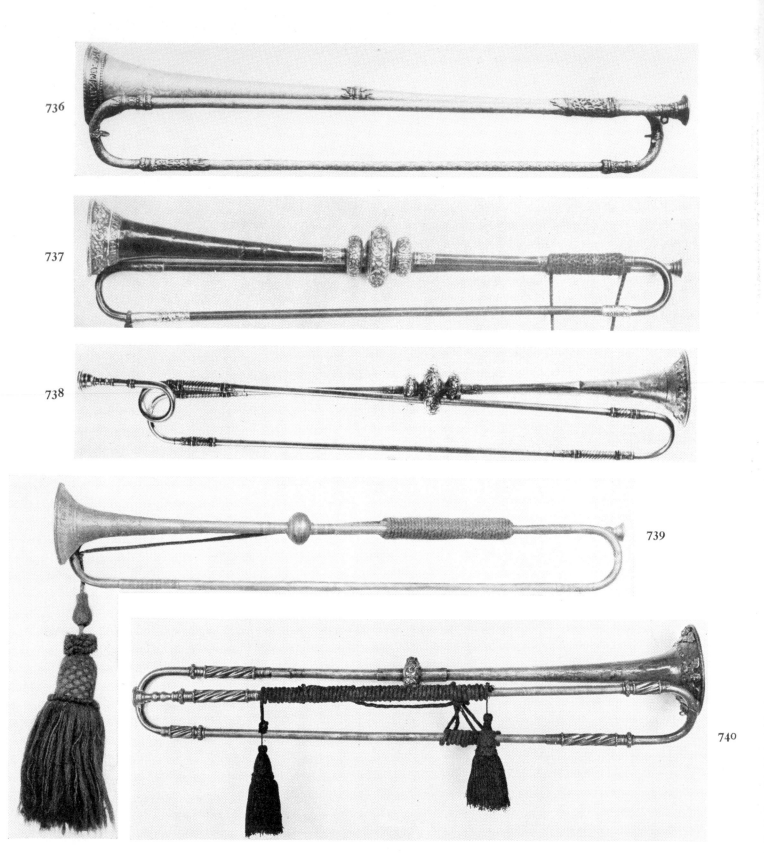

736 Trumpet. Anton Schnitzer, 1581. *Vienna, Kunsthistorisches Museum, Sammlung alter Musikinstrumente, A.258.* **737** Trumpet. Augustine Dudley, London, 1666. *London, London Museum.* **738** Trumpet. William Bull, London, late 17th century. *Oxford, Ashmolean Museum.* **739** Trumpet. Johann Leonhard Ehe, Nuremberg, 1746. *Nuremberg, Germanisches Nationalmuseum, MI.217.* **740** Trumpet. W. W. Haas, Nuremberg, first half of 18th century. *London, Wallace Collection, A.1333.*

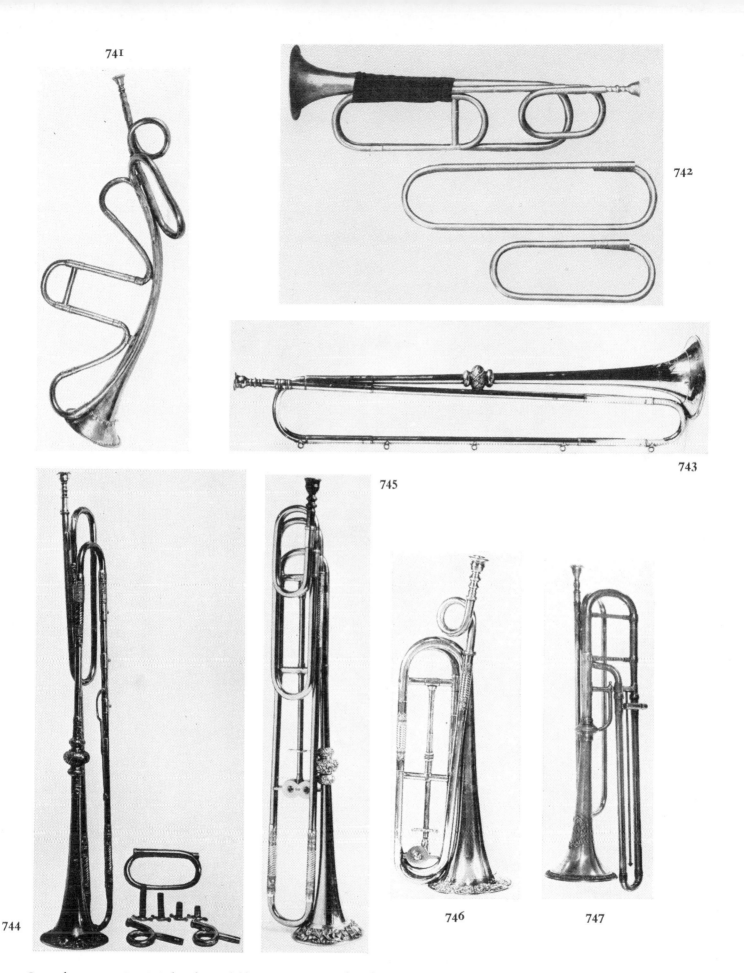

741 Curved trumpet. J. J. Friederich, Andelfingen, 1821. *Zürich, Schweitzerisches Landesmuseum, 1440.* **742** Trumpet. Carl Missenharter, Ulm, mid 19th century. *Nuremberg, Germanisches Nationalmuseum, MI.379.* **743** Trumpet. Henry Keat, London, third quarter of 19th century. *London, Royal Military School of Music, Kneller Hall.* **744** Trumpet. William Shaw, London, 1787. *London, London Museum.* **745** Slide trumpet. Köhler, London, c. 1830. *London, Royal Military School of Music, Kneller Hall, 70.* **746** Slide trumpet. James Power, London; hall mark of 1819–20. *London, Joseph Wheeler Collection.* **747** Slide trumpet. Antoine Courtois, Paris, 1840. *Paris, Conservatoire de Musique, Musée instrumentale, E.1541, C.1402.*

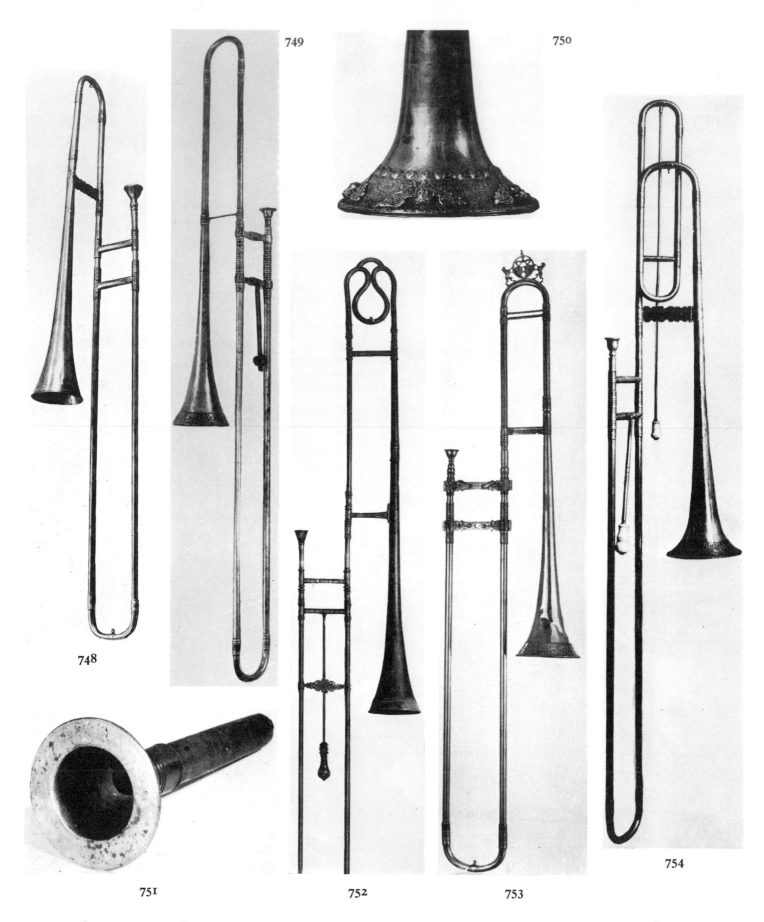

748 Trombone. Erasmus Schnitzer, Nuremberg, 1551. *Nuremberg, Germanisches Nationalmuseum. MI.170.* **749** Bass trombone. Pierre Colbert, Rheims, 1593. *Amsterdam, Rijksmuseum.* **750** Bass trombone. Johann Leonhard Ehe, Nuremberg, 1732. *Vienna, Kunsthistorisches Museum, property of the Gesellschaft der Musikfreunde in Wien, Inv. No. GdM 202.* **751** Mouthpiece of **749**. **752** Contrabass trombone. G. N. Oller, Stockholm, 1639 (? 1689). *Stockholm, Musikhistoriska Museet, 242.* **753** Trombone. Georg Ehe, Nuremberg, 1619. *Paris, Conservatoire de Musique, Musée instrumentale, E.754.* **754** Bass trombone. Wolf Wilhelm Haas, Nuremberg, first half of 18th century. *Berlin, Institut für Musikforschung, Musikinstrumenten-Sammlung, 567.*

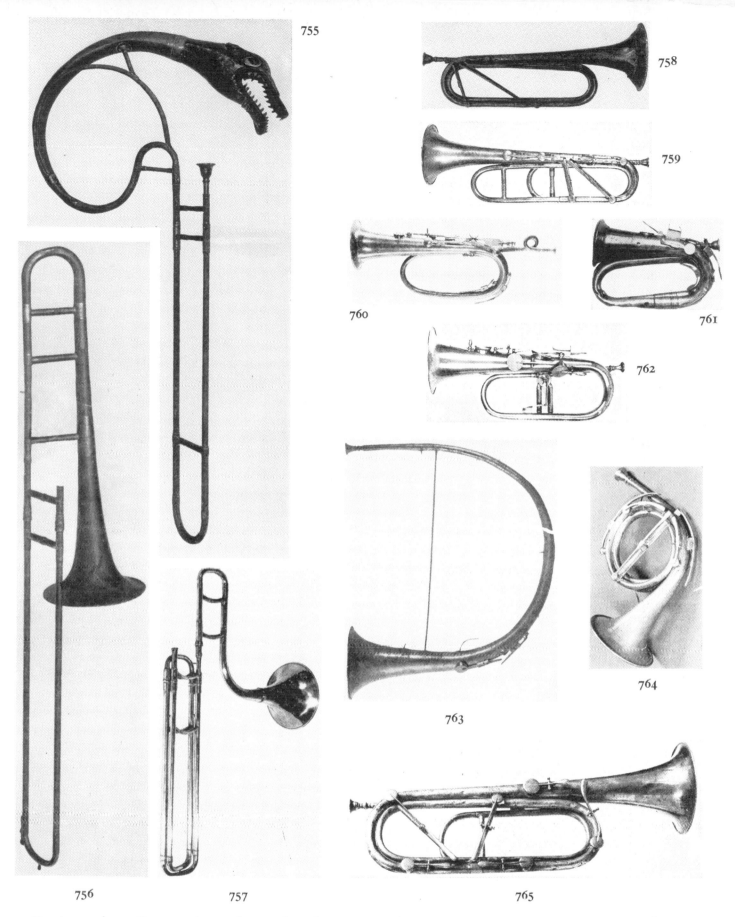

755 Buccin trombone. Bernareggi, Barcelona, early 19th century. *London, Horniman Museum, Carse 288.* **756** Trombone. Fasting & Wilde, Copenhagen, 1847. *Copenhagen, Claudius Collection, Musikhistorisk Museum, F.23.* **757** Bass trombone. Schmittschneider, Paris, 1823. *Ann Arbor, University of Michigan, Stearns Collection, 897.* **758** Key trumpet. Early 19th century. *Nuremberg, Germanisches Nationalmuseum, Rück Collection.* **759** Key trumpet. Coll, Barcelona, first third of 19th century. *Barcelona, Museo Municipál de Música, 57.* **760** Key bugle. Graves & Co., Winchester, New Hampshire, U.S.A., mid 19th century. *Yale, University, Belle Skinner Collection, 180.* **761** Key bugle. J. Fentum, London, c. 1840. *Keighley, Yorks., Museum.* **762** Key bugle. Joseph Higham, Manchester, after 1852. *Brighton, Museums, Spencer Collection.* **763** Key bugle (*Halbmond*). German, c. 1830. *Nuremberg, Germanisches Nationalmuseum, MI.180.* **764** Keyed post horn. German, c. 1830. *Boston, Museum of Fine Arts, Leslie Lindsey Mason Collection, 183.* **765** Tenor or bass key trumpet. Piatet & Benoit, Lyons, second quarter of 19th century. *London, Royal Military School of Music, Kneller Hall, 172.*

766 Ophicleide. George Wigglesworth, Otley, Yorkshire, 1856. *Halifax, Bankfield Museum.* **767** Alto ophicleide. Charles Sax, Brussels, *c. 1825. New York, Metropolitan Museum of Art, Crosby Brown Collection, 2411.* **768** Trumpet. W. Schuster, Carlsruhe, *c. 1820. Nuremberg Germanisches Nationalmuseum, Rück Collection, MIR.130.* **769** Trumpet. A. Barth, Munich 1834. *Nuremberg, Germanisches Nationalmuseum, Rück Collection, MIR.131.* **770** Trumpet. N. Adams, Lowell, Massachusetts, 1825. *U.S. Frigate Constitution, Navy Yard, Charlestown, Mass.* **771** Trumpet. Sandbach & Wyatt, London, 1832–5. *London, Horniman Museum, Carse 150.* **772** Trumpet. Charles Pace, London, 1830–40. *London, Horniman Museum, Carse 290.* **773** Trumpet. Köhler, London, *c. 1839. Cobham, Morley-Pegge Collection.* **774** Trumpet. C. Mahillon & Co., Brussels, after 1878. *Collection of the late C. Overy.*

775 Cornet. Halary, Paris, *c. 1835. London, Royal Military School of Music, Kneller Hall, 128.* 776 Cornet (Flugel horn). A. Heiser, Potsdam, *c. 1840. Eisenach, Bachhaus, Buhle 111.* 777 Cornet. C. A. Müller, Mainz, *c. 1850. Author's Collection.* 778 Cornet. Köhler, London, mid 19th century. *London, Royal Military School of Music, Kneller Hall, 173.* 779 Post horn. German, second half of 19th century. *Boston, Museum of Fine Arts, Leslie Lindsey Mason Collection, 214.* 780 Cornet. Thompson & Odell, Boston, Mass., late 19th century. *Collection of the late C. Overy.* 781 Pocket cornet. English, late 19th century. *Collection of the late C. Overy.* 782 Cornet. Graves & Co., Winchester, New Hampshire, *c. 1855. Yale, University, Belle Skinner Collection.*

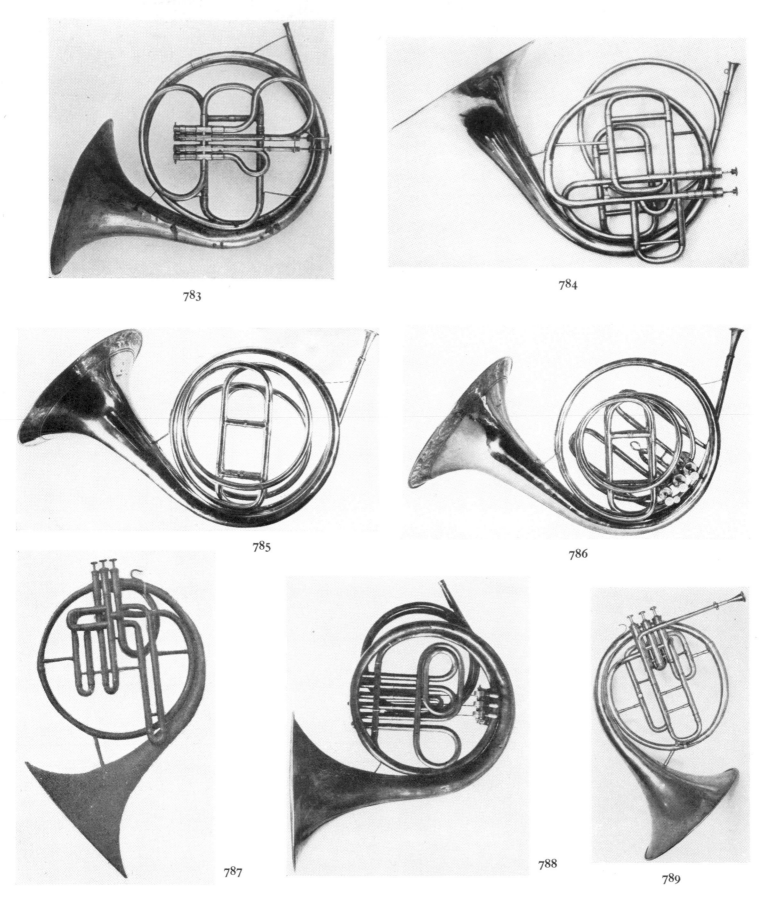

783 French horn. J. G. Kersten, Dresden, second quarter of 19th century. *Stockholm, Musikhistoriska Museet, 410.* **784** French horn. Thomas Key, London, before 1856. *London, Horniman Museum, Carse 156.* **785, 786** French horn. J. G. Moritz, Berlin, *c.* 1830. *Berlin, Institut für Musikforschung, Musikinstrumenten-Sammlung, 4366.* **787** French horn. Hawkes & Son, London, *c.* 1870. *Cobham, Morley-Pegge Collection.* **788** French horn. Joseph Riedl, Vienna, *c.* 1850. *Vienna, Kunsthistorisches Museum, Sammlung alter Musikinstrumente, N.E.356.* **789** Tenor cor. Couesnon, Paris, end of 19th century. *Barcelona, Museo Municipál de Música, 251.*

790 Clavicor. Guichard, Paris, after 1838. *London, Horniman Museum, Carse 206.* **791** Tenor horn. J. W. Wahl, Landskrona (Sweden), *c. 1845. Uppsala, Collection of Prof. C. G. Widstrand.* **792** Althorn. Köhler, London, *c. 1840. Brighton, Museums, Spencer Collection.* **793** Contralto saxhorn. Adolphe Sax, Paris, *c. 1850. London, C. R. Baines Collection.* **794** Flugel horn. J. Higham, Manchester, *c. 1860. Cobham, Morley-Pegge Collection.* **795** Ballad horn. Rudall, Rose & Carte & Co., London, *c. 1870. London, Horniman Museum, Carse 102.* **796** Tenor horn. E. Paulus, Berlin. 1874. *Berlin, Institut für Musikforschung, Musikinstrumenten-Sammlung, 4570.* **797** Cor alto. J. C. Labbaye, Paris, after 1862. *Collection of the late C. Overy.*

798 Bass tuba. J. G. Moritz, Berlin, 1852. *Berlin, Institut für Musikforschung, Musikinstrumenten-Sammlung, 4456.* **799** Tuba. Leopold Uhlmann, Vienna, 1839. *Salzburg, Museum Carolino Augusteum, Geiringer 152.* **800** Bombardon. Ahlberg & Ohlsson, Stockholm, 1859. *Uppsala, Hornboskapen Collection.* **801** Cornophone. F. Besson, Paris, late 19th century. *London, Royal Military School of Music, Kneller Hall, 77.* **802** Saxhorn. United States, c. 1860. *Washington, Smithsonian Institution, 55.589.* **803** Valve trombone. J. W. Wahl, Landskrona (Sweden), c. 1840. *Stockholm, Musikhistoriska Museet, 483.*

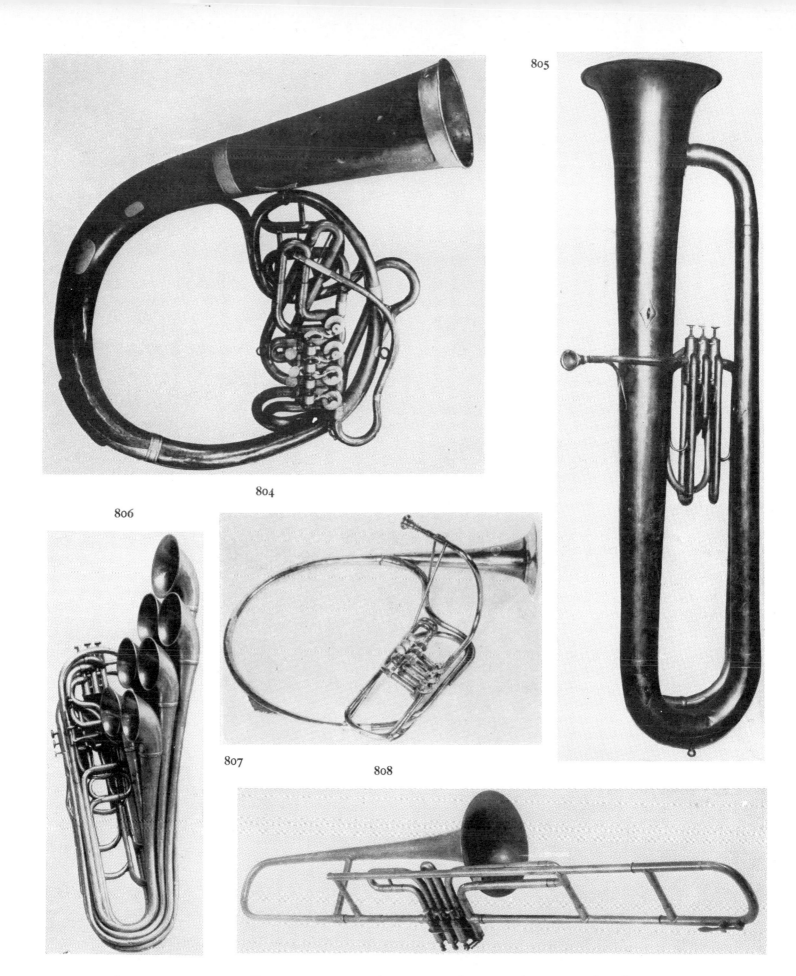

804 Helicon. Ignaz Stowasser, Vienna, *c. 1850. Nuremberg, Germanisches Nationalmuseum, Rück Collection, MIR.71.* **805** Saxhorn. Adolphe Sax, Paris, 1854. *Brussels, Conservatoire royal de Musique, 2459.* **806** Valve trombone. Adolphe Sax, Paris. *Brussels, Conservatoire royal de Musique, 1288.* **807** Helicon trombone. Ferdinando Roth, Milan, late 19th century. *London, Horniman Museum, Carse 314.* **808** Valve trombone. G. van Engelen, Lierre (Belgium), second half of 19th century. *Collection of the late C. Overy.*

809 Pair of kettle drums. German, 18th century. *Nuremberg, Germanisches Nationalmuseum, Rück Collection, MIR.630, 631.* **810** Set of kettle-drum sticks. German, 16th century. *Vienna, Kunsthistorisches Museum, Sammlung alter Musikinstrumente, S.267, 268, 269.* **811** Kettle drum. Cornelius Ward, London, *c. 1850. London, Royal Military School of Music, Kneller Hall, 232.* **812** Pair of kettle drums. Carl Friedrich Tzschiederich, Dresden, 1769. *Berlin, Institut für Musikforschung, Musikinstrumenten-Sammlung, 213, 214.*

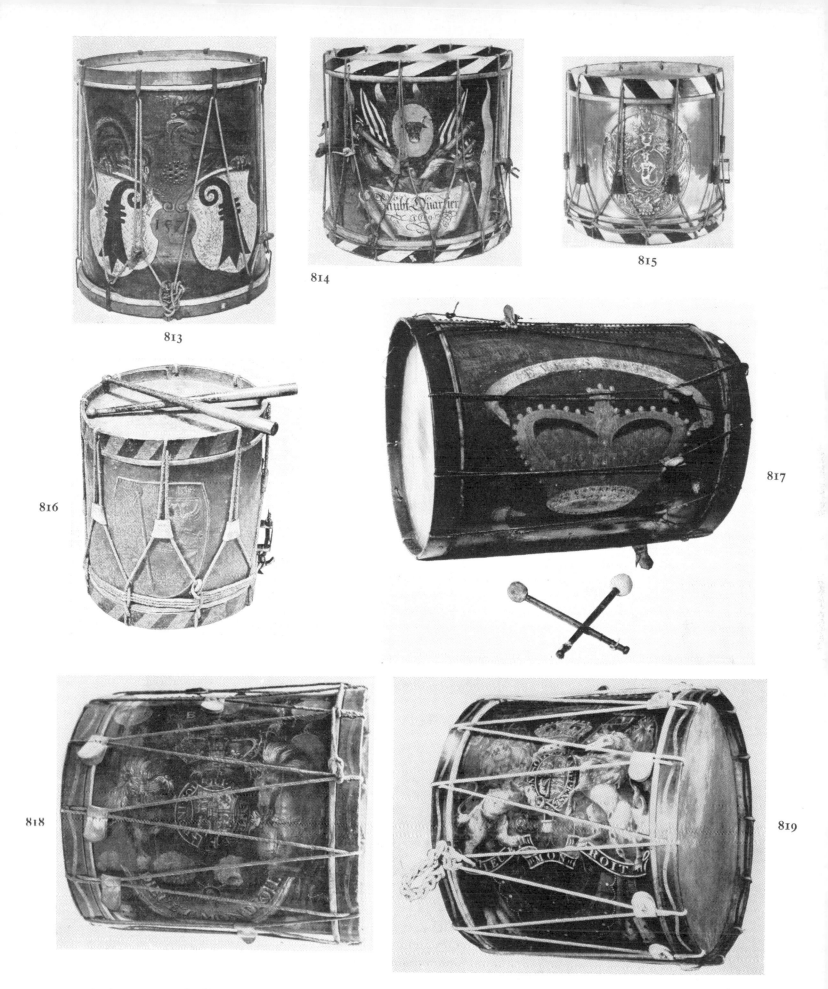

813 Side drum. Swiss, dated 1575. *Basel, Historisches Museum, 1874.120, Nef 232.* **814** Side drum. Swiss, dated 1689. *Basel, Historisches Museum, 1872.84, Nef 257.* **815** Side drum. Swiss, dated 1768. *Basel, Historisches Museum, 1894.138, Nef 262.* **816** Side drum. Probably Austrian, dated 1794. *Nuremberg, Germanisches Nationalmuseum, Rück Collection, MIR.640.* **817** Long drum. English, late 18th century. *Dorchester, Dorset Military Museum.* **818** Long drum. George Potter, London, 1811. *Messrs George Potter, Aldershot.* **819** Bass drum. Key, London, after 1814. *London, Royal Military School of Music, Kneller Hall, 233A.*

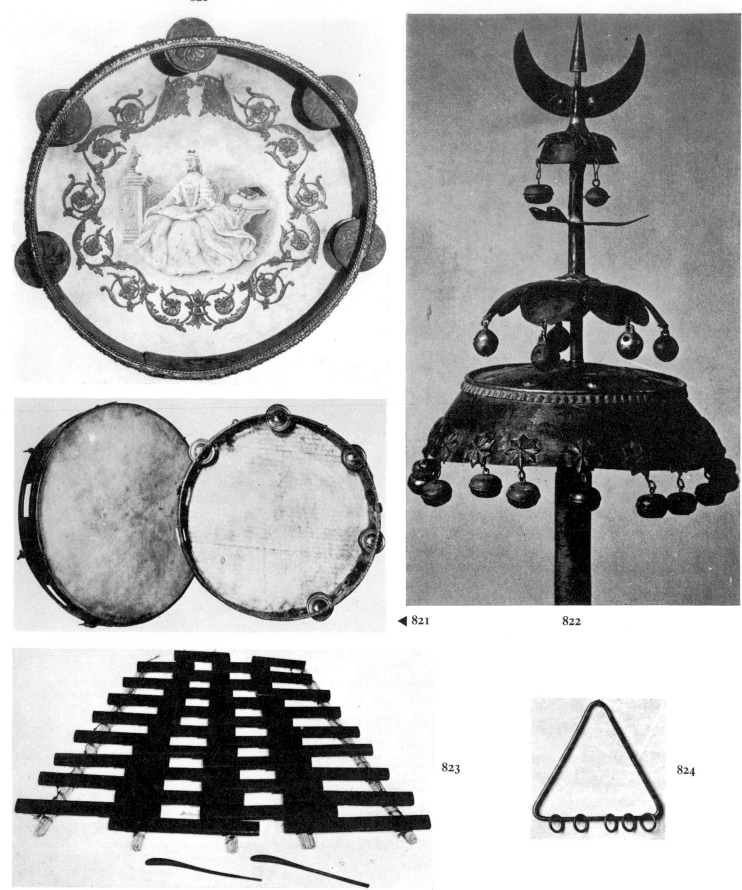

820 Tambourine. French, dated 1767. *Ann Arbor, University of Michigan, Stearns Collection, 404.* **821** Two tambourines. (Left) J. Dale, London, end of 18th century. (Right) Goulding & Co., London, *c.* 1805. *Norwich Museums.* **822** Jingling Johnny. German, 19th century. *Nuremberg, Germanisches Nationalmuseum, Rück Collection, MIR.563.* **823** Xylophone. Swiss, 19th century. *Oxford, Pitt Rivers Museum.* **824** Triangle. ? German, 17th–18th century. *Vienna, Kunsthistorisches Museum, Sammlung alter Musikinstrumente, C.271.*

III Brass Instruments

III Brass Instruments

In a generalized description, the operation of a brass instrument begins with the vibration of the player's lips under air pressure from the lungs. Between lips and instrument is the metal mouthpiece which, save in some small hunting horns, is detachable and contains a number of variable features, particularly the cup, varying from hemispherical as in the older trumpets to a deep funnel as in the older French horns. A mouthpiece may be supplied with a new instrument though generally players select their own. Where a contemporary mouthpiece is not present with an old brass instrument, enough representative examples of the most important kinds have survived in collections to make construction of a suitable replica possible.

The tubing of the instrument is assembled from lengths called joints or branches. A length which forms a U-bend is a 'bow'. The traditional making of the tubing is from sheet brass (or for ceremonial and presentation instruments, silver) formed round a mandrel and brazed; the method is still in some use although largely now supplanted through the availability of seamless drawn tube. The lengths meet in butt joints which are covered by ferrules, though lap joints also occur, especially in earlier work. The joints are normally secured with soft solder, allowing fairly easy taking apart for removal of dents, etc; silver solder is mainly reserved for things like valve assemblies. The branch into which the mouthpiece is inserted is termed the mouthpipe (or by some American writers, 'leader pipe'). This and other lengths of the tube are often required to be tapered, one old means of effecting this being to insert a tapered mandrel inside cylindrical tubing which is then pushed through a graded series of holes in a fixed block. For the bell flare the traditional construction is from a cut-out sheet, with addition of a triangular gusset if necessary. The bell mouth is strengthened by an added rim-band or 'garland', or by a wrapped-in wire, or by both together.

The grand acoustic feature of a brass instrument is the fact that for every sound that it is able to produce, the uninterrupted length of the air-column from mouthpiece to bell is in a state of full contributory vibration: every note is emitted from the bell and from nowhere else—save in the case of relatively short-lived keyed brass instruments like the key bugle. Bound up with this whole-length operation of a brass instrument is the expansion of the tube towards the bell. This is always present in some form, whether confined to a relatively short bell-joint terminating in a quick flare, as in trumpets, or whether the bell is simply a flare-less continuation of an expansion which occupies the entire length of the instrument, as in the old Prussian bugles and cornets (**707**). Between such extremes lie numerous other bore-profiles, and to all such differences, combined with considerations of mouthpiece shape and size, the brass tone-colours in their radiant variety are due, though to classify the instruments on a simple physical basis is difficult. The horn, often described as a 'conical-bore' instrument, may in some instances contain a higher proportion of cylindrical tube than a 'cylindrical-bore' trumpet. Sometimes it is difficult to decide precisely what the maker intended an early example to be, especially in cases where it is uncertain whether the instrument is complete as found or whether it was played with detachable components like crooks, which are no longer present and for which a specific bore-form cannot safely be assumed; the problem arises especially with the smaller kinds of circular horns, post horns and trumpets of the eighteenth century (e.g. **716**).

Identification of a specimen is often helped by measuring its tube length with a view to establishing its nominal pitch, i.e. the tonality that it is said to be 'in'. Allowance may have to be made for missing crooks, different tuning pitches, also the fact that narrow-bore instruments like horns and trombones may be up to 6 per cent longer in tube length than a wide-bore tenor horn or tuba. Yet the table below should be found a useful guide. With valved instruments, valve loops are not included in the total though they can give an independent indication of pitch: for example the first valve (for the first finger) —or if there are only two valves, the longer of the two—has a loop approximately equal in tube length to one eighth of the tube length of the instrument, and can be very quickly measured.

Pitch	Approx. tube length at modern pitch, less mouthpiece (cm)	Modern examples	Chief classical pitch zones
B flat	540–564	BB flat tuba	⎫
C	480–503		
D	–446	*Trompe (cor) de chasse*	
E flat	398–420	E flat tuba	
F	354–374	F horn	⎬ French horn
G	–333	G bass trombone	
A	–296		
B flat	262–280	Tenor horn, etc; Trombone; B flat horn	⎭
C	240–248	French horn minus crooks	⎫
D flat	–236		
D	–221		
E flat	197–210	Alto horn; Mellophone; State trumpet	⎬ Trumpet
F	177–186		
G	–164		
A flat	144–153		⎭
B flat	130–135	Trumpet; Cornet; Bugle	⎫
C	114–116		
D	–102	D trumpet	⎬ 'Bugle'
E flat	94–95	E flat cornet	⎭
F	85	F trumpet	
A flat	71	English post horn	
B flat	64	Piccolo trumpet	

The framework of brass-playing is the natural harmonic series of the note which the instrument is pitched in, and without mechanism (slide, valves or keys) an instrument can only produce notes which are contained in the series. Instruments like the horn and the trumpet, which have been used both with or without mechanism, are termed 'natural' when in a non-mechanized state. A chart of natural harmonics is given for reference since they will sometimes have to be referred to (Fig 17). This is for an

Fig 17 Harmonic series of C. Nos. 7 and 14 are a little flat. No. 11 is approx. a quarter-tone above F and no. 13 a quarter-tone below A

instrument in C with fundamental 'eight-foot' C (in organ terminology), i.e. the classical C trumpet or a horn in C alto. For other pitches this series must be appropriately transposed. It may be possible to sound enough notes on a specimen in order to find out which corresponds to a C in the chart, for this is the pitch note. The lowest note of the series, the fundamental, is seldom used in brass instruments other than orchestral tubas. The 'easy' range on most instruments is from the second or third harmonic to the sixth or eighth; ordinary bugle calls use the third, fourth, fifth and sixth. The full range of the French horn and classical trumpet runs from the second or third up to the sixteenth or even higher.

A fortunate circumstance with brass instruments as with woodwind is that in most cases the maker's name is indelibly engraved or stamped, usually on the bell. Again Langwill's *Index* is an indispensable companion.

1 Horns

The extensive family of horns may be said to embrace, at any rate up to the introduction of the new band instruments of the nineteenth century, all the brass instruments other than the trumpet and the trombone; or, putting it differently, the 'brass' instruments (simple horns being also of animal horn and ivory) which have served the signalling needs of town watchman, mail services, foresters, etc, and above all the hunting field, with later incursions into the areas of music and of the military. Cultivated musical use of horns is not attested before the late seventeenth century when the large circular horn first appeared, and military use, in the bugle horn (bugle), not until the mid eighteenth (save for archaic war-horns of the early Middle Ages), whereas of course the trumpet has always been military or ceremonial, and from the sixteenth century also musical, and the trombone was musical always. To classify horns in terms of function or purpose is not easy. Even today a new instrument which to English eyes might seem to be a military bugle may have been built in Germany for the hunt; and former post horns and hunting horns are in numerous cases indistinguishable on present knowledge. Research should eventually clarify such matters but has not done so yet, and the examples illustrated are therefore grouped mainly according to shape and size, the question of original function being often left open.

Illustrations

692 Hunting horn. Probably German, late fifteenth century. *London, Wallace Coll., 111.J.499.* The Horn of Saint Hubert, given by Louis of Bourbon to Charles the Bold after 1468. Horn, encrusted with gesso painted and gilt, with silver bands decorated with enamel of the fifteenth century. *Length 45 cm.*

693 Hunting horn. French, seventeenth century. *Munich, Bayerisch. Nationalmus., 227.* Attributed to Crétien. Oxhorn, with simple mounts.

694 Hunting horn. H. Grenser, Dresden, *c.* 1800. *Ann Arbor, Univ. of Michigan, Stearns 785.* Brass, covered with leather. *Length 53 cm. Diameter* of wide end 5·6 cm.

695 Hunting horn. Crétien, Vernon (Normandy), seventeenth century. *Paris, Conserv., E.133, C.577.* Brass, engraved.

696 Hunting horn. Crétien, Vernon, seventeenth century. *Paris, Conserv., E.792, C.576.* Marked *Vernon.* Chased brass, in two joints of octagonal shape. Conical mouthpiece. *Pitch D. Length* (of arc from mouthpiece to far edge of bell) 60 cm.

697 Bugle horn. German, late eighteenth–early nineteenth century. *London, Royal Coll. of Music, 137.* Copper, brass mounted. *Pitch C. Length* (as above) 61 cm.

698 Bugle horn. Hirsbrunner, Sumiswald (Switzerland), 1798. *Zürich, Schweitz. Landesmus.* Made for the band of the Helvetischer Legion. Copper, with dummy tube to complete a hoop. Tuning slide. Dragon bell with tongue. Cup mouthpiece possibly original.

699, 700 Two 'Russian horns'. German, early nineteenth century. *Berlin, Instit. f. Musikforschung, 490, 495.* The low G and high A instruments of a set. Each of brass, with curved mouthpipe and sharp-rimmed mouthpiece with hemispherical cup.

701 Hunting horn. German, 1803. *Nuremberg, German. Nationalmus., MI.374.* Silver, in two joints, one including curved mouthpipe. *Tube 52 cm. Length 46 cm. Bell diameter 7·4 cm.*

702 Hunting horn. English, early nineteenth century. *London, Royal Coll. of Music, 100.* Straight, of brass with ornamental mount and funnel mouthpiece soldered in. *Length 48·5 cm.*

703 Hunting horn. French, seventeenth century. *Paris, Conserv., E.296, C.566.* Spirally carved ivory, almost straight. *Length 28 cm.*

704 Post horn. Mahillon, Brussels, late nineteenth century. *London, Kneller Hall.* English straight model. Brass. *Pitch A flat. Length* 70 cm.

705 Coach horn. Köhler & Son, London, *c.* 1870. *Brighton, Museum.* Copper, with nickel-plated upper joint which telescopes into lower joint to fit into short leather case (on right). *Length* 91 cm. *Bell diam.* 6·6 cm.

706 Bugle. Wigley, London, early nineteenth century. *Bradford, Bowling Hall Mus.* Copper, brass mounted. One loop. *Pitch C,* with B flat crook. *Length* 36 cm.

707 Bugle. Russian, mid nineteenth century. *London, Horniman Mus., Carse 90.* With arms of Princess Tatiana Alexandrevna cavalry regiment. Brass. One loop. *Pitch C.*

Circular Horns

708 Horn. Jan Lechien, Antwerp, 1604. Replica. *Brussels, Conserv. royal, 3145.* Reproduction by Mahillon of original horn bought by the town of Malines in 1604 (Malines, Town Hall). Brass, single coil. *Pitch C. Tube* 120 cm. *Length* 54 cm. *Bell diam.* 10 cm.

709 Post horn. W. Schmidt, Halle, late eighteenth or early nineteenth century. *Berlin, Instit. f. Musikforschung, 4178.* Brass, single coil, bound with green cloth. Conical mouthpiece attached with chain. *Pitch C. Diam. of coil* 16·5 cm (inside). *Bell diam.* 10·6 cm. *Mouthpiece socket* 1·13 cm.

710 Post horn. Courtois frères, Paris, *c.* 1820. *Paris, Conserv., C.606.* Brass, single coil with tuning slide. Painted bell. With 'A' crook. *Diam. of coil* 20 cm. *Main bore* 1·09 cm. *Bell diam.* 12 cm.

711 Horn. Johann Wilhelm Haas, Nuremberg, 1682. *Basel, Hist. Mus., 1880.72.* Brass, single coil, diam. 20 cm. *Pitch A. Tube length c.* 145 cm. *Bore of mouthpiece socket c.* 0·75 cm. *Bell diam.* 12 cm. Much repaired.

712 Horn, Dresden, *c.* 1570. *Dresden, Staatl. Hist. Mus.* Marked *Gott is mein Helfer V.S. zu Dresden macht.* Brass, four coils with greatest width 16·5 cm. *Bell. diam.* 10 cm. *Pitch A flat.* Mouthpiece fits over mouthpipe.

713 Horn. A. Buchswinder, Ellwangen, 1738. *Salzburg, Mus. Carolino Augusteum, 225, Geir. 155.* Brass, six coils, diam. 21 cm. Bell painted black inside. *Pitch A flat.*

714 Miniature horn. Haas, Nuremberg, first half of eighteenth century. *London, Wallace Coll., A.1334.* Silver, single coil, diam. 7 cm. Silver gilt bell garland with applied winged cherubs. Outside diam. of cylindrical part of tube *c.* 0·5 cm. Small trumpet-like silver mouthpiece.

715 Horn. Hieronymus Starck, Nuremberg, 1667. *Copenhagen, Claudius Coll., F.99.* Single coil, diam. 33 cm, in three joints, each tapered. *Pitch F. Tube length c.* 176 cm. *Bore of mouthpiece socket* 0·9 cm. *Bell diam.* 10 cm.

716 Horn (or *Jägertrompete* ?). Balthasar Fürst, Ellwangen, 1770. *Nuremberg, German. Nationalmus., Rück Coll., MIR.122.* Two-coil, diam. (outside) 22 cm. In three joints, the first two cylindrical. *Tube* 190 cm. *Pitch E. Socket bore* 1·12 cm. *Bell. diam.* 13 cm.

717 Horn. Crétien, Vernon, *c.* 1700. *Paris, Conserv., C.578.* Single coil, diam. 95 cm. Blackened bell.

718 Horn. Georg Friderich Steinmetz, Nuremberg, pre-1740. *Berlin, Instit. f. Musikforschung, 4187.* One of a pair (both 'right-handed'). Two-coil in two joints, diam. (outside) 27 cm. *Tube length* 216 cm. *Socket bore* 1·16 cm. Blackened bell, diam. 17·5 cm. (Non-original mouthpiece in crook socket.)

719 Horn. Michael Leichamschneider, Vienna, 1718. *Basel, Hist. Mus., 1878.22.* Two coils, diam. 42 cm. *Pitch F.*

720 Horn. Nicolas Winkings, London, *c.* 1750. *Norwich, Museums.* Three-coil with leather binding, diam. 33 cm. *Pitch F. Bell diam.* 22·8 cm.

721 Horn. Carlin, Paris, *c.* 1755–60. *Cobham, Morley-Pegge Coll.* Three-coil, diam. (inside) 36 cm. In seven joints of which the middle five are cylindrical of three graded diameters. Blackened bell. *Pitch D. Tube length* 475 cm. *Bore of mouthpiece socket* 0·76 cm. *Bell. diam.* 26 cm.

722 Inventionshorn. J. G. Haltenhof, Hanau-am-Main, late eighteenth century. *The Hague, Gemeentemus., 773.* Two-coil, shown with plain slide and small mouthpipe crook.

723 Inventionshorn. C. Lobeit (? Bohemia, *c.* 1785). *Boston, Mus. of Fine Arts, 193.* Brass with silver alloy mounts. One coil. *Hoop diam.* (outside) 32 cm. *Socket* 0·8 cm. *Bell diam.* 29 cm. With crook marked *F.*

724, 725 Pair of horns. George Henry Rodenbostel, London, late eighteenth century. *Gloucester, City Museum,*
F.1536, F.1537. Bought in 1798 by the band of the Frampton on Severn Volunteers. The left-handed horn
shown with master crook and two couplers and the right-handed horn without crooks. Two-coil, in
two joints, the first (88 cm) cylindrical. *Hoop diam.* (inside) 24 cm. *Socket bore* 1·25 cm. *Tube* (without
crooks) 233 cm. Bell, lacquered red-brown, diam. 23 cm.

726, 727 Cor solo. Marcel-Auguste Raoux, Paris, *c.* 1826. *London, Victoria and Albert Mus., W.83–1926.*
Presented to Giovanni Puzzi (1792–1876) by Louis XVIII (or Charles X; see Morley-Pegge, 165). Brass,
silver mounted. Two-coil in four joints (the second cylindrical) plus crooks. *Hoop diam.* 28 cm (inside).
Socket bore 0·73 cm. *Main bore* 1·1 cm. *Bell diam.* 28 cm, lacquered green and gilt inside. Four coiled crooks
for F, E, E flat and D, and a G crook consisting of a simple bow.

728 Orchestra horn. Carl Gottlieb Schuster, Markneukirchen, *c.* 1800. *Nuremberg, German. Nationalmus.,*
Rück Coll., MIR.84. One coil. *Hoop diam.* 28 cm. *Bell diam.* 30 cm. With six crooks.

729 Omnitonic horn. Charles Sax, Brussels, 1833. *Boston, Mus. of Fine Arts, 194.* Eight fixed crooks (B flat
alto to B flat basso), selected by sliding piston of brass. Interior of bell lacquered dark red with flowers
and trophies in gold, diam. 29·5 cm.

Some examples of hunting horns of ox-horn, or of sheet or cast metal in an arcuate ox-horn shape
(**692–4**), illustrate the primitive horn proportions of wide-expanding unflared bore. Some finely decorated early mementoes of the hunt are known (**692**, preserved in honour of the patron saint of the hunt).
Later examples include some by well-known figures in wind-instrument history, as Grenser, the Dresden
woodwind maker (**694**, said to have been for the boar hunt) and the Crétien family from Vernon,
Normandy, who supplied horns, trumpets and drums to the French court in the seventeenth century
and early eighteenth (**693**). Ordinarily these small horns are good for sounding signals on one note only.
With lengthening of the tube more harmonics can be sounded effectively, giving a musical differentiation
between the various hunting calls, instead of merely rhythmic, and leading in due course to the hunting
music of the French horn proper. A modest step in this direction is marked by the *grand cor* figured in
Mersenne and illustrated here by a second Crétien horn (**695**), in which the primitive bore has given
place to a more gentle expansion complimented by a distinct bell flare. A third horn by Crétien (**696**)
brings the arcuate horn practically to the stage of the semicircular German hunting horn of the eighteenth
century and later, of which an early example is by Werner, Dresden, 1733 (Brussels, 3151) and on which
calls of the bugle kind can be sounded. This *Halbmond* horn was carried, in Saxony and North Germany,
by the wing men of the hunt (*Flügelhorn*), and has a pitch of around D, an octave above that of the
contemporary trumpet and two tones above that of the present bugle. At the middle of the eighteenth
century this horn began to be adopted by Hanoverian (1758) and Prussian Jäger regiments, to whom the
Halbmond no doubt recommended itself both through its association with the hunt and through the far-
carrying nature of its sound. This was the first military bugle (**697**), made of brass or copper and used by
English light regiments from the 1760s ('bugle horn'); the Brussels Collection has (1155) an American
specimen marked *John B. Dash, New York*, with the date 1783. The mouthpieces of these semicircular
bugles are, as with subsequent bugles, of a trumpet type with narrow rim, rather than of a funnel-
shaped horn type. A circular crook put the D horn into C when required, and the instrument was held
on parade by the strap, against the right side of the body with the bell uppermost and pointing forward.
The *Halbmond* remained in use in Germany, beside later bugles, through much of the first half of the
nineteenth century and was carried by Russian troops at the Crimea (example at Halifax, Bankfield
Museum). During the dragon bell period in band instruments the horn was sometimes made with a
bell of this kind for use with bands; the example shown (**698**) has a tuning slide, and is given a roughly
circular form by means of a length of dummy tubing.

Just after 1800 the London maker William Shaw, by whom examples of the semi-circular bugle
exist (e.g. in the York Museum), was also making the bugle in trumpet shape, with the tube folded in
one loop. The instruments are of copper, brass mounted, with a cylindrical mouthpipe and a pitch of C

(706). Crooks lowered this to B flat or A when required, e.g. for the 'bugle horn' solos which occur in light operas by Bishop. Germany began to adopt this folded bugle during the Napoleonic wars, and by 1822 the French *chasseurs* were also using it. Many Continental countries still make it, an old preference in Prussia and Russia having been for a flare-less model (707). The familiar twice-looped bugle, with reduced bell flare matching the general compactness, was adopted in England in 1858 and since came into use in America ('cavalry bugle') and to a smaller extent on the Continent, either as a duty bugle or, in Sweden and Germany, as a hunting horn.

Straight horns. A side development from the seventeenth century onwards has been a small hunting instrument, straight or nearly so, with smallish bore, a pretty French example being in ivory (703); a brass English example (702) illustrates an early size of the small horn introduced with fox-hunting, diminished during the nineteenth century to the hunting horn *c.* 23 cm long, still used. The English post horn, of brass, 70–80 cm long (704), came in with the early vogue for the valved cornet in the 1830s, being in bore and bell a straight-tubed 'octave' cornet which settled to a pitch of A flat. For use in band concerts—post-horn galops, etc—a tuning slide is provided midway along the tube. The instrument was also made by Périnet, Mahillon and others on the Continent for the English market, and variant models were not uncommon during the second half of the nineteenth century, in trumpet shape, in compressed twice-wound shapes, or again in small circular shape ('cyclist's bugle'). The English coach horn of the four-in-hand mail teams was, on the other hand, a kind of straight bugle of copper with wide conical bore without flare (705), and length *c.* 92 cm (E flat at the old sharp pitch), though longer instruments were built late in the century. (Latterly, copper semi-replicas have been manufactured commercially in quantities for wall decorations in hotels, etc, some also in a hoop form; the best genuine specimens have the stamp of Köhler, Keat, Swaine & Adeney, or other recognized maker of the last century.)

One of the many forms of hunting horn used in Germany is also straight, though with wide conical bore without flare and with a bent-round mouthpipe (*Jagd-Fanfare*, 701). This is also the model employed in the Russian horn bands of the period 1754–*c.* 1840, in which each of some 30 different-sized horns was used to sound one note only (699, 700). Some similar bands were also formed in eastern parts of Germany and probably many of the Russian outfits were built in Germany.

Small circular hunting and post horns. Lengthening the windway of a horn by means of a coil dates at the latest from the third quarter of the sixteenth century (Dufouilloux, *La Vénerie*) and in the early seventeenth century it appears both in Practorius and in Mersenne (*trompe*, the 'most-used' form of hunting horn), but early examples are very scarce. The horn in Praetorius (Fig 18) shows a primitive coil, visually dominated by the traditional ox-horn proportions. In a watchman's horn bought by the town of Malines in 1604 (708) the coil is already more decisive; this horn has the pitch, also the sound,

of a bugle in C. Further improvement to the shape is seen in the subsequent German post horn (709), occasionally introduced by eighteenth-century composers into their works and apparently used by some Hanoverian regiments from the late eighteenth century until *c.* 1830, a pair of these little horns being held forwards with the bells in the air. The mouthpiece sockets are wide and no doubt crooks were provided if desired. From the late eighteenth century also dates the rather similar *Prince Pless horn*, named after the Silesian patron of aristocratic musical pursuits and still one of the

Fig 18 Jägerhorn, after Praetorius, 1619

most popular hunting horns in Germany. It was introduced to give a 'more pleasant' (softer) sound than the older *Halbmond*, and is made of brass or nickel-silver, usually in two coils, with bugle-like bore and bell. It has also been made in various sizes for playing together in harmony, and often, like the circular post horns in the nineteenth century, with valves.

Differing from the above horns with bugle-like bore are small one-coil horns which have the narrow mouthpipe taper and mouthpiece socket of the French horn. The earliest dated examples are small instruments of the last third of the seventeenth century from the famous trumpet workshops in Nuremberg. One is by Starck, 1667 (**715**), pitched in F (classical F trumpet pitch). All three of its joints are tapered (Fig 19b) and the instrument sounds easily up to its twelfth harmonic with a faintly bugle-like tone. Another example, by Johann Wilhelm Haas, 1682 (**711**), has the smaller, post-horn size, and more pronounced flare. In its much repaired condition it stands at bugle pitch. From the eighteenth century a number of small two-coiled horns measuring about 24 cm across the coils survive from the neighbourhood of Nuremberg, by makers including J. G. Lindtner, Augsburg, and Balthasar Fürst, a horn maker of Ellwangen (**716**). Pitched in about F (trumpet pitch) they are in two or three joints, partly cylindrical, with wide sockets of 11 cm or more, perhaps for crooks, and bell diameter *c.* 11·6–13·2 cm. They have sometimes been described as circular trumpets (*Jägertrompete*), though 52 per cent of cylindrical tube is too little for a true trumpet, and the bell-joint profile and the tone quality both seem quite horn-like. Lacking crooks (if they had them) they are difficult to place but are probably hunting horns of a Bavarian type. A charming miniature one-coil horn by Wolf Wilhelm Haas (**714**), perhaps made as a keepsake, may properly fall into the 'circular trumpet' category; its mouthpiece is unequivocally of a trumpet pattern.

In France the circular post horn has the narrow taper and socket mentioned at the beginning of the last paragraph. With one or two coils it is said to have been used also in England with mail coaches in the eighteenth century to sound the departure signal. Extant French examples are of the early or later nineteenth century, including instruments by well-known Paris horn makers, e.g. Raoux and Courtois (**710**), these often with a painted bell as in French horns by the same makers. For playing with bands crooks were provided and often a tuning slide, as shown. The French name *cornet simple* or *ordinaire* distinguished this post horn from the valved cornet, *cornet-à-pistons*, developed largely from it during the 1820s.

'Helical' horns. A small horn, to which historians of the horn have drawn particular attention, is an early variety with four or more taper-bore coils wound like a Catherine wheel (**712**). It appears in pictures of *c.* 1600, and of two well-made specimens preserved in Dresden (at any rate up to the last war) the one illustrated has been attributed to the last third of the sixteenth century (Morley-Pegge, *The French Horn*, pp. 11–12). The bell flare is of an early character and the pitch is about A flat (bugle range); the companion instrument, possibly made a little later, has a longer tube and the old D trumpet pitch—the earliest known conical-bore brass instrument to have a pitch of this depth, at which tune-playing up to the sixteenth harmonic is for the trumpet a historical fact at this early period, though there is no evidence of it on horns until later. Multi-coiled horns of later periods include wide-belled French horns, e.g. six-coil (**713**), here with the black-painted interior of the bell commonly found in circular hunting horns as a precaution against reflected sun glare. In the nineteenth century there were also post horns made with many coils.

French horns without crooks. The hunting horn built in a wide circle with wide bell flare, known in England as 'French horn' before the end of the seventeenth century (in France, usually *trompe*) was introduced sometime within the years 1660–80, possibly first in France and if so probably at the hands of Crétien (Morley-Pegge, *op. cit.*, Chap 2). Whether the small early Nuremberg horns (**715**) lay behind it or not remains to be established. The instrument is made in one or more coils with mouthpiece socket bore *c.* 6·5–8 mm. The pitch varies from low F down to C, equal to the corresponding pitches of the classical orchestral horn and an octave deeper than the contemporary trumpets. There are, however, examples with higher pitches, up to high C. For the deeper pitches a *single-coil* horn needs a hoop diameter of *c.* 70 cm upwards; one of the largest is by Crétien, in low C (**717**). During sounding, such horns were held almost vertically to the side of the body, the arm on that side being nearly or fully extended downwards to grasp the coil above the bell. German and Austrian examples include one by the Viennese maker Leichamschneider, 1710 (Vienna Collection, with 68 cm hoop), and a fine one of similar size by the Haas grandson (born in 1723). This last (Brussels, 2443) is remarkable for being built, despite its size, in two joints only: an evenly tapered mouthpipe joint no less than 273 cm long, joined to a 130 cm bell pipe (Fig 19c). The single-coil horn was most popular during the first quarter of the eighteenth century. It may also have been the original pattern, though probably at one of the higher pitches; Morley-Pegge illustrates an unsigned French example attributed to the late seventeenth century, with 44 cm hoop and pitch high C. An early feature here is the comparative narrowness of the bell mouth by later standards, 14 cm as against 23–25 cm.

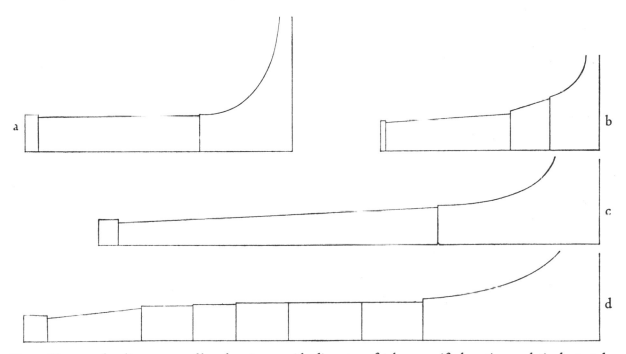

Fig 19 Horns: tube-diameter profiles, showing outside diameter of tube magnified 25 times relatively to tube length. Bell termination omitted. *a.* Steinmetz, **718**; *b.* Starck, **715**; *c.* Haas (Brussels, 2443); *d.* Carlin, **721**. (The first of these would have the addition of crooks)

The *two-coil* horn is also, at the deeper pitches, wide enough to be carried round the body while not being sounded, and in Germany was likewise known as *parforce* horn from its use in the mounted hunt which ran down the quarry. An early example is by Leichamschneider, 1713 (Hamburg Coll.), with 47 cm hoop. The example shown is five years later (**719**), and such horns were made right through the eighteenth century and into the next. The earliest *three-coil* horn is a copper instrument by Bull, London, 1699, with 37 cm hoop and pitch F (modern E; illustrated in Galpin, 1910, and in various other works). The strong and handy three-coil model, supported on the raised arm while blowing, became very popular in most countries by 1750, as illustrated by an English example of Winkings, who in 1740 was maker to the royal hunt (**720**), and a French one by Carlin (**721** and Fig 19d) which sets the pattern for the usual *trompe de chasse* in D up to today; its bore expansion after the mouthpipe is obtained by a number of cylindrical sections of increasing bore-dimension. An outstanding Paris maker of the second quarter of the nineteenth century is Périnet (Kneller Hall, 113, and other examples).

French horns with crooks. Horns of the types just described were much used for musical purposes in the first half of the eighteenth century, e.g. for hunting music performed in gardens, bandstand turns, and especially the three-coiled models, in the orchestra, in which French horns had already been used in Germany in the first decade of the century. The better to suit orchestral requirements, however, horns with crooks were introduced, the earliest record being in Vienna, where the leading maker was Leichamschneider, around 1718. Crooks, then already known on the trumpet, give the player a choice of different pitches using the same instrument. The socket of a horn with crooks (save for some of the later *Inventionshörner* mentioned below) is wider than that of a crookless horn, having a bore *c.* 11·5–12·5 cm (**725**) in order to receive the crooks, and the tube-length of the horn itself is relatively shorter, a part of the total windway being included in the crook. As with trumpets (**744**), and also the orchestral crookless horns, short tuning bits or shanks were available for tuning to other instruments and in a few cases some of these have been preserved.

The common type of crooked horn of the eighteenth century, employed during the second half of the century also in military bands, is in two coils with hoop diameter around 30 cm. Without crooks the tubing usually corresponds to about high C. The first joint of the horn may be slightly tapered, as in an example by Steinmetz (**718** and Fig 19a) or cylindrical, as in a pair of horns by Rodenbostel, London, before 1798 (**724, 725**). This pair is preserved with its original crooks, which are of the early type comprising a tapered master crook into which the mouthpiece is inserted, and four different-sized cylindrical-bore couplers which are inserted singly or in twos between master crook and horn to put the instrument into other keys than that given by the master crook alone. Some sets include two master crooks. Such crooks were still supplied in England up to *c.* 1850, though on the Continent they had long been superseded by other arrangements which followed the introduction of hand-horn playing in the middle of the eighteenth century.

In *hand horn* technique, formulated by the player Anton Hampl of Dresden in the middle of the eighteenth century, the right hand is placed in the bell so that by stopping the bell in various ways harmonics can be flattened or sharpened to supply all semitones absent from the natural harmonic series, save in the lower parts of the compass. The inevitable differences, faint or marked, in the quality of the stopped notes were on the whole accepted by audiences as adding to the charm of horn solos rather than the reverse, and in France particularly the hand horn was abandoned only with reluctance after valves came in. To suit the technique, a new system of crooks was devised by Hampl in 1755 in order to avoid the varying position of the mouthpiece relatively to the horn which was inevitable with the system of additive crooks described above. This is the *Inventionshorn* with fixed mouthpipe, first made by Werner, next by Haltenhof (**722**). The crooks are two-legged, and are inserted at a point about half-way along the main tubing to lie across the space enclosed by the coil of the horn. A specimen by Lobeit in the Boston Collection (**723**) illustrates the *Inventionshorn* of the latter part of the century in which the tubes leading to and from the crook are crossed (for the Bohemian attribution of this otherwise unknown maker, see Fitzpatrick, *GSJ*, XVII, 83). In Paris about this time the model was taken over by Raoux as the French *cor solo* (soloist's horn) with five crooks. In the fine example shown (**726, 727**) the crooks are cylindrical, and the mouthpiece is of the contemporary kind made from sheet metal, here silver. The German *Inventionshorn*, on the other hand, may have a full set of nine crooks, of which the higher ones may differ from the rest in including their individual mouthpipes (Morley-Pegge, Pl. IV), since provision of nine crooks with one on fixed mouthpipe would introduce difficulties of design.

In Bohemia and Austria during the third quarter of the eighteenth century horns were being made with mouthpipe crooks inserted into the terminal socket as with the old system but dispensing with couplers. Further along the tube a two-legged tuning slide is incorporated in the position occupied by the crooks of an Inventionshorn. This very practical model, permitting quick changes of crook, was described in those countries and in Germany as *Orchesterhorn* (**728**) and was extensively made in France and Belgium from the turn of the century onwards, many specimens having survived in their massive wooden boxes with compartments for nine crooks. Hand horn technique was again employed on these instruments. Austrian, Bohemian and many of the German examples are considerably wider in the throat of the bell than the French.

Omnitonic horns. These were devised chiefly in Paris and Brussels during the first half of the nineteenth century, though still advertised in a Lafleur catalogue *c.* 1870. They are hand horns with built-in sets of crooks or some equivalent means of securing changes of tonality without need for detachable components. They differ widely from one to another. The pattern shown (**729**) is said to have been the most successful; the desired crook is selected by a marked slide and plunger. (For the rest, see Morley-Pegge, Chap. 4.)

2 Trumpets and Trombones

The thirteenth-century trumpet was straight-built like a coach horn, resembling its parent instrument, the Arab *nafir*, this last being exemplified today by the Ramadan trumpet of Morocco. Sample particulars of this are: three brass or copper joints, the first cylindrical, the others tapered, with a total length of around 150 cm and a funnel-shaped bell 7·5 cm across; the instrument can be dismantled into its separate joints, but the mouthpiece is soldered to the first joint and has a thin rim often made simply by turning a flange in the sheet metal of which the joint is constructed. Such instruments, and others from India, etc, have sometimes been mistaken for medieval European trumpets (*buisines*) and have even been so exhibited.

In Europe the straight trumpet was obsolescent as a regular model by the fifteenth century, though made exceptionally up to the eighteenth century for use at pageants and the like. Some such examples appear to have been hurriedly assembled from bits and pieces. Others, however, are genuinely constructed, and have one or two balls decorating the tube. One example (Boston, 198) is engraved on the funnel-like bell with the name Sebastian Hainlein and the date *M.CDLX* (the two known Sebastian Hainleins worked, however, between 1565 and 1655). The example shown (**730**) by another of this famous Nuremberg dynasty of trumpet makers, in 1658, still has a fairly narrow bell. Of the first form of folded trumpet of the fifteenth century no genuine example is known: the tube is folded into a kind of 'S', with the bell pipe uppermost and, one would imagine, pretty tiring to hold. The classic model of natural trumpet, folded into one long loop (**731**), appeared about the middle of the same century and as a 'state' or 'fanfare' trumpet is manufactured still. There are also variant shapes and slide-trumpets. (For key and valve trumpets, see later sections.)

Illustrations: Natural and Slide Trumpets

730 Straight trumpet. Hans Hainlein, Nuremberg, 1658. *Frankfurt, Hist. Mus., 102.* Two balls. Bell with six cast angels' heads. *Pitch* E flat. *Length* 100 cm. *Bell diam.* 9·5 cm.

731 Trumpet. Philipp Schöller, Munich, mid-eighteenth century. *London, R. Coll. of Music, 194.* Banner with English royal arms. *Pitch* C. *Length* 80 cm.

732 Trumpet. Harris, London, *c.* 1720. *Author's Collection.* An instrument later converted to slide trumpet. Copper-bronze, silver mounted. *Bell diam.* 11 cm. (Detail of bell and outer bow.)

733 Trumpet mouthpiece. *Copenhagen, Musikhist. Mus.* With a trumpet by J. W. Haas (*F.105*). Brass. *Length* 10 cm. *Rim diam.* 2·85 cm outside, 1·68 cm inside. *Depth* 0·65 cm.

734 Trumpet mute. ? Eighteenth century. *Basel, Hist. Mus., 1956.309.* Wood.

735 Box trumpet. Adam Puchswinder, Ellwangen, 1731. *Berlin, Instit. f. Musikforschung, 298.* Brass. Tube coiled inside canister.

736 Trumpet. Anton Schnitzer, 1581. *Vienna, Kunsthist. Mus., A.258.* Silver, with cast ferrules gilt. Small cast bell ornament. The tube engraved with a scale pattern and with scenes of women playing musical instruments. *Pitch* D. *Bell diam.* 9·5 cm. With original long-stemmed mouthpiece.

737 Trumpet. Augustine Dudley, London, 1666. *London, London Museum.* Brass, silver mounted. Triple ball. *Length* 73 cm. Original mouthpiece.

738 Trumpet. William Bull, London, late seventeenth century. *Oxford, Ashmolean Mus.* Silver. Triple ball chased with floral motifs. Bell garland embossed with floral patterns. Ferrules with spiral fluting. *Pitch* D.

Bore 0·93 cm. With C crook and original silver mouthpiece, *length* 10·8 cm, *rim* 3·43 cm outside, 1·8 cm inside, *depth* 1·1 cm.

739   Trumpet. Johann Leonhard Ehe, Nuremberg, 1746. *Nuremberg, German. Nationalmus., MI.217.* One of a set of which three remain. Brass. Plain model. Winding of dark red cord and tassels over the wooden spacer block. Bell garland with the words *Ad Gloriam Dei. Pitch* C. *Bore c.* 1·1 cm. *Bell diam.* 11 cm. *Length* 75 cm. With contemporary mouthpiece, *length* 8·7 cm, *rim* (inside) 1·85 cm, *depth of cup* 0·8 cm.

740   Trumpet. W. W. Haas, Nuremberg, first half of eighteenth century. *London, Wallace Coll., A.1333.* Decorated model. Brass, with cast fluted ferrules and four angels' heads on bell garland. Cords and tassels of coloured silks and gold. Spacing block missing. *Length* 70·5 cm.

741   Curved trumpet. J. J. Friederich, Andelfingen, 1821. *Zürich, Schweitz. Landesmus., 1440.* With E flat crook.

742   Trumpet. Carl Missenharter, Ulm, mid-nineteenth century. *Nuremberg, German. Nationalmus., MI.379.* Short model with tuning slide. *Bore* 1·12 cm. *Bell diam.* 12·5 cm. *Length* 46 cm. With crooks for D, C, and B flat.

743   Trumpet. Henry Keat, London, third quarter of nineteenth century. *London, Kneller Hall.* Silver fanfare trumpet. *Pitch* E flat.

744   Trumpet. William Shaw, London, 1787. *London, London Mus.* Arms of George III. Silver. Triple ball. Spiral-fluted ferrules. Four 0·4 cm vents, three covered by rotating sleeves, one by a key mounted on saddle. *Pitch* E flat. *Bore* 1·0 cm. With crooks and tuning bits.

745   Slide trumpet. Köhler, London, *c.* 1830. *London, Kneller Hall, 70.* Brass. Slide with two spring boxes. With D and C crooks. Contemporary mouthpiece.

746   Slide trumpet. James Power, London; hall mark of 1819–20. *London, Joseph Wheeler Coll.* Spring box marked *Keat.* Short model with wide bell-bore. Silver, parcel gilt, in two coils. With E flat crook and original mouthpiece.

747   Slide trumpet. Antoine Courtois, Paris, 1840. *Paris, Conserv., E.1541, C.1402.* Brass. Slide with steel runners, max. extension 25 cm. *Pitch* A flat. *Bell diam.* 12 cm. *Length* 48 cm.

The trumpet up to the end of the eighteenth century was primarily a ceremonial instrument and made to look so, with stylized ornament giving dignity to the single loop of brass or silver tubing. The loop consists of three branches connected by two bows and measures about 75 cm from bow to bow for a D trumpet and about 60 cm for an F. The mouthpipe, lower branch, and bows are cylindrical with a bore of 11–12 mm. The bell pipe, sometimes in two sections, expands gently to its terminal flare, which in early specimens, as with the oldest examples of other brass instruments, is funnel-like (**736**). The junctions of the tubes are concealed inside ornamental ferrules and in many instances, especially with luxurious silver trumpets, they are unsoldered lap joints made air-tight with wax, possibly for the sake of dismantling for polishing. The bell rim is strengthened and embellished with a 'garland', often with applied ornament, like the cast angels' heads of Nuremberg trumpets (**740**, see also **750**). Fitted over the bell pipe about half way along is the 'ball', inherited from the Middle Ages (and found on traditional types of trumpet as far as China); the ball is hollow and is mounted on a long ferrule.

There are no cross stays. Instead, German practice was to place a wooden spacing block between mouthpipe and bell pipe, to the mouthpiece side of the ball. The block is concealed and held in place by the tasselled cord with which the player grasps the instrument. A wire loop holds the outer bow to the bell rim. In English trumpets the ball is much larger (**737**) and the mouthpiece passes loosely through a recess or hole in it. It has been suspected that these avoidances of organic rigidity are in the interests of free vibration of the air column; certainly in modern brass instruments where high harmonics are regularly employed, as the French horn, the siting of cross-stays can prove a delicate matter if all harmonics are to sound equally freely.

The pitch before the nineteenth century was normally D (with a crook for C), though from the latter part of the eighteenth century onwards a shorter trumpet in F (or higher) came in to cope, by means of several crooks, with the different keys required by military band and classical orchestral music.

Tuning was done with small tuning bits (**744**). The mouthpiece is long-stemmed compared with that of the nineteenth century, measuring about 10 cm in total length. It is heavy, with wide rim, hemispherical cup and sharp throat. An example shown (**733**) has a shallow cup as if for indoor use in the high register (though this view has been disputed). The register up to the sixteenth or even eighteenth harmonic is where diatonic melodies in the major key can be played on the natural trumpet—a faculty nobly exploited especially by J. S. Bach and his generation.

Among extant trumpets, German specimens are by far the most numerous, particularly of the celebrated Nuremberg trumpets, made by families some of which gave four or more generations to the craft, as the Ehe (**739**), of whom the earliest recorded died in 1632 and the last in 1794.[1] Instruments were purchased by the dozen for the numerous electoral and other courts, each of which had its trumpet corps, and over 60 trumpets survive from the three generations of the Haas family alone (**740**). Otherwise, only England has left fine and representative instruments from this great era in trumpet history (**737, 738**). By the end of the eighteenth century the dissolution of the old trumpet corps in Germany and the growth of military bands everywhere had brought changes in the form of the natural trumpet, though the traditional pattern has continued to be made for ceremonial and official use, sometimes still ornate, though generally becoming less so as the nineteenth century went on, as instanced by the state trumpets of Keat, London (**743**). An English trumpet of the time of transition, by Shaw, *c.* 1800 (**744**), is unique in possessing what Halfpenny (*GSJ*, XIII) has termed 'harmonic vents'; it appears that one vent is provided to suit each crook, and that it was uncovered for purposes which are not clear (though several can be conjectured).

Varieties of natural trumpet. An early variant is by Anton Schnitzer, Nuremberg, wound in the form of a loose knot, basically a figure-of-eight; a specimen at Verona is dated 1585 and some later imitations exist. A circular trumpet or (in Praetorius) *Jägertrompete*, though no good for carrying a banner, is thought by some historians to have had special importance in Germany as a solo instrument—a notion which arises from E. G. Haussmann's portrait of Gottfried Reiche, the leading trumpeter at Leipzig in Bach's time there. The best actual example, by Pfeifer, Leipzig, 1697 (Leipzig, 1819), is at present lost. It is in D, in three 'Catherine wheel' coils about 24 cm across, and with 11 cm bell; it was procured from a church along with a pair of kettle drums, and is illustrated in Menke and also in Grove, 5th edn (article 'Trumpet'). Other examples are doubtful (cf **716**, and p. **132**).

The *box trumpet* (**735**) has the tube coiled inside a brass canister about the size of a pint pot, with the bell mouth at the bottom. Examples are eighteenth-century and German.

'*Short model*' trumpets with the tube twice looped came in at the end of the eighteenth century. One form has loops of unequal size, the shorter comprising a tuning slide. Altenburg calls it *Inventions* trumpet (though specimens are provided with ordinary mouthpipe crooks) adding that it was used especially in Italy, by infantry regiments. It was common up to the mid nineteenth century (**742**), and even later as a French cavalry trumpet with tuning slide. (The ordinary E flat duty trumpet of the last hundred years is wound in two equal loops, without tuning slide.)

The *curved trumpet* is a pattern built in a curved loop with a tuning slide pointing towards the centre of the curve (**741**). The object of this *trompette demilune* is said to have been hand-stopping after the manner of the hand horn, whence the German historical term for it *Stopftrompete*. It was made in large quantities for bands in most Continental countries during the first third of the nineteenth century, usually in a high key admitting a wide choice of crooks.

[1] Particulars of the Nuremberg dynasties are summarized in the individual entries in Langwill, *Index*. For full biographical notes and details of extant instruments, see Wörthmüller, 1954–5, and for English trumpets, Halfpenny, *GSJ*, XV, XVI. The best contemporary source is Altenburg, 1795. Haas instruments generally bear the name of J. W. Haas, the founder of the business.

Slide Trumpets

While the early Renaissance trumpet in *S* form was a military and ceremonial instrument, pictures and musical sources from the early fifteenth century show that it was also built in a 'minstrel's' pattern with telescopic mouthpipe. By sliding the trumpet bodily outwards along the mouthpipe, the harmonics could be sounded at various pitches, enabling melodies to be played in the middle range of the harmonic series. This model gave place later in the century to the better-manageable trombone, yet it persisted in the background of German music up to the eighteenth century, known as *Zugtrompete* or, as in Virdung (1511), *Thurnerhorn* ('tower musician's horn'). The only genuine example is by Hans Veit, Naumburg (Prussia), 1651 (Berlin, 639). This looks like an ordinary natural trumpet, though with a wider bell pipe than most trumpets of its time and main tubing about a millimetre wider than the average, giving room for insertion of the loose mouthpipe. The latter is a replacement (the original presumably having partly vanished through corrosion) with length 65 cm, which allows pitch-lowering up to two whole-tones. Chorale tunes can be played quite well on this instrument, which is no doubt also the *tromba da tirarsi* of Bach's scores.

An English invention of the late seventeenth century is the slide trumpet with a two-legged slide comprising the nearer bow of the instrument and pulling back towards the player's head. This is the *flat trumpet* described in the Talbot manuscript and employed in Purcell's music for the funeral of Queen Mary. The term 'flat' here signifies that the instrument could execute melodies in the minor ('flat') key. No example from that period is known, but the idea was revived in London about the 1780s as the *slide trumpet*, publicized by the player John Hyde in 1798 and employed in many English orchestras up to the end of the nineteenth century (**745**). It is built in F, with a full set of crooks up to six in number. A hollow rod attached to the slide bow runs over a guide rod and has a short cross piece from which a length of gut passes to a clock spring enclosed in a circular case mounted on a cross stay near the bell. Thus the slide is pulled home when released. A second spring case is intended for a spare spring. The slide draws out far enough only to lower the pitch of harmonics by a tone or so, being intended for the correction of intonation of certain harmonics and for supplying a few useful semitones absent from the natural trumpet. After *c.* 1830 the clock spring began to be replaced by a length of elastic, a modification said to be due to the player Thos. Harper senior and executed by Köhler.

There are also a few 'short model' (twice looped) slide trumpets, including rare examples (**746**) with a wider-bore bell pipe than was customary (possibly the 'Regent's bugle' mentioned in some sources, see Morley-Pegge, *GSJ*, IX, 1956).

In Paris, *c.* 1840, Courtois brought out a more rational slide trumpet with a long spring-less slide pointing forwards somewhat as in the trombone (**747**). It was never much used, however, and examples are rare, since the French by that time had become more accustomed than the English to the valve trumpet.

Trombones

The trombone is a mid-fifteenth-century improvement of the earlier slide trumpet (above) through replacement of the sliding mouthpipe by a two-legged slide incorporating the outer bow of the trumpet.[1]

---

[1] Whence *trompette saqueboute*, one of the early names of the trombone ('trumpet with push-and-pull end'), retained in English, as 'sackbut', until the adoption *c.* 1800 of the Italian word *trombone*, also a fifteenth-century expression. The German name is *Posaune*.

To balance the weight and so make the slide manageable, the near bow is taken back behind the player's shoulder (normally the left) bringing the bell rim to a position about a foot in front of his head. And so the trombone remains today, save for valved versions (p. 152).

Illustrations: Slide Trombones

748 Trombone. Erasmus Schnitzer, Nuremberg, 1551. *Nuremberg, German. Nationalmus., MI.170.* Brass. Turned ferrules engraved with scale pattern. Slide with tubular stays, travel *c.* 64 cm. Bell in four joints with flat stay. *Tube length 252 cm. Bell diam. 9·4 cm. Height 114 cm.*

749 Bass trombone. Pierre Colbert, Rheims, 1593. *Amsterdam, Rijksmuseum.* Brass. Slide with flat stays with hinged clasps, lower stay with handle. Max. travel of slide 78 cm (inner legs 78·7 cm long). Bell in four joints with later solid stay. *Tube length 320 cm. Bell diam. 12·4 cm. Height 134 cm.*

750 Bass trombone. Johann Leonhard Ehe, Nuremberg, 1732. *Vienna, Kunsthist. Mus., Eigentum der Gesellschaft der Musikfreunde in Wien., Inv.No.GdM 202. Bell diam. 13·5 cm.* (Detail of bell, showing cast winged angels.)

751 Mouthpiece of **749**. Brass. *Length 9·7 cm. Rim diam.* 4 cm outside, 2·6 cm inside. *Depth of cup 1·8 cm.*

752 Contrabass trombone. G. N. Oller, Stockholm, 1639 (? 1689). *Stockholm, Musikhist. Mus., 242.* Brass. Slide with telescopic stays and handle 51 cm long. First leg of slide *c.* 1 mm narrower than second. Bell with involuted bow. Stay with pin clasp. *Pitch B flat. Tube length 550 cm. Bell diam. 16·5 cm. Height 205 cm.* With somewhat conical mouthpiece, rim 4·6 cm outside, 3·2 inside, *depth of cup 2·5 cm.*

753 Trombone. Georg Ehe, Nuremberg, 1619. *Paris, Conserv., E.754.* Brass. Slide with hinged clasps. *Bell diam. 12·5 cm. Height 130 cm.*

754 Bass trombone. Wolf Wilhelm Haas, Nuremberg, first half of eighteenth century. *Berlin, Instit. f. Musikforschung, 567.* Engraved on the bell *Iohann Wilhelm Haas in Nurnberg.* Brass. Slide with telescopic stays and ivory-knobbed handle 27 cm long. Max. travel 80·5 cm. Bell, with flat stay with pin clasp, includes three bows, incorporating a rearward-moving slide actuated by long ivory-knobbed rod; max. travel (limited by a brass stop on the rod) 19 cm. *Pitch E flat. Tube length 405 cm. Bell. diam. 14·7 cm. Height 148 cm.*

755 Buccin trombone. Bernareggi, Barcelona, early nineteenth century. *London, Horniman Mus., Carse 288.* Dragon bell. Tubular stays. Tuning slide at bottom of slide.

756 Trombone. Fasting & Wilde, Copenhagen, 1847. *Copenhagen, Claudius Coll., F.23.* Wide-bore bell with tuning slide. *Diam. 19·7 cm.*

757 Bass trombone. Schmittschneider, Paris, 1823. *Ann Arbor, Univ. of Michigan, Stearns 897.* Copper, brass mounted. Double slide. *Pitch G.* Sideways bell, diam. 17·6 cm. *Height 61 cm.*

The trombone has always been built in two parts which are disconnected after playing, for convenient portability and for the protection of the slide when not in use. The two parts are termed the slide and the bell; when assembled their respective cross-stays lie at 90 degrees to one another. The slide comprises two stationary inner legs (inner slide) each inserted into a ferrule at the upper end, these ferrules being connected by a stay. One ferrule includes the socket for the mouthpiece and the other the tapered tenon which receives the bell. Over these legs runs the outer slide, composed of two movable legs connected by a bow and by a stay with which the slide is moved. The maximum extension normally equals about a quarter of the total tube length of the instrument, this being the length required in practice to lower the third harmonic by six semitones, though in some early specimens the slide is shorter, lowering by only five semitones.

The second characteristic of the trombone is the mouthpiece, which at each period on the whole reproduces the form of the contemporary trumpet mouthpiece on a large scale: a traditional test of a good cup-diameter in England of recent years was for a trumpet a silver threepenny bit, but for a trombone a halfpenny. The effect of this difference is that a trombone can give greater weight to the lower harmonics compared with a trumpet of equal tube length (the tenor trombone having the same tube length as a classical trumpet crooked in B flat).

There exist at least six trombones with sixteenth-century dates, five being by Nuremberg makers, the earliest by Erasmus Schnitzer (**748**). The sixth is French (**749**) and, like a few of the others, is preserved with a contemporary mouthpiece (**751**), long-stemmed like an early trumpet mouthpiece, with hemispherical cup and sharp throat. Hemispherical mouthpieces were still in use in England up to the mid-nineteenth century, though a rounded throat had then come into use in Germany and an almost funnel shape in France. Trombones were made in the same workshops as trumpets and up to the beginning of the nineteenth century they may share the same forms of decoration, notably on the bell (**750**). The expansion of the bell was confined to the last branch, the rest being cylindrical, both slide and bell bows having about the same bore, which is, for an average early tenor trombone, about equal to the bore of a natural trumpet. As in trumpets too, the bell expansion of the earliest instruments is somewhat funnel-like (**748**) and develops a decided flare by the eighteenth century (**754**). Later, by *c.* 1830, German and German-style instruments had begun to be built with the bell expansion starting earlier, to include the bow and the first branch, the terminal flare also being increased (**756**). France and England, however, generally kept to the old mainly cylindrical bell profile until well into the present century. A tuning slide in the bell bow (**756**) is rare before the mid nineteenth century.

The early forms of stay are both flat and tubular. The flat stay (**753**) avoids rigidity by means of hinged clasps packed with leather, save on the bell joint where there is usually a clasp secured by a brass pin, though later repairs have often obliterated this feature. During the seventeenth century the slide was normally given tubular stays, that of the outer slide (the lower stay) being telescopic to retain flexibility and avoid binding on the inner slide. This telescopic stay is still sometimes found in the mid nineteenth century, though by that time inner legs fitted with steel bearing sleeves at the lower ends were coming in, reducing the length in contact with the outer slide to a few inches. With this development came stays of solid brass rod, though rigid tubular stays have persisted in Germany in a modified form.

The principal sizes of trombone have been alto (pitch from E flat up to F), tenor (the ordinary trombone in B flat or C), and bass (E flat up to G). The pitches are here cited as described in the nineteenth century and now, but there is some evidence that earlier trombones which sound in B flat or B today were considered in their day to stand in A, and so on. Treble trombones, an octave above the tenor, are mainly late eighteenth or nineteenth century, and are rarer than the others, the traditional treble to the trombones having in earlier times been the cornett. Contrabasses are rare before the Wagnerian epoch and the early example shown (**752**) may be unique.

Basses and tenors before the nineteenth century were sometimes supplied with a crook, inserted between slide and bell; the French bass shown, for instance, possesses a contemporary crook (not shown in the photograph) which is in one long loop and appears to lower the pitch of the instrument by a fourth to low D. Bass trombones usually have a hinged handle attached to the stay of the outer slide, owing to the great length from the top when fully extended. Sometimes they also have some kind of loop in the bell to save overall length. A curious feature found in several Nuremberg bass trombones from 1612 (by Isaac Ehe, the most beautiful trombone in existence; Nuremberg, Germanisches National-museum) to the first half of the eighteenth century (**754**; also **750**, of which only the bell is shown here—for this complete instrument see *Grove*, 5th edn, article 'Trombone') is a short slide incorporated in the bell, moved backwards by a long rod. It can be operated in both directions while the instrument is held to the lips so long as the main slide is in the first position (i.e. fully retracted), and in the Haas specimen shown it can lower the pitch by a little more than a semitone, just sufficient to make possible a low G (the instrument probably having been rated as a *Quintposaune* in D). Since no contemporary source describes its purpose, it may have been simply for tuning.

Another feature now and then found in trombones is a double slide, comprising four inner legs and four outer legs connected by two bows below and one above (**757**). With this, the slide shift for a given musical interval is halved. Instances before the nineteenth century do not seem to be wholly reliable, though the device is referred to by Praetorius. Nineteenth-century examples are not uncommon, mainly in bass or contrabass trombones.

Buccin and other nineteenth-century variants. The buccin, of the first third of the nineteenth century, is a trombone with the bell brought over in a wide curve to end with a dragon bell (**755**). Later in the century trombones were produced in which the bell points backwards, or sideways (**757**), either with the idea of causing the tone in the *forte* to blend better with an orchestra, or, according to other sources, for the sound to be heard better by the rest of the band marching behind.

3 Keyed Brass Instruments

Brass lever-keys with leather or stuffed pads similar to woodwind keys are provided on these instruments to give them a complete chromatic scale. They are principally closed keys, opened by the player's fingers to uncover holes in the tube, thus shortening the air-column and raising the pitch of harmonics by specific musical intervals. The chief objection is that once the distance between hole and bell rim exceeds a small amount the tone-making effect of the bell-mouth becomes much reduced and the notes lack much of the ringing quality of those which are emitted by the whole tube. This is least noticeable with instruments of wide, bugle-like bore, which are so to speak almost 'all bell', and consequently the key bugle and the ophicleide remained in use longer than the key trumpet. Of the keyed French horn, apparently the first of the group, having been reported as attempted by one Kölbel in St Petersburg from *c.* 1754 (*Amorschall*), no specimen has come to light.

Illustrations: Keyed Brass

758   Key trumpet. Early nineteenth century. *Nuremberg, German. Nationalmus., Rück Coll.* Two-coil. Left-handed. Four flat keys on saddles. *Pitch* E flat.

759   Key trumpet. Coll, Barcelona, first third of nineteenth century. *Barcelona, Mus. de musica, 57.* Two-coil, right-handed, with tuning slide. Six keys. *Length* 56 cm.

760   Key bugle. Graves & Co., Winchester, New Hampshire, U.S.A., mid nineteenth century. *Yale, University, 180.* Brass. Seven flat brass keys on saddles.

761   Key bugle. J. Fentum, London, *c.* 1840. *Keighley, Yorks., Museum.* Short model (two-coil). Copper. Flat brass keys on saddles.

762   Key bugle. Joseph Higham, Manchester, after 1852. *Brighton, Museum.* Copper. Four brass keys on posts, also a rotary valve (whole tone) for the left hand. *Bell diam.* 16 cm. *Length* 44 cm.

763   Key bugle (*Halbmond*). German, *c.* 1830. *Nuremberg, German. Nationalmus., MI.180.* Stamped No. 6. Brass, in two joints, with brass cross-stay. Three closed keys on saddles. Hook for right thumb. *Pitch* C. *Bell diam.* 16·3 cm. *Socket bore* 1·2 cm.

764   Keyed post horn. German, *c.* 1830. *Boston, Mus. of Fine Arts, 183.* Marked *A.K.* Brass in three coils. Five closed keys on saddles, one mounted on a cross-bar. *Pitch* G. *Bell diam.* 12 cm. *Socket bore* 0·9 cm.

765   Tenor or bass key trumpet. Piatet & Benoit, Lyons, second quarter of nineteenth century. *London, Kneller Hall, 172.* Brass. Two-coil with tuning slide. Cylindrical bore for first 134 cm., thence expanding. Six closed keys on pillars, two of them on cross-bars. *Pitch* G (bass trombone pitch). *Bell diam.* 17·5 cm. *Length* 60 cm.

766   Ophicleide. George Wigglesworth, Otley, Yorkshire, 1856. *Halifax, Bankfield Mus.* Presentation date 1856. Brass with nickel-silver mounts. Coiled crook. Eleven nickel-silver keys on brass pillars soldered to bed-plates. Ivory mouthpiece.

767   Alto ophicleide. Charles Sax, Brussels, *c.* 1825. *New York, Metropol. Mus. of Art, 2411.* Brass. Nine keys on saddles. *Height* 89 cm.

The *key trumpet* first featured—though not named as keyed—in Haydn's Concerto in E flat of 1796, and five years later, also in Vienna, the court trumpeter Anton Weidinger was playing a model made by Riedl. For over 40 years of the nineteenth century the key trumpet was built on the Continent, mainly for bands. It is usually in two loops, one often with a tuning slide (**759**). There are rarer 'long models' in one loop. Of the keys, numbering from four to six, one or two are generally mounted on flat cross stays. All are actuated by one hand, in some cases the left hand (**758**). The use of the keys when different crooks were attached was necessarily largely empirical. The early form of keys is flat with solid leather pads. Later they are cupped, sometimes cast in a decorative shell pattern, and fitted with stuffed kid pads. There are larger and deeper instruments than the ordinary, one of which is shown (**765**), though with only some 42 per cent of cylindrical tube this may have been intended as a neutral kind of band tenor like some of the so-called bass valve trumpets of Continental military bands. Only one English key trumpet is known, by Sandbach, London, with three keys and some key-bugle features of construction (Kneller Hall, 151).

Less common applications of keys are shown by a neatly made German keyed post horn (**764**), and a *Halbmond* bugle with three closed keys, placed to raise the pitch in diatonic steps from C to F (**763**).

The key bugle was patented by Joseph Halliday, Dublin, 1810. Whether he knew of the key trumpet is not recorded. The key bugle takes the model of the contemporary one-coil copper bugle (p. 130), and is likewise pitched in C or B flat with a tone or semitone crook provided. A clever thing about it is that the principal harmonic series, say of C, vents through an open key in the bell, which is extended forwards to give a B series when the key is closed. This key is near enough to the end of the bell for the quality of the C series not to be affected, while the adjacent semitones including the leading-note of the home tonality are sounded with matched quality. The closed keys were at first four, later five or more (**760**). A bridge over the third key helps the right hand to support the instrument. The early mounting of the keys on long brass saddles was by degrees replaced by brass pillars attached to stout bed-plates. A few years after its invention the key bugle reached the Continent, there made in brass, and in Germany (*Klappenhorn*) also in nickel-silver. But it was mainly in England and America that the instrument lasted as an important band instrument up to the 1850s. Some of the later models incorporate a whole-tone valve to provide a better low F (and by closing the bell key, E) than are given by the keys; Higham's pattern in fact has only four keys altogether (**762**), dispensing with those for F and E. From *c.* 1835 short models appear, in two loops (**761**), again sometimes with the valve. Conversely ordinary three-valve cornets of the mid-nineteenth century, especially in England, were often provided with one closed key, carried on a cross stay, for facilitating certain whole-tone trills ('clapper key').

The ophicleide, invented by Halary, Paris, 1817 (patent 1821), is essentially a bass key bugle in bassoon shape, said to have been directly inspired by the Halliday key bugle, like which it has the open key in the bell, the other keys being closed (**766**). There are from nine to twelve keys, in late models, after 1850, mounted partly on long axles with needle springs. The body is of brass, with a detachable mouthpipe (called a crook) which is either coiled or else made in a parallel-sided loop containing a tuning slide. The mouthpiece is often ivory, of about trombone dimensions, and the pitch is B flat or C. The ophicleide may be considered the most successful of the keyed brass in that it remained longest in use, mainly in France, Italy and England, still listed in a 1915 catalogue of Couesnon, Paris. It is in fact an excellent band instrument with a bright sound of considerable character, though the noise made by the keys can be obtrusive. The *alto ophicleide*, also introduced by Halary (as *quinticlave*), pitched in E flat or F, was far less successful and examples are quite rare. For some reason it was made with relatively narrow bore (**767**), similar to that found in some ophicleides of the normal bass pitch made in Germany, where the instrument was never widely adopted; an unsigned example of this German narrow-tube ophicleide is at Nuremberg (MI.250).

Other rare variants of ophicleide include a contrabass or 'monster' ophicleide, *c.* 150 cm tall, occasionally made from 1821 onwards, and Couturier's model, Lyons, 1852, with six keys and one valve. There are also freak instruments with the general look of an ophicleide but with many of the closed keys replaced by open keys for fingering in the woodwind or serpent manner, e.g. by Sautermeister, Lyons, 1827, and the *serpentcleide*, London, *c.* 1850. These are perhaps best considered as late forms of serpent. Some were in fact made of wood. (For a full account of the ophicleide in all forms see Morley-Pegge in *Grove*, 5th edn.)

4 Valved Brass Instruments

The valve is a sprung device actuated by the player's finger to connect instantly an auxiliary loop of tubing with the main tubing, the tube length of this loop being calculated to lower the pitch of the instrument by a specific musical interval. Of the three valves normally provided, the first lowers by a whole tone, the second by a semitone and the third by a tone and a half. Their combinations give further lowerings and render the instrument fully chromatic. Each valve loop normally includes its individual tuning slide.

The first news of valves is from Berlin, where the horn-player Heinrich Stölzel, previously in the employ of the Prince von Pless, is reported to have made a valve mechanism for the horn. Two years later Stölzel's horn is described as having had two sprung valves, and in the following year, 1818, a patent was taken out jointly by Stölzel and another player, Friedrich Blühmel, for a piston valve of a square pattern—or so the story goes.[1]

Square valves. In a Schuster trumpet shown (**768**), one of the very few known specimens with 'square valves', i.e. square- or rectangular-section pistons, the pistons are oblong cubes built from thick sheet brass, with channelled side faces to reduce friction. Each of the brass valve cases contains below the piston a coiled spring. Each piston is traversed by three inserted tubular ports of thin brass, one of which, functional when the valve is 'up', crosses the piston diagonally and conducts the windway directly through the valve. The other two lie above this and parallel with each other; when the valve is depressed they divert the windway into the valve loop and thence back into the main tubing and on to the bell. As with many early instruments with two valves only, the first valve (forefinger) lowers by a semitone and the second by a whole tone, not, as later, the other way about. After the mid-1820s square valves (*Kastenventile*) seem to have been abandoned.

Stölzel valves. The earliest known form of cylindrical piston (**771**, etc) is that which was known by this name, though the circumstances of its connection with Stölzel are not wholly clear. The direct passage, when the valve is up, is through the lower part of the piston and it continues down the casing. When depressed, the windway is diverted through the valve loop by means of two curved plates crossing the upper part of the piston. Since the casing forms part of the direct windway the coiled spring is housed above the piston inside the upper part of the casing. The Stölzel valve was introduced to Paris during the late 1820s, and up to the 1840s was the best known system in France and England. Often the valve stems have ivory tips for the fingers, and removable brass caps for protection when the instrument is not in use. Stölzel valves were still made in France early in the present century for cheap cornets. A horizontal version was made by Pace, London, *c.* 1835, with the idea of suiting players accustomed to the hand position of the slide trumpet (**772**).

Double-piston valves, also called **Vienna valves** (**769, 783,** etc), were known in Germany in the late 1820s, though the first recorded patent is by Leopold Uhlmann, Vienna, 1830. Each valve has two short tubular pistons, contained in parallel casings but linked externally by a cross-bar and moved as one. Again the casings form part of the windway, in this instance leading it through a valve loop which

---

[1] The story as so far known, patchily and confused by contradictory particulars and mechanically undetailed, has been told a number of times (Carse, *Musical Wind Instruments*, Section VIII; Morley-Pegge, *The French Horn*, Chap. 3; and in *Grove*, 5th edn, article 'Valve'). The present author, regretfully, can add nothing to it, though future research should fill the gaps and settle the points of doubt in the initial history of the most revolutionary and influential musical-instrument invention since Cristofori's invention of the piano.

connects their two ends. For this, the pistons are drawn outwards. The direct windway runs straight through a port in the upper part of each piston when these are at rest in the 'in' position. Thus the action is reversed as compared with other piston systems, and the valve assembly is normally placed on the instrument 'upside down' and actuated by external levers and springs. Early patterns use flat springs of brass or steel strip (**769**). These are mainly German, though there are French examples, e.g. by Courtois. Later arrangements have clock springs enclosed in drums (*Trommelwerk*) mounted beside rotating finger levers (as with the ordinary rotary valve described later). This became the usual arrangement in Austria and Germany and is still employed on the Viennese horn (**788**). Another version has spiral springs enclosed in separate tubular casings, which, coupled with simple push rods for the fingers, give the player more of the feel of other piston valves and became especially popular in Belgium later in the century (**808**).

Berlin valves (Berliner Pumpen), by Moritz, Berlin, 1835 (**779, 793**, etc), have single tubular pistons with an action recalling that of the old square valve. The casing forms no part of the windway and contains a coiled spring placed beneath the piston. The latter is short, but wide enough to take two ports side by side. These cross its upper part and lead to the valve loop when the valve is depressed. Below them is a third port, for the direct windway when the valve is 'up'. The direction followed by this port across the piston varies according to whether the designer found it convenient to place the entry and exit points of the main tube on opposite sides of the casing (**796**) or next to each other at 90 degrees (**779**). The external action is usually by direct finger pressure on the valve stem caps but occasionally by means of pivoted levers (**803**). These valves were widely used by Berlin makers on all instruments until displaced by the rotary valve late in the century. They have still, however, been provided on the traditional Berlin tuba until quite recently (**798**). In Paris, Adolphe Sax used both these and rotary valves in his saxhorns from 1843. Berlin valves are distinguished at a glance from the Périnet (modern) piston valves by the fact that all four entry and exit tubes are brazed to the casing at the same level.

Périnet Valves, the modern type of piston valve (**774**), were introduced by the Paris horn-maker François Périnet in 1839. The action resembles that of the Berlin valve but no two of the three ports lie side by side, so that the piston can be narrower. The spring is again placed beneath the piston, though from late in the century onwards many makers have preferred methods of putting it above the piston, especially for small instruments like trumpets and cornets. (In Germany the Périnet valve was built only in instruments for export until the advent of jazz, for which rotary valves on the trumpet are unsuitable owing to the difficulty of 'half-valving' with them.)

Samson valve ('finger slides') London, 1862, are totally enclosed piston valves (**795**), dispensing with the usual casing caps with holes for valve stems and for equalizing air pressure. The casing is part of the windway, the piston within it being moved up and down by a lug which emerges through a slot in the casing and is connected to an external push rod with coiled spring enclosed in a tubular case mounted parallel with the valve casing. The upper part of the casing leads to the valve loop. The piston itself is very short and is without inserted ports, having simply a closed upper end, open lower end, and one side orifice located immediately below the former. Instruments with these valves were sold by Rudall Rose & Carte, London, for a time but without much success owing to their expense and the difficulty of dismantling for the cleaning needed even by a fully enclosed valve.

Rotary valves. In these the piston is replaced by a rotor which turns in bearing plates at each end of a short casing. To actuate the valve external levers turn the rotor through a quarter-circle (**780**, etc). Something of this nature may have already been known in the late 1820s, possibly due to Blühmel, though the rotary valve well known today is credited to Joseph Riedl, Vienna, 1832. The rotor is normally made of a short, wide tube of brass, slightly tapered for grinding in; it can be inserted and removed only from the opposite end of the casing from the actuating lever (the cover plate at the lever end of the casing has, like the lower removable cap, a milled edge, but is brazed to the casing). The rotor tube is drilled with four holes to receive the two inserted ports. Some cheap versions, however, have the ports cut in a solid brass rotor. The external lever action is sprung either by leaf springs (**777**) or by the later enclosed clock springs (**780**) or (mainly on horns) exposed coiled springs. Other actuating mechanisms have been tried, as Higham's, Manchester, 1857, with simple push rods and springs enclosed in tubular casings (**794**). More important is the 'string action' introduced in America. Here a length of thread or fine gut is wound once round the projecting rotor spindle, replacing the customary cranks and levers (**782**). A patent for this in England cited by Morley-Pegge (*The French Horn*, p. 42) is by the Schreiber Cornet Co, New York, 1866.

Other rotary valves. Only two of these can be mentioned here. An early pattern in America, by N. Adams, Lowell, Mass., 1825 (*Permutation trumpet*), has twin rotary vanes of leather and brass for each valve, actuated simultaneously by flexible wires (**770**); a detailed account has not been published, but from the brief description by Christine Ayars (see Bibliography) America can perhaps claim credit for the first rotary valve. *Shaw valves* (*Patent lever* valves, later also referred to as 'disc valves') are due to John Shaw of Glossop, 1838, and are found on numerous mid-nineteenth-century instruments built by Köhler, London (**773, 778**). Each valve has a rotating brass disc which lies against a fixed disc. The former is turned through 90 degrees by a push rod, sprung either by a clock spring placed coaxially with the disc (**773**) or by an enclosed spiral spring on the push rod (**778**). Into four holes in the rotating disc are fixed, in the original design, the ends of the valve loop and of a semicircular port, the latter providing the air passage when the valve is at rest. Köhler improved on this by attaching the valve loop to the fixed disc beside the main entry and exit pipes (**773,** etc); to the rotating disc he fitted a second semicircular port, so that with the disc turned, the windway is led to the now stationary valve loop through one port and back through the other.

Independent and compensating pistons. Combinations of the customary three valves give pitches which are in theory too sharp, most so in cases involving the third valve. This is due to the fact that the loop of the first valve, for example, tuned to lower the pitch of the instrument by a tone, is not as long as it should be to effect the corresponding lowering when the instrument has been lengthened in the proportion 6:5 by depressing the third valve. The normal correction is by the player's ear and lip, but valve systems have been devised to remove or reduce the need for this. The first is Sax's six or seven independent pistons, 1852, mentioned later (p. 152). Theoretically less perfect but neater and quite effective in practice is the compensating system of D. J. Blaikley, London, 1874. Here the loop of the third valve is led through the other two Périnet pistons. To the casing of each of these is attached a second loop of small size. When either of these two valves is depressed *while the third valve is also depressed*, the windway of the third valve loop is led through the extra loop, counteracting the sharpness. Many of the deeper-pitched brass instruments have a fourth valve which lowers the pitch by a perfect fourth. In such cases the compensation can be connected to this valve instead of to the third.

Illustrations: Valved Brass Instruments Trumpets and Cornets

768 Trumpet. W. Schuster, Carlsruhe, *c.* 1820. *Nuremberg, German. Nationalmus., Rück Coll., MIR.130.* In E flat. Two square valves, the first semitone, the second whole-tone, travel 1·36 cm. *Bore of ports* 1·13 cm. Tubular stays. No tuning slide. *Bell diam.* 13·2 cm. *Length* 45 cm.

769 Trumpet. A. Barth, Munich, 1834. *Nuremberg, German. Nationalmus., Rück Coll., MIR.131.* In F. Two double-piston valves actuated by left hand (the instrument held with bell pipe lowermost), first valve semitone, second valve whole-tone. Flat brass springs. *Bell diam.* 11·2 cm. *Length* 39 cm.

770　Trumpet. N. Adams, Lowell, Massachusetts, 1825. *U.S. Frigate Constitution, Navy Yard, Charlestown, Mass.* 'Permutation trumpet.' Three valves of a rotary type.

771　Trumpet. Sandbach & Wyatt, London, 1832–5. *London, Horniman Mus., Carse 150.* In F. Two ivory-tipped Stölzel valves. *Valve bore* 1·12 cm. *Bell diam.* 11·5 cm. *Length* 36 cm.

772　Trumpet. Charles Pace, London, 1830–40. *London, Horniman Mus., Carse 290.* In F. Two horizontal Stölzel valves, the upper semitone, the lower whole-tone. *Length* 51·5 cm.

773　Trumpet. Köhler, London, *c.* 1839. *Cobham, Morley-Pegge Coll.* In F. Two Shaw valves, early improved pattern by Köhler. *Length* 43 cm.

774　Trumpet. C. Mahillon & Co., Brussels, after 1878. *Coll. of the late C. Overy.* In B flat. Silver plated. Three Périnet valves, bore 1·0 cm. *Bell diam.* 11 cm.

775　Cornet. Halary, Paris, *c.* 1835. *London, Kneller Hall, 128.* Two Stölzel valves. Socket bore of B flat shank 0·92 cm. Tuning slide bore 1·1 cm. Painted bell. Funnel-cup mouthpiece *c.* 0·2 cm deep.

776　Cornet (Flugel horn). A. Heiser, Potsdam, *c.* 1840. *Eisenach, Bachhaus, 111.* E flat soprano. Three rotary valves. Flare-less bell.

777　Cornet. C. A. Müller, Mainz, *c.* 1850. *Author's Coll.* In B flat. Silver plated. Three rotary valves with leaf springs. *Valve bore* 1·08 cm. *Socket of crook* (not shown) 0·98 cm. *Bell diam.* 12·5 cm.

778　Cornet. Köhler, London, mid-nineteenth century. *London, Kneller Hall, 173.* In B flat. Silver plated. Three Shaw valves of the later pattern.

779　Post horn. German, second half of nineteenth century. *Boston, Mus. of Fine Arts, 214.* Inscribed on silver bell rim *Ehren-Posthorn für dem Postillon Heinrich Bredemeier. Pitch* E flat. Two Berlin valves, bore 1·13 cm. *Bell diam.* 11·3 cm. *Diam. across coil* 20·3 cm.

780　Cornet. Thompson & Odell, Boston, Mass., late nineteenth century. *Coll. of the late C. Overy.* In B flat. Circular model. Three rotary valves, bore 1·12 cm. *Socket* 0·92 cm. *Bell diam.* 12·3 cm. *Diam. across coil* (outside) 16·6 cm. Tuning slide in mouthpipe.

781　Pocket cornet. English, late nineteenth century. *Coll. of the late C. Overy.* In B flat. Three Périnet valves. *Bell diam.* 9 cm. *Length* 23 cm.

782　Cornet. Graves & Co., Winchester, New Hampshire, *c.* 1855. *Yale, University Coll.* Bell-upwards model. Three rotary valves with string action and short flat springs under finger levers.

Horns

783　French horn. J. G. Kersten, Dresden, second quarter of nineteenth century. *Stockholm, Musikhist. Mus., 410* Two removable double-piston valves. Fixed mouthpipe.

784　French horn. Thomas Key, London, before 1856. *London, Horniman Mus., Carse 156.* Two Stölzel valves. Conical master crook. Seven cylindrical couplers (not shown).

785, 786　French horn. J. G. Moritz, Berlin, *c.* 1830. *Berlin, Instit. f. Musikforschung, 4366.* Silver plated and gilt. Fixed mouthpipe socket 0·87 cm. Detachable Berlin valves, bore 1·03 cm, and 'inventions' crook below the valves. *Bell diam.* 29 cm. Shown also with valves removed for hand horn playing (**785**).

787　French horn. Hawkes & Son, London, *c.* 1870. *Cobham, Morley-Pegge Coll.* Probably imported from Paris. Three Stölzel valves.

788　French horn. Joseph Riedl, Vienna, *c.* 1850. *Vienna, Kunsthist. Mus., N.E.356.* Three double-piston valves with clock-springs. With F crook. *Bell diam.* 29 cm.

789　Tenor cor. Couesnon, Paris, end of nineteenth century. *Barcelona, Mus. de Musica, 251.* Right-handed. With F shank.

Tenor Horns, Tubas, Valve Trombones

790　Clavicor. Guichard, Paris, after 1838. *London, Horniman Mus., Carse 206.* Brass, silver mounted. Removable mouthpiece and screw-off bell, diam. 22 cm. *Pitch* C. *Bore of right-hand valves* 1·16 cm; *of left-hand valve* 1·26 cm. *Height* 104 cm.

791   Tenor horn. J. W. Wahl, Landskrona (Sweden), *c. 1845. Uppsala, Coll. of Prof. C. G. Widstrand.* In B flat. Three rotary valves without tuning slides, bore 1·3 cm. Cylindrical mouthpipe. *Bell diam.* 14 cm. *Height* 79 cm.

792   Alt horn. Köhler, London, *c. 1840. Brighton Museum.* Marked *No. 904.* In C (high pitch). Detachable shank and deep mouthpiece. Tapered mouthpipe. Three Shaw valves with encased spiral springs over the push rods. Third valve is of wider bore than the other two. *Bell diam.* 16 cm. *Height* 79 cm.

793   Contralto saxhorn. Adolphe Sax, Paris, *c. 1850. London, C. R. Baines Coll.* In B flat. Three Berlin valves. *Bell diam.* 15·3 cm. *Height* 65 cm.

794   Flugel horn. J. Higham, Manchester, *c. 1860. Cobham, Morley-Pegge Coll.* Alto in E flat. Rotary valves actuated by push rods with encased spiral springs. Two tuning slides. *Socket and valve bore* 1·15 cm. *Bell diam.* 16 cm. *Length* 42 cm.

795   Ballad horn. Rudall, Rose & Carte & Co., London, *c. 1870. London, Horniman Mus., Carse 102.* In C. Samson valves.

796   Tenor horn. E. Paulus, Berlin, 1874. *Berlin, Instit. f. Musikforschung, 4570.* In B flat. Bell-front model. Three Berlin valves, the third valve for two tones. *Valve bore* 1·24 cm. *Bell diam.* 19·8 cm.

797   Cor alto. J. C. Labbaye, Paris, after 1862. *Coll. of the late C. Overy.* Right-handed, bell-up. Tapered mouthpipe. Coiled E flat crook in tuning slide. Three Périnet valves, bore 1·15 cm. *Bell diam.* 26 cm. *Across coil* (inside) 21 cm.

798   Bass tuba. J. G. Moritz, Berlin, 1852. *Berlin, Instit. f. Musikforschung, 4456.* In F. Brass, nickel-silver mounts. *Bell diam.* 19·3 cm. Five Berlin valves, bore 1·48 cm. *Height* 84 cm.

799   Tuba. Leopold Uhlmann, Vienna, 1839. *Salzburg, Museo Carolino Augusteum, Geir. 152.* In F. Three double-piston valves with clock springs. *Height* 145 cm.

800   Bombardon. Ahlberg & Ohlsson, Stockholm, 1859. *Uppsala, Hornboskapen Coll.* In F. Three rotary valves, bore 1·6 cm.

801   Cornophone. F. Besson, Paris, late nineteenth century. *London, Kneller Hall, 77.* In C, with B flat slide.

802   Saxhorn. United States, *c. 1860. Washington, Smithsonian Institution, 55.589.* Marked *J. Howard Foote, New York City* (dealer). Baritone in B flat. Bell-over-shoulder model. Rotary valves with string action.

803   Valve trombone. J. W. Wahl, Landskrona (Sweden), *c. 1840. Stockholm, Musikhist. Mus., 483.* F bass with coil in bell. Three Berlin valves actuated by pivoted levers.

804   Helicon. Ignaz Stowasser, Vienna, *c. 1850. Nuremberg, German. Nationalmus., Rück Coll., MIR.71.* In BB flat. Brass, nickel-silver mounts. Conical mouthpiece (socket 1·45 cm) leads direct to fourth valve. Four rotary valves, bore 2·19 cm. *Bell diam.* 24 cm.

805   Saxhorn. Adolphe Sax, Paris, 1854. *Brussels, Conserv. royal, 2459.* Contrabass in BB flat. With Regimental stamp and date *1854.* Three Berlin valves, the third lowering by two tones. *Height* 137 cm.

806   Valve trombone. Adolphe Sax, Paris. *Brussels, Conserv. royal, 1288.* Seven independent valves and bells.

807   Helicon trombone. Ferdinando Roth, Milan, late nineteenth century. *London, Horniman Mus., Carse 314.* In B flat. Three rotary valves, bore 1·17 cm. One coil. Short dummy tube next to bell. *Bell diam.* 17 cm. *Diam. of coil* 50 cm.

808   Valve trombone. G. van Engelen, Lierre (Belgium), second half of nineteenth century. *Coll. of the late C. Overy.* In B flat. Three double-piston valves with short parallel spring cases. Tuning slide at front end of valve joint. *Length* 109 cm.

Valve trumpets. Up to the end of the nineteenth century these were mostly built in F, sometimes G or A flat, like the natural and key trumpets of the first part of the century. As with other valved instruments, crooks were supplied for different tonalities through most of the century, even though valves might have been thought to render them unnecessary as history in due course has proved. G trumpets with crooks were still advertised in France after 1900 (by Chapelain). There were also military band trumpets in E flat (low) with and without crooks. The location of the valve assembly is on either the first or on the lower branch, largely according to the type of valve employed; Stölzel valves, inserted into the lower branch, can give the model a rather deep, cornet-like appearance (**771**). With double-piston valves on the first branch, the trumpet is played upside down (**769**). Some two-valve trumpets were still made after the mid-century (e.g. Berlin Coll., 4436, by C. W. Moritz, 1857), and in some instances the valves can be withdrawn and replaced by a plain bow for natural playing.

The high trumpet in B flat (bugle pitch, i.e. today's trumpet) was made in Berlin very soon after the invention of valves, and Wilhelm Wieprecht, the celebrated Berlin bandmaster, was using a two-valve model over the years 1824–33 together with deeper E flat valve trumpets. The B flat trumpet was also made in Paris by Sax and several mid-century specimens by various makers exist, e.g. by Joseph Riedl, Vienna, with three double-piston valves (Nuremberg Coll.). Their use seems to have been confined to bands until the end of the century. A late example by Mahillon (**774**) has a tapered mouthpipe as in modern practice, though short, with the valves set between it and the first bow as in many previous Périnet-valve trumpets and practically all German rotary-valve trumpets.

Valve trumpets designed specifically for performance of Bach's works date initially from the activities of 1885 in connection with the bicentenary of the composer's birth: a straight two-valve trumpet in A made by Silvani, Paris, for the English players (illustrated in *Grove*, 5th edn, 'Trumpet'), was followed by smaller three-valve instruments in high D, straight or looped, by Mahillon and others. Valved straight trumpets have also been built for fanfare and stage purposes, as in Verdi's *Aïda* (1870), where the Grand March needs stage trumpets with a whole-tone valve only.

Cornet. The *cornet à piston* ('post horn with valves') was brought out by Halary, Paris, 1828, apparently after the arrival of some Stölzel-valve instruments sent from Berlin by Spontini. It may be that Berlin makers had already made circular post horns with valves, which both German and French makers continued to do since (**779**). Seen in this light, the Halary cornet (**775**) is a bell-to-the-front post horn with Stölzel valves, and a slightly tapered mouthpipe into which tapered crooks may be inserted for different keys, the short straight shank shown being the B flat crook. Such crooks, down to F or lower, continued to be supplied with cornets for most of the century, though now only the B flat shank is retained. The valves are placed after the first bow and a tuning slide is contained in a short secondary loop (as in some F trumpets). The French cornet quickly reached England, known first as 'cornopean' and made with Stölzel or Shaw valves (**778**). The mouthpiece until late in the century had a funnel-shaped cup (**775**), not as deep as that of a horn but conferring a gentle, horn-like quality. By 1833 German makers were making instruments called by the French name, *Cornet*, or *Piston*, but which have wider bell pipes and keep the cylindrical mouthpipe characteristic of the German post horn. The shank leads immediately to the valves (**777**, the shank here removed) rather than to a long tapered mouthpipe as in the French cornet, and the instrument can be hard to distinguish at sight from a B flat trumpet, though this is usually made in a longer format.

The immense popularity of the cornet during the second half of the century, especially west of the Rhine and in America, led to many variant models: circular (**780**), similar to the valved post and Pless horns; with bell in the air (**782**); pocket cornets (**781**); cornets with built-in mute (echo cornets) and others.

The term *Flügelhorn* has denoted, since the introduction of valved instruments, what is to all intents and purposes a valve bugle, of most importance in Continental bands (English *flugel horn*, French *bugle*, Italian *flicorno*, etc). It was no doubt developed partly from the key bugle, and a 'chromatic *Signalhorn*' listed by Stölzel in 1828 may have been a valve bugle. In the flugel horn a short wide mouthpipe leads straight to the valves, permitting the bore-expansion to commence immediately thereafter, and the wide bell pipe is either flared or, in a Berlin type locally described as *Cornet* (**776**), flareless like that of the Prussian bugle. There are also small flugel horns in F or E flat, and altos in low E flat (**794**). So-called bass flugel horns usually have a relatively wider bore, being virtually bell-front tenor horns. The military bugle itself has been supplied in a model with detachable valves (Distin, London, 1855) and made in France and Italy with a single valve to provide a restricted diatonic compass.

Valve horn. Solo performances on the valve horn were heard in Germany during the early 1820s, though the success of the hand horn to some extent retarded its general adoption in orchestras. German makers accustomed to the *Inventionshorn* with fixed mouthpipe (p. 134) made a valve horn with similar fixed mouthpipe and with a valve assembly that can sometimes be replaced by a plain slide for hand horn playing (**783**). In a fine example by Moritz (**785, 786**) the third valve lowers by a whole tone a fraction bigger than that of the first valve; the only note which this unusual arrangement does not provide is the rarely written low C sharp. Later German horns were built in F, often with an 'inventions' crook for E flat. During the second half of the century the now prevalent German double horn was gradually developed, with dual valve circuits for F and high B flat, instantaneously switched by a thumb valve.

Vienna retained the old *Orchesterhorn* with mouthpipe crooks, adding double-piston valves (**788**). Analogously in France, two or three Stölzel, later Périnet, valves were added to the orchestral hand horn with mouthpipe crooks, the valves often being removable. Two-valve horns were made in Paris up to the end of the century as 'military models', and these and three-valve instruments were exported to, and copied in England, replacing, during the second half of the century, English designs with the ancient additive crooks (**784**, and p. 134). For use in Paris, the third valve, following Halary's invention of 1849, is ascending, raising the pitch by a whole tone. As with the previous French orchestral hand horn, the fixed tubing is short enough to allow the use of all crooks from high B flat downwards (**787**).

Tenor cor (in the U.S.A., **mellophone**) and **ballad horn.** These circular instruments are substitute and amateur horns of alto (F, E flat) or tenor (C, B flat) pitch, brought out from *c.* 1860 onwards. The tenor cor, in France *cor alto*, is intended to be easier to play on the march and by inexpert band boys; an early form is by Labbaye, Paris (**797**), with raised bell. The later form (Couesnon, after 1890) is horn-shaped (**789**). The valves are placed either for the right hand or for the left. The pitch is an octave above the French horn. The ballad horn, by Distin, London, *c.* 1870, and made there and in Paris for some years, has a larger bore, almost that of a tenor horn. It is usually pitched in C for easy reading from vocal music, whence also the name 'voice horn' (**795**).

Alto and **tenor horns.** The conical-bore valved instruments commonly employed in bands for the middle and lower parts of the harmony are of four principal pitches as follows (the nomenclature differing in the various countries): (1) Alto, in E flat (formerly also F), known in most countries as *alto horn* (but in England, 'tenor horn'). (2) Tenor, in B flat (or C), including one type with fairly narrow bore matched to the alto horn, and described in America and Germany as *tenor horn* (in England and France, 'baritone'); and a second type with wider, tuba-like bore and in fact a tenor-bass, called *baritone* (in England 'euphonium', in France, *basse*). (3) Bass in E flat (or F), in fact a tuba. (4) A larger bass in low B flat (or C), also a tuba. Instruments of pitches (2) and (3) were advertised in Berlin by Stölzel along with other 'chromatic' brass instruments of his own invention, in 1828 (the joint patent of 1818 having been for ten years). The advertisement does not say that he made them and is unillustrated, but the expressions *Tenor-horn, Bass-horn* which appear in it (further instances of recourse to the overworked name 'horn' for new band instruments) allow the supposition that the 'bell-up' brass-band tenor horn had by then appeared. It may indeed go back a few years earlier, since Wieprecht recalled using three-valved *Tenorhörner* and *Tenor-basshörner*, both in B flat, in the Prussian Dragoons band from 1824, when he was a young man of 20 (Kalkbrenner; for the full reference of this and of the Stölzel advertisement, see *Grove*, 5th edn, 'Tuba'). Whether any examples of such early dates survive—other than possibly a square-valve tenor by Schuster (Berlin, 3104)—is at present doubtful.

An unknown number of different valved tenors and altos appeared during the 1830s both in European centres and in America. A distinctive example is the *clavicor*, by Guichard, Paris, 1837 (**790**), a kind of tenor cornet in bell-up format with three Stölzel valves of which the whole-tone and semitone valves are for the right hand (placed lowermost) and the three-semitone valve for the left. In England, under the name 'alt horn' it came to play an important part in band arrangements of the mid-century, imported from France, or made in London by Pace and others, usually with the three valves placed normally (**792**). A Swedish tenor horn of the period illustrates a wider-bore type with unflared bell in Prussian tradition (**791**). The *saxhorns*, by Adolphe Sax, Paris, patented in 1845, were, as far as is known, the first homogeneous group of bell-up valved instruments covering the range from soprano to bass; the *contralto* (**793**) of the group has the pitch of the cornet. The short mouthpipe leads directly to the valves, which were at first of the Berlin or the rotary type, later Périnet. By degrees the model became more compact, and also to be copied, at least to some extent, by makers in most countries, and establishing the easily recognizable if not completely standardized alto and tenor horns of today. Sax also made the saxhorns in bell-to-the-front models. In Germany bell-front models may have been known earlier (e.g. Stölzel's 1828 advertisement) and altos and tenors have been made there ever since, known as *Trompetenform*, alternative to the usual bell-up (*Tubaform*) and 'oval' models. A bell-front tenor by Paulus, Berlin (**796**), has a two-tone third valve, as on some tubas. Among other designs, bell-over-the-shoulder models go back certainly to the 1830s, when in America the Dodworth band was using them, with rotary valves (**802**). Among later designs, the *cornophone*, by Besson, Paris, 1890 (**801**), has a narrow mouthpipe for use with a large horn-like funnel mouthpiece, perhaps suggested by the 'Wagner tubas' of *The Ring*, which are in fact played with horn mouthpieces.

Tubas. Seven years after Stölzel's 1828 list, Wieprecht and J. G. Moritz jointly patented the *Bass-tuba* in F, Berlin, 1835. This has a narrow flare and five Berlin valves (**798**). As built up to the early part of the present century the three lower valves (right hand) are the main set, the third valve lowering by two tones; the other two are for a whole-tone (transposing the tuba into E flat) and for a perfect fourth (giving notes below double-bass A). Some models have only four valves. A three-valve bass with flared bell (**800**) followed a few years later, known as *Bombardon*—a name which stuck for the ordinary E flat band tuba in many countries, as England, where instruments used to be much imported from Germany. Some other specimens mark independent ideas of what a brass bass might be in the early days, mostly German and Austrian (**799**). The deeper bass in low B flat (in band circles BB Flat, 'double B-flat bass') was constructed by Cerveny, the leading brass-instrument maker in Bohemia, in 1845, closely followed by Sax's corresponding addition to the saxhorn group (**805**).

The circular bass or *helicon*, in which the weight is taken on the left shoulder, was made by Stowasser, Vienna, 1849 (**804**). The American sousaphone, with wide bell raised above the player's head, is early twentieth century.

Valve trombones. Replacement of the trombone slide by valves was another idea of Stölzel and Blühmel (Carse, 258), put into effect certainly by 1830, especially in Vienna. From then the valve trombone has been made in most countries and is still widely used in East Europe, Italy, etc, in marching bands and theatres. It is normally built to retain something of traditional trombone appearance, with separate bell joint extending behind the player's head (**803, 808**). In some models this joint is slightly elevated to point forwards, while the valve joint is sloped downwards. Circular or 'helicon' trombones (**807**) have been made for mounted bands, and there are also bell-over-the-shoulder models. Sax's system of independent pistons, 1852, was applied with some success to the trombone, lasting in Belgium until not long ago. The six or seven independent valves and valve loops do away with the valve combinations and the intonation defects associated with them (p. 147). The original model with independent bells (**806**) understandably found less favour than the models with one normal bell.

IV Percussion Instruments

1 Drums

Drums consist essentially of skins and 'shells'. The drumskins are normally of calfskin ('vellums'). The shell is a hollow cylinder or a bowl, more rarely a frame of some other shape, across which the skin or pair of skins is stretched. Primitive means of attaching the skin by gluing or nailing is met in the West mainly in tambourines. The principal method is by lapping the skin while wet onto a thin wooden hoop termed a flesh hoop. The lapped drumskin and hoop fit over the rim of the shell, and tension is applied to a second hoop or counterhoop of wood or metal which is drawn down onto the flesh hoop. In kettle drums tensioning has traditionally been by short screw rods turning in brackets riveted to the bowl-shaped copper or brass shell. The tradition with the other principal drums, which have two skins, is for a rope, led through the holes in the two counterhoops in a zig-zag and passing through stout hide cuffs on the way. Adjustment of tension on both heads simultaneously is by shifting the cuffs to tighten or loosen the rope. From a little over a century ago rope tensioning began to be superseded, though never wholly, by rod tensioning fixed to the shell and allowing tension to be applied to the two heads independently. Rod tensioning can also, of course, be used on a cylindrical drum with a single head. (It has also recently been adopted, along with brass shells, in the Middle East for traditional drums like the pot drum *darabuka*, sometimes to give a deceptively European appearance.)

Illustrations: Drums

809 Pair of kettle drums. German, eighteenth century. *Nuremberg, German. Nationalmus., Rück Coll., MIR 630, 631.* On loose iron stand. Copper, with eight screws. *Diam. 49 cm and 60 cm.*

810 Set of kettle-drum sticks. German, sixteenth century. *Vienna, Kunsthist. Mus., S.267, 268, 269.* Ivory. Face of 'disc' heads carved in relief with the badge of Austria, with cardinal's hat, chain of the Golden Fleece, and an angel's head. Hole for wrist thong. *Length of stick 39 cm. Diam. of head 4·5 cm.*

811 Kettle drum. Cornelius Ward, London, *c.* 1850. *London, Kneller Hall, 232.* Smallest of set of three made for Queen Victoria's private band. Copper. Head removed to show internal rope tensioning by single handle (patent of 1837). *Diam. 51 cm.*

812 Pair of kettle drums. Carl Friedrich Tzschiederich, Dresden, 1769. *Berlin, Instt. f. Musikforschung, 213, 214.* Copper, with fixed iron legs. Seven and eight screws.

813   Side drum. Swiss, dated 1575. *Basel, Hist. Mus., 1874.120, Nef 232.* Emblazoned with two coats of arms supported by basilisks. Wood shell. Roped between iron hooks over the counterhoops. Rosette of seven air holes. *Diam.* 51·5 cm. *Height* 66 cm.

814   Side drum. Swiss, dated 1689. *Basel, Hist. Mus., 1872.84, Nef 257.* Arms of the Basel family Zäslin, surrounded by trophies and laurel wreaths and an inscription *Haubtquarteir 1689.* Wood shell. Single air hole. Hoops painted with barber's pole pattern. *Diam.* 50 cm. *Height* 51·5 cm.

815   Side drum. Swiss, dated 1768. *Basel, His. Mus., 1894.138, Nef 262.* Shield with arms (mermaid) of the Basel family Leissler, above a later inscription and the date. Presented to the *Basler Freikompagnie.* Brass shell. Single air hole. Barber's pole painting on hoops. *Diam.* 41 cm. *Height* 40 cm.

816   Side drum. Probably Austrian, dated 1794. *Nuremberg, German. Nationalmus., Rück Coll., MIR. 640.* With contemporary sticks.

817   Long drum. English, late eighteenth century. *Dorchester, Dorset Military Museum.* Drum of the Eversholt Volunteers. *Diam.* 58·5 cm. *Length of drum* 76 cm. With two padded sticks.

818   Long drum. George Potter, London, 1811. *Messrs George Potter, Aldershot.* Used at Waterloo. *Diam.* 66 cm. *Length of shell* 76 cm.

819   Bass drum. Key, London, after 1814. *London, Kneller Hall, 233A.* Made for the Royal South Gloucestershire Light Infantry. *Diam.* 72·5 cm. *Shell c.* 53 cm.

820   Tambourine. French, dated 1767. *Ann Arbor, Univ. of Michigan, Stearns 404.* Vellum inscribed *Marie Josephe de Saxe, Dauphine de France 1767* On obverse a portrait of the Dauphine. Painted wood with ten round jingles in a double row of five. *Diam.* of vellum 44·5 cm. *Depth of shell* 7·5 cm.

821   Two tambourines. (Left) J. Dale, London, end of eighteenth century. (Right) Goulding & Co., London, c. 1805. *Norwich Museums.* Five pairs of jingles.

See also tabors, **409** to **411**.

Kettle Drums

The bowl-shaped drums of the Middle East were known in Europe in the thirteenth century in a small form, *nakers*, with shells about 20–30 cm in diameter and played in pairs. No original specimens are known, though similar small kettle drums are still made in their home regions, e.g. for the reconstituted Janissary bands of the Turkish army, the two drums in this case being mounted rigidly together on a wooden spacing piece and beaten with a pair of short light sticks.

The large kettle drums introduced by the Arabs for mounted use, again played in pairs, were brought to Europe in the second half of the fifteenth century. They are shown at the beginning of the sixteenth century (Virdung) already with square-topped tensioning screws turned by a separate key, as remained standard for long afterwards and is found with cavalry drums still. Up to the end of the eighteenth century these drums were used almost exclusively in association with trumpets, providing a harmonic bass to these in trumpet corps, kettle drums being tunable; one of the pair was tuned to the C of the trumpets, the other to the G. They could be placed on an iron stand for performances in churches or theatres (**809**). The vellums were stouter than now (the pair shown has contemporary vellums). A unique early set of kettle-drum sticks of ivory, with the disc-shaped heads common up to the mid eighteenth century, is preserved at Vienna (**810**). Drums intended wholly for orchestral use (*timpani*) with fixed iron legs (**812**) were well known during the eighteenth century, though timpani on loose iron stands can still be found in orchestral use.

In diameter seventeenth–eighteenth-century kettle drums were generally small by later standards, 60 cm having been an average dimension for the larger of a pair whereas today it is near the average for the smallest drum of an orchestral set of three. Larger sets or 'great kettle drums' were also made, however, in the eighteenth century, even exceeding 100 cm in diameter (as in a pair from Strasbourg

IV Percussion Instruments

Cathedral, at Woolwich, Rotunda Museum). Handel is said to have preferred the larger drums for oratorio performances, and for military use they were borne on a special drum-carriage.

The first mechanical improvement of orchestral timpani was the attached T-shaped tuning handle for each screw, dating from early in the nineteenth century. Next followed inventions for simultaneous turning of all the screws. Many of these are given by Sachs (1930, 91–2, a work of special importance for the history of European drums and other percussion instruments). The earliest of these inventions traced by Sachs is by G. Cramer, Munich, 1812. It apparently foreshadowed in some respects the system of Cornelius Ward, London, 1837, which has internal rope and pulleys actuated by one master handle (**811**). Rotary tuning, by turning the drum on a screw stem, is attributed first to Stumpff, in Amsterdam, 1821, and tuning by pedal to Brod, Paris, in the 1830s.

Side Drum

The thirteenth-century *tabor*, used both with and without a tabor pipe (p. 82) was a small roped side drum with a gut snare stretched across one head. An occasional oblique view in miniatures of the time indicates a shell length about equal to the skin diameter—much as in the ordinary Basque tabor today. Enlargement of the drum came with the Swiss drum and fife military music of the fifteenth century, bringing the military side drums used since. A series of Basel drums over three centuries (**813–15**) illustrates among other things a progressive diminution in average size. In the earliest of the three drums the air holes in the shell are in the form of a rosette of seven small holes, a feature which vanishes during the seventeenth century in favour of a single hole. The shells are wooden up to *c.* 1700 when brass was introduced as an alternative. Another eighteenth-century side drum is illustrated with contemporary sticks (**816**). The first-recorded patent for rod tensioning is Ward's of 1837 (Sachs, *op. cit.*), soon followed by others in Germany. Shallow model side drums, with shell length half or considerably less than half the preceding drums, began to come in during the 1850s (in England, e.g. by Distin); for marching, a hinged wire thigh-rest is fitted. The *tenor drum*, a wide snare-less side drum played with soft sticks, appears to have been introduced in the 1830s.

Bass Drum

This entered the West with the 'Turkish music' in the second half of the eighteenth century; the earliest known dated specimen is of 1783 (at Lübeck; Sachs, p. 110). Whereas a full-sized side drum has a metal hook on one side of the upper counterhoop for carrying the drum against the thigh, a bass drum has a metal ring at the centre of the shell for carrying across the chest. Also it has no snare. The proportions of the bass drum changed in a striking way between the time of its introduction and *c.* 1850 when the modern military pattern came in. The early model, described in contemporary literature as *long drum* (**817**), has a wooden shell *c.* 65–75 cm in length (the overall length over the hoops being about 10 cm greater). The diameter is somewhat less, from 58 cm upwards. There are also smaller examples, *c.* 60 cm overall and only 48 cm in diameter. By the time of Waterloo, the drum was becoming wider (**818**), to produce, at any rate in the English service, a bulky model with shell length 53 cm and diameter up to 76 cm. At least two specimens of this size are by Thomas Key, London (**819**). The object of the change in shape was evidently to get more volume of sound without loss of portability, though these Key instruments come perilously close to the latter. They remained in use, as repair labels show, until near the mid-century, when the modern shallow-shelled bass drum was introduced, about 80 cm in diameter. Likewise some of the old long drums were still in use around the mid-century, e.g. in provincial brass bands; a number of English specimens are preserved at Snowshill Manor, Gloucestershire. Later there were also built (chiefly in London) single-skin orchestral bass drums or 'gong drums', *c*. 86 cm in diameter, with rod tensioning, still in use with some orchestras.

Tambourine

The thirteenth-century *timbrel* is frequently depicted with five pairs of circular jingles mounted in slots in the hoop-like shell—a device evidently borrowed from the Saracens. A snare is also shown in some instances, possibly indicating the presence of a second skin, as met still in some North African tambourines. The snare has not persisted, but five pairs of jingles, or two rows of five (**820**) remained usual up to the modern era when 12 or more pairs may be fitted, along with rod tensioning of the vellum. Several fairly large-diameter tambourines made around 1800 for the 'Turkish Music' have survived (**821**). Folk music knows other varieties, as the Portuguese ex-oriental square form with two skins and no jingles (*adufe*), and Italian single-skin circular instruments with jingle bells attached inside the shell in addition to the usual jingles.

2 Hard Percussion Instruments

Space allows only a glimpse of the vast range of instruments which includes bells, wooden substitute bells, horse bells, carnival and signal rattles of every description, drums which are not drums (for instance a large earthenware pot beaten over the orifice with a rush fan) and scores of others.

Illustrations

822 Jingling Johnny. German, nineteenth century. *Nuremberg, German. Nationalmus., Rück Coll., MIR.563.* Three sets of pellet bells.

823 Xylophone. Swiss, nineteenth century. *Oxford, Pitt-Rivers Mus.* Wooden bars in four rows loosely secured with string to five bunches of straw. Wooden beaters.

824 Triangle. ? German, seventeenth–eighteenth century. *Vienna, Kunsthist. Mus., C.271.* Iron. Five loose rings. *Height c.* 18 cm.

The *triangle* is medieval in origin. Early triangles, even to the beginning of the nineteenth century, were given three to five loose jingling rings (**824**). The *Jingling Johnny* or *Turkish Crescent* (**822**) is a traditional military band instrument in Turkey, where several may be used in a band, rocked up and down in time with the music. It was introduced into European bands at the beginning of the nineteenth century and in Germany it is used today, though it has largely given place to the *lyra-glockenspiel*, or upright glockenspiel mounted on a pole, surmounted by 'Turkish' horse-tails and crescent above the tuned metal bars.

The traditional European *xylophone*, the Alpine *holzernes G'lachter*, is recorded from the early sixteenth century. Unlike the now familiar 'piano style' xylophone, which basically follows the African arrangement of bars placed in a row like piano keys, this European type has three or more rows of bars placed in the opposite manner, the rows reaching away from the player (**823**). The bars are laid on thin rolls of straw. Such instruments, though primarily folk instruments, were made commercially in Germany in the latter part of the last century, and in improved forms are in use in some Continental orchestras still (e.g. in Russia). 'Metallophones', with tuned metal bars placed piano-wise (*Glockenspiel*), were known in the eighteenth century.

The use of friction to sound an instrument has appeared in several Western guises other than the fiddle and the hurdy-gurdy, though they can only be briefly listed here: friction drums (folk instruments), with a cane tied vertically in a central hole in a drumskin and rubbed up and down with the moistened hand; glass harmonicas and musical glasses, either with individual goblets or with a set of overlapping bowls rotated on a spindle, in each case touched with the moistened fingers; nail violins (from mid eighteenth century), with iron nails set in a circle on a flat round soundbox and sounded with a fiddle bow; and others could be cited. These cannot, of course, be described as percussion instruments, and it will be fitting to end these notes with a mention of the taxonomic improvement on our traditional 'strings, wind and percussion' due to Mahillon, followed by Hornbostel and Sachs, 1914 (English translation in *GSJ*, XIV, 1961), whereby instruments in which a stretched skin is set in vibration are *membranophones* and those in which a solid substance is made to vibrate are *idiophones*. For ethnological work these terms, along with *chordophones* (stringed instruments) and *aerophones* (wind) have proved most valuable. 'Percussion' here becomes divided in a new way and 'non-percussion' like the glass harmonicas find a place in idiophones along with further minor varieties of instrument, including those with flexible solid vibrating components like the widespread Jew's harp, which have also had to be passed over in this survey.

Select Bibliography

General

Agricola, M. *Musica Instrumentalis deudsch*. Wittemberg, 1528, etc. Reprint, Leipzig, 1896.

Alexandriu, T. *Instrumentele Muzicale Ale Poporului Romin*. Bucharest, 1956. (Rumanian folk instruments.)

Baines, A. (ed.). *Musical Instruments through the Ages*. London, 1961, 1963.

Berlioz, H. *Traité de l'Instrumentation*. Paris, 1844.

Bessaraboff, N. *Ancient European Musical Instruments*. Boston, 1941. 'An Organological Study of the Musical Instruments in the Leslie Lindsey Mason Collection at the Museum of Fine Arts, Boston.'

Bonanni (Buonanni), F. *Gabinetto armonico*. Rome, 1722.

Buchner, A. *Musical Instruments through the Ages*. London, 1955. (Illustrations largely drawn from the National Museum, Prague.)

Denis, V. *De Muziekinstrumenten in de Nederlanden en in Italie naar hun Afbeelding in de 15ᵉ eeuwsche Kunst*. Antwerp, 1944. (Translation of parts in *Galpin Society Journal*, II, 1949.)

Diderot and d'Alembert. *Encyclopédie*. Paris, 1767, 1776. (Section 'Lutherie'.)

Eisel, J. T. *Musikus Autodidaktos*. Erfurt, 1738.

Eppelsheim, J. *Das Orchester in den Werken Jean-Baptiste Lully*. Tutzing, 1961.

Galpin, F. W. *Old English Instruments of Music*. London, 1910, 1932, 1965.

Galpin, F. W. *A Textbook of European Musical Instruments*. London, 1937.

Galpin Society Journal. London, 1948 (in progress).

Geiringer, K. *Musical Instruments*. London, 1943.

Grove's Dictionary of Music and Musicians, Fifth edn, ed. Eric Blom. London, 1954.

Harrison, F., and Rimmer, J. *European Musical Instruments*. London, 1964.

Hipkins, A. J., and Gibb, W. *Musical Instruments, Historic, Rare and Unique*. Edinburgh, 1888, etc; London, 1945.

Kinsky, G. *History of Music in Pictures* (Leipzig, 1929). London, 1930, 1937; New York, 1951.

Kircher, A. *Musurgia universalis*. Rome, 1650.

Klier, K. M. *Volkstümliche Musikinstrumente in der Alpen*. Kassel, 1956.

Laborde, J. B. de. *Essai sur la Musique*. Paris, 1780.

Lesure, F. 'La Facture Instrumentale à Paris au Seizième Siècle.' *Galpin Society Journal*, VII, 1954; X, 1957.

Majer, J. F. B. C. *Museum Musicum*. Halle, 1732. Reprint, Kassel, 1954.

Marcuse, S. *Musical Instruments: a Comprehensive Dictionary*. New York, 1964.

Mersenne, M. *Harmonie Universelle*. Paris, 1636. Reprint, Paris, 1963. Latin edition (*Harmonicorum libri*, Paris, 1635) transl. Chapman, R. E., The Hague, 1957.

Minguet y Yrol, P. *Reglas y Advertencias Generales que ensenan el modo de tañer todos los instrumentos mejores*. Madrid, 1754.

Musik in Geschichte und Gegenwart, ed. Blume, F. Kassel, 1949 (in progress).

Norlind, T. *Musikinstrumens Historia*. Stockholm, 1941.

Ott, A. *Tausend Jahre Musikleben*. Munich, 1961. (With photographs of instruments in the Germanisches Nationalmuseum, Nuremberg.)

Pierre, C. *Les factures d'instruments de musique*. Paris, 1893.

Praetorius, M. *Syntagma Musicum*. Vol. 2, *De Organographia*, Wolfenbüttel, 1619. Reprint, Kassel, 1929.

Sachs, C. *Real-Lexikon der Musikinstrumente*. Berlin, 1913. Reprint, Hildesheim, 1962.

Sachs, C. *Handbuch der Musikinstrumentenkunde*. Leipzig, 1930.

Sachs, C. *The History of Musical Instruments*. New York, 1940; London, 1942.

Sauerlandt, M. *Die Musik in fünf Jahrhunderten der Europäischen Malerei*. Leipzig, 1922.

Schlosser, J. *Die Sammlung alter Musikinstrumente* (Kunsthistorisches Museum in Wien). Vienna, 1920.

Speer, D. *Grundrichtiger Unterricht der musikalischen Kunst.* Ulm, 1687, 1697.

Talbot, J. Manuscript Notes on Musical Instruments and their Dimensions (London, *c.* 1695). Printed in *Galpin Society Journal*: I, 1948 (Wind instruments); III, 1950 (Bowed instruments); V, 1952 (Bagpipes); XIV, 1961 (Plucked strings—the Lute family); XV, 1962 (The wire-strung fretted instruments and the guitar); XVI, 1963 (Harps).

Terry, C. S. *Bach's Orchestra.* London, 1932, 1958.

Tinctoris. *De Inventione et Usu Musicae.* ? Naples, 1487. Latin text and English translation of section on instruments in *Galpin Society Journal*, III, 1950.

Trichet, P., ed. Lesure, F. *Traité des instruments de musique* (*c.* 1640). Neuilly-sur-Seine, 1957.

Turrini, G. 'L'Accademia Filarmonica di Verona dalla Fondazione (Maggio 1543) al 1600 e il suo patrimonio musicale antico,' *Atti e Memorie della Accademia di Agricoltura Scienze e Lettere di Verona*, Series V, Vol. xviii. Verona, 1941.

Turrini, G. 'Il patrimonio musicale della Biblioteca capitolare in Verona dal sec. XV al XIX,' *ibid.*, Series VI, Vol. ii. Verona, 1950–1. (Photographs of instruments.)

Vertkov, K., Blagodatov, G., and Yazovitskaya, E. *Atlas Instrumentov narodov SSSR.* Moscow, 1963. (Folk instruments of the U.S.S.R.)

Virdung, S. *Musica Getuscht.* Basel, 1511. Reprint, Kassel, 1931.

Weigel, J. C., ed. Berner, A. *Musicalisches Theatrum* [*c.* 1720]. Kassel, 1961.

Wright, R. *Dictionnaire des instruments de musique: étude de Lexicologie.* London, 1941.

Stringed Instruments

Andersson, O. *The Bowed Harp.* London, 1930.

Armstrong, R. B. *Musical Instruments.* Part I, *The Irish and the Highland Harps.* Edinburgh, 1904. Part II, *English and Irish Instruments.* 1908 (English guitars, Light's instruments, etc).

Bachmann, W. *Die Anfänge des Streichinstrumentenspiels.* Leipzig, 1964.

Baron, E. G. *Historisch-theoretische und praktische Untersuchung des Instruments der Lauten.* Nuremberg, 1727. Reprint, Amsterdam, 1965.

Bermudo, J. *Declaración de Instrumentos musicales.* Osuna, 1549. Reprint of 1555 edn, Kassel, 1957.

Boyden, D. *The History of violin playing.* London, 1965.

Brandimeier, J. *Handbuch der Zither.* Munich, 1963. (Not seen.)

Burwell, M. 'Miss Mary Burwell's Instruction Book for the Lute' [*c.* 1668–72], ed. Dart, T., *Galpin Society Journal*, XI, 1958.

Dart, T. 'The Cittern and its English Music,' *Galpin Society Journal*, I, 1948.

Dolmetsch, A. 'The Lute,' *The Connoisseur*, viii, ix, London, 1904.

Dolmetsch, A. 'The Viol,' *ibid.*, x, xiii, 1904–5.

Dolmetsch, N. *The Viola da Gamba.* London, 1962.

Dolmetsch, N. 'Of the Sizes of Viols,' *Galpin Society Journal*, XVII, 1964.

Elgar, R. *Introduction to the Double Bass.* St Leonards-on-Sea, 1960. *More about the Double bass*, 1963.

Farga, F. *Violins and Violinists.* London, 1950.

Fruchtman, E. 'The Baryton: Its History and Its Music Re-examined,' *Acta Musicologica*, Vol. XXXIV, 1962. Basel.

Ganassi, S. di. *Regola Rubertina.* Venice, 1542. Reprint, Leipzig, 1924. (Viols and viol-playing.)

Gerle, H. *Musica Teusch auf die Instrument . . .* Nuremberg, 1532, 1546.

Hajdecki, A. *Die Italienische Lira da Braccio.* Mostar, 1892. Reprint, Amsterdam, 1965.

Hayes, G. R. *Musical Instruments and their Music, 1500–1750: II, The Viols, and other Bowed Instruments.* London, 1930.

Heartz, D. 'An Elizabethan Tutor for the Guitar,' *Galpin Society Journal*, XVI, 1963.

Hellwig, G. 'Joachim Tielke,' *Galpin Society Journal*, XVII, 1964.

Henley, W. *Antonio Stradivari*. Revised, Woodcock C. Brighton, 1961.

Heron-Allen, E. *Violin-making, as it was and is*. London, 1885, etc.

Hill, W. H., A. F. and A. E. *Antonio Stradivari: his life and work*. London, 1902, New York, 1963.

Hill, W. H., A. F. and A. E. *The Violin-makers of the Guarneri Family (1626–1762)*. London, 1931.

Gill, D. 'The Orpharion and Bandora,' *Galpin Society Journal*, XIII, 1960.

Jahnel, F. *Die Gitarre und ihr Bau*. Frankfurt-am-Main, 1963.

Huggins, Lady M. *Gio: Paolo Maggini, his Life and Work*. London, 1892.

Lanfranco, G. M. *Scintille di musica*. Brescia, 1533.

Lütgendorff, W. L. von. *Die Geigen- und Lautenmacher*. Frankfurt-am-Main, 1922.

Mace, T. *Musick's Monument*. London, 1676. Reprint, Paris, 1958.

Norlind, T. *Systematik der Saiteninstrumente: I. Geschichte der Zither*. Stockholm, 1936.

Panum, H., ed. Pulver, J. *The Stringed Instruments of the Middle Ages*. London (1940).

Prynne, M. 'A Surviving Vihuela de Mano,' *Galpin Society Journal*, XVI, 1963.

Rensch, R. *The Harp*, New York, 1950.

Rimmer, J. 'The Harp in the Baroque Era,' *Proceedings of the Royal Musical Association*, 90th Session, 1964.

Rimmer, J. 'The Morphology of the Irish Harp,' *Galpin Society Journal*, XVII, 1964.

Rimmer, J. 'The Morphology of the Triple Harp,' *ibid.*, XVIII, 1965.

Ritchie, H. *The Dulcimer Book*. New York, 1963.

Rousseau, J. *Traité de la Viole*. Paris, 1687. Reprint, Amsterdam, 1965.

Seeger, C. 'The Appalachian Dulcimer,' *Journal of American Folklore*, LXX, 278. Richmond, Virginia, 1957.

Sharpe, A. P. *The Story of the Spanish Guitar*. London, 1954.

Skeaping, K. 'Some Speculations on a Crisis in the History of the Violin,' *Galpin Society Journal*, VIII, 1955.

Simpson, C. *The Division Violist*. London, 1659, 1665, 1712.

Stainer, C. *A Dictionary of Violin Makers*. London, 1896, etc.

Usher, T. 'The Spanish Guitar in the Nineteenth and Twentieth Centuries,' *Galpin Society Journal*, IX, 1956.

Vannes, R. *Dictionnaire Universel des Luthiers*. Brussels, 1951; Vol. 2, 1959.

Walin, S. *Die Schwedische Hummel*. Stockholm, 1952.

Winternitz, E. Article 'Lira da braccio' in *Musik in Geschichte und Gegenwart*, VIII.

Wind and Percussion Instruments

Altenburg, J. E. *Versuch einer Anleitung zur heroisch-musikalischen Trompeter- und Paukerkunst*. Halle, 1795. Reprint, Dresden, 1911.

Askew, G. 'Origins of the Northumbrian Pipes,' *Archaeologia Aeliana*, 4th Series, IX. Newcastle-upon-Tyne, 1932.

Ayars, C. *Contributions to the Art of Music in America by the Music Industries of Boston, 1640 to 1936*. New York, 1937.

Baines, A. *Woodwind Instruments and their History*. London, 1957.

Baines, A. *Bagpipes*. Pitt Rivers Museum, Occasional Papers on Technology, 9. Oxford, 1960.

Baines, A. 'Shawms of the Sardana Coblas,' *Galpin Society Journal*, V, 1952.

Bate, P. *The Oboe*. London, 1956.

Bate, P. *The Trumpet and Trombone*. London, 1966.

Boehm, T. *The Flute and Flute-playing*, ed. Dayton C. Miller, Cleveland, 1922. New York, 1964.

Borjon, C. E. *Traité de musette*. Lyons, 1672.

Bridge, J. C. 'Horns,' *Journal of the Architectural, Archaeological and Historic Society for the County and City of Chester*, New Series 13. Chester, 1905.

Brömse, P. *Flöten, Schalmeien und Sackpfeife Südslawiens*. Brno, 1937.

Select Bibliography

Carse, A. *Musical Wind Instruments*. London, 1939; New York, 1964.

Dart, T. 'The Mock Trumpet,' *Galpin Society Journal*, VI, 1953.

Day, C. R. *Descriptive Catalogue of the musical instruments in the Royal Military Exhibition of 1890*. London, 1891.

Farmer, H. G. *The Rise and Development of Military Music*. London, 1912.

Fitzgibbon, H. M. *The Story of the Flute*. London, 1914.

Fitzpatrick, H. 'Some Historical Notes on the Horn in Germany and Austria,' *Galpin Society Journal*, XVI, 1963.

Fitzpatrick, H. 'An Eighteenth-century Bohemian School of Horn-makers,' *ibid.*, XVII, 1964.

Fitzpatrick, H. 'The Valveless Horn in Modern Performances of Eighteenth-century Music,' *Proceedings of the Royal Musical Association, 91st Session, 1965*.

Fröhlich, J. F. *Vollständige theoretisch-praktisch Musikschule*. Bonn, 1810–11.

Halfpenny, E. 'The English 2- and 3-keyed Hautboy,' *Galpin Society Journal*, II, 1949; 'The Tenner Hoboy,' *ibid.*, V, 1952; 'The French Hautboy: A Technical Survey,' *ibid.*, VI, 1953; VIII, 1955.

Halfpenny, E. 'Two Rare Transverse Flutes,' *ibid.*, XIII, 1960; 'The Bass Recorders of Bressan,' *ibid.*, XIII, 1955; 'Technology of a Bass Recorder,' *ibid.*, XV, 1962.

Halfpenny, E. 'The Evolution of the Bassoon in England, 1750–1800,' *ibid.* X, 1957; 'Early English Clarinets,' *ibid.* XVIII, 1965.

Halfpenny, E. 'William Shaw's 'Harmonic Trumpet,' *ibid.* XIII, 1960; 'William Bull and the English Baroque Trumpet,' *ibid.* XV, 1962; 'Two Oxford Trumpets,' *ibid.* XVI, 1963.

Halfpenny, E. 'Biographical Notices of the Early English Woodwind-making School,' *ibid.* XII, 1959; 'Further Light on the Stanesby Family,' *ibid.* XIII, 1960.

Heckel, W. *Der Fagott*. Revised, Heckel, W. H. Leipzig, 1931.

Hoover, C. A. 'The Slide Trumpet of the 19th Century,' *Brass Quarterly*, VI, no. 4. Durham, New Hampshire, 1963.

Hunt, E. *The Recorder and its Music*. London, 1962.

Julyan, Lt. Col. W. L. 'History of the Hunting Horn,' *The Field*, October 18th, 1947.

Kalkbrenner, A. *Wilhelm Wieprecht, . . . sein Leben und Wirken*. Berlin, 1882.

Kastner, G. *Manuel général de musique militaire*. Paris, 1848.

Kinsky, G. 'Doppelrohrblattinstrumente mit Windkapsel.' *Archiv für Musikwissenschaft*, 7, 1925.

Kirby, P. R. *The Kettle-drums*. London, 1930.

Kool, J. *Das Saxophon*. Leipzig, 1931.

Langwill, L. G. *An Index of Musical Wind-instrument Makers*. Edinburgh, 1960, 1962.

Langwill, L. G. *The Bassoon and Contrabassoon*. London, 1965.

Marx, J. 'The Tone of the Baroque Oboe,' *Galpin Society Journal*, IV, 1951.

Menke, W., transl. Abraham, G. *The History of the Trumpet of Bach and Handel*. London, 1934.

Morley-Pegge, R. *The French Horn*. London, 1960.

Morley-Pegge, R. 'The Anaconda,' *Galpin Society Journal*, XII, 1959. (Contra-serpent and bass cornetts.)

Morley-Pegge, R. 'The Regent's Bugle,' *ibid.* IX, 1956.

Neukomm, E. *Histoire de la musique militaire*. Paris, 1889.

Neuschel, J. Letters, 1541, etc. Published in *Monatshefte für Musikforschung*, 9, 1877.

Panoff, P. *Militär Musik*. Berlin, 1938.

Pompecki, B. *Jagd- und Waldhornschule*. Neudamm, 1926. (Hunting horns as used in Germany, nineteenth century.)

Rendall, F. G. *The Clarinet*. London, 1954.

Rockstro, R. S. *A Treatise on the Construction, History and Practice of the Flute*. London, 1890, 1928.

Russell, J. F., and Elliot, J. H. *The Brass Band Movement*. London, 1936.

Sachs, C. 'Chromatic Trumpets in the Renaissance,' *Musical Quarterly*, XXXVI. New York, 1950.

Smithers, D. 'The Trumpets of J. W. Haas,' *Galpin Society Journal*, XVIII, 1965.

Sunderlin, A. *Die Instrumentirung für das Orchester*. Berlin. 1828.

Weber, G. 'Abhandlung über die Verbesserung des Fagotts,' *Cäcilia*, II. Mainz, 1825. (On the Almenraeder bassoon.)

Welch, C. *History of the Boehm Flute*. London, 1883, 1896. Reprint, New York, 1961.

Welch, C. *Six Lectures on the Recorder*. London, 1911. (Reprint of the first three Lectures, with Introduction by
  Hunt, E., London, 1961.)
Wörthmüller, W. 'Die Nürnberger Trompeten- und Posaunenmacher des 17. und 18. Jahrhunderts,' *Mittheil-
  ungen des Vereins für Geschichte der Stadt Nürnberg*, 45, 46. Nuremberg, 1954–5.

Collections and Exhibitions: Catalogues and Guidebooks

Ann Arbor, University of Michigan. Stanley, A. A. *Catalogue of the Stearns Collection of Musical Instruments*.
  Ann Arbor, 1921.
Basel, Historisches Museum. Nef, K. *Katalog No. IV: Musikinstrumente*. Basel, 1906.
Berlin, Staatliche Hochschule für Musik. Sachs, C. *Sammlung alter Musikinstrumente*. Berlin, 1922. (Collection
  now incorporated in Staatliches Institut für Musikforschung, Musikinstrumenten-Sammlung, Berlin.)
Boston, Museum of Fine Arts. (See p. 161, Bessaraboff, N.)
Brunswick, Städtische Museum. Schröder, H. *Verzeichnis der Sammlung alter Musikinstrumente*. Brunswick, 1928.
Brussels, Musée Instrumental du Conservatoire royal de Musique. Mahillon, F.-V., *Catalogue descriptif et analytique*,
  5 vols. Ghent, 1893–1912; *Catalogue abrégé*. Ghent, 1911.
Cologne, Musikhistorisches Museum von Wilhelm Heyer. Kinsky, G. *Katalog, Vol. II* (Stringed instruments),
  Cologne, 1912; *Kleiner Katalog der Sammlung alter Musikinstrumente*, Cologne, 1913. (Collection later trans-
  ferred to Leipzig and now in the Karl-Marx-Universität, Leipzig.)
Copenhagen, Claudius Collection. *Carl Claudius Sammlung af gamle Musikinstrumenter*. Copenhagen, 1931.
Copenhagen, Musikhistorisk Museum. Hammerich, A. *Beskrivende illustreret Katalog*. Copenhagen, 1909.
Eisenach, Bachhaus. Buhle, E. *Verzeichnis der Sammlung alter Musikinstrumente*. Leipzig, 1913; Revised, Sachs,
  C., Leipzig, 1918.
Florence, Museo del Reale Istituto Luigi Cherubini. Bargagnana, L., *Catologo*. 1911.
Frankfurt-am-Main, Historisches Museum. *Sammlung alter Musikinstrumente*. Epstein, P. Frankfurt, 1927.
Ghent, Snoeck Collection. Snoeck, C. C. *Catalogue de la Collection d'instruments de musique*. Ghent, 1894. (Collec-
  tion later dispersed, a part to Brussels (q.v.), and a part to Berlin (q.v.).)
Halle, Saale, Händelhaus. Sasse, K., *Guidebook*, 1958. (Not seen.)
Hague, The, Gemeente-Museum. Balfoort, D. J. *De Muziekhistorische Afdeeling (Verz. D. F. Scheurleer)*, 1935.
  (Illustrated guidebook.)
Hamburg, Museum für Hamburgische Geschichte. Schröder, H. *Verzeichnis der Sammlung alter Musikinstrumente*.
  Hamburg, 1930.
Leipzig, Karl-Marx-Universität. (See Cologne.) Rubardt, P. *Führer durch das Musikinstrumenten-Museum*.
  Leipzig, 1955.
Linz, Oberösterreichischen Landesmuseum. Wessely, O, *Die Musikinstrumenten Sammlung*. 1952.
Lisbon, V Festival Gulbenkian de Musica: *Exposição internacional de instrumentos antigos*. Lisbon, 1961. (Instru-
  ments from the Conservatorio Nacional, Lisbon, and the Conservatoire royal de musique, Brussels.)
Lisbon, Museu Instrumental en Lisboa. Lambertini, M., *Catologo summario*, Lisbon, 1914. (Not seen.)
London, Horniman Museum and Library. Carse, A. *Catalogue of the Adam Carse Collection of Old Musical Wind
  Instruments*. London, 1951.
London, Music Loan Exhibition, 1904. *Illustrated Catalogue*. London, 1909.
London, Royal College of Music (Donaldson Collection). Dyson, Sir G., *Catalogue of Historical Musical Instru-
  ments, Paintings, Sculptures and Drawings*. London, 1952.
London, Royal Military Exhibition, 1890. (See above, Day, C. R.)
London, Galpin Society: British Musical Instruments, August 7–30, 1951. *Catalogue*, 1951.
London, Victoria and Albert Museum. Engel, C. *Descriptive Catalogue of the Musical Instruments in the South
  Kensington Museum*, London, 1874; Baines, A. *Catalogue of the Musical Instruments, Vol. II*.

Select Bibliography

Luton, Museum. *The Ridley Collection of Musical Wind Instruments*. Luton, 1957.

Milan, Museo Civico di antichi strumenti musicali. Gallini, N., *Catologo*. Milan, 1958.

Munich, Bayerisches Nationalmuseum. Bierdimpfl, K. A. *Catalogue*. 1883.

Munich, Ausstellung Alte Musik, 1951. Ott, A. *Katalog*. Munich, 1951. (Instruments from the Bayer. National-museum, Städtisches Instrumentensammlung, and elsewhere.)

New York, Metropolitan Museum of Art. *Catalogue of the Crosby Brown Collection of Musical Instruments of all Nations*. Hand-book No. 13, i, *Europe*. New York, 1902, 1904.

Paris, Musée National de Musique. Chouquet, G. *Catalogue descriptif et raisonné*. Paris, 1884. Supplements by Pillaut, L., 1894, 1899, 1903.

Prague, National Museum, Exhibition of Musical Instruments, 1950. Buchner, A., *Catalogue*, Prague, 1952. (Not seen.)

Salzburg, Museum Carolino Augusteum. Geiringer, K. *Alte Musik-Instrumente*. Leipzig, 1932.

Stockholm, Musikhistorisk Museet. Svanberg, J. *Catalogue*. Stockholm, 1902.

Vienna, Kunsthistorisches Museum. (See p. 162, Schlosser.)

Vienna, Gesellschaft der Musikfreunde. Sammlung der K. K. Gesellschaft der Musikfreunde in Wien. Mandyczewski, E. *Catalogue*. Vienna, 1912. (Collection on loan to Kunsthistorisches Museum.)

Washington, Library of Congress. Gilliam, L. E. and Lichtenwanger, W. *The Dayton C. Miller Flute Collection: A Checklist of the Instruments*. Washington, 1961.

Washington, Smithsonian Institution. *Handbook of the Collection of Musical Instruments in the United States National Museum*. Bulletin 136. Washington, 1927.

Yale, University. Skinner, W. *The Belle Skinner Collection of Old Musical Instruments, Holyoke, Massachusetts*. Holyoke, 1933. (Collection now on loan to Yale University Collection of Musical Instruments.) Marcuse, S. *Musical Instruments at Yale*. Yale, 1960.

York, Castle Museum. Wood, G. B. *Musical Instruments in York Castle Museum*. York, n.d.

Index

The numerals in **bold type** refer to the *figure numbers* of the illustrations